MITCHELL A. BYRD

A Synthesis of
Evolutionary Theory

A Synthesis

HERBERT H. ROSS

Principal Scientist
Illinois Natural History Survey
Professor of Entomology,
University of Illinois

of Evolutionary

Theory

Englewood Cliffs, N.J., PRENTICE-HALL, INC.   1962

A Synthesis of
Evolutionary Theory

Herbert H. Ross

Library of Congress Catalog Card No.: 62-8859

Printed in the United States of America

87994-C

To my graduate students
this book is affectionately and
gratefully inscribed

Preface

It is a remarkable circumstance that the quest of the ancient Ionian philosophers for a cosmic unifying principle should have remained somnolescent for over two thousand years and then be realized to a startling degree in the last two hundred. The Ionians recognized that both animate and inanimate matter have so much in common that they must be made "of the same stuff." The evolutionary theories of Lamarck, Darwin, and Wallace demonstrated the historical continuity of life and guessed at the transition from inanimate to animate matter. In more recent decades chemical and physical concepts have virtually bridged this transition and subatomic discoveries have linked matter as we see it on the earth with the earliest stages of cosmic evolution. When evolutionary ideas are extended into community and biome formation, there emerges a postulated continuity of events from the earliest cosmic conditions to the most highly organized communities in nature. This full sweep of evolutionary theory is indeed tantamount to a unifying principle of the universe.

Perhaps no field of study combines so many facts and theories from so broad a spectrum of science as does the study of evolution. It is a synthesis of facts and theories from zoology, botany, biochemistry, genetics, geology, ecology, and many other bordering fields. Presenting a general background in each of these contributing fields is, of course, outside the objectives of this book, but in some fields, such as genetics and ecology, an explanation is given for those facets needed to understand the basic concepts pertinent to evolution. These brief explanations are included so that the non-specialist in these fields may gain a grasp of this inter-disciplinary information to achieve a cohesive philosophy of evolution. Such a philosophy of evolution, embracing the entire scope of the evolutionary process, starts with pre-stellar evolution and continues by logical steps to the evolution of biomes.

By combining new ideas from different disciplines, evolutionary studies bring out new perspectives which in turn continuously generate new questions. Efforts to answer evolutionary questions lead to new ways of framing inquiries in affected disciplines. The analysis of whole communities, for example, has been considered by several writers (Andrewartha and Birch, 1954) as too complex a problem to be fathomed through the use of present ecological research methods. Because existing biotic communities are the products of past evolution, a knowledge of the principles of their evolutionary history will undoubtedly lead to new conceptual foundations valuable in community analysis. As the physicist, astronomer, and historian Rudolf Thiel has said, "Only knowledge of how a thing became what it is gives us a feeling of really understanding it. We are not satisfied with insight into the character of things; we must fathom their origins before we feel that we have begun to reach the ultimate truth about them."

The examples have been chosen carefully with two thoughts in mind. First has been the desire to choose those which would help to explain ideas with the greatest clarity. Second has been the hope that these examples would assist the reader in understanding how data from his investigations might fit into and augment evolutionary concepts.

The literature about evolution is voluminous, and it has been impractical to do more than cite a minimum number of papers bearing on the topics discussed. More extended bibliographies and treatment of special phases are contained in references listed in the bibliography.

ACKNOWLEDGMENTS

A book of this kind is in effect a distillation of information in the literature and the ideas from one's own research program extending over many years. It is therefore with deep thanks that I acknowledge my indebtedness to all those who have published on this subject and to the John Simon Guggenheim Memorial Foundation, the Research Board of the Graduate College of the University of Illinois, and especially to the Illinois Natural History Survey for generous support of research activities. I am grateful also to a host of scientific colleagues in many institutions and countries who have been of assistance in many ways and to all my students for vigorous stimulation.

During the preparation of the manuscript I have been greatly indebted to the following persons for valuable discussion, suggestions, and criticisms: S. J. Fox, University of Florida; Harlan Lewis, University of California at Los Angeles; Everett C. Olson, University of Chicago; H. B. Willman and David Swann, Illinois Geological Survey; J. B. Kitzmiller, J. R. Laughnan, and W. M. Luce, University of Illinois; and M. W. Sanderson, P. W. Smith, and L. J. Stannard, Illinois Natural History Survey.

I am especially indebted to Harlow B. Mills, Illinois Natural History Survey, and to Alfred E. Emerson, University of Chicago, for counsel and encouragement during the preparation of this book.

For scientific editorial assistance, I am extremely grateful to my wife Jean and also to my son Charles A. Ross and his wife June Phillips Ross.

I am grateful also to many publishers and authors for permission to reproduce a number of illustrations and to others who kindly loaned illustrations for use in this book. Specific acknowledgment is made under each such illustration. Finally I wish to thank the staff of Prentice-Hall, Inc., for the preparation of many original figures and for editing the manuscript.

Herbert H. Ross, Illinois Natural
History Survey. Urbana, Illinois

Contents

A Synthesis of
Evolutionary Theory

The Expansion

of Evolutionary

Concepts

1

From the earliest times of his recorded history, man has searched for an explanation of the earth, the things on it, the universe surrounding it, how they were formed, and the mechanisms they represent. Over the years he has had many notable successes, culminated in the last two centuries by the formulation of the theory of organic evolution. According to this theory, the present life on our planet has evolved from primeval ancestors by a process of change, and the direction of change has been channelled by an automatic interaction of organism and environment called natural selection.

Concepts of evolution began and evolved with the increasing development of modern fields of science. The first serious suggestions that present-day forms of life arose by a process of change from earlier prototypes were made in the middle and latter part of the eighteenth century. The French

1

writer Buffon and the English naturalist Erasmus Darwin were prominent authors who set forth such ideas, Buffon timidly, Darwin vigorously. Previously the scientific world had considered species to be unchanging or immutable.

It is undoubtedly no accident that the early suggestions of descent by change were made during the period when Linnaeus and others were developing a workable system for classifying living organisms. These classifications must have focused attention on the close similarity of many species and stirred speculation on the existence of some sort of relationship among the members of the biota. Perhaps contact with other progressive scientists of the time, such as the chemists Priestley and Lavoisier, was a stimulus to more objective philosophical efforts in biology. Good communication appears to have existed between the few scientists of that early period.

In the first decade of the nineteenth century, the French naturalist Lamark propounded a remarkably complete theory of the evolution of organisms by a process of change. As a mechanism to explain the change, he proposed that characters acquired during the individual's lifetime are inherited. A battle royal, led by Lamarck's compatriot Cuvier, began in opposition to Lamarck's idea of the inheritance of acquired characters, and the ridicule which smothered this idea threatened to engulf the whole idea of evolutionary change.

However, even while the idea of evolution was being bitterly contested, a battery of brilliant scientists were making great changes in the conservative intellectual attitude of Lamarck's time. In the first half of the nineteenth century, Humphrey Davy and Faraday established many of the modern concepts in electricity. In biology Owen brought forward the idea of analogy and homology of parts; Cuvier was solidifying the concepts of comparative anatomy already firmly introduced by Lamarck; Milne Edwards propounded the idea of division of physiological labor; Müller demonstrated the interrelationship of anatomy and physiology; Schwann and Schleiden demonstrated the cell theory; Bichat founded histology; Von Baer founded modern embryology; and Schultze defined protoplasm. That these discoveries were made in such rapid succession is not strange. Scientists had been on the verge of seeing them for years, and, as one fundamental was discovered, it served as a key to unlock the next half-anticipated secret. The whole spectrum of inquiry oriented scientific thinking in terms of dynamic processes and interrelatedness.

While these events were transpiring in the biological sciences,

Hutton, Lyell, and others were making great strides toward an understanding of geology. Lyell, especially, pointed out the gradual nature of the changes involved in geologic events. Contemporaneously, the English clergyman Malthus wrote a pioneering book on human sociology entitled *Essay on Population,* which emphasized the checks put on human population by war, disease, and famine.

In spite of the attacks on Lamarck's theories, even in the early nineteenth century, the idea of the origin of new species through change gained many supporters. Certain authors went so far as to postulate natural selection of favored variations as the mechanism involved in the individual examples or groups which had come to their attention. Climactic to these efforts, the naturalists Charles Darwin and Alfred Russell Wallace arrived independently at the conclusion that natural selection was a general theory explaining the evolution of all life. By prearrangement, their papers were read in London at the same meeting of the Royal Society in 1858. Darwin's classical exposition of this theory, *The Origin of Species by Means of Natural Selection,* was published in 1859. Although bitterly contested, this book established the Darwin-Wallace theory of natural selection and with it the theory of the evolution of life.

That some sort of hereditary mechanism existed was realized by Darwin and his colleagues, but its nature was unknown. Mendel, in his now famous study of peas, formulated the basic laws of inheritance in 1865 and made the first great stride in a knowledge of heredity. His work lay neglected and virtually unknown until 1900 when these same laws were rediscovered independently by Correns in Germany, De Vries in Holland, and Tschermak in Austria. A little later, Sutton and Boveri independently pointed out the probability that the chromosomes of the cell afforded a mechanism for the observed facts of hereditary characters. Soon after, commencing in 1910, T. H. Morgan demonstrated the fact that genetic determinants for many characters occur in a definite linear arrangement along the chromosomes. In the meantime, De Vries and others had outlined the mutation theory. Thus was born the field of modern genetics.

During the first decades of exploration in the new field of genetics, considerable controversy arose as to whether the laboratory mutants of the geneticists were the minute differences postulated by evolutionists as the kind of changes responsible for evolution. Although the controversy still is not entirely settled in the minds of some investigators, by the middle of the twentieth century, a practical synthesis of genetics and evolutionary theory had been achieved by notable investigators such as Theodosius Dobzhansky, Ernst Mayr, C. Darlington, and G. G. Simpson. By this time, A. E. Emerson had made the first serious efforts to extend evolutionary principles to multiple-species systems.

Geological studies after Darwin provided and continue to provide examples of what did happen in the evolution of many plant and animal groups. This mass of data has provided material of great interest relating to the actual products of evolution, including rates of change and patterns of dispersal, survival, and extinction.

In recent years, biochemistry has added a new dimension both to genetics and evolution. New insights into the chemistry of life have contributed valuable clues concerning the origin of life and what the first life might have been like, as well as the nature of the genetic material which carries the biochemical information that is heredity itself. Future discoveries in this area are sure to have a profound effect on many present ideas of inheritance and mutation.

It might seem that by now, over a hundred years after the announcement of the historic Darwin-Wallace theory, the process of evolution should be well understood. For its general outlines, this is true, but the advances made in these hundred years have served also to underscore deeper and little-explored facets which the advances have brought to light. There is today controversy on many points of evolutionary theory.

Difficulties in investigating the evolution of life and the controversies concerning its explanation stem in large part from two simple facts. First, the living world had evolved from non-living matter to the vast complexity of life as we know it before man and his historical pen had evolved. As a result, we have no choice but to attempt an explanation of past happenings on the basis of existing data. This hypothetical reasoning has definite philosophical limitations that frequently invite multiple explanations (hence controversy) and always requires the checking and rechecking of hypotheses in the light of new data or new perspectives. In the interpretation of fossils, for example, at least two sets of hypotheses are always involved. Fossils are not found bearing labels stating their identity; the strata in which they are found are likewise unlabelled. Both unknowns must be solved by comparative anatomy, comparative lithology, relative position in the geologic column, and other means, all of them based in turn on hypotheses or theories of homology or stratigraphy. Because of the necessity for reliance on hypothetical reasoning, the extrapolation of past evolutionary events cannot be proven in the mathematical sense of $x + x = 2x$ but can be judged only in terms of statistical probability, that is, on the probability that the data on the point in question support one answer rather than another.

The second simple fact concerning the difficulty of investigating evolution is that it is difficult to investigate life. The units of living matter are minute, yet each is composed of an unbelievably large number of atoms and molecules arranged in a fantastically intricate, yet orderly, architecture. Living matter is a curious type of self-replicating machine that must keep running continuously; it cannot stop and still be alive. So delicate is the balance between life and death in this living machine that frequently probing experiments destroy it, and the results are found to have dealt not with life itself but with a bit of mutilated corpse. Consequently, not only do we know relatively little about life, but much that we think we know may prove to be erroneous. In the use of whole organisms for experiment or observation, equal difficulties arise in manipulation of the organism and in planning experiments so that of a surety all unwanted variables are excluded. Investigators exhibit remarkable ingenuity in surmounting these difficulties.

In evolutionary studies to date, it seems that, when discovered, the answer to one question leads directly to another question. In effect, the more that is discovered about any given process of evolution, the farther back one must go into the history of that process to find its basic causes. It is becoming evident that all the happenings from the beginning of the cosmos to the present time are in reality changes in the organization of matter, changes peculiar in this respect, that the effects of one process become the cause of the next. For example, as investigators probe deeper into the mechanisms and probable origin of life, they have become more and more aware that life arose because of conditions and circumstances existing a long time ago in the pre-biological world of the earth. Certainly, primeval life could only contain the particular kinds of elements which occurred on the earth at that time and could use only the sources of energy then available. After life formed, it could not evolve beyond the limits imposed by conditions on the earth, and frequently the course of evolution was modified or channelled by the dynamics of the earth. Concurrently, life itself produced physical and chemical changes in the earth and its oceans and atmosphere. Thus, to understand life more fully, we are confronted with the necessity of knowing more about the earth itself, its nature, and its dynamics, both before and after life was formed. Attempts to gain an insight into properties of the earth lead to the question of how it was formed. So, step by step, the quest for knowledge about living things on the earth leads into the history of the entire cosmos.

The Evolution

of the Universe

Some measure of the size and organization of the universe is to be gained by considering the earth as a starting point. The earth is one of nine planets revolving around the sun. Approximately 8,000 miles in diameter, the earth weighs roughly 6,600,000,000,000,000,000,000 tons (6.6×10^{21}). The sun is about 3,000 times more massive. Compared with other stars, our sun is of only moderate size. It is part of a tremendous aggregation of stars known as a galaxy. The galaxy in which we live is only one of the myriads that comprise the universe. Our galaxy is lens-shaped and contains about 100 billion stars (Robertson, 1956) and great masses of interstellar dust and gas concentrated in the edge portions (Westerhout, 1959). The total mass of our galaxy is about 70 billion times that of the sun, 94 per cent consisting of stars, the remaining 6 per cent consisting of interstellar gas and dust. The chief concentration of stars is in the center of the galaxy, the light from these forming the Milky Way. The familiar constellations of our skies such as the Great Bear, or Big Dipper, and the Southern Cross are groups of individual stars situated between the sun and the Milky Way or in the peripheral region of our galaxy.

About a billion galaxies are within the range of the 200 inch Hale telescope; many of them are disc-like and resemble our own (Figs. 1 and 2); others are elliptic or nearly spherical in outline. The amount of gas and dust between galaxies has been computed to total almost as much mass as the galaxies themselves. The total amount of matter in the universe is incomprehensible in terms of weight measures we know.

Fig. 1. Galaxy NGC 3031 seen nearly face on, a galaxy with moderately tightly wound arms. In this and the next two pictures the individual bright areas of the galaxy consist of millions of stars which cannot be resolved individually by present-day telescopes. (Photograph from the Mount Wilson and Palomar Observatories.)

Fig. 2. Galaxy NGC 4565 seen edge on. The dark streak through the length of the galaxy is the disc of dust and gas. (Photograph from the Mount Wilson and Palomar Observatories.)

The distances encountered in the universe are likewise as incomprehensible as the weights. The distance from the earth to the moon is about 250,000 miles. Light, which travels at 186,000 miles per second, covers this distance in 1½ seconds. The distance from the earth to the sun is about 108 million miles, or 8⅓ light minutes, and the distance from the earth to the nearby star Alpha Centauri is a distance of 4.3 light *years*. The disc of our galaxy is some 80,000 light years across and 10,000 light years thick (Figs. 3 and 4). The distance to the nearest neighboring galaxy, the Andromeda nebula, is about 680,000 light years. Our galaxy belongs to a cluster of 17, the total group having a diameter of two million light years. Outside of this, the next cluster of galaxies is eight million light years away.

The universe and its parts are in constant motion. The earth rotates on its axis and, in addition, revolves around the sun. The sun and other stars also rotate, and, in addition, they sometimes have distinctive and highly individual paths, or orbits, within the galaxy. Each galaxy rotates as a whole. The various parts of our

Fig. 3. The Southern Milky Way photographed with a special 140° camera at Yerkes Observatory. This shows our galaxy edge on including the central core of stars and the disk of dust and gas. (Photograph by A. D. Code and T. E. Houck.)

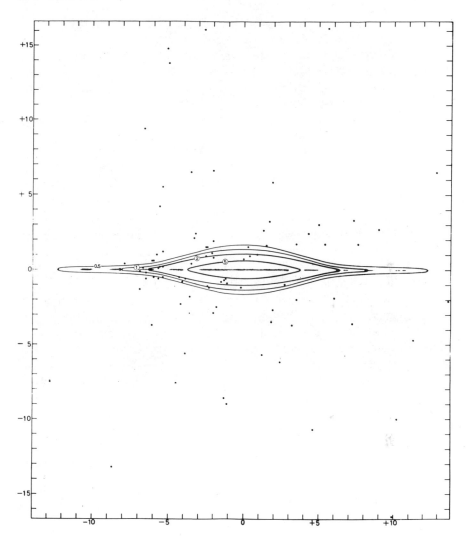

Fig. 4. Edge-on diagram of our galaxy. The sun is indicated by the small circle at the left, between the small numbers 0.5 and 1 in the left hand portion of the disc. The scale is in kiloparsecs; one kiloparsec is 3,260 light years. (After Oort.)

Milky Way galaxy rotate at different rates, the central portion making a complete revolution in 120 million years and the outer portion including our solar system in 230 million years. What effect this differential in speed will have on the future shape of the galaxy is not known (Oort, 1956).

The galaxies move in relation to each other but in a manner quite different from orbital or rotational movements. Studying peculiar shifts of red lines in the spectra of light emitted by celestial bodies and galaxies, Slipher, in 1920, deduced that the galaxies appear to be retreating from each other at rates proportional to their distances from us, and, soon after, Hubble concluded that the universe as a whole was expanding (Sandage, 1956). The optical explanation of the "retreating galaxies" can be readily visualized by the comparison made by Gamow (1951). If we imagine that the galaxies are black dots on a rubber balloon and that we are sitting on any one of the dots as the balloon is inflated, all the other dots will appear to be getting farther away from us. The more distant dots will appear to "retreat" faster than the closer ones.

This premise of the expanding nature of the universe is the basis for the two current theories seeking to explain the present form and content of the universe, the *explosion theory* (Gamow, 1951) and the *steady state theory* (Hoyle, 1950; Bondi, 1952).

According to the explosion theory, the beginning of our present universe started at a time when all matter had collapsed from space into a tremendous glob of primordial matter. In this presumed glob, pressures and temperatures became so high (the temperature is estimated to have been about a billion degrees) that matter was dissociated into neutrons. Presumably at this point of greatest contraction, the internal pressure literally blew the glob of neutrons apart, or started it expanding. This matter has been expanding ever since. As this expansion progressed, both temperature and pressure decreased and soon reached a point at which neutrons would disintegrate into protons and electrons which would combine in the form of stable elements. Physicists believe that within half an hour after the postulated expansion started, the entire mass would have formed into atoms, mostly into hydrogen but possibly some into helium as well.

Under the influence of gravitational forces, this tremendous expanding and turbulent mass of gas broke up into huge "gas balls," each gas ball continuing its movement from the center of the explosion into space but also developing an axial rotation of its own. Within each gas ball, the gases, again because of their turbulence, gradually aggregated into smaller and more dense spheres which condensed to become stars. Our sun is such a star.

If the explosion theory is correct, the time since the actual explosion can be computed from the rate of expansion in the universe.

Sandage (1958) gives a calculation of probably 13 to 20 billion years.

According to Sandage (1956), certain spectral shifts of distant galaxies may indicate that the expansion of the universe is slowing down. If this is true, it would suggest that the universe would eventually expand to a certain limit, then contract again into a titanic mass of neutrons and energy and thus start a new explosion. As a result, the universe as a whole would have a cyclical nature. A verification of the slowing down process would thus support the explosion rather than the steady state theory.

The *steady state theory* of the universe proposed by Hoyle, Bondi, and Gold postulates that new hydrogen is being formed constantly in inter-galactic space, that this new gas forms new great gas balls, and that these evolve into galaxies. The production of new galaxies theoretically equals the old ones which disappear over our horizon of space. According to this explanation, the universe would always look the same; it would have had no beginning and would continue for an infinite time.

EVOLUTION OF THE STARS AND ELEMENTS

The explosion theory accounts satisfactorily only for the theoretical production of hydrogen, the heavy isotopes of hydrogen (deuterium and tritium), and helium. The steady state theory postulates (but gives no theoretical basis for) the original production of hydrogen. In spite of their relative rarity on the earth, it is a fact that hydrogen (76 per cent) and helium (23 per cent) do comprise the great bulk of the matter in the entire universe (Fowler, 1956). However, in spite of their relatively low abundance (together, only 1 per cent of the weight of the universe) the other 90 chemical elements do occur and play important roles in the evolutionary processes of at least some parts of the solar system. Where these other elements (and possibly helium also) originated was for some years a mystery, but more recent studies show with little doubt that they had their origin in the dynamic processes occurring in stars. Lucid accounts of this entire topic are given by Fowler (1956) and the Burbidges (1958). A brief outline of their ideas follows.

If a portion of the cold, turbulent gas cloud of a galaxy that contains only hydrogen consolidates to form a star, the gravitation of the consolidating mass will compress the gas and, as a result, the star's interior will become denser and hotter. When the central temperature reaches about five million degrees, a series of nuclear reactions occur which convert hydrogen to helium with the production of large amounts of energy. This will heat the gases to a white luminosity. Thus the "cold jewels" we see in the sky are, in reality, extremely hot incandescent stars. Their heat radiates into space and is thus dissipated. When sufficient hydrogen is converted to helium, the star becomes unstable and contracts until its core may reach a temperature of 100 million degrees or more. Under these conditions, another set of nuclear reactions occur and helium is converted to carbon. When the amount of helium is sufficiently reduced, the star again becomes unstable and contracts still further. As higher core temperatures are reached, new nuclear reactions occur and heavier elements up to iron and its relatives are produced. Finally, when a star has exhausted all its fuel, it may explode or become what is called a white dwarf, or both. White dwarfs are unstable, if large, and will break up and lose matter until they reach the small size necessary for stability. In this fashion, the star begins as a ball of hydrogen aggregated from the gas cloud of the galaxy and ends as a small remnant composed chiefly of heavier elements. In this automatic, evolutionary process, a large proportion of the star's total matter is returned to the gas cloud of the galaxy but in a more complex chemical form than at the beginning.

Not all the stars in a galaxy form simultaneously. Star formation goes on continuously. Later generation stars have, in their original makeup, not only hydrogen but also some of the elements formed in earlier, now-exploded stars. Under these conditions, the nuclear reactions in the star may make different elements. Furthermore, stars may follow different evolutionary paths, each producing a different complement of elements during the life of the star. According to Fowler and the Burbidges, enough such element-making processes are known, or theoretically possible, to account for the formation of all the elements. From this they deduce that our sun, possessing all of the elements possible at its temperatures, is a third generation star.

THE SOLAR SYSTEM

The sun, composed chiefly of hydrogen and helium, is quite an ordinary star compared with others in the universe. Hoyle (1950) recognized that the earth and other planets of the solar system are "freaks" in the astronomical sense because they contain a high proportion of heavier elements such as iron and nickel. Many of these "freakish" conditions set the scene for the origin of life; hence it is pertinent to investigate the manner in which the solar system came into being.

The solar system consists of the sun, the nine planets which revolve around it, and moons revolving around six of the planets. The four small planets, Mercury, Venus, Earth, and Mars are closest to the sun; the four giant planets, Jupiter, Saturn, Uranus, and Neptune are located at much greater distances with the small planet Pluto beyond them.

According to earlier theories, the entire system resulted from a giant gas cloud, the edges gradually separating into gas rings around the resulting inner cloud. This inner cloud gradually condensed, more and more, until the pressure raised the heat of the interior to the point at which nuclear reactions occurred, giving the sun its present fiery nature. The gas rings were thought to have condensed into the planets. When the mechanics of the solar system were better known, however, it was discovered that the great distance of the giant planets from the sun combined with their relatively rapid orbital motion made this speculation untenable. The same circumstances also disprove the theory that explosions in the sun shot out huge gas balls which condensed to form the planets, or that another star passed sufficiently close to the sun as to tear away part of it in the form of a gas-dust cloud which, in turn, formed the planets (Jones, 1940).

According to the present consensus, the solar system arose from a pair of stars which were close together. Such twin stars are abundant in the galaxy. There is disagreement about the exact mechanics involved in the formation of the final (present) products in the system from such a twin origin. Some believe that when these twins were still gas-dust clouds, the larger (which became the sun) captured the smaller one in its gravitational field, and that the latter evolved into the planets. Others believe that the smaller star was the sun, and that the larger was a giant star. Giant stars burn with great rapidity and end by exploding as super-novae. According to this last theory, the sun's twin exploded in this fashion, blowing most of its mass far out into the galaxy but leaving behind a cloud composed chiefly of the giant's core of heavier elements. This cloud was then captured by the sun's gravitational field and evolved into the planets (Hoyle, 1950). On the basis of its radioactive materials, a meteorite presumably formed in this cloud has been calculated to be 4.95 billion years old. The meteorite fell in Richardton, N.D., in 1919 (Reynolds, 1960).

Hoyle believed that originally only a few solid planets condensed from this disc of dust and gas surrounding the sun but that these solid planets were too big to hold together after they had acquired a rotation of their own. They would have broken up, the fragments flying to various distances and ultimately evolving into the planets we now see.

Urey (1952), however, postulated that the planets became differentiated first as dust-gas clouds and that the earth cloud originally contained chiefly hydrogen, methane and inert gases, and large amounts of silicates, iron compounds, ice, and ammonia. He suggested the following course of events.

After the sun began emitting heat, the temperature of the earth cloud warmed up to the point at which the water and ammonia became liquid. These liquid particles in the cloud caused colliding dust particles to stick together; some larger pieces were formed, and by gravitational attraction the larger ones absorbed the smaller, until the first earth reached a stage (much smaller than it is now) when it was surrounded by a great number of small bodies called planetesimals revolving around it. At this time, the moon had almost reached its ultimate size. Both earth and moon were composed chiefly of siliceous material. The moon remained cold, but the earth, by virtue of its larger size and consequently greater internal pressure and larger total amounts of radioactive compounds, heated up. Under the high temperatures, most of its original gas atmosphere was lost. At some time the circling planetesimals fell onto the earth's surface and brought it up to its present size. Most of the earth's iron probably arrived by this means. Relatively few planetesimals fell on the moon, which presumably increased little in size. Those which did were responsible for the lines and craters which make up the curious present-day features of the moon's surface. When completely formed, the earth was chiefly composed of about 55 per cent silicates and 45 per cent iron, and had an atmosphere of water vapor, methane, ammonia, hydrogen, and some hydrogen sulphide.

Other theories as to how the planets were formed differ from the two above in various details. In particular some investigators believe that the early earth had no atmosphere and that the present hydrosphere and atmosphere, instead of dating from a primitive atmosphere, have accumulated gradually through geologic time by the escape of volatile substances from the interior of the earth (Rubey, 1955).

EVOLUTION OF THE PLANET EARTH

The earth is almost spherical, slightly flattened at the poles, and slightly pear-shaped by virtue of the southern hemisphere being a little larger than the northern hemisphere (O'Keefe *et al.*, 1959). The surface of the earth is highly irregular, marked by high mountain ranges, deep ocean troughs, and lesser relief features in between. The total relief from the deepest ocean trough to the highest mountain, however, is less than 13 miles, minute compared with the approximately 4,000 mile radius of the earth as a whole (Fig. 5). Almost three-fourths of the earth's surface is covered by

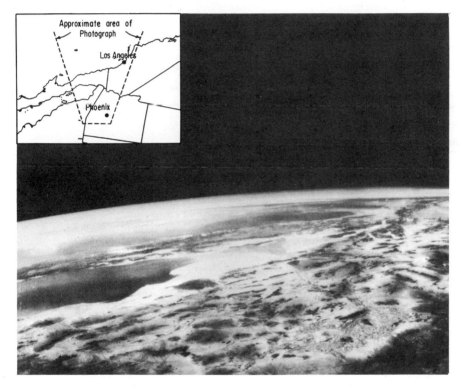

Fig. 5. The surface of the earth as seen from an altitude of 143.4 miles, showing its irregularities. The photo shows parts of Mexico, the Gulf of California, Arizona, and California to north of Los Angeles, shown in inset map. The mountains near the horizon on the right include peaks ranging from 5,000 to over 10,000 feet high. Photo taken from the U.S. Navy's Viking 12 rocket. (Official U.S. Navy Photo; inset added.)

ocean; if the earth's surface were completely levelled, it would all be covered by oceans several thousand feet deep.

The specific gravity of the whole earth is about 5.5 but that of its outer crust is only 2.7, indicating that it becomes more dense with depth. The exact internal composition of the earth is not known, but the study of both shear and compressional waves associated with earthquakes, the density of the earth, and the composition of the crustal rocks has led to several generally accepted interpretations as to the internal structure (Fig. 6). The core is a fluid sphere, possibly composed of nickel-iron (Urey, 1952) and having a diameter of about 2,500 km. Extending about 2,900 km above the core, is the

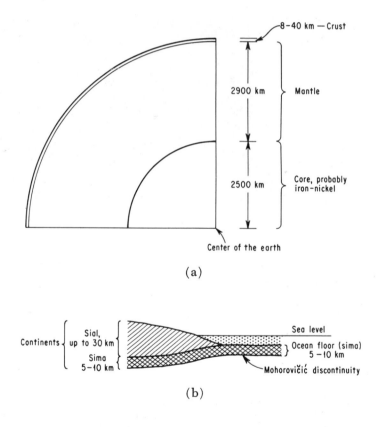

(a)

(b)

Fig. 6. Diagram of the supposed cross-section of the earth. (a) A quadrant of the earth, diagrammatic. (b) The earth's crust, diagrammatic.

mantle which shears under concentrated, short-term stress but which flows plastically under diffuse, long-term stress. The crust, 8 to 40 km thick, is the outermost part of the earth. It flows plastically only under extremely long-term stress. Each of these parts of the earth's interior is separated by more or less abrupt discontinuities which may be related to their density and physical properties.

The crust is extremely complex, and although we live on its surface and know much more about it than about the mantle and the core, we have only begun to unravel its structure. The crust extends under the oceans and across the continents. The oceanic areas of the crust lie beneath the great ocean basins and are 8 to 10 km thick. The rocks which compose this part of the crust are believed to be Fe-Mg-rich silicates, such as rock basalt, having a specific gravity of 2.9 to 3.1. They are commonly termed sima. These rocks are usually covered by only a few hundred feet of sediments consisting in part of fine clay particles washed in from the continents and in part of atmospheric dust and organic shells which form vast areas of "oozes."

The continental areas of the crust are believed to be strikingly different in most respects from those of the ocean areas, although locally there may be a gradation between the oceanic and continental types of crust. The upper portions of the continents are believed to be composed primarily of aluminum silicate rocks, such as granite, having a specific gravity of about 2.7. They are commonly termed sial. These low density rocks are about 30 km thick and rest on sima. The mountains of the world commonly have greatly thickened "roots" of sial and sima which extend into the mantle to much greater depths than is normal for continental areas, in much the same manner as icebergs extend farther beneath the water surface as they grow higher. Thus the thickness of the crust beneath the Himalaya Mountains, India, is nearly twice that of the crust beneath the Great Plains area of the United States.

Early History of the Earth

Age determinations from radioactive elements indicate the crust of the earth is at least 4 billion years old. The earth itself probably was formed about 4.5 or 5 billion years ago (J. T. Wilson, 1959; Hales, 1960). Hypotheses as to the process of its formation are about as numerous as the number of students of the field. Some believe that the earth started as a hot object and cooled with time, others that its temperature changed little with time, and still others that it began as a cool object and has since become warmer. Some believe it was molten; others believe it was solid. Depending upon their various premises, some believe it is shrinking, others that it is expanding, and still others that the earth has reached an equilibrium in its size and that its heat production and heat loss are in equilibrium. The origin of the three divisions of the earth, core, mantle, and crust, is also a major problem and has been discussed by Urey (1952), Wilson (1959), and Kennedy (1959) to name only a few. Some including Urey (1952) believed the earth was originally more homogeneous and that the three divisions of the earth are the result of density segregation of minerals as the earth cooled.

Crustal Changes

Perhaps one of the most significant realizations in the study of earth history has been the discovery that continental areas are far from being as stable as we commonly envisage. Indeed, in the geologic past, almost the only land areas persistent at any one place have been the continental shield areas, such as those found in eastern Canada, Brazil, Australia, and Siberia. Mountain ranges and huge troughs in the surface, called geosynclines, commonly formed at the edges of the continental shield areas. Shallow but extensive seas commonly flooded the interior of the shield areas. The end of the Cenozoic era in which we are living is perhaps exceptional because it is a time of widespread glaciation and because it has an unusual amount of emergent land. The continual changes of surface features and redistribution of land and sea areas on the continental blocks show that the crust is by no means a stable structure. Earthquakes, fault movement, and volcanic activity are but a few phenomena which give us day-by-day evidence of the dynamics of crustal instability.

The many diametrically opposed theories attempting to explain this instability fall into two major schools of thought. According to one school, the continents are essentially fixed in their relative positions and the crustal instability is the result of compressional forces in the earth's crust or mantle. According to the other school, the continents are not stationary but are "floating" blocks which respond to long-term stress and are free to "drift" over the sima. Various hypotheses modify these premises. According to Gamow's views (1948), the continental shields may have become fixed in their present position at a time before the possibility of the existence

of life on the earth. Others, however, believe that the drifting has
been much more recent and still continues (Wegener, 1924; DuToit,
1937; Runcorn, 1959; and Irving, 1959).

The hypothesis that continents occupy fixed positions rests chiefly
on interpretations of the folding of the crust resulting in island arcs
and linear mountain ranges associated with adjacent deep troughs
and geosynclines. Geosynclines are usually relatively narrow but
long depressions (Figs. 7, 8) which gradually fill with sediments
washed in from adjacent highlands. As they fill, the geosynclines

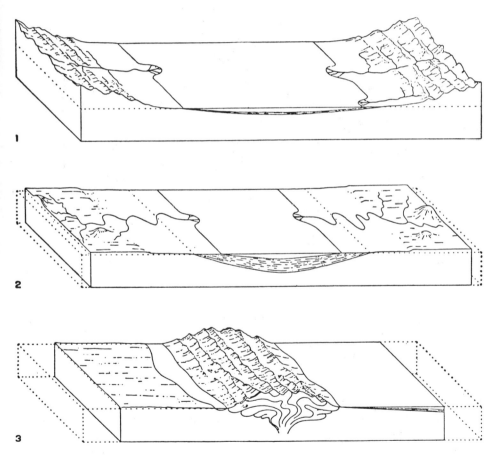

Fig. 7. Diagrammatic representation of a geosyncline. 1, original depression;
2, depression filling with sediments washed in from the adjacent highlands and
simultaneously sinking; 3, sedimentary rocks of geosyncline elevated into
mountains. Umbgrove depicts lateral compression accompanying these steps.
(After Umbgrove, *The Pulse of the Earth,* by permission of Martinus Nijhoff.)

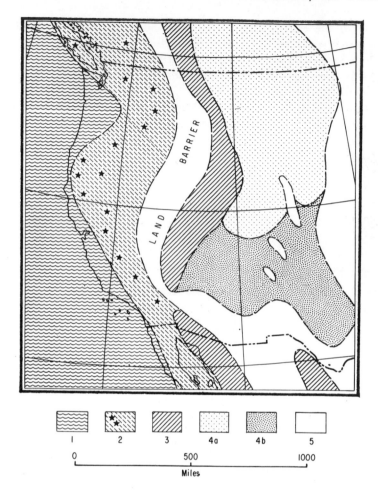

Fig. 8. Map of western United States showing generalized conditions during Triassic and Early Jurassic times. 1, ocean; 2, geosyncline west of the land barrier (stars indicate volcanic centers); 3, geosyncline east of the land barrier; 4, areas receiving lesser amounts of deposits; 5, protruding highland areas. (After King.)

sink deeper into the crust, thus becoming able to receive more sediments. Eventually the sinking trend is reversed and the entire geosyncline is folded and elevated to form linear mountain ranges. Thus, the Himalaya Mountains are composed chiefly of sedimentary rocks formed in the old extensive geosyncline (called the Tethys Sea) which occurred from at least middle Paleozoic time to the middle of Tertiary time, a span of 250 million years or more. The present Mediterranean Sea is the western remnant of the Tethys

Sea. The Gulf Coast of North America is the site of a geosyncline which has persisted since Cretaceous time. The Coast Ranges of the Western United States are folded and faulted strata representing a geosyncline which originated in Jurassic time and continued through the Cretaceous into late Cenozoic time (King, 1959). In the Pliocene and Pleistocene epochs, relatively recently geologically speaking, the sediments of this geosyncline were greatly deformed and uplifted to form parts of the Coast Ranges.

Mountain chains, island arcs, and geosynclines occur chiefly along continental margins or around old shield areas (Fig. 9). This

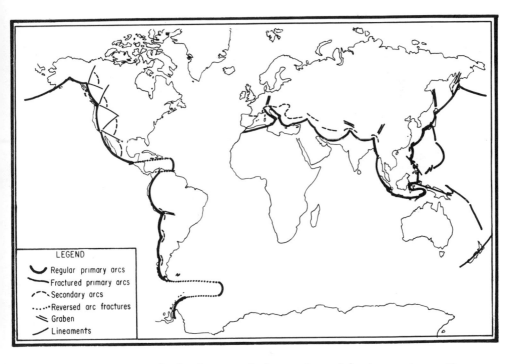

LEGEND
⌣ Regular primary arcs
⌐ Fractured primary arcs
⌢ Secondary arcs
···· Reversed arc fractures
⌇ Graben
╱ Lineaments

Fig. 9. Mountain and island arcs and the continental fracture system active at the present. (After J. T. Wilson.)

distribution is one of the chief points used by J. T. Wilson (1959) in his postulate that continents have enlarged through geologic time by the addition of geosynclinal sediments to primeval "shield" areas or nuclei of sialic material.

Umbgrove (1947) believed that these arcs of elevated areas and troughs result from crustal buckling created by hypothetical convection currents in the mantle. He suggested that deep in the mantle, rocks become hotter and thus less dense as a result of thermal expansion and that these rocks then move plastically upwards toward the crust where they cool and sink again. In this way convection currents in the mantle would develop. Urey (1952) suggested that the separation of iron from nickel compounds at the boundary between the core and the mantle releases heat and that this energy may initiate convection currents in the mantle.

Several writers since 1952 have disclaimed the existence of convection currents in the mantle, but Menard (1960) demonstrated that many lines of evidence concerning the East Pacific Rise are explainable on the basis of such currents. The East Pacific Rise is a vast low bulge of the ocean floor, about 2,000 to 4,000 km wide with its crest arising northward off the coast of British Columbia and Washington, cutting under the western edge of the North American continent to about midwestern Mexico, from there extending across the Pacific first south and then irregularly to near New Zealand. In a lucid, remarkable synthesis, Menard pointed out how the convection hypothesis (Fig. 10) explained the observed

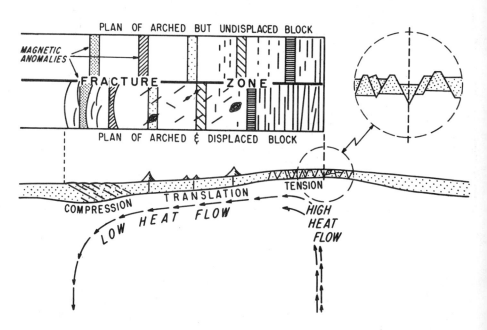

Fig. 10. A diagram of the crustal features associated with the East Pacific Rise and their supposed relation to the convection-current hypothesis. The circle in the upper right depicts block faulting and rifting caused by the supposed up-welling of the crust. (After Menard.)

differences in heat radiation from the ocean floor, the apparent differences in thickness of the crust in the Rise area, and the submarine topographic features of upthrust, slumping, and faulting.

Few hypotheses have caused as much controversy as Wegener's hypothesis (1924) of continental drift. Followers of this hypothesis believe that South America, Africa, India, Australia, and Antarctica once fitted together as one large continent, Gondwana land, which has since broken up and drifted apart. Jardetsky (1954) postulated that the difference in rotational speeds between equatorial and polar regions would provide a mechanism for such continental fragmentation and reported supporting experiments on the rupture of thin plates under the influence of such simulated conditions.

Wegener (1924) and Du Toit (1937) believed that the separation of the African mass from the South American mass had occurred within the last 40 or 50 million years, at least within the Cenozoic. Studying polar wanderings, as deduced from rock paleomagnetism, Runcorn (1959) and Irving (1959) arrived at figures that suggest little drifting in the northern hemisphere since the Cretaceous (about 70 million years ago) and an amount of drifting that would bridge only a third of the Atlantic Ocean since the Cambrian, some 600 million years ago (Fig. 11).

Origin of the Hydrosphere and Atmosphere

Two other components of the earth are of vital importance to the process of organic evolution: the oceans and the atmosphere. Urey (1952) believed that the hot period of the earth's crust lasted only a short time. He deduced that, as temperatures in the earth's atmosphere rapidly cooled to their present state, the various gaseous elements combined to form an atmosphere of water vapor, hydrogen, ammonia, methane, and smaller quantities of other gases. A large part of the water vapor condensed and filled the low areas to form the oceans. Urey also asserted that the water comprising possibly 95 per cent of the oceans has escaped from the interior of the earth during geologic time. Thus the early oceans would have been small and would have supplied only a limited amount of rain to erode areas of the cooled earth. As the volume of surface water increased, so would the amounts of rain, ice, and snow, bringing about great erosive forces constantly tending to level the highland areas of the earth's crust.

Other investigators believe that the primeval earth lost all its

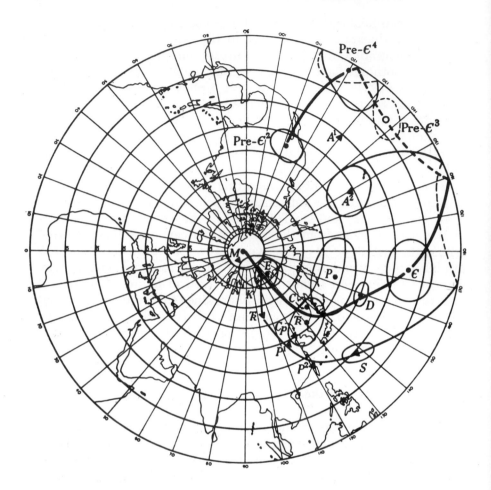

Fig. 11.   Polar wandering paths postulated from pre-Cambrian to the present on the basis of rock magnetism. *A*, pre-Cambrian of the United States; *Pre-ϵ*, pre-Cambrian of Great Britain; ϵ, Cambrian; *O*, Ordovician; *S*, Silurian; *D*, Devonian; *C*, *Cp*, Cambrian or Pennsylvanian; *P*, Permian; *Tr*, Triassic; *K*, Cretaceous; *E*, Eocene; *M*, Miocene. Solid lines, paths in Northern Hemisphere; broken lines, paths in Southern Hemisphere. Thick line, paths inferred from British rocks; thin line, paths inferred from American rocks. (After Runcorn.)

surface gases and that the present oceans and atmosphere are the result of gases escaping from the earth's interior (Rubey, 1955). Rubey believes that a dense primitive atmosphere would have had geological effects not now found on the earth and that several postulated conditions of early earth history can account for the escape of all its original atmospheric gases. He believes that the progenitor of our present atmosphere was composed chiefly of water vapor, nitrogen, and carbon dioxide and agrees with Urey that the present high content of atmospheric oxygen is the result of biological activity. Bernal (1951) believes that some methane and ammonia were present, and Revelle (1955) would consider likely the presence of some carbon monoxide. Rubey (1955) adduces evidence that the chemical composition of the atmosphere and oceans has varied little since early in geologic time.

A review of this chapter emphasizes the sketchy and controversial nature of our knowledge and opinions concerning many facets of the origin and evolution of the present universe and particularly of the earth. Yet a general theme can be discerned even if the details are obscure. Whatever the start of the process, laws of physics and chemistry coupled with laws of probability have led, step by step, from gas masses to stars and planets. Under the conditions set by one situation, the next result occurred automatically and in turn created the conditions which led to the next evolutionary development. When we finally learn the truth about the evolution of the earth, we will unquestionably find that its present properties are the result of changes set in motion by its original chemical composition and physical characteristics.

Two items concerning the earth are of unusual evolutionary interest. In the first place, the earth's crust, and probably its interior as well, is not static but highly dynamic. As will be seen later, this dynamic aspect of the earth's crust has been, and is, one of the most important features in shaping the course of biological evolution. Secondly, from early in the earth's history to the present, the gases occluded in its formative materials have leaked through the crustal layers, bringing reactive gaseous mixtures containing the elements carbon, hydrogen, oxygen, nitrogen, and sulphur and discharging these and their products above the crust to form or influence our oceans and atmosphere. These masses of escaping gases likely played a responsible part in the initial formation of life on this planet.

Life: Its Nature

and Origin

3

Life did originate on this planet some two or more billion years ago but exactly how we do not know. Two avenues of investigation, however, are beginning to provide tangible clues as to its probable mode of origin. One consists of an increasingly more detailed knowledge of the structure, chemistry, and physics of life, and the other consists of a better appraisal of the possible and probable course of chemical and physical reactions which would have taken place under conditions existing on the pre-biological earth. When these two avenues meet, a plausible and relatively complete hypothesis should emerge to explain how life began on the earth.

THE NATURE OF LIFE

As more has been learned about life, it has been found to be a physico-chemical mechanism com-

plicated almost beyond the limits of our imagination. The search
for those properties of life which will throw light on its origin has
been an arduous undertaking complicated by many factors. The
total evidence of phylogeny shows clearly that life began as a
simple cell suggesting that a study of the simplest unicellular
organisms may be the chief avenue for deducing the properties of
the primeval cells of first life; but here difficulties arise. In the first
place, it is highly unlikely that any living cell is as primitive as the
primeval cell because each persisting kind of cell has been evolving
to some extent during the two billion or more years that life has
existed. In the second place, it is difficult to study life. The bacteria
and viruses are excellent objects of study for many experiments on
chemical and physical properties, but they are too minute for
observation and manipulation beyond a gross degree. Experimenting with many of the unicellular nucleate organisms circumvents
a number of these difficulties but presents the same problem in that
the various functions of the organisms are crowded together in a
small space. From this standpoint, the multicellular organisms are
better subjects for study because certain cells such as muscle tissue
or nerves may become so highly specialized for the performance
of one biological function that in them the processes of particular
functions may be studied to special advantage. Yet these specialized
cells are so different from the primeval cell that great care must
be exercised in extrapolating from one to the other.

By bringing together information from these various sources, it
is possible to reconstruct a sort of idealized cell combining properties basic to all life and in its essential features probably approach-
ing closely the primeval cells which were the beginning of all the
existing life on this planet. Life progresses and continues from
generation to generation by the growth and division of cells and in
no other way. Our problem, therefore, is resolved into two parts:
How do cells grow, and how do they divide? The answers to these
questions are essential not only to deductions concerning the origin
of life but also to an understanding of its evolution.

The cell has three principal structural components: the cell wall,
essentially a membrane which separates the contents of the cell
from its external environment; the nucleus, the central dense portion containing the highly complex genic material; and the cytoplasm, usually a viscous aqueous colloid containing a tremendous
assortment of simple and complex molecules, including proteins,
free amino acids, carbohydrates, fats, and metallic compounds.

The living cell has a most precise life history, as is demonstrated by the careful studies of Mazia (1956) on unicellular animals. Typically the cell grows until it doubles its weight; then, without further weight increase, it undergoes a period presumably occupied by some sort of maturing activity; then it divides. If some cytoplasm is removed from a newly full grown cell, this cell will grow some more until its doubled weight is restored, then go into the dividing sequence. However, Mazia found that there is a time point near the beginning of the maturation period after which the cell, if injured, will not stop to replace its weight, but will proceed with the division process. In other words, there is a triggering point which starts the actual division of the cell, and, after the trigger is pulled, the process can go only toward completion.

The physical process of division occurs in certain well-defined stages (Fig. 12). The boundaries of the nucleus disappear and the chromosomes, diffused within the nucleus during the growing period, condense into compact threads (C). Simultaneously, a mitotic center forms and divides, and a daughter center moves to each pole (A and B). Each of these centers is a protein gel oriented into a system of aster-like rays. During this development, the chromosomes come to lie in a flat equatorial plane between the poles, and the centromere of each chromosome is attached to a ray of a mitotic center (D). These connecting rays become greatly strengthened to form distinctive fibers. The entire system of fibers is called the spindle. By this stage, each chromosome is double, composed of two daughters. Next the daughter chromosomes separate into two identical sets (E) and each set moves to a pole (F). During this movement the chromosome-to-pole fibers shorten and the equator-to-chromosome fibers lengthen; it is a moot point whether the chromosome sets are pulled apart, pushed asunder, or are moved by a combination of both. Finally the walls of the cell pinch in (G); the mitotic centers and the spindle structures disappear, the chromosomes loose their obvious identity to form a well-defined nucleus, and the division is complete (H). Each daughter cell now starts the cycle of growth all over again.

The formation of the mitotic centers and the spindle is a real puzzle. Mazia advanced the interesting hypothesis that these centers and their rays and fibers arise through the formation of bundles of connected protein molecules, each pair joined by a sulphur-to-sulphur bond known as a disulphide bridge. He suggested that, in a series of chemical reactions involving the sub-

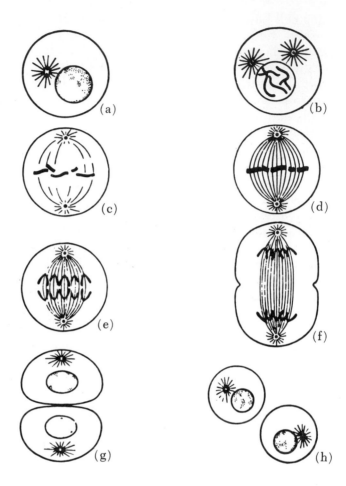

Fig. 12. The stages of mitosis shown diagrammatically. For explanation of stages see text. (After Mazia.)

stance glutathione, disulphide bridges which originally connected parts of the same protein molecule are switched around to connect adjacent molecules.

The phenomena of cell growth, spindle formation, and division are visible manifestations of a series of highly complex chemical reactions occurring in the cell. However, the sum of these reactions requires both raw materials and energy which must be present in the environment of the cells and which must be in such states that the cell can absorb them. These ingested raw materials are the nutrients of the cell. Nutrient material passes through the cell membrane into the cytoplasm. These nutrients may first be broken down to simple compounds. Gradually they are built up into more complex compounds and finally into duplicates of the structures of the original young cell. When the cell has exactly doubled in weight, it undergoes maturation and division again, as was described above.

Simple though these steps sound, each is highly complex. The cell membrane is a series of meshes of proteinaceous and other molecules oriented by inherent physical properties of attraction and repulsion into a precise network. Conditions either outside or inside the cell cause the network to change the "mesh" so that different compounds can pass through it at different times. Only molecules in aqueous solution can go through the membrane, and they do it according to the physical laws of diffusion. Diffusion unaided could not supply the cell as we know it with the large amount of nutrients needed for its growth. Several methods for supplementing diffusion have evolved. In one method, the size of the mesh of the membrane decreases, preventing the diffusion of certain substances out of the cell. This causes differences in solution concentrations in the two sides of the membrane, effecting an automatic flow of the solvent into the cell (osmosis). In another method (Weinstein, Robbins, and Perkins, 1954; Thomas, 1956) it is thought that complex, organic bonding agents (chelating compounds) combine with needed molecules to form compounds which will diffuse into the cytoplasm. Then they release the captive compounds to other compounds in the cytoplasm. The freed molecules of the chelating agents then diffuse back to the outer regions of the membrane, and the process can start over again. This process is in reality a miniature molecular machine, kept going by material arriving from the external environment and being consumed within the cell, geared by automatic chemical and physical conditions inherent in the cell.

Once inside the cell, these nutrients are consumed in two types of reactions. In one, the enormously varied and complex compounds of the cell are built up, that is, doubled, from the ingested raw materials. In the other, the raw materials take part in reactions which produce the energy to perform the synthetic reactions involved in this replication.

Of all the compounds in the cell, the proteins are the largest and most complex. A tremendous number of proteins have been observed in living systems. The basis of proteins are amino acids, of which 22 kinds have been identified (Fruton, 1950). Individually these are relatively simple, as shown in the diagrams of the common amino acids glycine and alanine (Fig. 13). Each amino acid

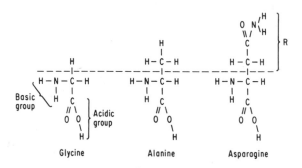

Glycine   Alanine   Asparagine

Fig. 13. Structural formulae of three amino acids. The portion of each above the dotted line is called the side chain or *residue*, R.

molecule has both an acidic carboxyl group (—COOH) and a basic or amino group (—NH₂). Several amino acids (either all one kind or a mixture) may join together, base to acid, base to acid, and so on, lose H₂O in the process, and form linear chains called peptides. These chains become aligned so that the atoms —C—C—N—C—C—N— form a central axis (called a polypeptide chain) from which hydrogen and oxygen atoms and the distinctive residues of the amino acids stick out as branches (Fig. 14). Proteins are essentially very long polypeptide chains whose size may be judged from their molecular weight which ranges from 2,000 to 10,000,000. The amino acid residues may occur in a variety of combinations along the chain, each combination with potentialities for entirely different physical and chemical behavior. The best known protein is insulin (Fig. 15), one of the smaller proteins with a molecular weight of about 6,000 (Sanger, 1959). Entire chains may become bonded together or combined with other types of compounds.

What is the role of proteins? They form many of the structural elements of cells, such as collagen in bone and myosin in muscle fiber; they constitute those tremendously varied groups of compounds, enzymes and hormones. Certain complex types, the protamines, form what is believed to be an important part of the genetic structure. Linderstrom-Lang (1953) and Pauling, Corey, and Hayward (1954) gave instructive accounts of other features of proteins.

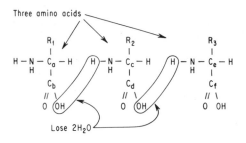

Three amino acids

Lose 2H₂O

And form a peptide chain

Fig. 14. The formation of peptide chains. The carbon atoms have been designated individually from *a* to *f* to aid comparison between the amino acids and the peptide chain.

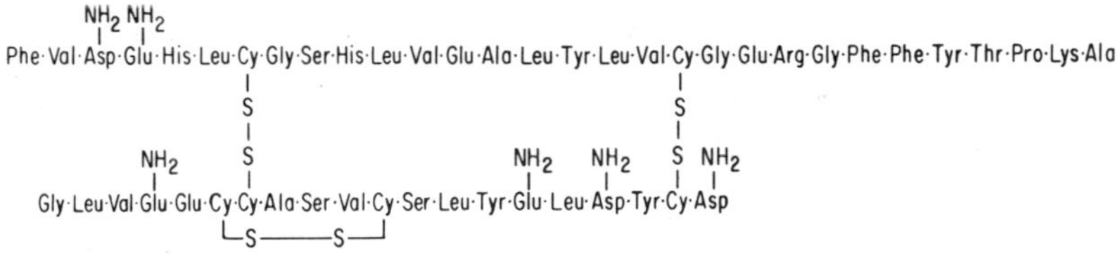

NH₂ NH₂
Phe·Val·Asp·Glu·His·Leu·Cy·Gly·Ser·His·Leu·Val·Glu·Ala·Leu·Tyr·Leu·Val·Cy·Gly·Glu·Arg·Gly·Phe·Phe·Tyr·Thr·Pro·Lys·Ala
S   S
NH₂   S   NH₂   NH₂   S NH₂
Gly·Leu·Val·Glu·Glu·Cy·Cy·Ala·Ser·Val·Cy·Ser·Leu·Tyr·Glu·Leu·Asp·Tyr·Cy·Asp
S——————S

Fig. 15. The arrangement of amino acid residues in the molecule of the protein insulin. The abbreviations indicate the identity of the amino acid residues. (After Sanger.)

Proteins are not the only groups of highly complex organic compounds found in the living cell. A group of complex alcohols called steroids comprise some of the important hormones and vitamins necessary for cell functioning (Fieser, 1955). Complex sugars, certain phosphorus compounds active in respiration, a wide assortment of pigments, and many other molecules may contain nearly a hundred or more atoms per molecule. Among the largest molecules in the cell are the nucleic acids, which are long chains of sugar molecules with other groups attached to them.

These compounds and many more must be doubled between each

cell division. All available information indicates that the manufacture proceeds along exact chemical paths and in a predetermined chronological order, yet consists of the usual type of chemical reactions: combining two molecules into one, dividing one into two, or rearranging the bonds within the same compound. Thus it may take dozens of steps to build up a single complex molecule. Remembering that it occurs at relatively low temperatures, the surprising feature about this synthesis is that it is so rapid. In a mosquito larva, for example, practically all the cells in the full grown body may arise by successive divisions of an egg in five or six days. The growing tips of corn plants have been known to lengthen nearly a foot overnight. A bacterial cell may mature and divide in 20 minutes. It borders on the fantastic to try to imagine the rapidity with which the millions of chemical reactions must tick off in their precisely ordered sequence to bring about these results.

This apparent miracle is due to the enzymes which catalyze these biological reactions at speeds far beyond their ordinary rate of occurrence at biological temperatures. About a hundred enzymes have now been isolated, each one catalyzing a particular type of reaction. We have no idea of the number of specific reactions in the cell which require an enzyme, except that it is tremendous. We do know that the same enzyme may participate in more than one reaction, but presumably in each of such reactions the basic mode of action is the same, for instance, the addition or removal of hydrogen or the addition or removal of an —OH ion. It is of interest to note that, whereas the enzyme is a large protein molecule, in at least some enzymes the only known reactive part is their lone atom of iron or copper in each enzyme molecule (Mahler, Baum, and Hübscher, 1956).

Present research indicates that enzymes increase the rapidity of action in the following general fashion. Suppose compounds A and B are the raw materials from which the cell synthesizes essential compound AB, but that A and B unite directly at only a slow rate. Enzyme C, however, unites with A rapidly to form compound AC. Unlike plain A, the compound AC unites rapidly with B to form AB and C. Thus the two reactions $A + C = AC$, $AC + B = AB + C$, progress at a fast rate to produce AB, with the original enzyme C restored to its original condition. The parallel will immediately be obvious between this chain of events and the action of chelating compounds mentioned a few pages earlier. Each enzyme forms part of a machine which will run continuously as long as A and B are "fed" to the enzyme C, and presumably AB is removed in some fashion.

This example is an extremely simple one used to illustrate the general principle of enzyme action. In the cell many of these reaction chains are extremely complex. Theorell (1956) gave an interesting account of the mode of action of several enzymes and pointed out that in some cases the chain of reactions may go through as many as nine steps before the enzyme is free again. He also pointed out that in certain reactions a second enzyme must first activate or condition the primary enzymes. These accessory coenzymes act like a self-starter on a car, a little motor starting the big motor. Energy is always either released or consumed in a chemical reaction. If, therefore, one of the enzymatic reactions *consumes* energy, it must be linked in some fashion with another reaction which *produces* energy. The energy-giving reaction itself will be a machine-like one involving an enzyme system, and may indeed be a whole system of systems, such as the ATP-ADP system (Fig. 16).

We can make a simplified analogy between one of these complicated situations and an automobile engine. The battery supplies the energy to rotate the starter (a co-enzyme) which in turn starts the motor, which then turns the generator to produce electric power which recharges the battery. This recharging is a by-product of the main work done by the motor. The entire system, however, is dependent on receiving from the external environment fuel in the form of gasoline and oxygen. However, not any indiscriminate amount will work; the motor is a machine in such delicate balance that the correct amounts of its fuels must be applied and at the right time and intervals. This is accomplished by accessory machines, the carburetor and valving system. Also like a living cell, the automobile motor must dispose of its waste products.

Bearing in mind the vast number of compounds in the cell, the complexities of the enzyme systems, and the meticulously accurate organization of the cell, it is possible to visualize it as an intermeshed series of molecular machines. From the original intake of raw materials from the environment to the duplicating of the last molecule in the mature cell, these tiny machines must lead from one to the other, the last dependent on the first and the first on the last. A failure of even one could conceivably bring the whole chain to a halt, resulting in the death of the organism. For one fact is true about life: *it must keep going to stay alive* (Ruzicka, 1919; Nilsson, 1953).

The ultimate and critical products of cell growth would seem

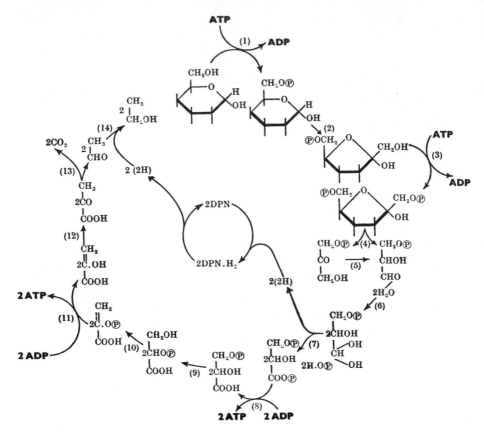

Fig. 16. A summary of the complex cyclic reactions associated with biological oxidation in which energy-poor ADP (adenosine diphosphate) is converted into energy-rich ATP (adenosine triphosphate). These summarize a set of "molecular machines" which provide energy for other biological reactions. (From E. Baldwin, *Dynamic Aspects of Biochemistry*, 3d. Ed., Cambridge: Cambridge University Press, 1948.)

to be the main components of the nucleus, the protamines and nucleic acids. These two groups of compounds comprise the chief bulk of the mature nucleus and are believed to constitute the great bulk of the genic material of the cell.

In most mature cells the most abundant nucleic acids are ribonucleic acid (RNA) and the more complex desoxyribonucleic acid (DNA) (Fig. 17). The basic structure of DNA is composed of alternating pentose sugars and phosphate groups linked together to form an extremely long chain; to each sugar group is linked an organic base. Each chain probably contains a thousand or more sugar groups, yet commonly only four kinds of bases are present in the chain; two of them are larger structures called purines (adenine

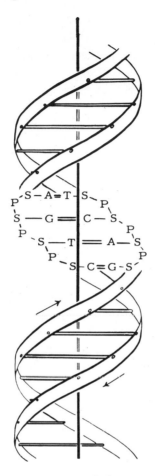

Fig. 17. Diagrammatic representation of the Watson-Crick model of DNA. P, phosphate group; S, pentose sugar group; A, adenine; T, thyamine; G, guanine; C, cytosine. Horizontal parallel lines symbolize hydrogen bonding between complementary bases A, T, G, and C. (After Beadle.)

and guanine), and two are smaller bases called pyrimidines (thymine and cytosine) (Fig. 17). In DNA two of these chains occur parallel with each other, with the sugar-phosphate chains on the outside and the bases of opposing sides not only directed toward each other but opposite members of each pair probably also joined with weak hydrogen bonds (Crick, 1954). Watson and Crick (1953) calculated the spatial arrangements of the atoms in such a compound and further postulated that in these pairings of bases, one space must be small, the opposite large, and that only the two pairs adenine-thymine and guanine-cytosine could occur. X-ray photographs of purified material led to the final postulate that this ladder-like double chain is actually coiled into a helix, one complete circle to about every ten sugar groups. The molecular weight has been estimated at 800,000.

The protamines are proteins peculiar to nuclei, with calculated molecular weights ranging from 2,000 to 12,000. Each protamine molecule contains eight or ten kinds of amino acids of a select known group of about 12, of which proline, alanine, and arginine are common. The proportions of the various amino acids and the exact order of their arrangement varies from species to species. Felix (1955) indicated that, according to present knowledge, there are possibilities in these molecules for the existence of literally millions of different compounds. Felix calculated that in the nucleus there are about 100 protamine molecules per molecule of DNA, and he suggested that protamine and DNA are actually combined in this ratio of 100:1 to form enormous nucleoprotamine molecules. He further calculated that each trout sperm nucleus has space for about 4,660,000 of these nucleoprotamine molecules, which would be an average of 233,000 per chromosome. Other investigators believe that the DNA and protamines are not actually combined chemically but lie together in some fashion (Kacser, 1956; Serra, 1958). Serra pointed out that the protamines form the main backbone of the chromosome strands, that the DNA is distributed unevenly along it or among its strands (Fig. 18), and that DNA, at least in the form identified by current techniques, may be greatly reduced in quantity during the growing stages of the cell.

The duplication of the giant nucleoprotein structures is poorly understood. Many models have been proposed for the synthesis of the duplicate member (Crick, 1954; Kacser, 1956; Steinberg, Vaughan, and Anfinsen, 1956; Taylor, Woods, and Hughes, 1957; Hoagland, 1959). However, the relationship between RNA, DNA, and protamines has not yet been established. Serra (1958) emphasized that synthesis of the protamine must precede synthesis of new DNA and concluded that none of these compounds reduplicate themselves directly but that one is formed by the other.

Although the exact processes are still obscure, enough is known about them to suggest that final duplication at cell maturity of RNA, DNA, and the protamines is in some fashion associated with the climactic molecular machines which trigger the reactions leading to cell division (Burns, 1959) and that the products of this

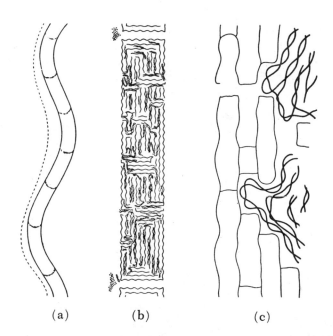

(a)   (b)   (c)

Fig. 18. Possible arrangement of protamine and DNA in strands of the mature nucleus. (a) Scheme of a chromonema strand, composed of a sequence of threadlike monomers (nemameres) The interrupted line represents other components which may exist in chromosomes during some stages of the cell cycle. (b) Longitudinal section of one monomer of (a). The nemamere is not represented to scale; only parts of the chains, in length and in diameter, are shown. Nucleic acid chains are represented as double helices and protein chains as single helices. The chains are folded many times, although their disposition along the chromonema axis predominates. At the junctions of contiguous nemameres dots represent types of compounds which help in the bonding of such monomers, which should take place, however, chiefly through secondary forces. (c) Scheme of two genic sites with specific geometry, composed of mutually adapted protamine chains and complementary nucleic acid chains. (After Serra.)

division restore the molecular machines that initiate a new period of growth.

There is little doubt that the molecules in the cell must be arranged in a precise physical architecture. Otherwise, it is difficult to conceive of the proper molecules being in reactive positions which will permit the even flow of chemical reactions necessary for the rapid growth exhibited by many cells and especially for the operation of the many "molecular machines" which are cyclic in nature. Indeed, this consideration suggests that the interior of the cell is a continuous system of exactly spaced boundaries forming an orderly array of interactive components. This idea is supported by histological studies (Fig. 19). This architecture must be dynamic because various parts such as the chromosomes change in size and shape during the cycle of growth.

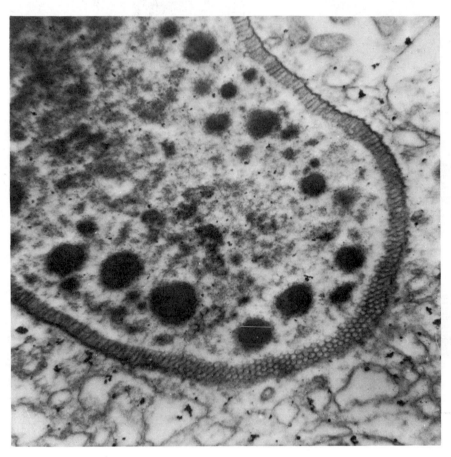

Fig. 19. The nuclear membrane of *Amoeba proteus* as photographed with the electron microscope. Note the remarkable orientation of the units. (Photograph courtesy of George Pappas and the Upjohn Company.)

An entirely different aspect of cell architecture arises from studies made by Szent-Györgi (1956) concerning energy used in the cell. Although it is known that this energy arises from changes in chemical bonding, the question remains: How is such *chemical* energy converted into *mechanical* energy in a form available for cellular processes such as muscle contraction? Szent-Györgi offered strong evidence that the chemical energy produced in the cell can be converted into electromagnetic energy, which can be used for work and which also can produce work (for example, the clumping of molecules in muscle) elsewhere than at the site of production. He pointed out, however, that the only known basis of such electronic conversion is through certain phenomena of electron excitation called phosphorescence. This phosphorescence does not occur in ordinary fluid water, in which the water molecules are moving at random, but can occur in appreciable amounts in ice, which is a crystal having a highly organized and non-random arrangement of the water molecules. On this basis Szent-Györgi postulated that the water molecules in living systems are not randomized, but are highly organized and oriented.

He suggested that further study of three factors will contribute greatly to our understanding of biological reactions: water structures, the electromagnetic field, and forms of electron excitation made possible by water structure. The resultant findings might aid in explaining the molecular clumping which forms structures of the spindle at cell division, the gathering and organizing of material to duplicate macromolecules, and other cellular puzzles.

Our idealized cell has one additional property of great importance. With only minor and infrequent exceptions, when the cell divides it produces daughter cells exactly like the parent cell, generation after generation. This is borne out by the exactness with which progeny resemble their parents through all classes of living things. Daughter amoebae look like the parent amoeba, daughter oaks like parent oaks. It seems established beyond all doubt that the macromolecules of the nucleus forming the chromosomes (chiefly DNA and the protamines) are the structures responsible for this continuity of similarity and, therefore, that these molecular structures are duplicated with extreme accuracy during cell division. This topic forms the subject of the next chapter.

At this point we can visualize some of the properties and habits of the cell, the unit of life. The cell consists of many kinds of molecules, some of them extremely complex, held together in an aqueous colloidal gel, having at least some properties suggestive of a crystalline state, and separated from the external environment by an enveloping membrane which is essentially the outside layer of the gel. The whole is essentially a multiplicity of tiny molecular machines so organized that they proceed radially from the edge of the cell to a culmination in those processes which ultimately re-duplicate the protamines and nucleic acids in the nucleus.

Environment

Life, however, cannot be considered apart from its environment because this must provide both nutrients and other suitable conditions for life's existence. These two environmental items may therefore be of interest in a consideration of plausible pre-biological conditions.

If, as seems to be the case, primeval life came into existence before photosynthesis had evolved, we may assume that its minimum nutritional requirements were those common to all but the green plants. It is significant that these minimum requirements are strikingly similar for bacteria, protozoa, insects, and mammals (Trager, 1953; Johnson, 1956; Lea, Dimond, and DeLong, 1956). Using these minimum requirements as a basis, the needs of our primeval cell were (1) water (the first cell presumably originated in an aqueous environment); (2) a large selection of amino acids; (3) some nucleic acid derivatives such as guanine or cytidine; (4) a number of vitamins, generally at least six and commonly many more; and (5) a large number of inorganic substances including phosphorus, potassium, iron, copper, zinc, cobalt, and calcium. Although the energy foods (carbohydrates and fats) are used by many organisms, some of the other organic compounds may be "burned" by the tissues for energy. Except for water, our cell requires building blocks from which protein and nucleic acid are manufactured and a few other elements and compounds vital to the chemical reactions of such manufacture.

Suitable factors for the existence of life in water, which is the habitat of pre-biological interest, comprise chiefly temperature and chemical composition. The upper temperature limit for most known living aquatic organisms ranges from slightly above 0°C (32°F) to about 48°C (120°F), but a few algae living in thermal springs tolerate 85°C (185°F). Individual species in water vary greatly in chemical tolerances. In general, each species can tolerate only certain concentrations of various ions in solution. Above or below these critical values, the organism loses or absorbs too much water to maintain a proper internal organization or suffers other losses or absorptions which produce the same effect. Thus the highly ionized metallic salts or inorganic acids such as sodium chloride or sulphuric acid produce much greater environmental effects than comparable amounts of the many much less reactive organic salts and acids.

In summary, the miniature physico-chemical universe called the living cell, if situated in its proper environment, ticks along automatically like a watch, first growing and finally dividing into two daughters, each like the original and each automatically repeating the processes of growth and reproduction.

ORIGIN OF LIFE

A plausible explanation for the origin of life must account for three items: (1) the simple elements or molecules of the pre-biological world which formed the building blocks for life, (2) a logical set of chemical reactions which would lead to the formation of life, and (3) a source of nutrient materials for the persistence of life.

Available Materials

As was indicated in Chapter 1, there has been considerable controversy about the pre-biological composition of the atmosphere and the oceans, but most authors agree that the atmosphere contained little or no oxygen and was essentially a reducing or at least a non-oxidizing medium. It probably contained chiefly water vapor, carbon dioxide, and nitrogen, with small quantities of hydrogen sulphide, methane, and ammonia. The oceans probably contained dissolved carbon dioxide, ammonia, and hydrogen sulphide, with various metallic compounds, chlorides, and phosphorus compounds in solution.

Pre-biological Syntheses

Oparin (1938) believed that, during a time when atmospheric temperatures were from 300°C to 1,000°C, a certain proportion of these compounds would combine to form simple hydrocarbons such as acetylene and that later, when the oceans formed, they would contain quantities of these hydrocarbons in solution.

In 1953 S. L. Miller pumped a mixture of ammonia, methane, water vapor, and hydrogen (the mixture believed by Urey to constitute the primeval atmosphere) past an intermittent electric discharge and found that at the end of a week the condensed water vapor had become red and turbid. On analysis, the products proved definitely to contain three amino acids, glycine, *a*-alanine, and *b*-alanine, and possibly a fourth, aspartic acid. Because amino acids are the building blocks of protein, these results aroused great interest in the question of the origin of life. Since Miller's historic experiment, many amino acids have been synthesized by using various mixtures of gases activated by electricity, ultra-violet irradiation, and heat (Miller and Urey, 1959). It is therefore evident that amino acids would have been formed by a variety of processes in the reducing gas mixtures of the pre-biological world.

Once formed, many of these products would have had a long life. Abelson (1954) isolated amino acids from fossils up to 300 million years old and estimated that under today's climatic conditions alanine would have a life of many billions of years.

As Blum (1957) and Fox (1956) pointed out, it is a long step from the production of amino acids to that of protein, and it is protein which is practically synonymous with life. For amino acids to polymerize into a protein-like chain, they must lose a molecule of water at each linkage, and, outside biological systems, this loss of water can be accomplished only by the addition of considerable energy in a nearly anhydrous environment. Blum pointed out that both Katchalski (1951) and Fox and Middlebrook (1954) had achieved some success with protein synthesis under these hot dry conditions. From this he suggested that, under pre-biological conditions, pools containing dissolved amino acids might dry up, and in this concentrated dry state, with the aid of solar energy, the amino acids could have formed long polypeptides, that is, primeval proteins.

In later experiments Fox and Harada (1958) reported the production of a true protein-like substance, called a proteinoid, by heating mixtures of amino acids at temperatures of 170°C. These proteinoids are split by proteolytic enzymes and have other properties of natural proteins. Fox and Harada also found that an excess of aspartic and glutamic acids was necessary for the success of the reaction, and that the addition of phosphoric acid increased the yield. In the presence of a polyphosphoric acid, proteinoids resulted from mixtures of 15 amino acids at temperatures as low as 70°C (Fox, 1960). One of their proteinoids had a mean chain weight of 4,900, and the proteinoids as a whole contained residues of 18 amino acids. A large number of different non-random combinations were obtained.

When hot saturated solutions of these proteinoids cool, they form huge numbers of uniform, microscopic elastic spherules (Fig. 20) (Fox, Harada, and Kendrick, 1959). At room temperature these

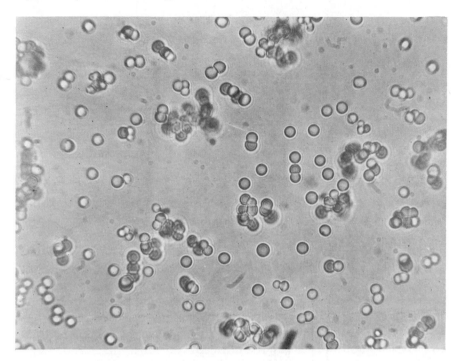

Fig. 20. Individual and aggregated spherules formed by synthetic protenoid in a hot solution of salt potassium thiocyanate. 1550 X. (After Fox.)

cell-like spherules retained their individual integrity for several weeks.

When aspartic acid was heated alone or with other amino acids, additional amino acids were formed through rearrangement of the atoms of the original molecules. The simple organic compounds malic or fumaric acid and their ammonium salts similarly converted in part to aspartic acid. When malic acid was heated with urea, the chief product was ureidosuccinic acid, one of the precursors of nucleic acid. These are only a few of the many organic compounds formed in the thermal experiments (Fox 1956, 1957).

The basic biological staples such as amino acids, vitamins, pyrimidines, and carbohydrates arise through steps involving the addition of energy and the loss of water. Furthermore, the biological macromolecules such as proteins, nucleic acids, and polysaccharides arise from these staples by exactly the same two processes. Both staples and primitive types of biological macromolecules have arisen stepwise in the thermal experiments. Hence, Fox believes that these reactions may be the true original source of the primary ingredients of primeval life. Because organisms almost certainly originated in water, it is significant that Fox's proteinoids form cell-like spherules that persist over a moderate temperature range and have an outer membrane through which water is lost or absorbed with changes in salt concentrations in the environment.

Because proteins normally have a fairly short life in water, the persistence of these proteinoid spherules for several weeks may be all that could be expected of such a structure composed of protein alone. Among the most effective substances which protect proteins from decomposition are the nucleic acids. Perhaps some nucleic acid precursors such as ureidosuccinic acid, which was formed in the thermal experiments, would be effective protectors likewise. Living cell membranes are thought to be composed of oriented lipoproteins (Upjohn, 1958), in which the protein fraction is presumably protected by fat molecules (lipid); whether such protection was available and involved when life first started is not known.

Fox (1957, 1959) has proposed an interesting hypothesis from the results of his thermal experiments. He suggests that in pockets of hot, compressed gas rising through fissures in the crust of the earth, simple compounds recombined to form biological staples, and these staples likewise recombined to form macromolecules. Furthermore, if the gas escaped through a crustal fissure into a warm or hot ocean, the proteinoids would form "cells" containing proteins and nucleic acid precursors. Thus a primeval protein-nucleic acid system embodied within the confines of a membranous "cell" wall would be formed *automatically* and *rapidly* from gases arising from within the earth.

A description of idealized cells must stress the orientation as well as the chemistry of molecules. Hence, the physical as well as the chemical properties of macromolecules such as proteins must be fitted into any explanation of the origin of life. Some proteins approximate a crystalline organization under certain conditions. Thus fibrils of collagen, from cartilage or muscle (Fig. 21*a*), may be dispersed in weak acetic acid in such a manner that the molecules of collagen are completely randomized (Fig. 21*b*). When the proper amount of sodium chloride is added to this mixture, the collagen molecules spontaneously reassemble into long fibrils in which the molecules are arranged in a crystalline type of organization (Fig. 21*c*). Thus, under certain conditions of the environment, a great deal of order is inherent in the physical nature of some organic molecules, an order resembling that found in living organisms (Fig. 21*d*).

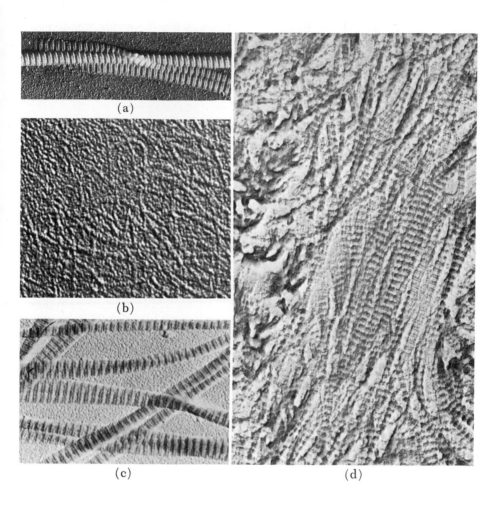

(a)

(b)

(c)

(d)

Fig. 21. Collagen, a protein of muscle, cartilage, and bone. (a) Normal collagen fibrils. (b) Collagen dispersed as thin filaments by immersion in dilute acetic acid. (c) Collagen fibrils formed spontaneously from filaments such as those in (b) when 1 per cent of sodium chloride has been added to the suspension of dispersed filaments; the resulting long fibers are identical in appearance but not quite in structure to the fibrils in (a) which were dispersed to form the filaments in (b). (d) Collagen fibers in human leg bone after removal of calcium. These electron microscope photographs represent a magnification of about 30,000 X. (Photographs of (a), (b), and (c) courtesy of F. O. Schmitt, *Proc. Am. Philos. Soc.* **100**:478, 1956; photograph of (d) courtesy of R. A. Robinson.)

We mentioned earlier that certain properties of energy transfer theoretically require a highly oriented system of water molecules and that such mechanisms have apparently been demonstrated in living systems (Szent-Györgi, 1956). Proteins and similar organic, highly organized molecular substances have such an orienting ability when in aqueous colloidal solutions. Each colloidal particle is surrounded by highly oriented water molecules which are held in place by electrostatic forces generated by various parts of the colloidal particle. In mixtures of mutually attracted (oppositely charged) colloid particles such as the protamine clupein and nucleic acid, the particles may clump to form tiny cell-like droplets called coazervates, much like Fox's spherules, each droplet surrounded by a rigidly delimited membrane of highly oriented water molecules (Oparin, 1938).

It is, of course, a long step from a simple primeval system like that just described to one embodying growth and division, followed by exact replication of the mother cell by the daughters. But the raw ingredients are all there, including the possibility of a primitive nucleo-protein which on division could conceivably release enzymes embodying precise peptide or nucleotide arrangements that would repeat exactly the anabolic pathways of their parents. For these reasons, the thermal origin of pre-life compounds is a field offering great possibilities for further investigation.

Nutrients

Three environmental circumstances make a thermal hypothesis of the origin of life especially attractive. First, S. L. Miller's experiments (1953) indicate that the ocean would have a continuing supply of amino acids and other organic substances resulting from the action of ultra-violet light and electric discharge on the components of the atmosphere. Second, if Rubey (1955) and Fox (1957) are correct, the ocean would receive through fissures in its floor a continual supply of many biological staples and macromolecules formed in the passage of gas mixtures from the interior of the earth through the crust. The proto-organisms and primeval organisms would need a continuous food supply to persist indefinitely, and these two sources would provide it. Finally, the sea contained in solution the many inorganic radicles ultimately incorporated into living systems.

FIRST LIFE

Different authors have considered life to begin at various steps in the chain of chemical evolution. It seems most reasonable to consider that life began when a cellular protein-containing system arose which, at some definite point in its growth, automatically and inexorably divided to form daughter cells which just as inexorably grew into forms exactly like their parent.

This concept does not require the premise that life was monophyletic. Many living lines could have arisen independently (Keosian, 1960). The first might have perished from a variety of nonpredatory causes, or it might have been destroyed by other more virile types. Certain lines may have fused. However, a polyphyletic origin is not at all a necessary prerequisite of this theory. If a single organism arose answering our description of life, this could have been sufficient to begin the whole subsequent sequence of living forms. Whether or not the first life was monophyletic or polyphyletic, uninterrupted generations of some lines must have succeeded each other from near the dawn of life, some billion or more years ago, down to the present. Until photosynthesis evolved, the biochemical staples formed in the air and in the escaping gases of the earth must have provided the energy and food needed for growth and reproduction.

Whether or not the facts and theories presented above indicate the path along which life evolved, they indicate that in the prebiological world a complex organic chemical and physical evolution occurred that could have led ultimately to the evolution of life. It would seem also that, before life evolved, complex chemicals underwent a natural selection based on longevity, ability to absorb other chemicals, and ability to withstand changing ecological stresses of the environment. The ultimate surviving macromolecules, those which made the transition to living matter, unquestionably imposed on life certain restrictions concerning its future evolution. Any subsequent single change would have to be compatible with the already existing chemistry.

EVOLUTION OF THE MODERN CELL

Because the form of the first living organisms is not known, it is difficult to do more than speculate on the evolution of primeval living things into the complex structure represented by even the simplest known complete living entity, such as a bacterium. The primeval organisms were undoubtedly in the form of cells. They must have been much simpler chemically and probably physically, for just as highly specialized composite flowers arose by small steps from a simple buttercup-like type, so existing cells must be the result of many changes from a much simpler progenitor.

If this supposition is true, at least three general facets of evolutionary change can be postulated: elaboration of chemical compounds, increase in complexity of chemical organization, and evolution of sex.

Elaboration of Chemical Compounds

The frequency of occurrence of chemical families of compounds suggests a great deal of channelling of chemical evolution, presumably conditioned by the inheritance of precursor substances. All authors of chemical evolution are agreed on this point. Blum (1951) gives examples of familial tetrapyrole structures in the blood pigments of animals and certain photosynthetic pigments in plants (Fig. 22). Several investigators have pointed out that analyses of proteins bring out strong familial relations in a chemical sense. For example, Fox (1956) reported that in proteins of soy bean, corn, wheat, and rye only the amino acid radical lysine occupies the "N" end of the protein molecules in significant and substantial proportions; the radicle arginine predominated in the penultimate position on these protein chains. Alanine occupies the same "N" end position in three proteins of chick egg (Fraenkel-Conrat, and Porter, 1952); and the protamines in the sperm nuclei of five fish species bear proline (Felix, 1955). Fox concluded that the actual number of protein types in cells is relatively small, only an infinitesimal fraction of the theoretically possible number of amino acid combinations which would satisfy the empirical formula of the proteins.

These and many other examples suggest that in organisms the evolution of chemical compounds has followed to a remarkable degree an elaboration of several early basic types.

Complexity of Organization

Oparin (1938) and others have expressed the opinion that the earliest cell contained only a small number of macromolecules, presumably nucleoproteins for the most part and that this aggregation absorbed and fed on macromolecules only slightly less complex. Under these conditions, only a few steps in chemical

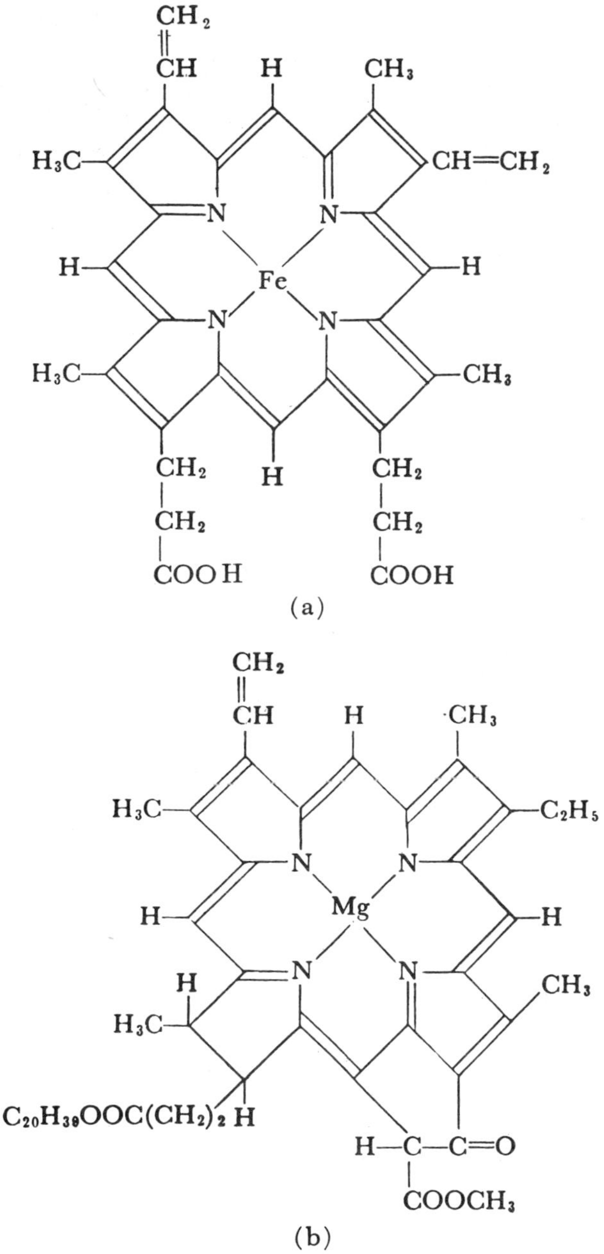

CH$_2$
CH   H   CH$_3$

H$_3$C—   CH=CH$_2$

—N   N—

H—   Fe   —H

N   N

H$_3$C—   —CH$_3$

CH$_2$ H   CH$_2$
CH$_2$ CH$_2$
COOH   COOH

(a)

CH$_2$
CH   H   ·CH$_3$

H$_3$C—   —C$_2$H$_5$

N   N

H—   Mg   —H

N   N

H$_3$C—   CH$_3$

H

H$_3$C—

C$_{20}$H$_{39}$OOC(CH$_2$)$_2$ H

H—C—C=O
COOCH$_3$

(b)

Fig. 22. Tetrapyrole structures in biological pigments. (a) protoheme, combined with protein in the red respiratory animal pigments hemoglobin and erythrocruorin; (b) chlorophyll A, found in green plants. In each of these complex structures the four bonds of the central metal atom represent a resonant or highly reactive condition. (Adapted from Blum, *Time's Arrow and Evolution*, Princeton University Press.)

synthesis would have occurred in the cell. In other words, of the great procession of syntheses which make up the chain of growth in a modern cell, only the last two or three steps would have occurred in the primeval cell. These authors believed that during the evolutionary process more and more of these syntheses became incorporated in the cell itself in an orderly fashion starting backward from the point at which synthesis began inside the parent cell. According to this view there is some basis for speculating that the nuclear membrane (Fig. 19) may represent the primeval cell membrane and that the cytoplasm represents all the molecular machines which have been added subsequently and then invested with a second membrane of their own during the course of evolution. The evolutionary mechanics adding a whole "outside layer" are, however, difficult to visualize.

That new processes, or molecular machines, have been added to the cell seems certain. One of the most important was the process of photosynthesis, by which carbon dioxide and water are converted to carbohydrate with the liberation of oxygen. This addition provided a new source of food for life and changed the atmosphere to an oxidizing one, thus creating new environmental conditions affecting the process of natural selection.

A second important development probably followed the evolution of photosynthesis. Most authors agree that the early organisms obtained energy by the chemical process of fermentation. In this process only a small amount of the chemical-bond energy is extracted from sugar, but without using free oxygen it is as far as an organism can carry the energy-extracting process. After the advent of photosynthesis, oxygen was added to the atmosphere and aquatic medium. In some organism an enzyme system evolved which was able to utilize the oxygen in oxidizing sugars down to their ultimate compounds, CO_2 and H_2O, and to utilize this added energy for activating living processes. This oxidation process, called respiration, releases 30 times as much energy as fermentation from a given quantity of sugar.

Mechanics of respiration in living organisms indicate that respiration was added to an original fermentation process which is still the first step in energy production in protoplasm. Indeed, present-day cells may lose their oxidative machinery and still exist at a reduced tempo on their fermentation facilities alone. Dramatic demonstration of this ability was given by Warburg (1956), who showed that cancer cells are simply normal cells damaged to a critical point at which respiration (oxidation) is stopped, but at which the cell is left alive and still in possession of enough of its fermentation system to provide energy for growth. Although not necessarily evidence for it, this demonstration at least is in harmony with the idea that primeval cells evolved by adding molecular machines (or perhaps occasionally groups of machines) one after another to the earlier and less inclusive organism.

These are only a few highlights of the events which must have occurred in the evolution of primeval life. Other aspects, details, and speculations on this subject may be found in papers by many investigators, including Blum (1951, 1955), Calvin (1959), Fox (1960), and Wald (1954)

Evolution of Sex

We may presume that changes leading both to elaboration of chemical compounds and to incorporation of new molecular machines into the structure of the organism arose by genetic mutation and that they were associated with enzymatic compounds controlling inheritance. This means that individuals possessing these new physiological characters would have, for example, better enzymatic action, better buffering, or new sources of food available. Natural selection for such improved traits would be strong.

An even stronger selection pressure would have been exerted if different but compatible improvements, arising as unit characters in different individuals, could have been combined in a single cell. It is therefore plausible to assume that some sort of recombination mechanism, that is, sex, arose fairly early in the evolution of life.

How a sexual mechanism started is unknown. Perhaps it originated in the form of small, freed genetic particles similar to the "combining principles" of bacteria. Dougherty (1955) suggested that the boundaries of early cells broke down at maturity, freeing into the aqueous medium bundles of genetic material which later recombined to form new cells and that during this process different combinations of characters resulted. It is also possible that tendencies for occasional diploidy arose in some line and that the first sexual types arose from this beginning.

Implicit in a regular sexual process are two mechanisms: one insuring that a diploid cell divides into haploid cells, another insuring that haploid units combine to form diploid units. The exact mechanism triggering the chromosomal halving has not yet been discovered, but a mechanism bringing about the fusion of haploid units has been partially demonstrated in certain yeasts. It has been known for some years that in these organisms the haploid cells are of two types identical morphologically and metabolically but with different mating reactions. Cells of like type will not mate with each other but only with cells of the opposite type. Experiments with surface solvents suggest very strongly that each type has a distinctive surface chemical and that the two kinds of chemicals form a loose bonding with each other. The surface compound of one haploid type is believed to be a protein, that of the other a polysaccharide, two compounds which would theoretically unite by weak hydrogen bonds (Brock, 1959). Whatever the exact nature of the chemicals, when two haploid cells of opposite type come in contact, an agglutination occurs embracing the touching surfaces and holding the two cells together. After the two haploid cells agglutinate, they unite to form a diploid cell.

However these things came about, eventually there did evolve living organisms having the properties of our idealized cell and having some kind of a sexual mechanism by which characteristics of one parent could be combined with those of another.

The Time Scale

It is difficult to date the events outlined in this and the preceding chapter accurately. Cosmologists use data associated with nuclear reactions and spectrographic analysis of heavenly bodies to arrive at ages for celestial events. Geologists and physicists use isotopes of radioactive elements in rocks and sediments to date early periods of the earth's history (Aldrich, 1956). Certain isotopic ratios in elements may also give clues to some past environmental conditions (Lowenstam and Epstein, 1954; Emiliani, 1955).

Life as we know it did not appear until the earth's crust had formed and its climate had reached a stage approximately like that prevailing today. Also life must have formed during the period when the atmosphere was in its non-oxidizing condition, with no free oxygen. This period is estimated to have occurred more than two billion years ago. The fossil record proves that life had become highly diverse as early as the Precambrian era, at least 600,000,000 years ago (Glaessner, 1961). Weighing these factors, it seems probable that life originated at least two billion years ago.

Summarizing the best-founded estimates and calculations gives the following chronology for the events which occurred from the beginning of the universe to the first fossil beds of the Paleozoic era:

Origin of universe . . . . about 13–20,000,000,000 years ago
Origin of oldest known stars . . . . 6,500,000,000 years ago
Origin of solar system . . . . 5,000,000,000 years ago
Origin of earth . . . . 4,500,000,000 years ago
Origin of continents
  and final cool stage . . . . 3,500,000,000 years ago
Origin of life . . . . 2,000,000,000 years ago
Origin of oxidizing atmosphere . . . . 1,000,000,000 years ago
First well-marked fossil beds
  of Paleozoic era . . . . over 600,000,000 years ago

The last 600 million years have been divided into three long eras called the Paleozoic, Mesozoic, and Cenozoic. Each of these three eras is divided into periods and these into epochs. The following list gives the periods and epochs of the Cenozoic and the periods of the Mesozoic and Paleozoic. The number to the right of the time divisions is the approximate number of million years ago that each subdivision began. At the extreme right are listed phenomena for which the various time divisions are best known. The dates are from Kulp (1961).

Cenozoic—Modern life

Quaternary—Pleistocene	1	The ice ages, to the present
Tertiary—Pliocene	13	
Miocene	25	Dominance of flowering
Oligocene	36	plants; diversification of
Eocene	58	mammals
Paleocene	63	

Mesozoic—Medieval life

Cretaceous	135	Dominance of cycads, tree
Jurassic	181	ferns, and conifers; era of
Triassic	230	dinosaurs

Paleozoic—Ancient life

Permian	280	Evolution of modern insect orders
Pennsylvanian	310	The Carboniferous; first great
Mississippian	345	tropical forests
Devonian	405	Beginnings of land animals
Silurian	425	Predominance of marine
Ordovician	500	invertebrates; rise of land
Cambrian . . . . ?	600	plants

The Source

of Variability

Life has developed into an amazing array of types, ranging from bacteria to elephants, with millions of other kinds around and between. To produce such an array, a tremendous amount of genetic character change had to occur, so much that at first thought one would expect to find our natural species literally evolving before our eyes from one generation to another. Yet, here we encounter another of the many apparent paradoxes of nature, for we find that the streams of life have an orderliness and stability akin to those of the cell. Examination of parents and off-spring discloses only few and small differences between them, and a museum specimen 200 years old will match character for character a freshly caught specimen of the same species.

A closer scrutiny of numerous progeny or large samples shows that small variations do occur in a surprising variety of characters. Occasionally a "sport" appears as well, a variant of greater degree, such as a black sheep among the white, a red-eyed fly among a black-eyed species, or an eight-legged flea among the normal six-legged individuals (Fig. 23). Experimentation shows that many of these vari-

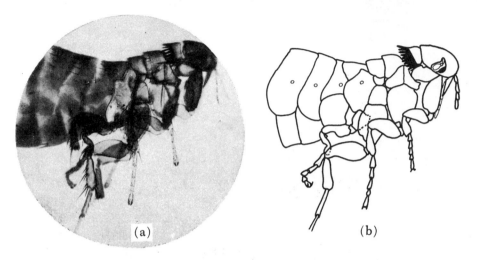

Fig. 23.   An eight-legged flea (fleas normally have only six legs). (a) photograph showing all eight legs of the flea. (b) Drawing showing the four legs on one side in proper relation to each other. (After Sanjean and Travis.)

ants breed true and represent inherited changes in the genetic make-up of the individual. These genetic variants, both large and small, resulting from a wide variety of causes, are in essence the building blocks of evolution.

Fossils record the fact that various kinds of life have changed radically from eon to eon, attesting the continuous origin of new genetic variants since the record began. The great diversity of life which had already evolved when the existing record began, now some 600 million years of age, is excellent testimony that new genetic variants have been arising ever since life began. This leads to the questions: What caused the variants? How did these variants accumulate and bring about changes in the kinds of life? Did everything change gradually and methodically at the same rate, resulting in a sort of orderly and predictable flow of new types, or was the process of change irregular and unpredictable?

Examining the geological record in regard to these questions specifically, we find that in the past certain phylogenetic lines evolved into highly specialized creatures, such as the dinosaurs, and then became extinct; that other lines seemingly arose and supplanted older groups, as the birds and mammals seem to have supplanted the dinosaurs; but that, by way of contrast, other groups such as cockroaches and molluscs, already old when the dinosaurs were young, are even now successfully continuing several hundred million years of existence. Many of the marine Mollusca and unicellular organisms afford a surprising number of examples of these long-lived types. Examining the composition of living categories, we note that some genera contain only one or two species, whereas other genera of comparable age may have a thousand species. These conditions of unequal evolutionary development in different phylogenetic lines do not fit a picture of the evolution of life from the accumulation of equal radial paths of variation. Rather, the situation indicates some influence or combination of influences that results in a drastic deviation from either the production or the survival of an orderly, automatic radiation of life.

All the known evidence indicates that these influences comprise two great sets of factors. One set constitutes the origin of new variants. Its causes arise within the hereditary mechanism of the organism, including both changes in the genetic material itself and recombinations of these changes. The other set of factors involves the fate of the variants. It includes effects of both the internal and external environments which in one way or another determine which genetic types survive.

In the past several relatively simple explanations have been given for both sets of factors. The more these phenomena are studied, however, the more difficult it becomes to find a satisfactory explanation for how the hereditary mechanism works, or how it changes, or how the more selective factors are identified in the environment. One fact, however, has been confirmed by almost all of the experiments performed. That part of the external environment (such as weather, predation, and food) which exerts a selective action on genetic types, has at most a very limited effect in causing genetic mutation. It seems that in almost all instances genetic variants arise as some function of the individual independent of its environment. Whatever their origin, however, only after spontaneous changes have occurred in the individual can the environment influence their survival.

It is therefore pertinent to consider first the spontaneous phenomena associated with the production of variation, in other words, the material basis of evolution. Primarily this involves the identification of the genetic determinants and the mechanisms by which they change and cause character change.

THE GENETIC MECHANISM

Typically all organisms begin as single cells. This is obviously true of single-celled organisms such as *Amoeba,* and is equally true of the multicellular organisms. Oak trees and horses alike start from a zygote, the single cell resulting from two gametes. Incredible though it seems, the single cell initiating a new generation of the most complex organism carries within it a physico-chemical code of some sort which sets in operation and maintains a precise set of complex reactions resulting in a daughter organism essentially like the parent. If an alternation of generations occurs in the life history, the coded information in the spores or eggs originates the series of physiological reactions that produce the members of the life cycle in their correct order. These happenings always presuppose an environment suitable for the existence of the organism. New types of organisms, or genetic variants, presumably arise because changes occur in the coded information called the genetic material or genome.

According to present knowledge the great proportion of this genetic material occurs in the chromosomes, situated in the nucleus. A great volume of published information chronicles the existence of literally thousands of genetic determinants or *genes* on the chromosomes and explains the manner and proportions in which the various determinants are passed on from one generation to the next. A lesser proportion of genetic material is apparently located outside the chromosomes, and this proportion is classed as cytoplasmic inheritance. The units of cytoplasmic inheritance are sometimes called plasmagenes but more frequently are simply called genes. Relatively few instances of cytoplasmic inheritance have been established, but this may be due more to the pioneering state of the field than to the existence of only a small number of cytoplasmic genes.

Chromosomal Inheritance

The chromosome number varies from 2 in some plants of the family Compositae (Jackson, 1957) to over a hundred in some animals (White, 1954) and over 200 in some plants (Manton, 1950).

Chromosomes are relatively similar in structure and behavior throughout the protistan world. Each chromosome has a definite structure, consisting of the mechanical center or centromere and the arms, the latter typically having areas considered to contain genic material of specific function (*euchromatin*) alternating with areas for which only a more general type of genic activity has been demonstrated (*heterochromatin*).

The chromosomes have distinctive areas each of which exerts specific genic effects. In the crossing-over of chromosomes, breaks normally occur between these areas and not through them. These seemingly unitary areas of genetic action are called genes, so that each chromosome may be considered a succession of areas of specific genic action, in truth a "gene string."

ALLELES

Many genes occur in two or more forms, called *alleles*. These may form the two complementary units of the paired chromosomes in diploid generations and the separate units in the gametes of the haploid generation. A classical example of alleles occurs in Mendel's peas, one allele being for red flowers, the other for white. If the two alleles in the zygote are both of the red type, the flower is red, if both are of the white type, the flower is white. If the zygote is heterozygous for red and white, the flower is red. This is an example of complete dominance. As more examples are studied, this phenomenon of complete dominance is proving to be relatively rare, because most heterozygotes produce an effect either intermediate between the two homozygote expressions or quite different from either. In fowl, for example, *black* crossed with *splashed white* produces *Andalusian blue*.

The inheritance of many characters once thought to be controlled by a single pair of alleles is now known to involve a large complex of alleles (called *pseudoalleles*) situated so close together on the chromosome that crossing-over seldom occurs between them (Glass, 1955). Eye color in wasps of the genus *Mormoniella* is controlled by two major genes each having several pseudoalleles. As a result of the large number of resultant distinctive genetic combinations, a dozen or more distinct shades of eye color can be recognized (Whiting, 1955).

COMPOUND EFFECT OF GENES

A single gene may produce two or more quite different phenotypic effects in an organism. The two principal types of such correlation are pleiotropy and allometry.

Pleiotropy is the condition in which one allele has a direct effect on more than one trait. Thus in *Drosophila* the allele causing vestigial wings also causes other slight morphological differences from normal flies and in addition causes lower fecundity (Dobzhansky, 1955); the allele *scabrous* produces both bulging eyes and additional sets of certain body bristles; and the allele *giant* produces both larger size and slower development (Patterson and Stone, 1952).

Allometry, or heterogonous growth, is the condition in which different parts of the organism grow at different rates so that at different size stages of the individual the body proportions are not the same. An excellent example of this phenomenon occurs in humans. In the human embryo the head is very large compared with the trunk, but as the individual grows the trunk increases in size

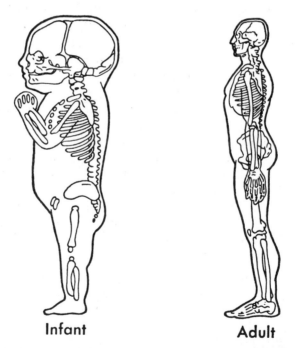

Infant   **Adult**

Fig. 24. Allometry in the human head and trunk. The effects of differences in the relative growth of parts of the body are strikingly brought out by a comparison of the proportions of infant and adult. (From Simpson, Pittendrigh, and Tiffany, *Life: An Introduction to Biology*, Harcourt, Brace and Company, 1957. Adapted, with permission, from Etkin, *College Biology*, Thomas Y. Crowell Co.)

at a greater proportionate rate than the head. Thus at maturity the human head and trunk have different proportions than at an early stage in development (Fig. 24). There is a similar difference in growth rate between the muzzle and cranium of horses (Reeve and Murray, 1942). This differential development in relation to absolute size has been plotted for (1) the ontogenetic development of the domestic horse, (2) horse breeds of different sizes, and (3) fossil horses ranging from the small ancestral horse *Hyracotherium* to the living, much larger horse, *Equus* (Fig. 25). In

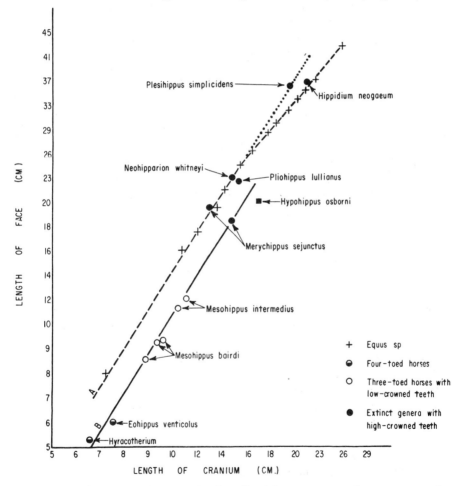

Fig. 25. Allometry in horses. The length of face increases disproportionately as the skull increases in size. A, growth pattern in the modern horse *Equus caballus;* B, growth pattern of slightly different proportions which fits *Hyracotherium* and certain other genera. (From Reeve and Murray.)

Equus (Fig. 25, line *A*) the face grows at a much faster rate than the cranium (the remainder of the head) until the cranium attains a length of about 16 cm. After that, the two parts of the head grow at more nearly equal rates. Several extinct horses appear to fit this pattern, and one of these, *Plesihippus simplicidens,* may follow an extention of the steep part of the heterogonic slope beyond the 16 cm. "bend" shown by *Equus.* Several other genera of extinct horses have head measurements which agree with a pattern of heterogonic growth different from, but roughly parallel with that of *Equus* (Fig. 25, line *B*). Thus in a small horse such as *Hyracotherium,* mutations resulting in larger body size would automatically cause a change from a short-faced head to a long-faced head such as that found in the larger species *Merychippus.*

DOSAGE AND DOMINANCE

It was formerly considered that pairs of recessive and dominant alleles were different from each other, but this apparently is not always the case. In *Drosophila melanogaster* a certain bristle on the thorax occurs as the normal long form or as an abbreviated form called "bobbed." A single pair of alleles controls this condition, the allele for the normal type being completely dominant over the "bobbed." Experimenting with replicates of the sex chromosome in this species, Stern (1929) was able to produce a zygote containing not the normal single sex chromosome but three or more sex chromosomes each bearing a recessive "bobbed" allele. Zygotes with three or four "bobbed" alleles produced not the recessive phenotype, but a fairly long spine, and zygotes with even more "bobbed" alleles produced the typically dominant long form. It is therefore concluded that in this case the dominant allele represents simply a larger dosage of the same material represented by the recessive allele. The same phenomenon is displayed in many types of sex determinants, especially the XO, XY male, and XX female class (White, 1954). Here only one dosage of X produces males, but a double dosage produce females. Thus many pairs of alleles simply may represent dosage effects of the same unitary genetic attributes.

Added support for this view comes from cases of unequal crossing-over. The sex-linked character *Bar* (reduced number of eye facets) in *Drosophila* is caused by a tandem duplication of the 16A region of the X-chromosome, a duplication which is caused by unequal crossing-over. Occasional further unequal crossing-over results in a tandem triplication of region 16A which in its homozygous condition produces an extreme bar condition called *Ultrabar.*

POSITION EFFECTS

In some instances the same alleles have a different effect if they occur in different positions. An example concerns the *Bar* and *Ultrabar* alleles described above. Female flies heterozygous for *Ultrabar* contain the same number of *Bar* units as those homozygous for *Bar,* four per nucleus, and hence might be expected to have similar phenotypes, but this is not so. The number of eye facets is definitely lower in the heterozygous *Ultrabar.* It appears that in this case the extra *Bar* regions are more potent in their effect when situated on the same chromosome. This exemplifies *position effect,* to wit, that the same units produce a different genetic effect in different positions.

SUPPRESSION EFFECTS

Blum (1951) pointed out that mutations should be the result of a chemical reaction, that this reaction should be reversible to some extent, and that as a result mutations should occasionally mutate back to the original condition. Apparent reverse mutations have indeed been recorded on many occasions. Stadler (1955) warned, however, that observed phenotypic reversions may be due not to a reverse mutation but to an inhibitor gene which blocks the expression of the mutant effect, although the mutant gene is still present. Glass (1957) gave two interesting examples of such an effect concerning mutant alleles in *Drosophila* which produce abnormal adult eyes or tumors in the larvae. Glass and his colleagues investigated the biochemical pathways involved in the expression of the alleles in this genetic complex and concluded that so-called "suppressor" genes may be channelling agents for substrates needed for the expression of many genes rather than being modifiers of any particular gene under study. In this situation, apparent suppression of a gene would be the suppression of its effect because of competition for substrates.

ENZYMATIC EFFECT

Investigations of the mold *Neurospora* by Beadle and Tatum (Beadle, 1945) and of the bacterium *Salmonella* by Zinder and Lederberg (Zinder, 1953) demonstrated the occurrence in these species of alleles whose absence resulted in the inability of the organisms to synthesize specific essential chemical materials such as thiamine, cysteine, and tryptophane. Further research demonstrated the presence of many alleles, each necessary for the production of a specific step in the biosynthesis of some one required compound. For example, Demerec (1955) found that the action of four sets of alleles in *Salmonella* corresponded to the four known steps in the synthesis of tryptophane from anthranilic acid.

These and other examples of biochemical genic effects have given rise to the concept that genes act through controlling the production of specific enzymes. Each gene is presumed to produce, or cause to be produced, a specific enzyme which in turn brings about a specific chemical reaction in the cell.

MODE OF GENIC ACTION

Cases of position effect and genes affecting single enzymatic reactions have contributed greatly to the current view of how genes act, whatever the genetic determiners are called. The following is a summary of this view. The genetic determiners activate adjacent substrate compounds which in turn produce enzymes catalyzing still other reactions, and so on until the organism and its parts are fully formed. How many such chemical steps occur between the original action of the genetic material on the first substrate and any one final product is not known. In some cases a few of the final steps have been determined. In the bacillus *Salmonella* the final synthesis of tryptophane is known to involve at least four steps: from anthranilic acid to an unknown intermediate to indole to tryptophane (Beadle, 1955). A different enzyme seems to be involved at each step, and for each enzyme a different gene is involved. Thus, products resulting from the action of one gene appear to combine with the products of other genes to form distinctive substances, the whole integrated to form the mesh of biological synthesis. In some cases a different character results not from the action of a distinctive gene, but from interference with chemical pathways due to the competition between genes for identical substrates (Glass, 1957).

It can readily be seen that character determination becomes extremely complex in multicellular organisms having a well-developed soma. In an oak tree, the leaves, roots, and structures of the flowers are removed by many physiological processes and by many cell divisions from the original zygote. Yet, the genetic makeup of that zygote in some fashion effected the differentiation of cells and tissues through the control of chains of chemical reactions leading to the completed individual. The same type of control is responsible for the growth of highly specialized animals such as whales with their massive structures and insects with their different and peculiar life history stages which together form the ontogeny of a single individual.

SIZE OF A GENE

Little success resulted from efforts to calculate the possible size of a gene by measuring the cross-over distances on highly organized chromosomes such as those of *Drosophila*. The measurable units were microscopic but even so were immense in terms of the submicroscopic units represented by even such large molecules as protamines. More meaningful figures resulted from studies of viruses, especially the phages. Studying inheritance in the phage known as T4, Benzer (1955) found that each phage consisted of a simple molecule of DNA, that abundant mutant alleles occurred in a specific region of this molecule, and that these mutants crossed over readily. By calculating accurately the locus of each allele on the DNA molecule, Benzer found that the average distance between loci which crossed over was essentially identical with the calculated length of one complete whorl of the DNA molecule, a distance including about a dozen nucleotide pairs (see Fig. 17). Benzer points out that these distances are suggestive only of the minimum distances that might be involved in chemical changes of genic material but that much greater distances may be involved in the amount of genic material necessary to accomplish a specific function.

DEFINITION OF THE GENE

Because both the operation and the physio-chemical nature of genes are unknown, probably the gene can be defined best in terms of its effects. Efforts to formulate theoretical models or hypotheses of genic action have resulted in highly divergent opinions of what a gene is and how the term should be defined.

The controversial views concerning the gene fall into two schools of thought, one implying that specific molecules of the genic material control each character (Dobzhansky, 1955; Beadle, 1955) and the other that interactions between all parts of the genome are responsible for the production of each character (Goldschmidt, 1955). Stadler (1954) pointed out that the differences of opinion arise because one school defines the gene as an operational unit whose action can be demonstrated by experiment, whereas the other school defines the gene in a hypothetical physico-chemical sense.

In an operational sense, the gene can be defined only as the smallest segment of the chromosome that can be shown to be associated consistently with the occurrence of a specific genetic effect. As Stadler pointed out, such demonstrations are a function of the limitations of whatever experimental methods are employed; improved or new methods could conceivably demonstrate an "operational gene" quite different from that recognized now.

Unquestionably there are differences in some structure of the chromosome at the molecular level which distinguish one gene from another. Ideas as to what these differences are constitute the hypothetical gene.

The operational gene, therefore, is based on what a gene *does*, a hypothetical gene on what it *might be*. Except for parts of the discussion on gene change later in this chapter, I am using the term *gene* in the sense of Stadler's operational gene.

Cytoplasmic Inheritance

Information concerning cytoplasmic inheritance is meagre at best, but what is known about its occurrence and action is highly intriguing. Examples of this type of inheritance in plants include series of genes influencing pigmentation of the plastids and other series of genes influencing resistance to or dependence on certain chemical compounds such as streptomycin. Some of these cytoplasmic elements appear to be under the ultimate control of chromosomal genes (Darlington, 1958), but in other cases there is no evidence of such a relationship. Sager (1960) pointed out that in the alga *Chlamydomonas* certain cytoplasmic elements controlling streptomycin resistance could combine with chromosomal genes also controlling streptomycin resistance and produce an additive effect. From this circumstance she concluded that the cytoplasmic elements fitted the terms *gene* and *allele* as applied to chromosomal elements which behave similarly.

In mites of the genus *Tetranychus*, Boudreaux (1959) discovered a cytoplasmic element causing a reduction in the number of hairs on the legs (Fig. 26). This element could be destroyed by heat, hence Boudreaux drew attention to its virus-like quality. This fact of heat-intolerance, however, does not necessarily militate against the view that the element is a true allele.

In this regard certain observations on viruses are pertinent (Hayes and Clowes, 1960). Certain phage viruses apparently can exist either as a cytoplasmic inclusion or attached to the nucleus

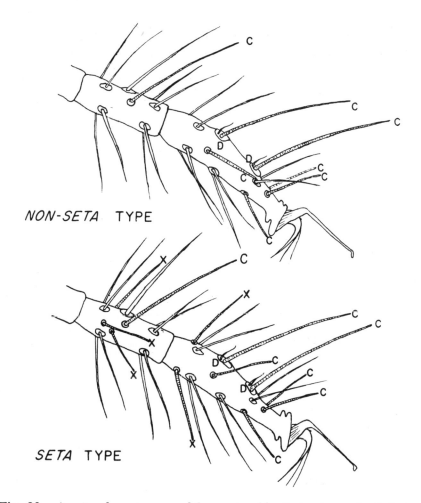

Fig. 26. A mite character caused by a virus-like factor transmitted through the mite's cytoplasm. *Seta* type, normal setae on leg, especially including those marked *x; Non-seta* type, setal pattern lacking the four marked *x*, caused by virus-like factor. (After Boudreaux.)

of their bacterial host. When occurring in the cytoplasm, the phage virus multiplied at a prodigious rate and killed its host. When it occurred as a molecule of virus DNA on the host nucleus, the virus DNA molecule duplicated only in unison with its host and acted as if it were a normal part of the genome of the host. Sager suggested from this that perhaps many mutants originate in the cytoplasm and eventually become incorporated into the chromosomal organization.

Most recorded cytoplasmic alleles exhibit a uniparental mode of transmission. In higher plants and animals having large ova (macrogametes) that contain large amounts of cytoplasm but having only minute male pollen or sperm (microgametes) with essentially no cytoplasm, only the macrogametes transmit the cytoplasmic alleles. This situation, called transovarian transmission, results in a pattern of segregation in which all the progeny of the pair have the maternal condition, but only the female progeny can transmit the cytoplasmic characters to the succeeding generation. In the alga *Chlamydomonas* the same uniparental transmission of cytoplasmic genes occurred, even though both gametes (called *plus* and *minus*) are of about the same size. This raises puzzling but as yet unanswered questions concerning the mechanism of transmission in these forms. Certain cytoplasmic factors in *Chlamydomonas* demonstrate that this uniparental transmission is not changed even when the cytoplasmic allele is in company with a chromosomal allele with which it interacts physiologically (Sager, 1960).

CHANGE IN GENETIC EFFECT

The tremendous increase in diverse types of life from the primeval, simple organisms of a billion years ago to the biotas of the present reflects concurrent increase in character change. This change must have been due to changes in the genetic system.

These changes are considered to be of three kinds: (1) change in chromosomal architecture (chromosomal mutation), (2) change in the genes themselves (genic mutation), and (3) changes in the combinations of genetic determinants (recombination).

1. Chromosomal Mutations

Mutations of the chromosomes fall into two groups: changes in chromosome number and changes in gross chromosome structure. Mutations of the genes are also changes in chromosome structure because genes are parts of the chromosomes. Yet it is possible for the chromosomes to become reorganized without change in the genes, and it is this type of rearrangement which is called chromosomal mutation.

CHANGES IN CHROMOSOME NUMBER

Chromosome sets may vary because of the addition or subtraction of one or two chromosomes or by the addition of complete normal sets of chromosomes.

In the normally precise process of meiosis, each chromosome pair divides, one of the pair going to each daughter cell. Extremely rarely, an occasional pair of chromosomes fails to divide, so that one daughter cell receives an extra chromosome and the other loses one. Frequently the progeny of these mutants (called *aneuploids*) are inviable, but in many known cases, especially in organisms

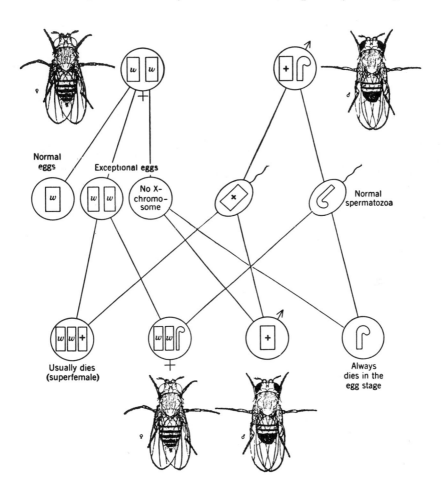

Fig. 27. Aneuploidy in *Drosophila melanogaster*. The progeny of the unusual eggs *ww* or lacking *w* are aneuploids, in that they have more than or less than the normal number of chromosomes. (From Dobzhansky, *Evolution, genetics, and man.* John Wiley & Sons, Inc.)

having many small chromosomes, they are viable. Dobzhansky (1955) noted that in the blue grass *Poa* aneuploids are common in natural populations. The change in numbers of specific chromosomes will shift the gene balance and dosage levels for all the characters influenced by the chromosomes involved (Fig. 27)

How commonly aneuploids serve as the basis for changes in chromosome numbers in different phylogenetic lines is not known. Consulting tables of the chromosome numbers of related animals (see White, 1954, pp. 186, 193–195, 198–200), it is apparent that small changes in chromosome numbers are the rule in many animal groups, and it is quite possible that aneuploids have been instrumental in initiating some of these changes.

On occasion the entire chromosome assemblage fails to divide during meiosis, so that a germ cell is formed with double the normal genome complement. These, under various circumstances, give rise to offspring having 3*n*, 4*n*, or higher multiples of chromosomes, such individuals being termed *polyploids*. Polyploids have been produced experimentally by use of the drug colchicine, which inhibits spindle formation in dividing cells but does not interfere with the duplication and separation of the chromosomes on the equatorial plate.

Polyploidy has played an important part in plant evolution, but only a minor role in animal evolution. In plants whole large groups such as the ferns may be primarily polyploid (Manton, 1950). In animals few cases of polyploidy have been demonstrated (White, 1954), and most of these are parthenogenic forms such as certain weevils and earthworms.

CHANGES IN CHROMOSOME ORGANIZATION

During meiosis various segments of the chromosome may become broken or detached and then rejoined in an order different from the original. If a rejoined unit has either no centromere or two centromeres, it is incapable of proper mitosis and ultimately disappears. If the rejoined unit has a single centromere it can, other factors permitting, continue to divide and persist normally.

The rearrangement is expressed and detected as a rearranged order of genes in the gene string. Four types are recognized (Fig. 28).

1. A deficiency (B). Here a gene or gene sequence has dropped out (*efg* becomes *e*). In the homozygous condition, deficiencies are usually lethal, but even these types may persist in heterozygotes.

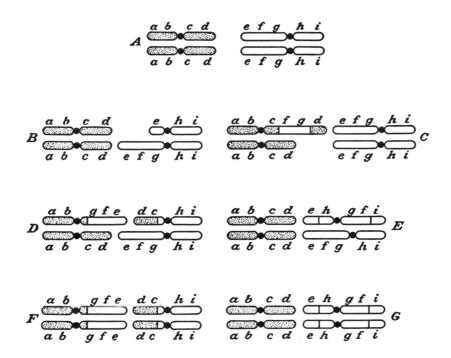

Fig. 28. Changes in chromosome arrangements, schematic. A, two pairs of original or "normal" chromosomes. B, deficiency. C, duplication. D and F, examples of translocations. E and G, examples of inversions. (From Sinnott, Dunn, and Dobzhansky, courtesy of the McGraw-Hill Book Company.)

2. *A duplication* (*C*). Here a gene or gene sequence is added to the normal complement (*cd* becomes *cfgd*). Duplications in general are much more viable than deficiencies.

3. *An inversion* (*E, G*). Sometimes a chromosome will break in two places. *efg-hi*, for example, may fragment into *e*, *fgh*, and *i*. The middle section may turn end over end and the chromosome reunite to form the order *eh-gfi*, in which *f*, *g*, and *h* are now inverted in comparison with the original condition. In many species of *Drosophila* inversions occur commonly.

4. *A translocation* (*D, F*). Sometimes two different chromosomes will break and reunite in an exchanged order, for example, *ab-cd* and *efg-hi* will produce *ab-gfe* and *dc-hi*. These translocations are usually not viable, presumably because of difficulties in synapsing during meiosis. Translocations occurring between two chromosomes each with a single long arm, may produce one chromosome with two arms plus a degenerate chromosomal element.

Such a translocation, called a *centric fusion* by White (1954), may be quite viable and in a heterozygote may synapse normally with the unfused two, homologous, one-armed chromosomes.

In animals several cases are known in which translocations and inversions occur or have occurred. According to White (1954), translocations occur naturally in certain scorpions and in wild populations of certain grasshoppers. In *Drosophila,* Patterson and Stone (1952) found that centric fusions had occurred continuously throughout the evolution of the genus but that no good evidence existed for supposing that other types of translocation had ever become established.

In *Drosophila* and other true flies (Patterson and Stone, 1952; White, 1954) inversions are extremely common. In certain species of *Drosophila* one inversion has followed upon another, and in the *Drosophila virilis* group these inversions were the data needed to determine the phylogeny of the species. Investigators have found only inconclusive evidence of inversions in other animals, but White pointed out that the necessary demonstration is extremely difficult to detect in forms lacking the giant salivary chromosomes found in the *Diptera.* A few cases of inversions have been reported in the plants (Stebbins, 1950).

EFFECT OF CHROMOSOME MUTATIONS

Although from these data it is apparent that chromosomal mutations have accompanied the evolution of many groups, little is known concerning their exact genetic effect. Additions and deletions of chromosomes or sets of genes alter the gene dosages, and certain of the effects of these additions and deletions have been established. In some polyploids of both plants and animals, for example, there is little observable difference from the diploid form of the same species, but in some plant polyploids either the whole plant or its individual parts may be about twice the size of those in the diploid form (Stebbins, 1950; White, 1954). In plants of the genus *Clarkia* additional chromosomes are associated with ability of the species to inhabit more xeric situations than species having lower, more primitive chromosome numbers (Lewis, 1953*b*). On the basis of an evaluation of evolutionary mechanisms in *Clarkia,* Lewis (1953*a*) suggested that structural rearrangements of chromosomes were of great evolutionary importance in linking different genes into persistent combinations of unusual adaptive value.

In some species of *Drosophila,* inversions are associated with an unusual adaptive effect. Dobzhansky (1946, 1948*a*) found that in

Drosophila pseudoobscura and *persimilis* heterozygotes of various inversions possessed greater vigor than their respective homozygotes and further that the proportions of the various gene arrangements varied in cyclic fashion throughout the year. It appeared therefore that the inversions represented gene rearrangements having slightly different adaptive qualities in different temperature bands, but later Dobzhansky (1948*b*) found indications that the explanation might involve gene change.

In spite of the lack of experimentally proven adaptive effects, chromosomal mutations have occurred in many species; they have become homozygous in the population and have continued in their new arrangement through long phylogenetic lines. This is the only plausible explanation for the diversity of chromosome numbers and arrangements found in many groups of organisms such as in *Drosophila* (Fig. 29) and the series of extreme chromosomal reductions found in the plant genus *Crepis* (Babcock and Jenkins, 1943).

2. Gene Mutations

In practically every population under careful genetic observation, individuals appear which have a character not previously seen in the population but a character which breeds true through subsequent generations. Some of these characters are associated with a change in chromosomal conditions or with the cytoplasm. The others, constituting the great bulk of those observed, are presumed to be caused by a change in the genic material itself and are called gene mutations.

So universal is this occurrence of gene mutations that mutability, the ability to change, is considered an innate property of life. Observed rates of mutation vary from group to group, from species to species, and from gene to gene within a species (Beadle, 1955). Beadle gives values for the incidence of mutations ranging from one mutation in a thousand genes per life cycle to less than one in a billion. Certain genes are said to increase the rate of mutation; Schmalhausen (1949) contended that any mutations increase this rate.

LETHAL MUTATIONS

A high proportion of all mutations are lethal. They produce a sufficient disruption of normal physiology that they cause the death of their carrier individuals before the latter reproduce. In nature these mutations are weeded out of the population immediately. Examples

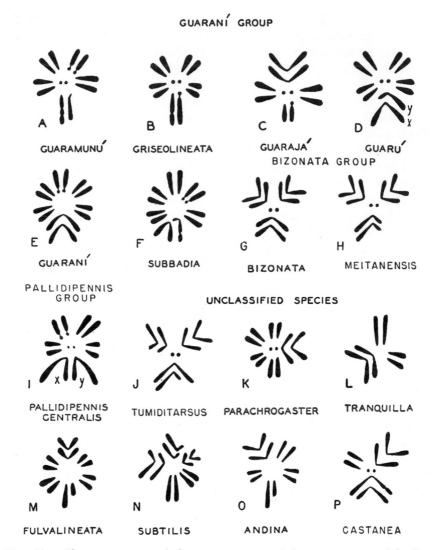

Fig. 29. Chromosome morphology in a portion of the genus *Drosophila* illustrating the great diversity in organization. (From Patterson and Stone, *Evolution in the genus Drosophila*, courtesy of the Macmillan Company.)

of lethal mutations are the enzyme-deficient mutants of bacteria and molds. Their normal environment lacks the essential substances which the mutants cannot produce; if these compounds were not added to the experimental nutrient solutions, the mutant organisms would never develop. The exact physiological failure causing many mutants to be lethal is not known, but, under proper conditions of observation, the presence of these "lethals" can be detected by the failure of eggs to hatch, seeds to germinate, or individuals to reach full development.

VIABLE MUTATIONS

A large proportion of the viable mutations in both plants and animals are of a deleterious nature, often expressed as reduced fertility or vigor. Even if the homozygotes of these mutant alleles are lethal or nearly so, the heterozygotes combining a mutant with a normal allele may be nearly as productive and vigorous as normal homozygotes. In this heterozygous fashion sublethal alleles may be carried in populations almost indefinitely.

Viable mutants have been observed for practically every gene studied and therefore affecting every character studied. Many exhaustive studies and compilations provide long lists of these mutant types (Goldschmidt, 1940; Lerner, 1958; Stebbins, 1950; and many others). An enumeration of this tremendous array of spontaneously arising mutants would convey the impression of a fountain of new variability sufficient to account for the changes inherent in the evolutionary mechanism.

One point concerning these mutants is of special interest. In any one line, the same mutant will appear independently many times. Also homologous mutations have been observed in entirely different species (Spencer, 1949). This fact provides a possible explanation for the appearance of the same character in different phylogenetic lines. It also supports the plausibility of Blum's (1951) contention that the basis for mutation is a relatively simple chemical change in the genic material.

A number of investigators have speculated on the nature of this change in the genic material which produces a new mutant. Several authors have assumed that DNA is the genic material and have postulated various mechanisms by which changes in the arrangement of nucleotides might occur (Watson and Crick, 1953; Beadle, 1955) and how this might control the composition of proteins synthesized through DNA activity (Gamow, 1955). When, however, one considers the possibility that DNA may be only one link in a sort of ultimate molecular machine involving protamines, DNA, and likely other compounds, it seems feasible that changes in any member of the machine might be responsible for the origin of mutations.

In extremely detailed studies of several genes, however, Stadler (1954) pointed out that the mutants he observed were due to unequal crossing-over. When this process occurs at meiosis, one chromosome of a dividing pair has a tandem duplication of a gene, and the other has a complete loss of that gene (as is diagrammed in Fig. 30). Thus no chemical change in the gene need have taken

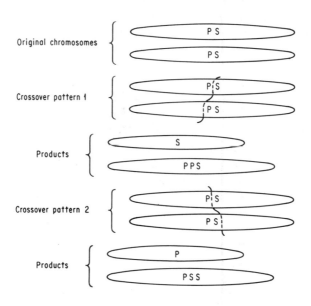

Fig. 30. Diagram of the mechanism of unequal crossing-over and the resulting tandem duplication of genic elements in some gametes and the loss of genes in others. (Modified from Stadler.)

place. Stadler pointed out that unequal crossing-over of minute and essentially undetectable areas could theoretically account for all observed mutations.

These conflicting ideas are not necessarily mutually exclusive, but they do emphasize our lack of knowledge concerning both the mechanism and causes of gene mutation. We know that mutations arise and that the inheritance of those on the chromosomes is associated with a definite spot or condition of the chromosome. Beyond that we are in the realm of speculation.

ENVIRONMENT AND MUTATION

To date, no evidence has been reported which indicates that the normal environment produces genic mutations. Several instances are on record, however, in which abnormal additives to the environment have increased the mutation rate. Unusual dosages of ultraviolet rays, gamma rays, and other wave-lengths, and various chemicals such as mustard gas and streptomycin have produced increased mutation rates in many organisms. The mutations induced by streptomycin are particularly interesting. Sager (1960) found that one particular streptomycin-resistant, cytoplasmic mutation of *Chlamydomonas* appeared only in certain strains of *Chlamydomonas* exposed to hyper-toxic dosages of streptomycin. Thus the drug apparently induced a mutation in some way linked with the drug itself. Although only this one instance of such action is known, it nevertheless indicates the possibility of new discoveries and concepts in this intriguing relationship between environment and mutation.

3. The Mixing Process

In addition to a process of change, the sexual processes of the genetic system have an inherent behavior which effects a mixing and recombination of characters. The component parts of this mixing process include crossing-over of homologous chromosomes at meiosis and independent segregation of chromosomes at meiosis.

CROSSING-OVER

In typical crossing-over two strands or chromatids of homologous chromosome pairs exchange pieces (Fig. 31). This effects a changing

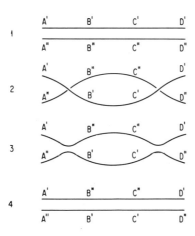

Fig. 31. Diagram of a simple pattern of crossing-over occurring between homologous chromatids during meiosis. Letters indicate the position of hypothetical genes.

combination of alleles of different genes situated on the same chromosome. Thus two exchanging chromatids starting out with alleles A′B′C′D′ and A″B″C″D″, respectively, may end up after crossing-over as A′B″C″D′ and A″B′C′D″, respectively. The sequence of the genes ABCD is unchanged, but the combination of alleles is different. If, in one meiotic division, crossing-over occurs between a certain pair of chromatids, then the chances are that at the next such division crossing-over will occur between the other pair. In this fashion an almost complete recombination of alleles may occur within the same chromosome.

Several circumstances inhibit crossing-over. It does not occur in areas of chromosomes bearing inversions or in the chromosomes of male Diptera. White (1954) cites other examples but points out that in at least some cases genic mixing lost by this inhibition of crossing-over is partially regained by an increase in number of chromosomes.

CHROMOSOME SEGREGATION

A mixing of the chromosomes also occurs at meiosis in the following fashion. If the gametic chromosomes of one parent are A and B and those of the other are A′ and B′, then the fertilized individual will have the chromosome pairs AA′ and BB′. When these chromosomes divide at reduction division they do so independently of their parental origin and strictly by chance. In other words, if A goes into one gamete, it is pure chance whether B or B′ goes with it. Hence a large number of gametes will have all the possible recombinations, in this case AB, A′B′, and A′B, AB′.

CYTOPLASMIC SEGREGATION

The various alleles associated with cytoplasmic inheritance exhibit either no segregation or uniparental segregation. If no segregation is manifest, then all the progeny of a given pair transmit their cytoplasmic alleles to all their offspring. Under these circumstances, in the absence of selective factors, cytoplasmic genes would spread gradually and completely through the entire interbreeding system. If, as is usually the case, the inheritance were uniparental, the cytoplasmic alleles would become distributed continuously through lines arising from one parental type, such as ova or *plus* mating cells, but these alleles would not pass to the next generation in unions in which the character occurred only in the other parental type, such as sperm, pollen, or a *minus* mating cell.

EFFECTIVENESS

A combination of crossing-over, chromosome segregation, and parental differentiation thus provides mechanisms which can theoretically produce every possible combination of alleles in a breeding population. So great, however, is the total number of alleles in an individual that tremendous populations and large numbers of generations would be necessary to bring about this complete mixing.

The mixing process is theoretically random and complete in species having bisexual reproduction. In other species the mixing process ranges from being more restricted to nonexistant. In organisms which may be facultatively self-fertilized, as many plants may be, genetic mixing between individuals is restricted to those individuals of the species which are cross-fertilized. No genetic mixing occurs between individuals in obligate self-fertilized or in apomyctic species. In self-fertilized species, free recombination of the genes of a single individual is theoretically possible, as it is also in types of parthenogenesis involving meiosis. In all other types of reproduction, such as simple fission involving mitosis or various types of vegetative reproduction, no genetic mixing occurs. The name *apomixis* is usually applied to all types of reproduction in which normal fertilization does not occur and means, literally, "without mixing."

Free and complete mixing of the genes in a population demands that all progeny be fertile and that they cross back and forth with each other. This appears to be the case in a species population in any one locality. Hybrids arising from crosses between individuals of distant populations may have greatly reduced fertility, and hybrids between distinct species very frequently have low fertility or none. Hybrids between distinct genera or higher categories are seldom fertile. In any group of organisms there is a point of taxonomic divergence beyond which no effective hybridization occurs. Beyond this point no gene mixing is possible.

The greater the genetic difference of hybridizing parents, the more the characters are inherited as blocks from each parent, and the fewer are the block combinations which produce fertile hybrids (Darlington, 1958). Thus hybridization at the point of near-incompatibility between parents tends to produce progeny having mosaics of the parental characters rather than intermediate conditions of these characters. This situation may be exemplified by the leafhopper *Erythroneura alicia* (Fig. 32), thought to be a hybrid between *E. metopia* and *E. trivittata* or their immediate antecedents.

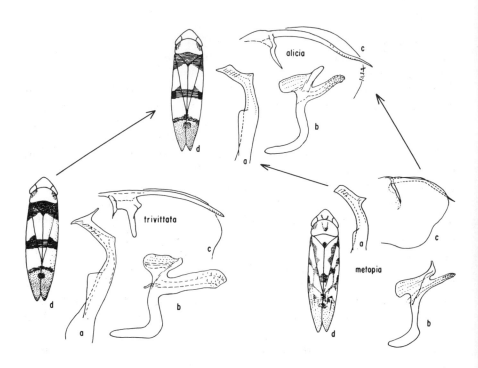

Fig. 32. A comparison of the salient characters of the presumed hybrid species *Erythroneura alicia* and representatives of the two phylogenetic lines which were its probable parents.

E. alicia combines the specialized, banded color pattern (*D*) of *E. trivittata* with the style (*A*) and pygofer hook (*C*) of *E. metopia;* its aedeagus (*B*) is somewhat intermediate between the presumed parental types. The same type of mosaic mixtures of characters occur in other species of *Erythroneura* and several species of mosquitoes thought to be of hybrid origin (Belkin and Hogue, 1959).

In spite of the genetic difficulties against hybridization between well-separated species, viable hybrids between such parents occasionally arise and produce a mixing of characters between phylogenetic lines. In animals there is evidence indicating such a hybrid mixing in the leafhopper genus *Erythroneura*. In the *maculata* group of this genus four probable hybrids species have been detected, each between species belonging to different species complexes (Fig. 33) (Ross 1958a). In the plants hybrid mixing has occurred in many groups, most commonly perpetuated through the mechanism of

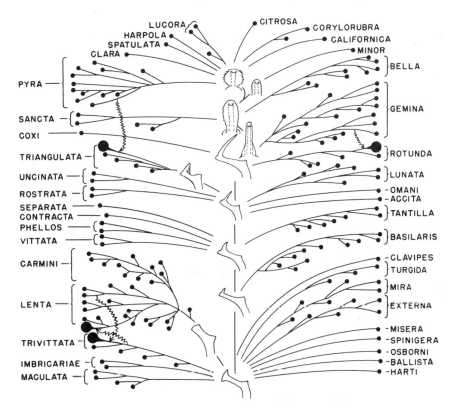

Fig. 33. Family tree of the *Erythroneura maculata* group of leafhoppers showing the four species thought to be of hybrid origin (each indicated by a large black dot) and the phylogenetic line contributing the smaller number of characters to each (shown by zigzag line).

polyploidy (Fig. 34) (Babcock, 1957; Anderson, 1949; Lewis and Lewis, 1955). This mixing of characters through hybridization has thus resulted in the origin of many highly successful and novel character combinations and must therefore be considered an important facet of evolution (Stebbins, 1959).

GENETIC VARIABILITY IN NATURAL POPULATIONS

Because of the extremely high proportion of lethal, sublethal, and deficiency mutants arising in experimental populations, the idea is frequently expressed that the type of mutation observed in the genetics laboratory does not provide a basis for the kind of char-

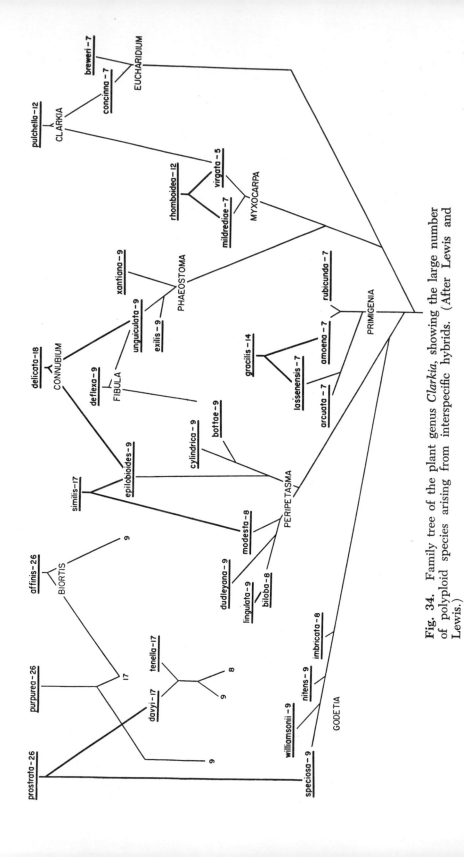

Fig. 34. Family tree of the plant genus *Clarkia*, showing the large number of polyploid species arising from interspecific hybrids. (After Lewis and Lewis.)

acter change observed in evolutionary studies. Two lines of evidence show the fallacy of this idea.

In the first place, every natural population adequately tested contains an abundance of mutant alleles of the same types as those found in the laboratory. Regarding *Drosophila*, Spencer (1947) states that wild or semi-wild populations carry many more than the 1,000 or more mutants reported from experiments and that certain kinds of mutants can be obtained more easily from wild populations than by radiation or other laboratory methods. This coincidence of wild and artificially induced mutation indicates that all the different alleles occurring in nature arose originally as mutant types such as are studied in the laboratory. Special techniques of detection have shown also that the lethal and sublethal alleles also abound in natural populations (Spencer, 1947).

Numerous natural alleles have been observed. In humans, a mutant for a six-fingered hand occurs with some frequency. Mosquitoes show many allelic components similar to those found in other organisms (Lavan, 1957).

Many natural physiological traits are allelic in nature, suggesting that they arose as mutations in nature. Harvey (1954) found that in the spruce budworm *Choristoneura fumiferana* about 20 per cent of some populations did not diapause, and that by mating selection this fraction could be increased to 80 per cent. In the larch sawfly *Pristiphora erichsoni* one race possesses an allele for encapsulating and killing the larvae of certain internal parasites (Muldrew, 1953). Examples in the plants include mutants of wheat rust which will attack previously resistant races of wheat, and mutants of the mold *Penicillium* which produce different amounts of the antibiotic penicillin.

The second major point concerning these mutations is that many of them do represent the kind of differences found between natural taxa.

In the plant *Primula sinensis* an assortment of laboratory mutant types of leaves, bracts, calyx, and corolla display differences in shape much like those found between distinct plant species (Fig. 35). In the fly *Drosophila*, laboratory mutant types include the addition or loss of setae, juxtaposition of wing veins, and many color characters on almost all parts of the body (Patterson and Stone, 1952), and these are the type of character used to differentiate many species of the genus. Stebbins (1950) lists many more examples for plants.

The short-winged mosquito mutants observed by Lavan (1957)

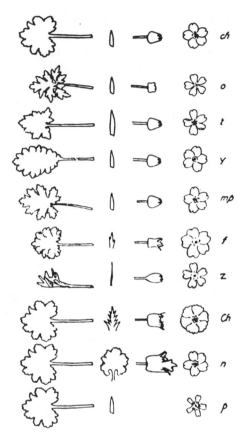

Fig. 35. Leaf, bract, calyx, and corolla of the "wild" type (ch) of *Primula sinensis* and of nine mutants affecting leaf and inflorescence shapes. All are shown on a wild type background except the calyx of *nn,* which is shown on a *ChCh* background. (After Anderson and DeWinton.)

exemplify exactly the type of difference found to be established as specific, generic, or even family characters in many orders of insects (Fig. 36). The ancestors of many wingless insects such as fleas and lice were undoubtedly normally winged insects bearing analogous if not homologous alleles for shorter wings.

Similar observations are on record for chromosomal mutations. In natural populations of *Drosophila,* chromosomal inversions are abundant and of many kinds, and similar inversions have become established as distinctive features of some species of *Drosophila* (Patterson and Stone, 1952). In the plants many natural populations show aneuploidy, and in some cases this is considered to be the

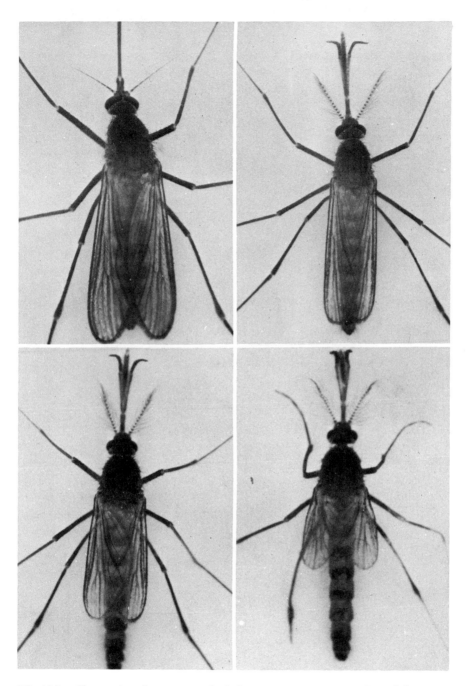

Fig. 36. Short-winged mutant of *Culex pipiens,* segregated in laboratory cultures. Upper row, normal female and male. Lower right, male homozygous for short-winged mutant allele. Lower left, male heterozygous for short-winged mutant allele. (After Lavan.)

basis of the establishment of different chromosome numbers in different species of plants (Stebbins, 1950; Clausen, 1951).

We therefore have every reason to believe that mutants similar to laboratory types exist and are spontaneously and continuously arising in all natural populations. We may also assert that these are the true building blocks of evolution.

MAGNITUDE OF CHARACTER CHANGE

A lively controversy has progressed for many years concerning the magnitude of character change involved in evolution. Darwin (1859) believed that evolution proceeded by the accumulation of small differences. Goldschmidt (1940, 1948) argued that such small changes cannot lead to the large differences found between major groups and that the latter must arise by the occurrence of large mutant differences (saltation or macroevolution). Because of discontinuities in the geologic record, Clark (1930) also argued that major groups must arise by saltation. Simpson (1944) took the position that saltation is not necessary to explain the discontinuities in the fossil record and agreed with Dobzhansky (1937) that evolution proceeds on the basis of genetic changes of small magnitude. Later both Goldschmidt (1955) and Dobzhanky (1955) pointed out that large differences in *characters* might arise from relatively small differences in genetic makeup.

In discussing character change at the inter-generic level, experimental genetic analysis is usually impossible because either the organisms are too different to produce fertile offspring, or they represent extinct groups, or they cannot be reared under suitable experimental conditions. Hence, any extrapolation from characters to genetic makeup must be by inference. In spite of these difficulties the phylogenetic analysis of certain groups does offer interesting speculation regarding magnitude of character change.

Small Changes

The evolution of the male claspers in one branch of the caddisfly genus *Helicopsyche* can be traced through a series of small steps from the ancestral type *H. mexicanus* to the specialized type *H. vergelana* (Fig. 37). In mosquitoes of the genus *Culex* many evolutionary lines can be followed in each of which only a small morphological step separates one species from another, as is shown by characteristics of the male genitalia in one of these lines

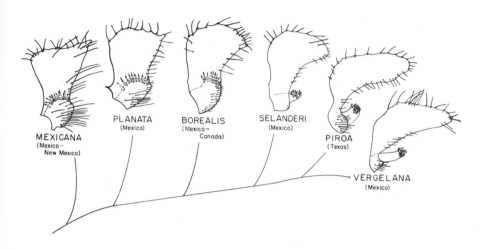

Fig. 37. Family tree of the *borealis* branch of the caddisfly genus *Helicopsyche*, showing the evolution in the shape of the clasper from a primitive species resembling *H. mexicana* to the specialized species *H. vergelana*.

(Fig. 38). Innumerable examples of similar sequences of small steps in evolutionary change could be cited in both plants and animals.

If in these cases the intermediate conditions became extinct and only the extremes survived, it might appear improbable for the end results to have arisen from a succession of small changes. So many graded series of this sort occur, however, that the accumulation of small character changes must be extremely common in evolution.

Large Changes

Ever since their discovery, investigators have wondered if the homeotic mutants of *Drosophila* presaged a type of character change important in evolution. These mutants include the one called *tetraptera* in which the halteres are wing-like, *proboscipedia* in which certain mouthparts are antenna-like or foot-like; and *aristipedia* in which the antennae are leg-like. In each case these changes from normal are brought about by some structure coming under the developmental influence of the determiners for another structure. In *aristipedia*, for example, the cells which would normally become an antenna have come instead under the control of the

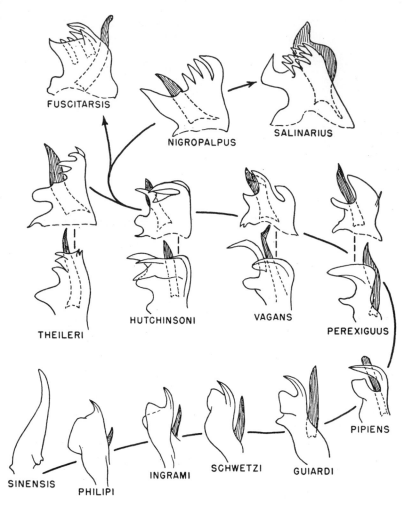

Fig. 38. A structure of the male genitalia of selected species in the mosquito *Culex pipiens* line. The basal species *C. sinensis* is a member of a primitive, closely related line and is added for purposes of comparison. Upper two rows, lateral aspect; lower two rows, ventral aspect. (Modified from Barraud, Edwards, and others.)

system of developmental enzymes which produces a leg. Furthermore this change has occurred in one jump, or mutation. The best explanation to date is that the mutant represents some simple switch in physiological pathways early in ontogenetic development. In nature, several cases suggest some such mechanism as the cause of new characters.

In primitive caddisflies the larvae have a sclerotized hard dorsal shield on only the first of the three thoracic segments (Fig. 39*a*). In four completely unrelated phylogenetic lines, the second and third

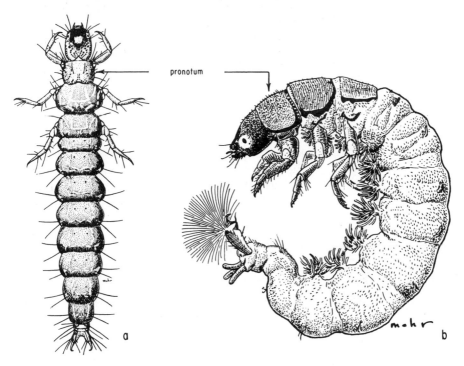

pronotum

a

b

Fig. 39. Larvae of two caddisflies. (a) *Rhyacophila,* having pronotum sclerotized, the succeeding two segments membranous; (b) *Hydropsyche,* having pronotum and succeeding two segments sclerotized dorsally. (From Illinois Natural History Survey.)

thoracic segments also have a sclerotized dorsal shield extremely similar to that of the first segment. Three of the four cases each represent an entire distinctive family, the Hydropsychidae (Fig. 39*b*), Hydroptilidae, and Limnocentropidae, respectively. In the latter family the dorsal shields on the second and third segments are similar to that on the first in so many small details that the influence of a homeotic mutation is strongly suggested. In the fourth case, the genus *Ecnomus* in the Psychomyiidae, the adults resemble those of a related genus *Tinodes* so closely that one would expect only a trivial difference in the larvae. Yet the larva of *Tinodes* has the second and third thoracic segments completely membranous with no indication of an intermediate stage leading to the three-shield condition in *Ecnomus*. This array of circumstantial evidence points strongly to the occurrence in each of these four lines, of parallel, homologous, homeotic mutations, bringing the dorsal region of the second and third thoracic segments under the same developmental control as the first.

Concerning horse evolution Robb (1936, 1937) and Simpson (1944) thought that the change from a three-toed horse to a one-toed horse (the two side toes represented by splints) occurred in one stage and in one step, due to a change in the proportionate development of the toes. This would imply the possibility of a single mutation causing drastic change, but it is possible that a series of progressive mutations were involved (Simpson, 1953).

Another type of large mutation is the duplication of parts. Occasionally a specimen shows a striking duplication such as the flea having an extra pair of legs (Fig. 22), reported by Sanjean and Travis (1955). This condition may have been caused by a somatic mutation. Less striking but heritable is polydactyly in humans, in which a single mutation causes the production of an extra finger or toe.

Taken together, these examples and circumstances indicate that, although small character mutations may be the rule, some much larger character mutations do occur and become established in their respective populations. It is probable that, as far as chemical reorganization of the genic material is concerned, these mutations producing larger phenotypic changes are no more complex genetically than those producing small changes.

THE ORDER IN GENETIC CHANGE

The observed continuity of mutation in experimental populations, the occurrence of similar mutations in nature, and the diversity of undoubtedly genetically-controlled characters in organisms back to the earlier fossil records, together tell a story of constant genetic change since life began. This change has not been random but, like pre-biological change before it, has moved in the direction of a kind of order peculiar to itself.

The order in pre-biological chemical evolution was determined by temperatures, the possible kinds of chemicals mixed together, and the inherent chemical and physical properties of the resultant units.

The order in genetic change also is restricted in one direction by its chemical nature in that only certain new bondings or breaks can be made in a complex biological compound without destroying it. However, the primary influence regarding genetic change is physiological. A change must act harmoniously in relation to the rest of the genome with respect to initiating and controlling the many chemical pathways involved in duplicating the organism. If the organism or colony bearing the change is not duplicated, the change is not perpetuated. Lethal mutants represent such changes. Thus the fact that a change is possible chemically does not necessarily mean that it will produce a balanced genetic system. Changes in chromosome structure have the added physical prerequisite that they must produce a mechanical assemblage capable of synapsis and division at meiosis. Many chromosomal and genic mutations do occur that are not perpetuated because of these several physiological processes. The genetic changes which are effectively introduced into the living population are thus restricted by the physiological framework into which they must fit.

Natural Selection

5

Although spontaneous changes or mutations in the genetic system are normally produced independently of the environment, their fate is ultimately determined by the forces of the environment. The organism cannot be divorced from its environment which contains the necessities for the growth and reproduction of the organism and at the same time imposes a rigorous test of the fitness of the organism. The environment therefore is the testing ground for genetic changes, and its action determines which changes will persist and which will perish. This sifting is the process of natural selection.

The process of natural selection is difficult to measure on a short-term basis. Few contemporaneous cases have been observed or adequately tested in nature. Experimental evidence has contributed much knowledge concerning the selective forces exerted by simple laboratory variables on a few characters. Through the fossil record it is possible to obtain some understanding of the long-term results of natural selection (Fig. 40). Some lineages living today have existed with little change for

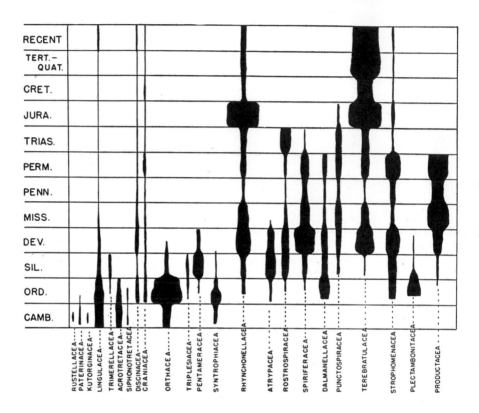

Fig. 40. An example of the results of natural selection. The range and development in time of the superfamilies of the animal phylum Brachiopoda, illustrating the differences in taxonomic size, time of "flowering," and patterns of survival. The thinnest line drawn (for example, Lingulacea from Pennsylvanian to Tertiary times) equals one genus. (After Cooper and Williams.)

many millions of years—the American opossum for possibly 100 million and many marine clams for possibly 350 million. Other existing lineages, such as that which eventually evolved into the horse *Equus,* have been changing fairly steadily for the last 100 million years. Their primitive ancestral forms are long extinct. In *Equus* it appears that change is synonymous with survival, but this is not universally true of other lineages. The reptilian dinosaurs and pterodactyls represented lineages which changed rapidly but all of which were extinct by the end of Mesozoic time.

These examples demonstrate that some of the continuing flow of genetic changes become established in the population; others do not. Further, over long periods of time much-changed and little-changed lineages alike may persist or become extinct. Thus there is no necessary corollary between amount of change and persistence.

In broad outline, current explanations of natural selection follow the pattern of reasoning laid down in 1858 by Darwin and Wallace (Darwin, 1859). Genetic information has increased greatly since that time, as has knowledge concerning other facets of evolution, and these changes have modified a number of evolutionary concepts.

The action of natural selection is simple in theory but tremendously complex in operation. The root of the selection starts in the innate ability of living things to reproduce. There are such tremendous environmental hazards between the time of being born and that of reproducing, that of the many young produced by an individual, only one or a few survive in the long run. Theoretically, these survivors will be those with genetic constitutions producing individuals best fitted to cope with the environments; those which perish will have genetic constitutions producing individuals inferior with respect to critical environmental factors. The complexity arises from the fact that the collective progeny of one individual or pair have many genetic variables, as does the environment have many variables. The complexity of natural selection lies in the many combinations of circumstances arising from the interplay of these two sets of variables.

The empirical action of natural selection may be explained by a hypothetical example. If a breeding population of snakes consists of 1,000 specimens, 500 of them spotted and 500 banded, what will be the proportion of spotted to banded snakes in the thousand specimens which will survive to form the next generation? We will assume that predators see the banded snakes more easily than the spotted ones and catch more of them. In this case the second generation might contain 750 spotted and only 250 banded. Thus the selective action of the predators on the phenotypes has changed the genetic composition of the snake population. More snakes bearing the genetic makeup for "spotted" survived to breed than did those bearing the genetic makeup for "banded."

If "banded" were new in the population, arising as a spontaneous mutation, then this selection would rapidly weed it out. If, in contrast, "spotted" were a new mutant character, the selection would eliminate the old character "banded" and establish a changed genome.

This type of action selects the phenotypes of one generation and in so doing determines the genetic composition of the next.

FACTORS OF NATURAL SELECTION

The factors of natural selection fall into two categories: those contained in the inner workings of the organism and those of the environment. In certain cases it may be difficult to assign selective action to one or the other alone because the selective response to a factor in one category may result in an action involving a factor in the other category. This interlocking situation is exemplified in a few of the examples given.

Selection by Internal Factors

The great proportion of all mutations, as was mentioned in the preceding chapter, is sufficiently harmful to the genetic organization that progeny bearing them die before reproducing. Such mutant individuals would leave no offspring and thus would be eliminated immediately by natural selection caused by internal factors. Many mutations have drastic effects on viability or reproductive rate as homozygotes but are only moderately deleterious as heterozygotes. Individuals bearing these mutant types will leave fewer progeny than others, and this differential reproduction will exert a strong selection pressure against the mutant type. If, however, the heterozygote is as viable or reproductive as the homozygote of the original type, the trait may be carried in the population for a long time.

Viability and reproductive rate are affected adversely by rigid experimental selection for some one trait. In chickens Lerner (1958) found that intensive selection producing unusually long legs also produced almost complete loss of reproductive capacity. Following extreme selection for individual traits, a similar reduction or loss of reproductive capacity has occurred in many other organisms (Stebbins, 1950). It is possible that if equally rigorous selection for individual adaptive traits operated in nature, comparable losses in reproductive capacity might ensue. Should such losses reach critical proportions in regard to maintaining population numbers, then selection for fecundity (resulting in greater heterozygosity) would outweigh the selection pressure for the trait becoming homozygous.

Other examples indicate that intensive selection may result in establishing the homozygous condition of an advantageous trait without reducing the general population level. In certain regional populations of mosquitoes and house flies exposed to intensive control programs, single-allele factors for insecticide resistance have risen from an extremely low initial level to a practically homozygous condition without causing a perceptible drop in field populations (Brown, 1960). These instances of the establishment of insect resistance are striking examples of rapid evolution at work. They provide evidence supporting Carson's (1959) view that heterozygosity lost through intense selection for one trait may be offset by heterozygosity associated with other traits.

Occasionally freakish mutations arise which would seem to be at a great selective disadvantage because of their inability to function mechanically. For example, in a population of the foxglove aphid *Myzus persicae* on Presque Isle, Maine, several individuals of a mutant having wings on only one side appeared in 1956 and 1957. These can fly but only in a curious spiral pattern (Wave, 1958). Because these aphids normally migrate between hosts, it is difficult to see how this mutant type can survive many years in nature unless it is carried as a recessive trait which does not appear phenotypically in the heterozygote. Possibly, wind currents may be the chief agents both of propulsion and direction in the migratory flights of aphids. If this is the case, these lopsided aphids can at least become airborne and may not be at as much of a mechanical disadvantage as it would seem.

Selection by Environmental Factors

The environment has a most complex selective action on the genetic makeup of a population. From the standpoint of the organism the environment is composed of many factors: food, water, and shelter; physical conditions such as temperature, humidity, pH, wind velocity, water current, and light; parasites and predators, usually of many kinds; and competitors for food, shelter, mates, and other requirements for successful growth and reproduction. In contrast, the organisms of a population may possess collectively great variation in genetic makeup, representing differences for which any factor of the environment may have a selective effect.

The following cases are relatively simple examples of the selective action of environmental factors.

1. SICKLE-CELL

In certain African Negro populations the allele for the blood cell condition known as sickle-cell disease was found to be common. This disease is the product of a gene which causes the blood cells to assume a sickle-like shape in a medium deficient in oxygen. In the heterozygous state this gene causes at most a mild anemia but in the homozygous state causes a lethal anemia. Why sickle-cell persisted in these populations was a mystery until it was discovered that individuals carrying the sickle-cell allele were more resistant to malaria than those with normal alleles. Therefore, the individuals homozygous for sickle-cell were depleted by the pathologic blood condition, and those homozygous for normal blood cells were decimated by malaria. Heterozygous individuals survived best, and therefore natural selection favored carriers of this genetic makeup (Allison, 1955).

2. CHROMOSOMAL INVERSIONS AND CLIMATIC ADJUSTMENT

Another simple example in the operation of selection involves inversions in the chromosomes of the fruit-fly *Drosophila pseudoobscura* (Dobzhansky, 1955). Natural populations of these flies sampled at different elevations in the Sierra Nevada of California each had a distinctive proportion of several inversions in its genetic pool. Laboratory tests showed that individuals heterozygous for these inversions possessed sufficient heterosis or hybrid vigor to be more successful than either homozygote. Further, each combination of inversion heterozygote was most effective within particular temperatures. Thus each elevation had a different range of temperatures, and this in turn brought about the selection of that proportion of the different inversions most successful within that particular temperature range (Fig. 41).

3. PROTECTIVE COLORATION AND MIMICRY

The potential selective value of these has long been established by experiment. Especially startling examples include the many patterns of edible Cerambycidae beetles (Fig. 42) which mimic patterns of stinging wasps or distasteful Lycidae beetles occurring in the same habitats (Darlington, 1938; Linsley, 1959) and the protection given to various cryptically colored grasshoppers against predation by birds (Isely, 1938). The realized value of such selection is afforded by two cases involving populations of a species of snake and a species of moth, respectively.

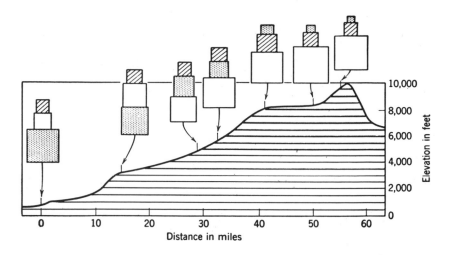

Fig. 41. The relative frequencies (symbolized by the dimensions of the squares) of three different types of chromosomes in populations of *Drosophila pseudoobscura* which live at different elevations in the Sierra Nevada in or near Yosemite Park, California. Stippled, white, and shaded squares represent three different kinds of chromosomes. (From Dobzhansky, *Evolution, Genetics and Man,* John Wiley & Sons, Inc.)

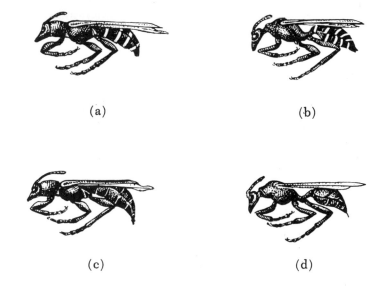

Fig. 42. Mimicry in the beetle family Cerambycidae. Two flower-visiting species of beetles (a) *Sphecomorpha murina* and (c) *Acyphoderes odyneroides* mimic two wasps which visit the same flowers in their respective localities (b) *Polybia nigra* and (d) *Polybia liliacea.* (From Linsley.)

The widespread North American water snake *Natrix sipedon* has a population on a small island in Lake Erie which differs from the heavily banded mainland populations in that it ranges from a less conspicuously banded condition to a uniform limestone grey or beige color. The snakes are active on the limestone rocks which line the shore of the island. Camin and his colleagues found that a high proportion of the young snakes were banded, but that the proportions of the different color classes of the mature snakes had shifted towards the unbanded type; about twice as many adults were unicolorous as compared with the young. Because the unicolorous specimens are relatively inconspicuous on the limestone, whereas the banded types are seen much more readily, these authors believed that predation has been greater on the more conspicuously banded individuals and thus that natural selection has favored the unicolorous types (Camin, Triplehorn, and Walter, 1954; Camin and Ehrlich, 1958).

In the vicinity of various cities in Europe, melanistic individuals of several species of moths occurred in increasing numbers. Experiment showed that on the dark surfaces in and near industrial areas these darker forms had a marked cryptic protection from predators. The melanistic individuals of at least the species *Boarmia repandata* have a greater fecundity than the light form. In non-industrial areas the moths frequent light-colored and mottled tree trunks. Here the preponderance of light forms is maintained by a strong selection pressure for protective coloration, in spite of their reproductive disadvantage (Goldschmidt, 1940; Ford, 1955; Kettlewell, 1955, 1956*a,b*).

Darwin (1859), Dobzhansky (1951), Simpson (1953), Stebbins (1950), and others have summarized many additional examples of known or inferred natural selection. The gist of this mass of information is that every factor in the environment may produce some selective action on the organism, and that in the long run this action leads to the survival of the better fitted phenotypes in a population.

The "long-run" product, however, must be an average of the devious and complex pattern of selection which surely occurs. Taking a hypothetical example, an abundant insect population might strip its food supply so that progeny of later emerging and reproducing females died of starvation; only the progeny of the earlier emerging females reached maturity. This would result in a positive selection pressure for genotypes associated with early appearance. If late lethal spring frosts occurred the next year, the earlier emerging individuals would be killed, and selection would be for late emergence, the opposite of the previous year. Undoubtedly many conflicting sets of selection pressures are in operation.

Identical selection pressures may not reoccur for many generations, especially for organisms with a life cycle of a year or less. Competitive selection pressures and weather extremes are often separated by periods of five to 25 years. Thus genetic factors rigorously selected in one year may become diluted due to counter-selection or many other causes before any additional identical selection becomes operative. However, many selection pressures occur continuously for considerable periods of time, especially in the case of structures adapting an organism to better success in a new environment. Thus an animal which had recently adopted a subterranean, digging mode of life might have feet not especially adapted to digging. In this case it would seem that natural selection would favor any genetic change producing feet better suited for digging. Immediate selection, however, might be hindered by pleiotropy and genic competition.

Many genes are pleiotropic, each affecting several characters, and there is always the possibility that conflicting selection pressures may result from this situation. In chickens, as was stated earlier, rigid selection for long legs results in reduced vitality and fecundity (Lerner, 1958).

Different genes may themselves be in competition for nuclear substrates, as shown by Glass (1957), so that unforeseen results may follow selection for different combinations of alleles. Here and in pleiotropic conflicts natural selection might result in a biological compromise.

It is probable that natural selection never produces perfect adaptation. As Simpson (1949) pointed out, many possible variations around a central theme may work equally well to such a degree that any one variant would have little or no selective advantage over the others. He cited as an example the horns of African antelopes (Fig. 43); those of no two species are exactly alike, but all seem to function satisfactorily.

The correlation of seemingly linked adaptive characters may not be perfect. In several stonefly groups the females have short wings and the extra body segment thus exposed is sclerotized like the other exposed end segments, presumably conferring some kind of protection. In the winter stoneflies of the American genus *Allocapnia* this correlated change has evolved independently in two lines. In one of these lines, represented by *A. vivipara*, the wings of the female vary from fairly long wings to short pads (Fig. 44), resem-

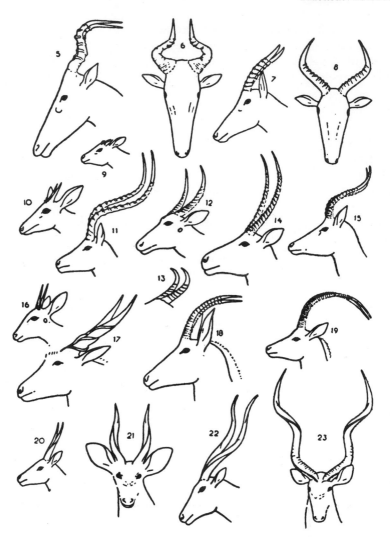

Fig. 43. Heads of the principle types of antelopes in the Congo. The horns of all function satisfactorily, indicating that there is no one perfect type for these stuctures. (After Schouteden.)

bling the series of short wing mutants discovered by Lavan in the mosquitoes (Fig. 36). Also, an extra terminal segment is variously sclerotized. In these *A. vivipara* females, however, the two characters are not correlated. In populations over a wide part of the range, a third of the females with the shortest wings have the most extensively sclerotized abdomens and a third have the least sclerotized; conversely, of the females with the most extensively

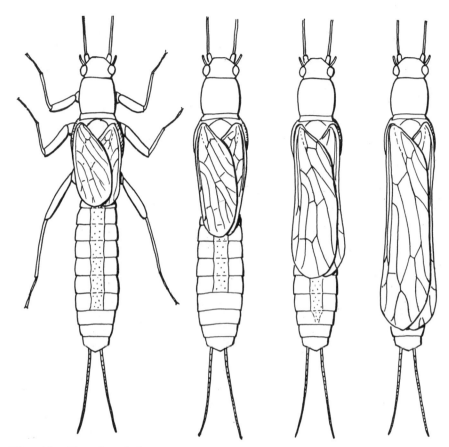

Fig. 44. Females of the stonefly *Allocapnia vivipara* showing differences in wing lengths found in nature. The stippled area on the abdomen is membranous.

sclerotized abdomens, a third have unusually short wings and a third have the longest wings. In spite of this lack of adaptive correlation, both traits are being carried in many populations and are available for selection pressures to influence.

At any time and through a variety of causes new viable genetic components or combinations may occur and become a part of the gene pool of the population. In other words, the genetic composition of a population is dynamic and constantly adding an element of variability into the relationship between gene frequency and natural selection. Such changes might modify old selection pressures or establish new ones.

DIRECTION OF SELECTION

Evolution takes one of two courses: toward stability of the existing phenotype or change away from it. The selection pressures producing these courses are called *centripetal* and *centrifugal,* respectively, by Simpson (1944).

Centripetal Selection

If an organism is well adapted to its environment, the chances are great that any new mutations would produce phenotypes less well adapted. Selection would remove these new elements and restore the population to its original genetic composition. In this case of selection the direction would be toward stability of existing phenotype.

There seem to be considerable grounds for thinking that the genetic system as a whole is sufficiently intricate to exert a strong stabilizing selection pressure regardless of the environment. This idea revolves around the concepts of genetic balance or homeostasis (Lerner, 1954, 1958) and implies that any genetic change will tend to create physiological imbalance even though it produces a trait beneficial ecologically. Such a concept suggests that the environment would have to exert a certain minimum selection pressure toward change before the innate "inertia" of genetic homeostasis would be counterbalanced.

Theoretically centripetal selection over a long period of time would result in an unchanged lineage of great age. The living American opossum *Didelphis virginicus,* which is remarkably similar to its Cretaceous ancestor, might be such a product.

Centrifugal Selection

If an organism were in a new environment, the chances are great that of the many mutations occurring, some would produce new characters better adapted to the new environment than the old ones. The classical example to illustrate this situation concerns the teeth of the horse and its ancestors. The early horses had generalized teeth, but later types of horses had cusped and furrowed teeth. Presumably the early horses fed on many kinds of vegetation, and later types fed primarily on grass. The grass-feeding habit supposedly exerted a strong selection pressure toward teeth more efficient for masticating grass and led to changes from the ancestral types of teeth.

If the same centrifugal selection pressure is maintained in the same direction over a long period of geologic time (what is termed *straight-line selection*), changes continue in the same direction and form trends. Simpson (1953) stated that in paleontological data long-term trends are extremely common in some characters. As an example he cites the sea urchin *Micraster* from the English chalk of the late Cretaceous. A continuous series of overlapping fossil populations show trends for increasing relative breadth and height, anterior migration of the mouth, and development of a deep anterior notch at the margin. The evolution of horse teeth is another example. In phylogenies based on living species similar trends are common. Good examples are the series of changes in the claspers of the caddisfly genus *Helicopsyche* (Fig. 37) and in the genitalic parts of mosquitoes (Fig. 38).

Trends in unrelated lineages may follow parallel courses in what appear to be adaptive changes in each line to identical environmental conditions. In cave species of fish, salamanders, crustaceans, and insects, for example, eyes are usually reduced in size or absent; in burrowing forms such as the gopher, mole, and molecricket some sort of digging foot is usually developed; and in large swimming animals almost the same sort of paddle-like appendages, streamlined body, and large tail are evolved. In many desert plants spines evolve and the leaves become thick and relatively impervious to desiccation.

These trends usually involve only a few radical structural changes; the great bulk of the characteristics of the species vary around a constant pattern. In animal phyla in particular the great base of "conservative" characters provide the information for deducing the relationships of the groups. Thus the skull and skeletal parts can be homologized within broad limits through the entire series of vertebrate animals and in considerable detail through any one class such as the Reptilia, Aves, or Mammalia. Although it seems that this circumstance may be more easily recognized in the animals than in the plants, in the latter, detailed histological studies demonstrate remarkable evidence of relationships in stem and leaf structure and other parts (Bailey and Nast, 1943; Prat, 1936).

RATE OF CHANGE

Rate of change has two distinct aspects: the occurrence of advantageous mutations, and the intensity of the selection pressures influencing their subsequent incorporation into the gene pool.

Production of Advantageous Mutations

Because many species, like the oppossum, have existed with little change for millions of years, there is good reason to believe that each group has an optimum possible adaptedness to its environment. This optimum should not be confused with perfect adaptedness (as was explained previously in this chapter). The optimum possible adaptedness is the best phenotype that results from the mutational possibilities of the organism. If the species comes to occupy a new environment in which the species was initially far from its optimum possible adaptedness, the chances are that many new mutations would be advantageous. As the mutations were incorporated into the genetic structure, the species would evolve closer to its optimum possible adaptedness. As this advance progressed, the chances are that fewer and fewer mutations would be advantageous, hence, more and more mutations would be weeded out of the species by natural selection.

Observations on mutations in general indicate that the rate of occurrence of mutations in a species is fairly constant. Because the number of mutations occurring in a unit of time is relatively constant, whereas the proportion of these which are advantageous theoretically decreases with length of occupancy of a new habitat, it therefore follows that theoretically the number of advantageous mutations occurring per unit of time would decrease. On the basis of this reasoning, the rate of occurrence of advantageous mutations would be highest during the period of most pronounced centrifugal selection. The rate would decline exponentially as the species approached its optimum possible adaptedness, which would represent a state of centripetal selection. Simpson's (1944) analysis of rates of change observed in the fossil record for the mammals fits this reasoning.

Selection of Mutations

Strictly speaking, the "selection" part of centripetal or centrifugal selection cannot and does not operate until a new mutant character has occurred in the species. After its occurrence the rate of selection will be individual with regard to each new mutation and will be expressed as changes in the proportions of the new allele in the gene pool. Theoretically, if selection for the advantageous mutation were relatively constant, the proportion of the new mutation would rise exponentially by a function determined primarily by the size of the species population, the fecundity of the species, and the rigidity of selection for the new mutation. Thus if a mutation conferred unusual adaptive benefits on an individual bearing it, that individual would leave more offspring than others in the population, and all of its progeny bearing the mutant allele would do likewise. However, if the whole population were large, the individuals bearing the mutant would at first be only a small proportion of the total. With the difference in survival rates, however, the new type would tend to increase by a geometric proportion, whereas the old type would tend to increase by an arithmetic proportion or lower, and with time the new type would replace the older type at an increasing rate.

Some measure of the possible speed of these changes in genic proportions is afforded by the results of campaigns to eradicate certain mosquito and house fly populations by chemical control. In some instances, under the powerful selection pressure of the insecticides, alleles conferring resistance to the control chemicals rose from negligible proportions to virtual homozygosity in two years (Brown, 1960).

Studies of insecticide resistance afford excellent examples of the phenomenon called *preadaptation*. Some and probably all of the kinds of alleles conferring insecticidal resistance occurred in wild populations of the insects before these populations were ever exposed to insecticides. In mosquitoes and house flies which had not been exposed to insecticides, the resistant alleles occurred in extremely low frequencies but built up to much higher ones as soon as control applications superimposed a selective factor for them. Many evolutionists have suggested that in natural evolution the same type of circumstance has operated frequently. They believe that many mutations conferring little or infrequent advantage may persist at low frequencies and that subsequently changed circumstances (either in the environment or in the genome) exert strong selection pressures for the previously rare mutations. Such considerations indicate a possible indeterminate period of low selection pressure preceding the exponential increase of many alleles after they become highly advantageous to the species.

Thus in time every trend tends to end at a point where the organism is as well adapted to its environment as is possible within its genetic framework. This means that centrifugal selection gradually leads to a condition of centripetal selection.

SELECTION IN APOMICTIC ORGANISMS

In apomictic species, natural selection operates solely by its effect on each individual. In these reproductive types there is no opportunity for genetic mixing between individuals. The members of the species form clones or pure lines rather than an interbreeding population. Selection in these species has certain distinctive features.

The genetic variability in one individual is thought to be extremely small. In asexual types it will be nil except for an occasional viable diploid or polyploid mutant, but this will immediately give rise to two homozygous types of offspring. In diploid unisexual types undergoing meiosis, there is the theoretical possibility that a considerable number of allelic heterozygotes would be formed, but White (1954) believes that even in these forms homozygosity predominates. If true, it is theoretically possible to delete a genetic trait from the population by removing one certain individual.

Because apomictic species lack a mechanism for accumulating mutants from different parents in one individual offspring, maximum rate of change in them should theoretically be much lower than in bisexually reproducing types. If, however, an unusually well adapted mutant arose it should be able to supplant older types with great rapidity.

SELECTION IN BISEXUAL POPULATIONS

In bisexually reproducing populations natural selection acts by removing individuals, but in one sense the population as a whole is involved. The reason for this lies in the large store of variability in an entire population, and the fact that in the mating process an effective mixing of genetic variants takes place. It is highly likely that (1) in most cases no offspring are exactly like either of their parents and (2) the removal of one individual will not delete any genetic trait from the genetic makeup of the population. Selection, therefore, operates on the total gene pool of an interbreeding population.

This interbreeding or Mendelian population, called a *deme,* may be either small and local or large and regional, depending on the continuity of the range and the ability of the organisms to disperse or be dispersed (called their *vagility*). It may include the entire population of the species or only one minute segment of the species. The size of the deme is important in selection.

Large Demes

Geneticists estimate that so much genetic variability occurs in a deme that even in the largest populations it is almost impossible for every possible genetic combination to occur. The larger the deme, however, the greater would be the realized number of these genetic combinations upon which natural selection could act. Combinations of great selective advantage might appear in a large deme which would never appear in a small one. Also, the larger the deme, the greater would be the possibility of the occurrence of advantageous new mutations.

It has been calculated by Wright (1949) that genetic recombinations or new mutations of high selective value would spread and become established faster in large demes or at least in populations of large numbers. In contrast genetic elements having only slight selective value would move more slowly through a large deme than through a small one.

Small Demes

From the preceding remarks concerning large demes, it is clear that small demes are considered to have few selective advantages. The principal advantage seems to be that genetic factors of only slight selective value can theoretically become established more rapidly in small demes than in large demes.

Because local populations vary in population density, some differences in selection pressures should occur between the high and low density phases. Theoretically, the smaller the deme in number of individuals, the greater the chance for the population density to cross and re-cross a point critical for switching from large-deme to small-deme selection effect.

SUMMARY

The contents of this and the preceding chapter emphasize that the inherent genetic mechanism produces spontaneous inherited changes continuously and that the phenotypic results of this genetic change are sifted by forces of natural selection occurring both within the organism and in its environment. The constant input of genetic change and the action of natural selection are highly complex, and their interactions are the product of their individual complexities. A few of these complexities are outlined in these and later chapters of this book; many have been expressed as mathematical models by Fisher (1930), Haldane (1932), and Wright (1949). By these mechanisms and processes, individuals which are better adapted to their environment tend to survive. The physiological and morphological attributes which increase the adaptedness of an individual are called *adaptations*.

The result is that natural selection acts on the individuals of one generation and in so doing determines the genetic composition of the next.

One aspect of the relationship between genetic change and natural selection is of especial interest from an over-all view of the evolutionary process. Because of its own innate properties, the genetic change mechanism introduces into the population new units which are random as regards selective value. The process of natural selection selects and discards these random units in such a fashion that the persisting units are essentially ordered in a finite number of character changes having definite physiological and ecological orientations.

Species and

Species Change

6

Although natural selection directs change in individual local populations, it is the establishment of change in species as a whole which has led to the great variety of living types that constitute the vast family tree of nature. Each line of this family tree is one species thick. During the passage of species through time, two evolutionary processes occur (Fig. 45): (1) species change and become new and often radically different kinds of organisms, and (2) species give rise to daughter species and in this way increase the number of phylogenetic lines. In this chapter we will discuss the change in species progressing through time.

RECOGNITION OF SPECIES

The species are the different kinds of plants and animals. Typically each kind breeds true generation

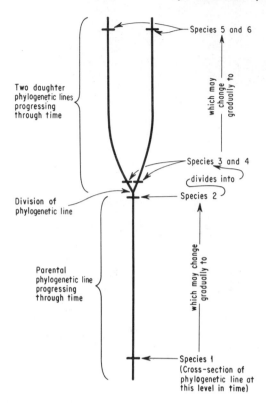

Fig. 45. Diagram of hypothetical phylogenetic line to illustrate the relationship between phylogenetic lines and species.

after generation; individuals cross freely with others of their own kind but do not interbreed with individuals of other kinds. This repetitive and essentially genetic concept of a species is old, without doubt dating back at least to the prehistoric time when man began keeping flocks and sowing seeds. In spite of the antiquity of the species concept, confusion still exists as to what is a species and how the term should be used properly. Much of the confusion stems from the fact that species are for the most part dynamic, not static, and it is frequently difficult to find readily understood terms which will define species in respect to their changing nature.

Genetic isolation has been stressed above as a criterion of species. In the processes leading to an increase in the number of species, however, daughter species of certain types may pass through stages in which they appear to be species on the basis of recognizable characteristics but are not genetically isolated from each other. This situation, which is explained in more detail in the next chapter, leads to much confusion in defining species. What these in between categories are called is not important as long as they are recognized as evidence of a dynamic phase of evolution.

A further point of confusion about the definition of species is encountered in the geological record. If fossil representatives were available for every few generations in a phylogenetic line, the samples would grade into each other and form a gradually changing series, as from Species 1 to Species 2 in Fig. 45. When it is desirable to divide such a series into species categories, this must be done on a purely arbitrary scale. Usually the fossil record of any one phylogenetic line represents forms far apart in time and hence moderately different from each other. In these cases, however, new fossil finds may unearth populations tending to bridge the previously known morphological gaps, necessitating the use of arbitrary measures in defining the species (Simpson, 1951).

Individuals in species which reproduce asexually do not form an interbreeding population and cannot be tested regarding genetic similarity with individuals of other species thought to be different. Asexual lines sometimes possess marked physiological differences but no other diagnostic criteria. Many of the lines breed true in remarkable fashion and in this respect may form unusually stable phylogenetic lines. These asexual species can be defined only arbitrarily on the basis of designated standards of difference and similarity. These similarities may include both morphological and physiological traits (Hoare, 1957).

Asexual lines appear to have arisen as side branches from bisexual lineages at various times in evolutionary history. The great bulk of evidence indicates that most of the continuing lineages in evolutionary history comprise bisexually reproducing organisms, a conclusion greatly strengthened by discoveries concerning sex in microorganisms (Wenrick, Lewis, and Raper, 1954). The bisexual species, therefore, are of special evolutionary importance and are the type discussed in this chapter.

Most of the species found living together (that is, sympatric species) are genetically isolated from each other in rigid fashion, with the result that each species forms a distinctive interbreeding population. The remarks in this chapter apply especially to these species well defined in this genetic sense.

Reproductive Characteristics

In both plants and animals, hybrids between sympatric species are rarely observed in nature. Experimental evidence indicates that almost invariably some physiological reaction, ecological circumstance, or mating behavior pattern prevents cross-mating between different species. Examples of physiological reactions include the failure of pollen grains to grow properly on foreign pistils and the dying of the sperm of certain *Drosophila* species when transferred to the spermatheca or sperm storage gland of a foreign species. Ecological circumstances preventing cross-breeding include different times of sexual maturation in both plants and animals, the pollination of flowering species by different species of insects, and the differing times of day during which species are sexually active.

If cross-mating does take place, varying degrees of intersterility can be found between the species, ranging from complete intersterility to moderate interfertility. In the latter cases, the hybrid progeny are generally either sterile or have reduced viability. Thus not one but many circumstances tend to reduce interbreeding between species. The proportionately rare occurrence in nature of hybrids between sympatric species is evidence of the effectiveness achieved by all these circumstances acting together. The result is that each species is an interbreeding system continuing from generation to generation, sufficiently isolated reproductively from other species that it maintains it own identity. Hence, although different species may be able to exchange characters to a limited extent, each species is independent in an evolutionary sense.

Visible Identification Characteristics

Almost without exception even closely related species differ in some visible trait. Frequently these differences are of small magnitude. A remarkable example was demonstrated by Price (1958). His studies showed that in eastern North America the fresh water copepod commonly referred to as *Cyclops vernalis* comprises at least seven species reproductively isolated from each other, three differentiated by minute but constant characters, the other four by only average differences.

In some instances, the diagnosis of species requires techniques involving special preparations and characters inaccessible to the student of museum specimens. In the insects of the black-fly family Simuliidae, for example, many apparently distinct genetic species cannot yet be diagnosed on the basis of conventional taxonomic characters but differ in chromosomal arrangements (Rothfels, 1956). These different chromosomal arrangements may be seen readily in specially collected and prepared salivary gland chromosomes of the larvae (Duncan, 1959; Basrur, 1959).

In a few instances, no known reliable distinguishing features of a visible nature have been detected between related species. In field crickets of the genus *Acheta* of eastern North America, five sympatric native species differ to the eye only in average characters of color and proportions (Fig. 46), but in each species the males have a distinctive mating song (Fulton, 1952; R. D. Alexander, 1957). Breeding colonies set up on the basis of these songs behave reproductively as any good "morphological" species.

It is therefore possible for genetically distinct species to differ physiologically or biochemically but to lack traits affording visible identification. Ever since this situation was appreciated, alarm has been expressed that perhaps our identifiable species are in truth conglomerates of undetected but genetically distinct species. However, in the case of several previously unidentifiable species known to be distinct by genetic tests, intensive search has unearthed either previously unobserved differences or a distinctive modal distribution of characters. In insects of the genus *Drosophila*, for example, the species pair *pseudoobscura* and *persimilis* were long considered inseparable except by genetic tests, as were five species in the *D. willistoni* group. However, Spassky (1957) found reliable identification characters in several parts of the male genitalic structures in these species of *Drosophila*. In plants, two genetically distinct species of *Uvularia*, *grandiflora* and *perfoliata*, were long considered indistinguishable on any reliable basis; Anderson and Whitaker (1934) showed that individuals of the two species could be sorted accurately by using statistical indexes involving combinations of several characters. Several investigators have found that various biochemical assays such as paper chromatography and electrophoresis (Cassidy, 1957; Sibley, 1960) have value in separating species otherwise difficult to identify (Micks, 1954; Lewallen, 1957). It seems that eventually diagnostic characters will be found between all species.

Biological and Ecological Characteristics

A detailed study of two or more species always discloses some biological difference between them. In many cases the difference

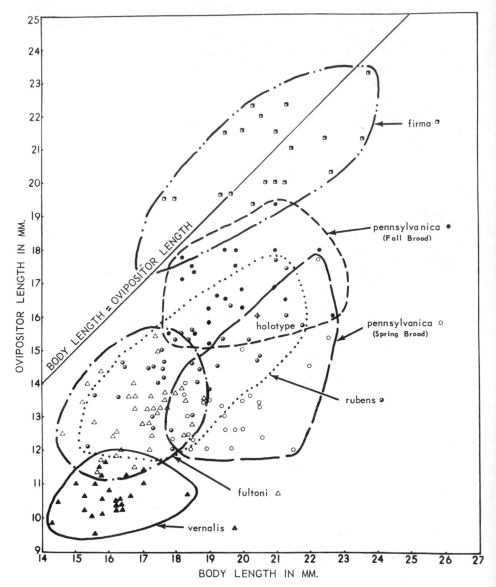

Fig. 46. Differences in body proportions between genetically distinct species of field crickets of the genus *Acheta* (oviods fitted by eye). To date these are the best morphological criteria for the separation of these species. (Modified from R. D. Alexander.)

is one of ecological zonation, for example the upland versus the lowland species of *Salix* (willows). In animals the difference may be in food habits, such as is found in many moths, sawflies, leaf-hoppers, and certain other insects in which closely related species feed on different host species (Clarke, 1952). If no other difference is noted, each species has some difference in range or population density, both of which are expressions of physiological differences and their ecological manifestations (Fig. 47). Many of these biological differences are modal rather than absolute, especially those concerning range, density, or ecological segregation within the same area. Only in the examples of food specificity and behavior

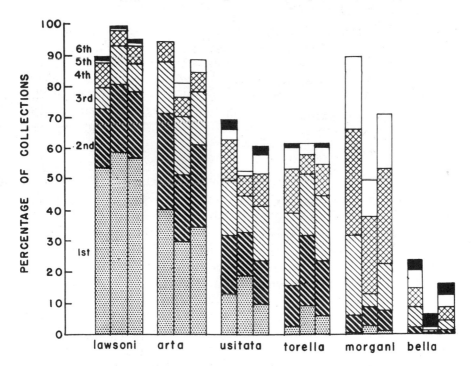

Fig. 47. Order of abundance of leafhopper species of *Erythroneura* coexist-ing on sycamore in Illinois. In the tabulation of each species, the left column represents collections made prior to and during 1954; the center column, collections made in 1955; the right column, total of all collections. The per-centage of these rankings gives a measure of the differences in population density between the six species, all of which have greatly overlapping ranges.

are there many known instances of absolute biological differences between closely related species.

In summary, bisexual species represent cross-sections of phylogenetic lines moving through time. Each species is usually distinct on the basis of some recognition feature and has distinctive biological and ecological attributes. Above all, each species is genetically distinct to a high degree, and for this reason each one changes genetically independently of other species. Thus each species is independent in an evolutionary sense.

THE SPECIES AS A PHYSICAL UNIT

The species is the total of the individuals forming its populations. These populations occupy space and are the tangible expression of the continuity of the genetic basis which controls and directs the growth of the individual. This total population is the result of the interaction between the dynamic genetic composition of the column and the dynamic environment. Certain aspects of this total population are important to an understanding of adaptability in the species as a whole.

Range

The range of a species is the sum of all the areas in which the species lives. It is also the total inhabited area of all the local populations. Where the species can live is determined by certain ecological requirements, including food, climatic and physical factors, and a place to live and reproduce. These ecological factors are extremely complex in their action, both singly and in combination. An excellent summary of this topic is given by Allee and Schmidt (1951). Each species can exist only between certain maximum and minimum values for each ecological factor of its environment. This total possible band is the *ecological tolerance* of the species. A species can occupy only those areas which occur within its ecological tolerance.

GROSS EXTENT

Ranges of organisms vary from very small to practically worldwide. The range of the Kankakee mallow *Illiamna remota* occupies an island of only a few hundred square yards in the Kankakee River near Kankakee, Illinois, and a few hundred square yards on Peter's Mountain, Virginia. This latter colony may be a distinct species (Jones and Fuller, 1955), in which case each species would be known from only a single small colony. Many insect species each occupy only one or a few adjacent caves, as for example do the ground beetles *Horologion speokoites* (Valentine, 1932) and *Nelsonites jonesi* (Valentine, 1952). The giant sequoia *Sequoiadendron giganteum* and the redwood *Sequoia sempervirens* occur in narrow strips only a few hundred miles long (Fig. 48). Every intermediate can be found between these small ranges and the much larger transcontinental and intercontinental ones.

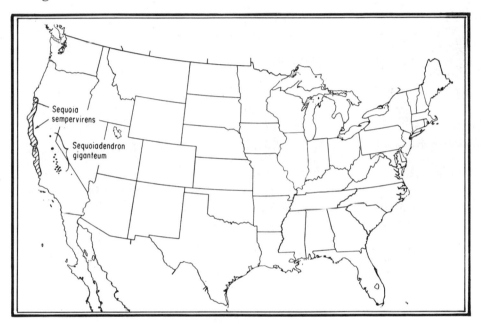

Fig. 48. Geographic ranges of the giant sequoia *Sequoiadendron giganteum* and the redwood *Sequoia sempervirens*. (After Munns.)

Although the range of any one species varies markedly in extent, observations over a number of years can be used to predict its limits and fluctuations with reasonable accuracy. This predictability indicates that the genetic changes within a species seldom build up sufficiently to change their observed ecological tolerances within short periods of time. Most of the observed exceptions are inferred and concern species introduced into a foreign environment (Elton, 1958). These exceptions may represent simply changes in the frequency of genes already in the genome rather than the origin and success of new mutant types.

A range map, such as that in Fig. 48, seldom represents an area over which the species is uniformly distributed but almost invariably includes a series of discontinuous local populations. This discontinuity is due to a combination of three factors: (1) each species can exist only in certain ecological conditions; (2) an area of any sizable geographic extent contains ecological differences sufficient that any one species could not exist over every square foot of it; and (3) a species is at times annihilated from local pockets within its normal range. If the area of the range is extremely small, such as the small island abode of the Kankakee mallow or a beetle known from only a single cave, the species may indeed occur uniformly over the entire range. If, however, the range is much larger than these local examples, it will include differences in elevation, water areas which cut up the land surface, local differences in soil types, and differences in climatic factors from one edge of the range to another. Any one species within this whole area is adapted to live in only certain ecological conditions; where those conditions exist, there the species may be. In the American grasslands, for example, the grama and buffalo grasses occur only on the better drained areas which are not too sandy. In the sloughs another set of plant species occur and on the sand ridges a third set is found. Some species of marine plankton probably approach most closely a uniform distribution of individuals over the entire geographic range, but these species also encounter ocean currents or areas having inimical ecological conditions which result in lacunae within the species range. As a result each species occupies only certain habitats; the exact areas in which these specific habitats occur will be interrupted or separated by habitats of other types.

RANGE OSCILLATIONS

The range of a species is dynamic; its edges continually change to a greater or lesser extent in amoeboid fashion. Peripheral demes may become connected with or disconnected from each other and more central populations. As Andrewartha and Birch (1954) explained in detail, the dynamic nature of a range is caused by two factors: the dispersal of the species and fluctuations in ecological factors limiting the geographic distribution of the species.

Fluctuation is as much a characteristic of each ecological factor as genetic change is characteristic of a species. Some fluctuations such as daily, seasonal, or annual rhythms of temperature or rainfall are predictable in general, but the exact quantitative values of these fluctuations fall into more random oscillations. Unusual quantitative values such as lack of rainfall or late freezes may kill entire local populations of a species, causing peripheral contraction or internal lacunae in the range. Again because of ecological fluctuations, by the next season or even only a few hours later these same depleted areas would again be perfectly habitable for the species if it reached the area.

Local extinction by unusual ecological fluctuations would eventually exterminate every species were it not for the inherent property of every species to disperse. By dispersal, depleted areas may be repopulated and the range reconstituted. Areas which are only temporarily suitable ecologically may also be populated periodically, thus affecting another variable in range periphery.

Because dispersal is at least partly random, many individuals of a species will spread into areas outside the habitable range and perish. However, over the years this is not really a loss to the species because, by this mechanism, the species maintains what might be called a constant expansion pressure at the edge of its range.

How far species habitually disperse beyond the border of their ranges is not completely known, but it is undoubtedly different from year to year and species to species. Many kinds of flies are known to disperse readily for distances of five to 30 miles (Schoof, 1952). In the case of the migratory high plains grasshopper *Dissosteira longipennis*, Wakeland (1958) reported dispersal with some regularity in an arc of several hundred miles radius beyond the area where breeding occurs (Fig. 49). Wind-borne seeds may have an even greater radius of regular dispersal. More sedentary organisms have correspondingly lower dispersal potentials. For snakes and terrestrial amphibians some writers have estimated the net annual dispersal distance of an individual at only a mile or two, representing the total of its day-to-day travels. Plants with heavy seeds such as oaks and hickories normally have a dispersal distance limited to the daily activities of squirrels, but a tornado or flood might carry an occasional nut many miles. For rare species such as animals confined to caves or local streams, valleys or peaks, little is known concerning dispersal, although it surely occurs.

The exact oscillations in ranges are poorly known, but several examples in the insect order Orthoptera give some idea of the potentials involved in the interplay between ecological fluctuations and dispersal. The range of the North American high plains grass-

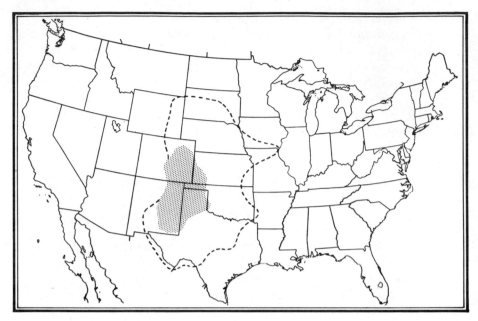

Fig. 49. Known range of the high plains grasshopper *Dissosteira longipennis*. The dark central area indicates the greatest extent of breeding; the broken line indicates the extent of adult dispersal beyond the breeding area. (Modified from Wakeland.)

hopper *Dissosteira longipennis* increased and decreased greatly during the period from 1937 to 1940 (Fig. 50) (Wakeland, 1958). Both the spread and contraction of the range were somewhat concentric around the earlier small range.

Population

The average population of most species runs into astronomical numbers, but for a few species it is small. Among those species whose range may have been little affected by man, the population of Ross' goose *Anser rossii* was found to be 1,951 in 1949 (Hanson, Queneau, and Scott, 1956), and the total breeding population of the gannet *Sula bassana* was found to be approximately 78,000 pairs in 1935 (Edwards, Lockley, and Salmon, 1936). The lowest possible population before the species is in danger of becoming extinct is not known. Interesting in this connection is the North American whooping crane *Grus americana*, whose total population has oscillated between about 15 and 30 individuals since the 1940's.

Fig. 50. Known distribution of the high plains grasshopper *Dissosteira longipennis* before and after the outbreak period of 1937 to 1939. The range decreased rapidly after 1940 also. The shaded area indicates the breeding range; the dotted lines indicate known areas of adult dispersal from that year's breeding range. (Modified from Wakeland.)

OSCILLATIONS

Population densities of natural populations are constantly oscillating, as a whole, regionally, and locally. In species having a large geographic range, populations in different areas of the range prob-

ably seldom oscillate synchronously. For example, outbreaks of the
African migratory locust *Locusta migratoria* occurred from 1928 to
1934 (Fig. 51), but the occurrence and spread of outbreak areas

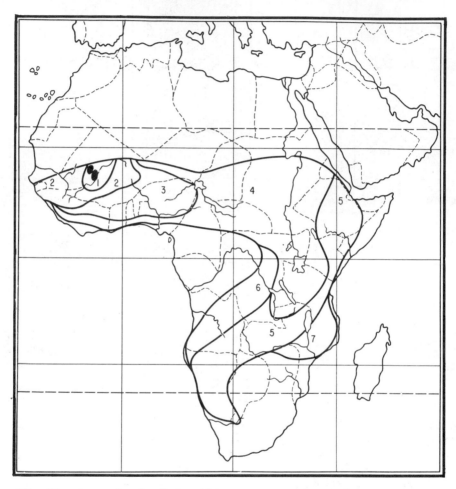

Fig. 51. An outbreak of the African migratory locust *Locusta migratoria
migratorioides*. The area on the middle Niger where the outbreak commenced
in 1926-27 is shown in black. The successively numbered areas indicate annual
expansion of the invaded area in the period 1928-34. The distribution of low-
density areas of the species is not indicated. (After Uvarov.)

was highly irregular (Uvarov, 1951). The entire population of several fur animals show fairly regular oscillations (Fig. 52) (Mac-
Lulick, 1937), and moderately large segments of many species

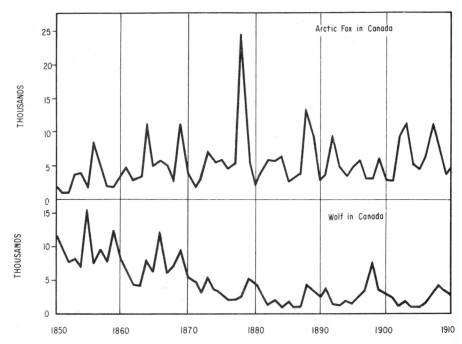

Fig. 52. Fluctuations in the estimated total populations of the arctic fox and wolf in Canada. (Adapted from Hewitt.)

ranges, such as the Illinois chinch bugs (Shelford and Flint, 1943), show similar oscillations. Attempts have been made to resolve these into regular cycles of three and one-half, four, six, eight, ten, and up to twenty-five years between peaks of abundance. Portions of most charts do fit this cyclic concept. Cole (1951) suggested that these natural population oscillations are random rather than regular. Other analysts believe that beneath many of the seemingly inconsistent gross oscillations there is some sort of regular cyclic population rhythm affecting many kinds of organisms synchronously (Errington, 1945, 1954; Mills, 1953). As a possible factor responsible for this basic cycle, Shelford (1951) and others have suggested ultraviolet light correlated with the ten or eleven-year sunspot cycles. As Shelford and Mills have pointed out, however, oscillations of other factors in the environment such as humidity or temperature (which are irregular and not synchronous with sunspots) would reduce or augment, or lengthen or shorten, any basic regular cycle. If the gross population oscillations are the result of many independent factors, some regularly cyclic and others irregularly (aptly termed *polyvalent* by Mills), then we would expect both total and regional oscillations to approach the random character described by Cole (1951).

From the standpoint of understanding genetic changes in an entire species, it is necessary to know whether certain areas of the range have habitual high population densities from which individuals and therefore also genetic variability flow into areas of low density or whether some other pattern prevails. An extremely large body of recorded data suggests that almost every conceivable pattern occurs and that these patterns are governed by ecological factors and the species vagility. In the example previously cited of the high plains grasshopper *Dissosteira longipennis* (Fig. 50), the general trend of individual movement is almost certainly from the small and fairly stable minimum range outward (Wakeland, 1958). In the African migratory locusts *Locusta migratoria migratorioides* (Fig. 51) and *Schistocerca gregaria,* high population densities develop in widely scattered small areas and flow out over a tremendous total range (Uvarov, 1951).

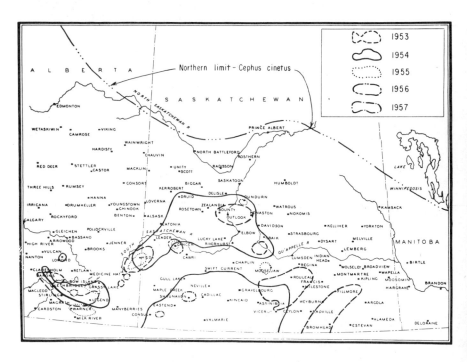

Fig. 53.   Areas of high population density of the wheat stem sawfly *Cephus cinctus* during the years between 1953 and 1957 in the Canadian portion of its range. (Adapted from Farstadt.)

In many other species local or regional population peaks appear irregularly over the entire range, and there appears to be little movement from such peak areas into less densely populated surrounding areas. This situation is exemplified by the high density of the North American wheat sawfly *Cephus cinctus* in the Canadian portion of its range between 1953 and 1957 (Fig. 53) (Farstadt, 1953–1957). In 1953 these high density areas formed seven small- to medium-sized areas roughly arranged along a wide arc. In 1954 the high density areas formed two large, one medium, and one minute area, of which the southern large one was displaced considerably westward from the two southeastern highs of the preceding year. In 1955 there were only six small high areas, arranged somewhat along the arc of the 1953 series; the large southern and eastern highs of 1953 and 1954 had dropped to lower population levels. In 1956 high populations appeared in only one small area which dropped to a lower level in 1957. In this latter year, high populations appeared in only four minute southern areas. Because the wheat sawfly is non-migratory, these data indicate that the population level of each area rose and fell independently of surrounding areas. This point is strengthened by an examination of the population density maps for 1953 and 1954. In 1953 (Fig. 54a), the total area of heavy infestation (high population density) was small, but the area of light infestation was large; in 1954 (Fig. 54b), the "heavy" areas were much larger, but the northwestern and extreme eastern "light" areas were at a lower population level. Obviously this series of population changes is not a build up in the middle accompanied by a radial expansion but was caused by density changes occurring independently in each area. These changes occur in an area having habitual kaleidoscopic fluctuations in climate.

Shift in Geographic Position

During the past, climates have changed repeatedly in different parts of the world. New ranges of mountains, for example, have caused xeric conditions over previously wetter areas and have restricted mesic situations to local pockets such as ravines. Climatic bands may shift. Seas may retreat, uncovering large new areas for terrestrial living, or seas may advance, supplanting previous terrestrial habitats with new areas available for marine life.

Species ranges have shifted with the climatic or other ecological changes. The movements of these ranges in geologic time took place

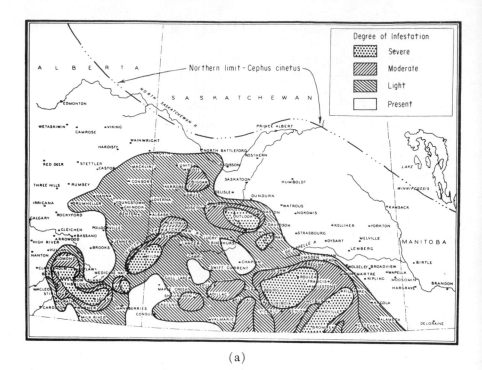

(a)

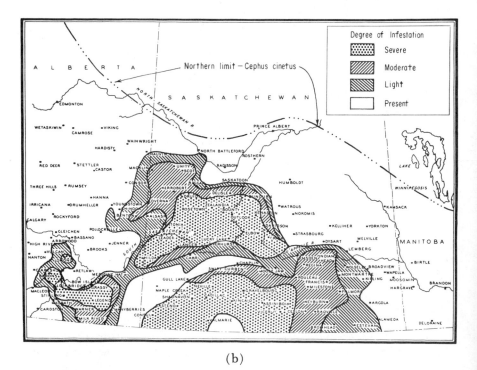

(b)

Fig. 54. Relative intensity of infestation of the wheat stem sawfly *Cephus cinctus* in the Canadian prairie provinces (a), in 1953, (b) in 1954. (After Farstadt in the *Canadian Insect Pest Survey*.)

gradually and are the accumulation of small changes similar to those occurring contemporaneously.

An example is the shifting of ranges which accompanied the glacial advances and dissipations during the Pleistocene. When glaciers and presumably cooler climates moved southward, the ranges of affected species changed radically before them; many species lived in southern areas inimical to them today. When warmer climates and the ice margin moved northward, the ranges of many species enlarged northward also (Fig. 55) (Deevey, 1949;

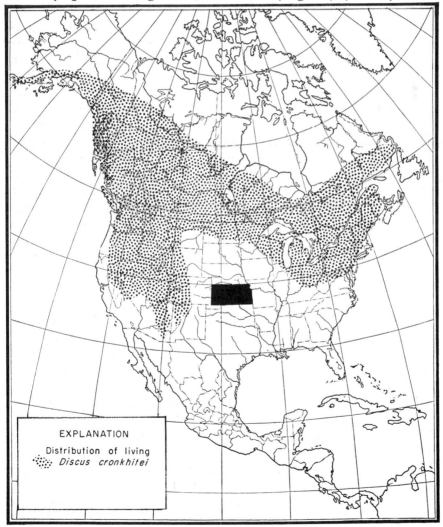

EXPLANATION

Distribution of living
Discus cronkhitei

Fig. 55. Changes in the distribution of North American Mollusca during the Pleistocene. During one of the advanced glacial stages, prior to 12,000 years ago, the snail *Discus cronkhitei* was widespread in Kansas (black area on map). Now it is known only much to the north and east or at high elevations in the mountains. (After Leonard.)

Frye and Leonard, 1952, 1957; P. Smith, 1957). The present biota of previously glaciated terrain represents such range shifting.

The Wisconsin ice sheet in North America seems to have melted back moderately rapidly, geologically speaking, yet in the last 8,500 years its edge has moved north little over 2,000 miles. This averages one fourth of a mile per year. Undoubtedly in some years the retreat was more rapid, and numerous readvances increased the total mileage covered. Although it is possible that during certain periods the ice margin melted back as much as a mile per year, organisms following in its wake would need to have averaged only a fourth of a mile a year (440 yards) to keep up with glacial regression. Presumably *average* climatic conditions moved at the same tempo. Compared with local and annual differences observed in any one place today, these small changes would have been imperceptible from year to year along the ice margins and the movement of the range would have been an extremely slow process.

The mechanics of the range movements were unquestionably like those observed today. In times of northward movement, the populations on the extreme southern edge of the range of cool-adapted species would be reduced by adverse conditions at a rate greater than counter fluctuations would permit recolonization of depleted southern areas; the populations on the extreme northern edge of the range would be able to colonize new areas to an extent greater than adverse cycles cut them back. The populations in the middle would fluctuate in the same fashion that they do today. In other words, by amoeboid oscillations of peripheral populations, the range of a species gradually follows the movement of the ecological conditions to which the species is adapted.

In this context size of present range becomes an ephemeral character. A species called "successful" because today it is widespread and abundant may simply be inhabiting an unusually large acreage having ecological conditions to which it is adapted; in the geological tomorrow the area over which these conditions prevail may be much smaller and the range of the species correspondingly reduced. Yet, in its own habitat, the species would be no less "successful." The abundant species of migratory ducks and geese nesting in the marshes and tundra of North America may now have available a greater area of suitable habitat than ever before. It is entirely possible that, during the maximum extent of Wisconsin glaciation, areas suitable for them were small, and the total populations of these species accordingly were small. Furthermore, it is possible that when the ice recedes even more than now their present range may shrink again, and the birds will become relatively rare (Mills, 1951). Following the same reasoning some of the rare, "less successful" species of today might be adapted to conditions which tomorrow would cover a much more extensive area with a consequent enlargement of the species range.

THE SPECIES AS AN ADAPTIVE UNIT

A comparison of living and fossilized biotas demonstrates that, in their passage through time, phylogenetic lines have changed in all manner of characters, manifested morphologically, physiologically, or ecologically. The genetic composition therefore changed to a comparable extent through natural selection. The theoretical action of natural selection, outlined in Chapter 4, would seem to be a straightforward, albeit complex, mechanism. When the known or inferred natural products of evolution are examined in relation to this theory, however, many paradoxes appear. The explanation of many changes in phylogenetic lines is therefore still on a speculative basis. A working hypothesis combines the concepts of genetic homeostasis with ideas arising from phylogenetic analysis.

Genetic Composition

The genetic variation demonstrated experimentally in controlled populations appears to extend throughout the species' natural range. The variation may be conspicuous, as in the American butterfly *Glaucopsyche xerces* (Fig. 56) (Downey and Lange, 1956), or inconspicuous and demonstrable only by careful experiment and observation. In species with a low vagility or other attributes which result in little inter-population mixing, the genetic variation may be segregated geographically; this is true especially of many birds (Pitelka, 1951) and small mammals having well-marked subspecies (Hoffmeister, 1951; Hall and Kelson, 1959). In other instances the selection exercised by local environments has produced the same result in the face of moderate vagility; this has been demonstrated best in plants (Clausen, 1951). In the great bulk of vagile organisms, such as many insects, the characteristics and genetic composition tend to be either similar over the whole range, or to grade from one edge to the other.

Little information is available concerning local short-term changes in genetic composition over an entire species range. The observed changes concerning industrial melanism in moths, cited in the

Fig. 56. Variation in the pattern on the undersurface of male wings in the recently extinct California butterfly *Glaucopsyche xerces.* (After Downey and Lange.)

preceding chapter, are associated with artificial changes in the environment. Even so, they give an insight into the possible rate of spread of strongly adaptive traits in a population. Dobzhansky (1958) has demonstrated marked changes in chromosome type over the range of *Drosophila pseudoobscura.* During a period of twenty years, chromosome type PP increased greatly and type CP decreased in almost all tested populations in the western portion of the range (Fig. 57). A trait which gives the larch sawfly *Pristiphora erichsoni* immunity from its chief parasite has spread extremely rapidly through many thousands of square miles in the Canadian portion of its range (Muldrew, 1953). The trait is a blood-clotting behavior by which internal parasite larvae are encapsulated and killed inside the body cavity of the larval sawfly. This again is a highly adaptive trait conferring high survival which is contrasted with no survival among individuals not possessing it.

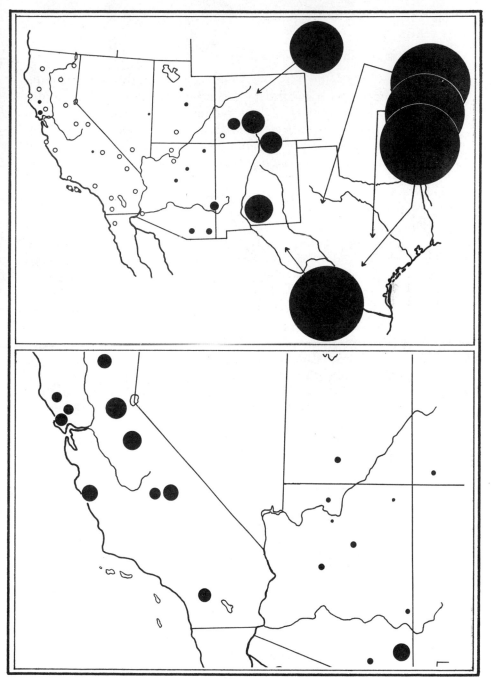

Fig. 57. Increase in frequency of chromosome type PP in the southwestern United States populations of *Drosophila pseuoobscura*. Above, samples made during 1940 and earlier. Below, samples made in 1957. The relative proportion of PP in the population is indicated by the size of the black circles. Although the geographic scale is different in the two maps, the scale of circle size is the same and comparable in the two. (After Dobzhansky.)

The species was defined as an assemblage of interbreeding populations. In species with small compact ranges or with a high vagility
it is likely that members of any population will interbreed effectively with any other. In species with large ranges and low vagility
members of adjoining populations interbreed effectively, but individuals from widely separated localities frequently reproduce much
less effectively. Experimenting with the American leopard frog
Rana pipiens, Moore (1949) crossed individuals from Vermont,
New Jersey, Oklahoma, Florida, and Texas. Matings from two successive locations produced normal offspring, but matings between
frogs from Vermont and Texas or Vermont and Florida produced
young which died before completing development. Through the
avenue of interbreeding between adjoining populations, however,
genetic changes in the populations at either end of the range can
theoretically spread through the entire species. Similar conditions
occur in the fly *Drosophila pseudoobscura,* in which the vigor of
the F_2 generation decreases when populations from California,
Nevada, Utah, and Colorado are intercrossed. In spider mites of
the species *Tetranychus telarius,* Boudreaux (1957) found that
crosses between colonies from various states exhibited little to moderate inviability of eggs, but crosses between European and North
American strains exhibited moderate to complete inviability of eggs.
A highly graphic expression of the same circumstance is shown by
the "ring species." The range of the herring gull *Larus argentatus*
extends around the Arctic Ocean and the two ends of the range,
represented by different subspecies, meet in northwestern Europe.
These two forms do not hybridize but live together like two distinct species even though they are connected genetically through
a ring of intermediate interbreeding populations.

Thus, with time and through progressive accumulation of genetic
changes, individuals in different populations may come to have
genetic systems too different to produce a physiologically balanced
zygote. If a species has a high vagility, presumably the mixing of
new characters is sufficiently thorough to prevent such large local
divergence. If a species has a low vagility or a narrow mixing
radius, local changes can accumulate to form distinctive local types.
The situation emphasizes that a species forms a genetic system
which permits genetic traits to diffuse through all parts of it,
although distant populations may be inter-sterile.

Considering the tremendous potential for change inherent in the processes of genetic mutation and natural selection, one might suppose that the variation in a species would be infinite, but this is not the observed state of affairs. Simpson (1944) calculated the coefficient of variation for several characters in diverse groups of mammals and other animals and for 70 characters in man and found that almost every case fell within a narrow range of variation. Exceptions to this low range of variation are well known, especially in polytypic butterflies (Downey and Lange, 1956) and in plants (Clausen, 1951; Stebbins, 1950). In the mammals Simpson (1944) noted two examples of high variability, one the tail of the opossum, another the length of a multituberculate tooth of a mammal. Simpson believed this latter case to represent a degenerating structure and hence one which might be expected to be unstable genetically. In these examples of unusually great variation, it is almost invariably only one structure which is involved—the wing pattern of a butterfly, the leaf of a plant, the degenerating tooth of a mammal, the tail of a marsupial. In the same species, literally thousands of other characters will have a low value of variability.

Simpson's data (1944) bring out another important fact. Although a given structure may evolve considerably within a phylogenetic line through a portion of geologic time, at any one time during this evolution, the structure has the same small coefficient of variation.

THE FUNCTIONING PHYLOGENETIC LINE

From these various considerations the species is seen to represent a phylogenetic succession of parent-offspring generations progressing through time. At any point in time this phylogenetic line has a dynamic range, a dynamic population density, and a dynamic genetic constitution, all directly under the influence of a dynamic environment. The compounding of these elements endows the phylogenetic line with tremendous possibilities for change. However, the phylogenetic line may have a finite limit to its total amount of genetic variability at any one time and concomitantly a finite limit to its total phenotypic range of ecological tolerances and adaptive adjustments.

Adaptive Change

Adaptation is expressed in some phylogenetic lines by great stability, in others by great change. On the basis of fossil data, Simpson (1944, 1953) demonstrated that evolutionary change is multipaced. There is every reason to believe that the same differences in rate of change hold true between phylogenetic lines in existence now. A satisfactory theory of evolutionary change must, therefore, provide for both stability and change. Such a dual explanation must take two circumstances into account: (1) that the amount of variation in a species is usually low and (2) that any phylogenetic line maintaining viable populations today is well adapted to the ecological situation within its range.

STABILITY IN ADAPTATION

Considering the dynamic nature of both phylogenetic lines and the environment, it might seem as if change should be the rule and stability the exception. In many groups of organisms the opposite is found.

In the caddisfly tribe Philopotamini the primitive and near-primitive forms include 90 species, all occurring only in cold water streams; from this complex set of lineages (Fig. 58), dating back probably to the Cretaceous, only two surviving lines became adapted to warm water streams (Ross, 1956). Even greater stability is found in the tropical caddisfly genus *Leptonema* in which some 80 known species have evolved during the Cenozoic, but none has yet become established more than a few miles beyond tropical areas. If the phylogenetic lines of the genus *Leptonema* could be joined end to end, the result would represent something like three billion years of continuous genetic reproduction without more than minor and local adaptive changes. Comparable stability is suggested by the great age of many living marine genera, many tracing back over 400 million years with little structural change and probably little ecological change (Schrock and Twenhoffel, 1953). These examples give credence to the idea that, in evolving phylogenetic lines, stability is the rule and that some unusual circumstance is necessary for the line to change.

Stable phylogenetic lines appear to remain within the same ecological range, in other words, to live under nearly identical conditions generation after generation. In the coelenterates, Bayer (1955) reported from the lower or middle Eocene of Trinidad remarkably well-preserved fossil sea pens *Virgularia presbytes* which are apparently the same species as recent populations in the Gulf of Mexico. This phylogenetic line thus seems to have persisted without change in the same general area and presumably under the same ecological conditions for some 40 or 60 million years. Even so, most if not all ranges encompass some average ecological variation and have local and periodic ecological oscilla-

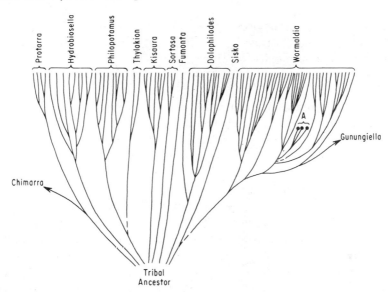

Fig. 58. Family tree of the known species of the caddisfly tribe Philopo-tamini. All the surviving lines are cool adapted with the exception of the two leading to *Chimarra* and *Gunungiella* which gave rise to warm adapted forms. A indicates three species known from Baltic amber.

tions. In such a situation at least some selection factors would differ on each segment of the periphery of the range. At any one time the species would therefore contain a sort of internal tug of war, the selection factors on one periphery tending to pull the genetic mode in that direction, the selection factors on the opposite periphery tending to pull the mode in that direction.

Species in general exhibit pronounced genetic homeostasis, which causes, essentially, an inertia to genetic change. This homeostatic condition is a balanced heterozygosity buffered by modifying genes or other elements so that essentially the same phenotype is produced by a wide range of genotypes (Lerner, 1954). After a species had been in the same environment for a long time, presumably it would have reached a homeostatic condition in which the genetic extremes of the edges had been molded by polygenic action and buffering into a well-coordinated meshing of physiological reactions. Small mutations would be damped and absorbed by the buffering action or polygenic complexities and have no perceptible phenotypic effect.

To initiate adaptive shifts in a phylogenetic line would require changes sufficient to counteract the damping effect of genetic homeostasis. On the basis of present evidence and inference these changes fall into two categories: new unusual genetic constituents, and reduction in complexity of the gene pool.

NEW UNUSUAL GENETIC CONSTITUENTS

The type of mutation most likely to be perpetuated would have only a slight effect on the physiology of the genetic system but a marked positive selective effect on the phenotype. Two examples illustrate this possibility. Discussing the rapid early evolution of the dipnoian fishes, Westoll (1949) suggested that the early forms may have had some simple genetic mutations which acted on early developmental processes and produced relatively large or varied phenotypic effects. He pointed out that if these were selectively advantageous, they could have changed the spectrum and action of further selection to a high degree. In the caddisfly order Trichoptera, the evolution of the entire case-making suborder appears to fit Westoll's premises perfectly. The adults of the entire order are essentially terrestrial-aerial; the larvae are aquatic and in one line are either naked or make portable cases. The mature naked larvae build an outer cocoon, shaped like a tortoise shell, from small stones and cemented to a support. Within it they spin an inner cocoon in which they pupate. From this type arose a form which builds the outer stone cocoon when very young and carries it around as a case; when full grown the larva cements its outer cocoon or case to a stone, spins the inner cocoon within it, then pupates. From a form making this crude type of case evolved a great number of lines making cases progressively better constructed from many utilitarian standpoints (Fig. 59) (Ross, 1956).

Starting from a naked-larva parent, the entire case-making line could have begun with a single mutant individual in which the instinct for building the outer cocoon had been switched from the mature larva to the newly hatched larva. For survival such a mutant would need to be favored by a strong positive selection pressure, and this circumstance was presumably protection from predation afforded by the stone case. Such protection also allows these larvae to crop diatoms, their chief food, not only from their protected hatching areas but also from exposed surfaces in the stream. The added grazing area would result in increased population size with its impetus to a greater rate of adaptive genetic change.

The postulate in both the fish and caddisfly examples is that mutations occurred having (1) slight genetic effect hence a mini-

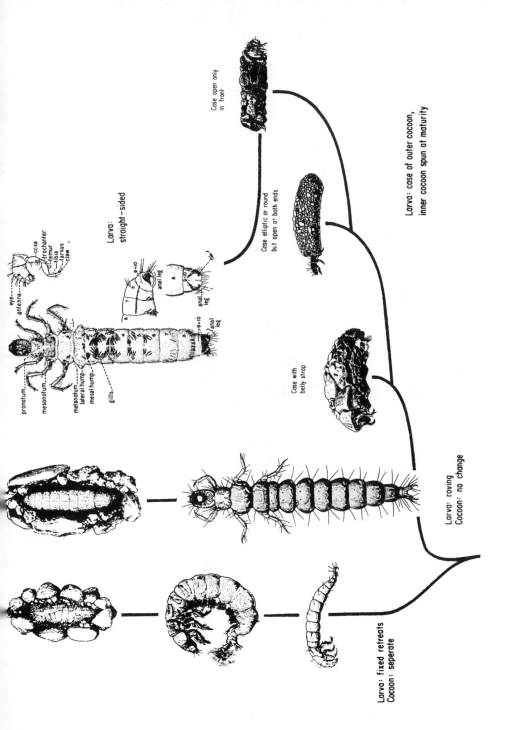

Fig. 59. The evolution of case-making by the larvae of caddisflies.

mum of physiological imbalance, and (2) phenotypic characteristics bringing a large part of the genetic column into the field of influence of a new environmental situation. Another example perhaps falling in this category is found in rabbits (Hoffmeister and Mohr, 1957). The North American Lagomorpha are terrestrial, including the cottontail *Sylvilagus floridanus,* but the swamp rabbit *Sylvilagus aquaticus* spends much time in the water and is an excellent swimmer. Some sharp change in behavior has brought this species into the selective orbit of the aquatic habitat. An almost identical example occurs in North American voles of the genus *Microtus* of which all but one species are strictly terrestrial or essentially so. The Richardson vole or water rat *M. richardsoni,* while living in meadows, is much like a small muskrat in general behavior, swimming and diving well (Cowan and Guiguet, 1956). In this new environment will the future phylogenetic lines of the swamp rabbit and water rat evolve into distinctive obligatorily aquatic groups such as the muskrats and beavers?

Another phenomenon may be classed in this category of unusual genetic change. In both plants and animals it is commonplace to find that a cluster of closely related species have approximately the same range or at least that the ranges appear to occur within the same band of climatic conditions. In certain examples of this sort, one species has a range occupying this common band but in addition extends far beyond into a markedly different climate. The American *borealis* branch of the caddisfly genus *Helicopsyche* contains such an example. This branch comprises 12 or more species, all but one confined to streams in virtually frost-free areas or to outpost springs with warm winter temperatures. One species, *H. borealis,* occurs in these warmer streams in company with some of its 12 relatives but in addition occurs north almost to subarctic regions (Fig. 60). In some fashion a genetic change must have become established in the northern peripheral populations of this species, a change which produced either winter hardiness or peculiar competitive advantages. As a result, this one species extended its range into a climatic zone new to the entire genus. In a sense this is not a great change. The northernmost populations are identical morphologically with the southernmost, indicating that up to the present little has happened beyond an extension of range and that this probably occurred relatively recently. The important circumstance is that the largest part of the species range is now under a set of selection pressures markedly different from the set which has acted on the entire genus up to this time. This should break effectively the homeostatic balance that was previously reached between the species and the old environment.

Why did this ecological extension happen to only one species in the entire branch? It appears to be unrelated to phylogenetic specialization because *H. borealis* is intermediate between more primitive and more specialized types in its own branch (Fig. 37). It may be of significance that even in the warmer parts of the range where its ancestors occurred, *H. borealis* far outnumbers its congeners. The tenets of population genetics hold that such larger populations would have a greater prospective incidence of mutants having adaptive benefits and greater potentialities for the occurrence of all possible genic combinations. This is a plausible explanation.

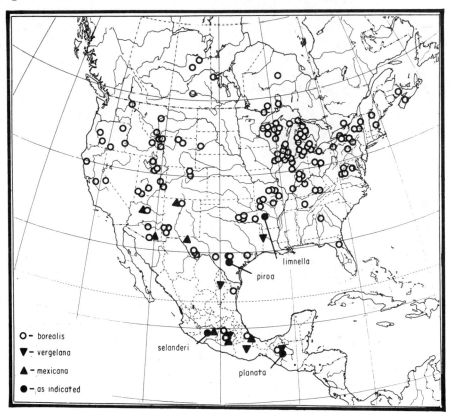

Fig. 60. Distribution of the six most northern species of the caddisfly genus *Helicopsyche* (because of morphological similarity, *H. limnella* is considered an outpost population of *H. mexicana*). Other members of this complex occur from southern Mexico south.

According to one of Wright's models (1949), the best chance of adaptive change would occur if the species were divided into local populations having only limited breeding between them. The distribution of *H. borealis* through much of Mexico and southwestern United States fits this model well, occurring primarily in springs which may be 50 to 100 miles apart. It cannot, however, be the only critical factor because the ranges of the other species of *Helicopsyche* in the area have exactly the same type of distribution. Perhaps this discontinuity factor *plus* large population size caused the unique evolutionary development of *H. borealis*. If so, then the root of this development must have started with whatever circumstances produced the initial relatively large populations of *H. borealis*. There is no clue to these circumstances.

In the *Helicopsyche borealis* example there is no suggestion as to the specific genetic change involved. In the American plant genus *Clarkia,* an unusual extension of climatic tolerance in *C. lingulata* is associated with additional chromosomal units in the genome (Lewis, 1953c). Lewis suggested changes in quantitative gene dosages as the probable basic cause of this change in ecological tolerance.

REDUCTION IN GENETIC COMPLEXITY

The total genetic complexity of the species would seem to be related to the ecological divergence encompassed in the total range. Starting from this premise, any physical, chemical, or biotic change which reduced the range in an ecological sense would reduce the complexity of the gene pool. As a hypothetical example involving a physical change, a terrestrial species might occupy the annual rainfall gradient from 20 to 40 inches, with its range bounded by a mountain range on the 20 inch side and by an ocean on the 40 inch side. If the mountains become more elevated and their rain shadow more intense, the rainfall gradient would move out over the ocean so that the species would have available only the rainfall gradient 20 to 30 inches. This would eliminate the genetic factors having a high selection factor on the former 30 to 40 inch part of the rainfall gradient and presumably would reduce the complexity of the gene pool and the interactions contributing to homeostatic balance.

Under these conditions of decreasing homeostatic complexity, smaller and smaller genetic changes should theoretically produce phenotypic changes sufficiently great to have a selective value. As a result, in the example above genetic changes could become established conferring advantages at points lower on the rainfall gradient, say at 19 inches, then 18 inches, and so on, even though these mutations would have been swamped out in the more complex homeostatic balance adjusted to the old 20 to 40 inch range. The net result would be a change in the species by which it became adapted to a new climate. Axelrod (1958) cited this as the probable mechanism for the origin of the xeric flora of southwestern North America. He suggested that possibly large segments of the ranges of mesic species became trapped in the more mesic highlands, surrounded by xeric lowlands (Fig. 61) and that subsequent increase in aridity of the whole area brought the mesic-adapted species under extremely strong and inescapable selection pressure for adaptations to xeric existence.

Among biotic changes, competition is known to restrict the range of a species to less than it would be in its absence. A demonstrated example concerns two European sawflies of the genus *Cephus* whose larvae bore within wheat stems. Both were introduced accidentally into the United States. *Cephus tabidus* arrived in 1889 and by 1936 occupied a range extending from southern New York to southern Virginia. *Cephus pygmaeus* arrived prior to 1899, probably in New Jersey, spreading chiefly northward, then westward. Finally it outcompeted *C. tabidus* where the two species overlapped, and by 1941 *C. tabidus* was restricted to the more southern and western parts of its former, larger range (Fig. 62) (Udine, 1941; Elton, 1958). Thus competition narrowed the climatic selection pressures acting on *C. tabidus*.

An inferred example illustrating a different plane of restriction concerns the Canidae (dogs) and Felidae (cats). The common ancestor of the two could have been a rather omnivorous species inhabiting a wide vegetation gradient, from relatively open country to forest edge and into the forest itself. Some of the skunks have essentially these wide ecological tolerances. In such a wide habitat gradient, small mutations favoring swift, short bursts of speed (advantageous in the forest portion of the range) would be mixed continuously with mutants favoring slower but sustained running (advantageous in the open portion of the range). A compromise between these would be established by the simple process of genetic mixing, with no opportunity for specialization advantageous solely for life in one part of the habitat.

The situation undoubtedly changed after the canid-felid ancestor had first evolved into many species which then moved into

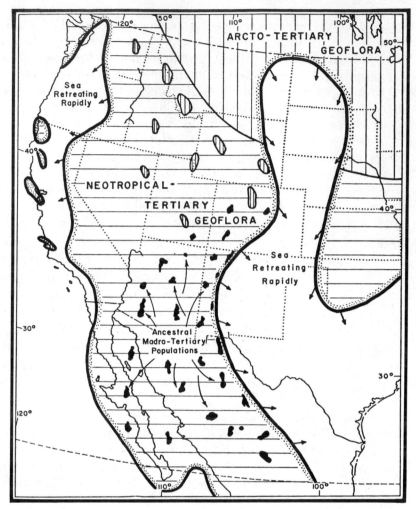

Fig. 61. Inferred distribution of ancestral Madro-Tertiary plants in pre-Eocene time, in which isolated populations became exposed to locally hotter and drier climates. (After Axelrod.)

the same geographic area. Competition for food could have resulted in a restriction of the habitats of the species along local ecological lines. Because the species would have had at least some ecological differences, each would have tended to follow its own advantages. With one species this could have led to greater success in more open country, with another to greater success in more heavily vegetated areas. In this fashion the ecological range of

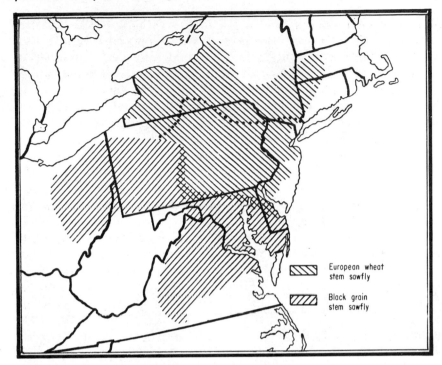

Fig. 62. Distribution of the black grain stem sawfly and the European wheat stem sawfly in the United States in 1937. The dotted line marks the former northern extension of the black grain stem sawfly. (Adapted from Udine.)

each species would have been rigidly reduced from a wide to a narrow band. In the line which eventually became chiefly a heavy-cover or forest group, selection pressures for waiting and springing would not be diluted constantly by pressures for coursing and running. Under this newly restricted ecological setting, slight genetic changes favoring waiting and springing, silent tread, and other habits adaptive to the now more restricted environment would have had an opportunity for phenotypic expression.

GENETIC MECHANISMS AND POPULATION SIZE

The examples cited for unusual genetic change are associated with large populations, whereas those cited for a reduction of genetic complexity are associated with a decrease in population size. This latter circumstance suggests a parallel with the models of adaptive change based on small populations proposed by Wright (1942, 1949) and Simpson (1944). In their models, the population is postulated to be at a precariously low point, poorly adapted to its immediate environment, and close to the extinction point of the population. Under these conditions it was supposed that adaptive genetic mutants which might be swamped by a larger population could, by rare happenstance of matings, suddenly become homozygous and thus phenotypically effective. The events suggested in this chapter would achieve the same result through ecological restriction without necessarily reducing the population to a figure which could be described as small. Nor would the populations pass through an "inadaptive" stage because they would never be less well adapted to their environment than they were initially.

If population size were to reach the extremely low levels of the Wright-Simpson model, it is possible that interspecific hybridization would follow. Certainly in many groups of animals it is likely that two closely related species would be in the same range and that extremely low population density would result in stress mating. The peculiar similarity of head markings in the mice *Peromyscus maniculatus triangularis* and *Microtus townsendi cowani,* both restricted to tiny Triangle Island off the coast of British Columbia (Guiguet, 1955), suggests that small populations have here resulted in intergeneric hybridization. As has long been appreciated by botanists but generally disregarded by zoologists, the unpredictable results which are possible in hybrid progeny could account for a great deal of the observed shifts in the adaptiveness of species (Stebbins, 1959).

DIRECTIONAL FACTORS IN ADAPTATION

After a species has moved into a different environment and come under the influence of a new set of selection pressures, these pressures will continue to select adaptive changes, as was explained in the preceding chapter. From the standpoint of the long-term phylogenetic line, two types of consequence are of special interest: the evolution of characters prerequisite for later changes, and the occupation of new adaptive situations.

PREREQUISITE CHARACTERS (PREADAPTATION)

It is evident that certain characters could not have evolved until some other character had evolved previously. For example, insects evolved from a multilegged, centipede-like ancestor and became six-legged creatures in which the locomotor function was centered near the anterior part of the body. Because of this position of the legs, later insects were able to evolve a rapid gait and the ability to spring from a vertical surface. Later some such insects evolved flight but only because they already had evolved locomotor muscles near the anterior part of the body giving aerodynamic balance and had strong legs giving propulsion at the take off. In the insects the body balance and the few, strong legs were prerequisites to the evolution of flight.

A simple case can be postulated for the cats or felids involving successive specialization of food. The early felids, as do many of them today, probably fed on a variety of small foods such as insects, small rodents, and rabbits (Hoffmeister and Mohr, 1957). As the number of felid species increased and mixed in the same habitat, food specialization undoubtedly occurred, the larger felids eating the larger prey species, the smaller felids eating the smaller prey. Subsequent to this food specialization, a selection for larger size probably acted on the larger species because larger size would enable the felid to catch full grown animals with their increased food poundage where only juveniles had been accessible to the felid before. Thus after the first food specializations, successive sets of selection pressures moved the adaptive mode of some phylogenetic lines along a gradually ascending food gradient to points far beyond the utilization bands of earlier stages of the lines.

The examples of insect flight and felid food specialization involve the evolution of prerequisite characters which have permitted phylogenetic lines to establish new adaptive relationships. Westoll attributed the great burst of specialization of the dipnoian fishes to the same processes. In many cases, as was indicated in Chapter 4, these changed phylogenetic lines become better and better adapted to their new environment and finally become extremely stable over long periods of time.

REVERSIBILITY OF EVOLUTION

In one sense, evolution is irreversible in that the changes in a phylogenetic line never change back to their original genetic state. In an ecological sense, however, evolution is frequently reversed. Both the dogs or canids and the cats or felids offer examples. The canids became specialized for open country and running down prey, but in the fox branch of the family at least one line, represented by the American gray fox, has reversed the group specialization and has become a forest animal with many cat-like habits (Hoffmeister and Mohr, 1957). One line of the felids, represented by the cheetah, displays the reverse of other lines, being a running plains animal with many dog-like habits (Wright, 1960).

The caddisflies *Sortosa* and *Chimarra* offer an example of temperature reversal. The progenitor of *Sortosa* was undoubtedly a cool-adapted species, as the many living members of *Sortosa* still are. From this form evolved the warm-adapted genus *Chimarra*. In its early evolution *Chimarra* became a widespread and abundant tropical caddisfly, but at a later time one of its branches evolved into a group of cool-adapted forms now living in company with *Sortosa*. The phylogenetic line of each of these later species traces back through a tropical ancestor to the original cool-adapted parent.

THE ROLE OF BIOTIC FACTORS IN ADAPTIVE CHANGE

In many of the examples of natural selection and evolutionary change mentioned in this and the preceding chapter, competition is mentioned prominently. It may also have been important in some examples such as *Chimarra*. Competition, however, is not the only biotic factor which will change the pattern of selection pressures operating on a species. In parasitism, predatism, symbiosis, commensalism, and other circumstances, ecological interaction between different species may affect profoundly the future evolution of one or all of the species involved. Biotic factors therefore loom as tremendously important in the processes of adaptive change. It is also evident that the more species there are, the greater will be the complexities of this relationship. Thus attention is drawn forcefully to the subject of the increase in number of phylogenetic lines, or species.

Increase in

Number of Species

7

The taxonomic intricacies of ecological communities and the adaptive relationships between species emphasize the fact that a large number of evolutionary patterns and processes are conditioned by the multitudinous array of past and present species. Because life presumably began from a few simple types of organisms, the number of species must have increased continuously, accompanied by survival or extinction to produce the existing biota.

Viewed in this light, the processes which lead to an increase in the number of species have a unique evolutionary importance. They first explain the origin of the great number of these evolutionary "building blocks" called species and in addition offer clues in explaining the resultant interspecific adaptation and community evolution.

153

IN APOMICTIC ORGANISMS

In the completely apomictic or parthenogenetic species the population consists of numerous lines or clones of mother-daughter relationships, but these lines do not exchange genic constituents through the sexual process. Thus each individual is an independent evolutionary line in contrast with the situation in a bisexual species in which the entire system of interbreeding populations is the evolutionary line. Each viable mutant in an apomictic line produces a new kind of line which is immediately and permanently distinct from sister lines in respect to the new character. One might expect, therefore, that apomictic lines would vary too much to be grouped into assemblages of like individuals, in other words, into species in the usual sense. However, apomictic species are frequently extremely constant both morphologically and ecologically over a wide geographic range. Pathak and Painter (1959), for example, have segregated four distinctive apomictic strains or species within the corn leaf aphid *Rhopalosiphum maidis,* all four abundant and widely distributed in Kansas and probably over most of North America.

It has been asserted by many writers that apomictic species may be unusually well adapted to some particular situation but that eventually their lack of plasticity with reference to character mixing will lead to their early extinction. For this reason apomictic species seem to be dismissed by many as of little evolutionary importance. The large number of existing apomictic species may have only a short tomorrow, geologically speaking, but they certainly are important ecologically today. There probably never was a time when apomictic species did not occur in goodly numbers and by their presence exert influential selection pressures on the bisexual species whose lives they touch either as competitors, predators, or benefactors. Because of these considerations, every new apomictic species is a unit of potential evolutionary importance.

An increase in the number of these species may occur by two processes: the origin of new apomictic species from bisexual forms, and the differentiation of new distinctive lines from parental apomictic species.

New Apomictic Species from Bisexual Parents

New apomictic species may arise from bisexual parents in two general ways: (1) by restriction to vegetative reproduction, or (2) by complete circumvention of normal fertilization.

(1) In some cases, an asexual mutant may arise from a normally sexual parent. Such action probably explains the origin of the curious oligochaete species *Enchytraeus fragmentosus* which reproduces only by fragmentation (Bell, 1959). In organisms having an alternation of sexual and asexual generations, a strain might lose the sexual generation and so become an apomictic species. The trypanosomes in the Protozoa probably arose in this fashion. Examples are much commoner in the plants, in which many species scattered through many families persist and reproduce only vegetatively by runners, underground stolons, bulb division, or other means. In a large proportion of these plants, the apomictic species originated as an interspecific hybrid individual which retained its vegetative viability but which was infertile. Manton (1950) has found that the European *Equisetum litorale, E. trachyodon,* and *E. Moorei* belong to this category. The most conspicuous cases reported in nature are polyploids. The lily *Fritillaria camschatcensis* is a tetraploid which reproduces only by offsets from its bulbs. Many sterile grass polyploids reproduce only by underground stolons or runners.

(2) A truly remarkable array of mechanisms have evolved which produce apomictic species by the complete suppression of normal fertilization. In some cases meiosis never occurs in gametogenesis; in other cases the products of meiosis may re-unite before the reduced cells divide, thus restoring the $2n$ chromosome number; in others the early cleavage nuclei unite in pairs to bring about the same result; in still others the egg unites with a polar body to restore the chromosomal complement. These and other ways of circumventing cross-fertilization are described by Stebbins (1950) and White (1954). To this category belong the greatest number of existing apomictic species.

Splitting of Apomictic Species

In apomicts having only mitosis in their life histories, theoretically the occurrence of a single, distinctive, viable mutation would result in a new homozygous type. In apomicts having meiosis plus chromosome number restitution, there might be a possibility for gene recombinations; hence the elimination of heterozygotes by natural selection might be necessary for the formation of a distinctive species. Although the splitting of apomictic species seems so simple, in general only a few cases occur here and there among the various taxonomic groups. In many instances either only one species in the genus is obligatorily apomictic, as is the sawfly *Diprion polytomum,* or a genus contains only a single species which is apomictic, as is the sawfly genus *Endelomyia*. The four known apomictic (parthenogenetic) species of black flies (Simuliidae) occur in three genera, indicating that in these insects the phenomenon occurred independently three and perhaps four times, with no observed subsequent increase in the number of species in any one of the phylogenetic lines (Basrur and Rothfels, 1959). In these cases it is highly probable that no species splitting has occurred since the evolution of the original apomictic parent.

In other instances of apomixis subsequent splitting has occurred. One of the most extensive apomictic evolutionary developments in animals is found in the trypanosomes. These protozoans evidently arose from a form parasitizing insects, in which a mammal host became included in the life cycle. By successive stages (Fig. 63), the protozoans evolved into a form in which their entire life history occurs in the mammalian host (Hoare, 1957). Some 20 species and many other races and strains are known, ranging from the primitive

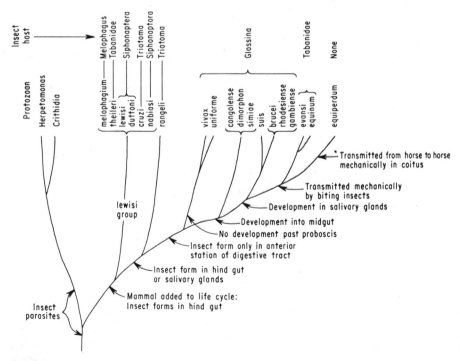

Fig. 63.   Probable phylogeny of certain trypanosomes, an example of extensive evolutionary development within an apomyctic group. The large right branch is the genus *Trypanosoma*. (Based on data in Hoare, 1957.)

T. lewisi group to the highly specialized venereal species *T. equiperdum*. Observations made to the present indicate that this entire development is the result of strictly apomictic evolution because no sexual stages have ever been observed in this branch of the Protozoa. Quite possibly similar series occur in simple plants, especially the Fungi Imperfecti, but little seems to be known about the relationships of these forms.

In the plants the greatest pyramiding of apomictic species accompanies hybridization combined with polyploidy. A few examples of this combination occur in the weevils. In the weevil subfamilies Otiorhynchinae and Brachyderinae numerous apomictic polyploid species have evolved, including triploids, tetraploids, and pentaploids. It is probable that in these weevils a diploid parthenogenetic species evolved first and that polyploidy followed as the result of occasional fertilizations of the parthenogenetic eggs by sperms from a male of one of the related diploid bisexual species (White, 1954). The earthworms of the family Lumbricidae contain several short polyploid series of species (White, 1954).

In the plants, however, large numbers of hybrid and polyploid apomictic species have evolved which together form morphological and ecological "bridges" between the parental diploid sexual parents (Stebbins, 1950). Such a situation has been investigated in detail for many genera including *Crepis, Poa,* and *Taraxacum* (Babcock and Stebbins, 1938; Stebbins, 1950).

IN BISEXUAL ORGANISMS

Because bisexual organisms form interbreeding systems in which the whole population is the local genetic unit, an increase in the number of species results from circumstances which do not affect apomictic organisms. These circumstances include geographic isolation, hybridization, ecological isolation, and spontaneous genetic isolation.

Geographic Isolation

The two essential features of species fission by geographic isolation are (1) a species comes to occupy a divided or disjunct range in which practically no genetic interchange occurs between the isolated portions, and (2) the population of each isolated portion gradually changes genetically until the population of one segment is no longer genetically compatible with that of another segment. A divided range may be initiated either by critical range movements caused

by long-term changes in the ecology of the region or by colonization of an area which is physically isolated from the parent range
but which can be reached on rare occasions by stragglers. The importance of geographic isolation in species fission has been recognized by many authors (Wagner, 1868; Jordan, 1905; Rensch, 1929)
and was accorded an extended treatment by Mayr (1942) and
Stebbins (1950).

DIVISION BY RANGE MOVEMENTS

Species fission by range movements is a simple extrapolation of two
dynamic aspects of ranges. Frequently in large ranges populations
from different areas are intersterile; this intersterility is a force which
tends to tear the species apart but which is counteracted by interbreeding through adjacent parts of the range. Ranges move with
time and in doing so may be broken into two or more fragments
by ecologically inimical areas encountered in the range movement.
This fragmentation then breaks the continuity of gene flow, and
each part of the range is free to evolve even greater genetic indi-
viduality.

The extremely common operation of this process is manifest by
the large number of known disjunct ranges and by closely related
species occupying different ranges which can be explained satisfactorily only on the basis of the fragmentation of a previously
continuous range.

Examples of such disjunct ranges are common. The range of the
boreal forest race of the smooth green snake *Opheodrys vernalis
vernalis* (Fig. 64), has a large eastern segment and a small western
segment restricted to the Black Hills of South Dakota. Presumably,
late in the last glacial advance this snake had an unbroken and more
southerly range; as the ice dissipated, the range moved northward,
and ultimately a segment was left isolated in the Black Hills forests
surrounded by relatively xeric areas (Smith, 1957). Range fission
must be invoked to explain the disjunct range of many plants such
as the purple skunk cabbage *Symplocarpus foetidus* which has isolated populations in Asia and eastern North America (Fig. 65) and
to explain the disjunct ranges of many animals each having isolated
populations in Florida and other areas (Neill, 1957).

To match these patterns of disjunct ranges, there are a remarkable
number of instances in which exactly the same sort of division of
species ranges has resulted in the evolution of two or more species
from each parent species. Many pairs of sister species of the caddisflies have one member in western North America and the other in

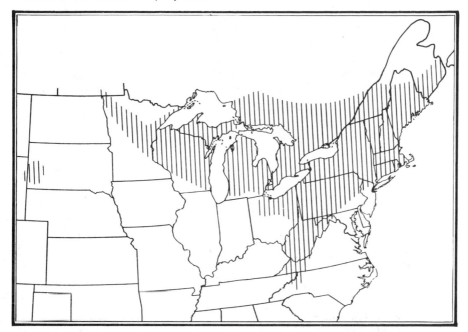

Fig. 64. Range of the smooth green snake *Opheodrys vernalis vernalis* showing the small isolated population in the Black Hills of South Dakota. (After P. W. Smith.)

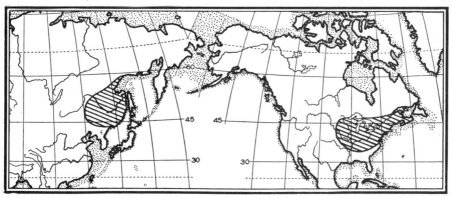

Fig. 65. The disjunct range of the purple skunk cabbage *Symplocarpus foetidus*. (After Fernald.)

adjacent Asia, and other pairs (matching the skunk cabbage distribution) have one species in Asia and the other in eastern North America (Ross, 1956). In the plants a pair of North American sister species of the genus *Senecio* are the undoubted result of range disjunction, one species now occurring in the western mountains and the other in the Appalachian mountains of the East (Stebbins, 1942 *b*).

A comparison of large numbers of "before and after" sets of distribution patterns shows that in general (but by no means universally) a rough correlation exists between deduced duration of isolation and amount of difference between the isolated populations or species. On this basis the process of increase in number of species by range division may be visualized as outlined in Fig. 66. Four steps are involved in the process.

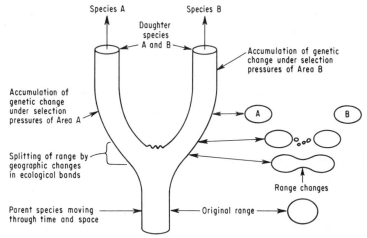

Fig. 66.   Diagram of the splitting of a species to form two daughter species.

(1) The initial step is the parent species, constantly changing genetically and having a dynamic fluctuation in density and range responsive to ecological changes in the environment, as was explained in Chapter 6.

(2) The range becomes divided when it flows around what might be termed an ecological "obstacle," an area of conditions adverse to the species which has the same effect on the species movement as a boulder in a stream (Fig. 67). The unsuitable area separating the isolated portions of the range may be of many types, either a land bridge arising and dividing ocean areas, a mesic area separating xeric areas, or a xeric area separating mesic areas. The only common denominator is that the ecological conditions in the "obstacle" area are unsuitable for the continued existence of the species in question. The result is the production of two or more populations isolated geographically and therefore independent genetically from each other.

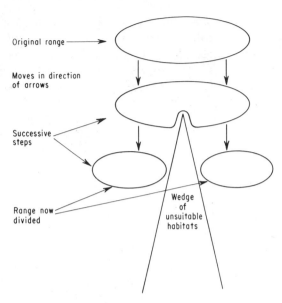

Original range

Moves in direction
of arrows

Successive
steps

Range now
divided

Wedge
of
unsuitable
habitats

Fig. 67. Diagram of the mechanics of a simple type of range division.

(3) After becoming separated, the isolated populations diverge genetically because each will start with at least a slightly different genetic composition due to the geographic variation within the parental species and because continuous spontaneous genetic change would accentuate the original differences. In addition the ecological selection pressures would be different for each daughter population. This stems from the fact that no two separated geographic areas are *exactly* alike ecologically. If a sufficiently detailed examination is made, differences of several kinds can be detected between such areas, perhaps small differences but differences which are nonetheless perceptible. Points of dissimilarity might be diurnal or seasonal rhythms of precipitation or temperature, soil types, seasonal changes in length of days, among many other factors. As a result, the direction of selection and the consequent adaptive changes would be at least slightly different in each isolated population.

Opportunities for genetic change through hybridization might be different in each isolated population. In the mosquitoes *Aedes aedes* and *A. albopictus*, hybridization apparently does not occur on the Philippine Islands but can occur between populations from Indo-China. Thus the potential flow of genetic material from one to the other is different in various isolated populations of the two species (Mattingly, 1953).

If this period of separation and increasing genetic divergence is sufficiently long, the isolated daughter populations will become genetically incompatible with each other. In other words, they will evolve into two distinct species, and each of these new species will be at least slightly different ecologically from its sister species.

(4) The final step in this process of species fission is the development of sexual isolation. Many distinctive species which evolved in isolation and are still isolated will hybridize freely if brought together artificially, even though the hybrids are sterile or inviable (Stalker, 1953). In much more closely related sympatric species, interspecific matings seldom or never occur. In these latter species cross-mating is prevented by a variety of behavior patterns to which one or both sexes of the species respond actively. Distinctive courtship patterns have been studied in *Drosophila* (Spieth, 1952), fish (Gordon, 1947), mice (Blair and Howard, 1944), and various birds and crickets. Under normal conditions females reject suitors belonging to other sympatric species, and frequently males do not court females of other sympatric species. In these same species the discrimination frequently breaks down when the sexes of isolated but closely related species are brought together experimentally. From these data the inference seems clear that distinctive interspecific courtship patterns do not evolve as rapidly between two species in isolation as between species whose ranges have come into contact and overlapped.

The mechanism leading to these different behavior patterns is natural selection operating through the medium of gametic wastage. If the ranges of two species met and the species hybridized to form unsuccessful progeny, selection pressures would immediately favor those individuals breeding with their own species, for those individuals which cross-bred would leave no progeny. The effectiveness of the selection has been demonstrated experimentally in the genus *Drosophila*. Koopman (1950) mixed two species of *Drosophila* which mated almost as readily between the two species as within each species. In each generation he discarded all hybrids so that continuing generations were composed only of the offspring of those individuals which had mated with their own species. In succeeding generations the number of hybrids decreased rapidly; hence this rigid selection against cross-breeding actually increased the intensity of sexual isolation between the populations of the two species.

For such a rapid response to selection pressure, it is necessary to suppose that pertinent differences in genetic factors affecting behavior already existed before the experiments were made and that these behavioral characters possessed a slightly different mean or mode in each species. The selection would therefore remove the overlapping bands of gene frequencies, producing in each species a new distinctive mode for these characters. Figure 68 shows diagram-

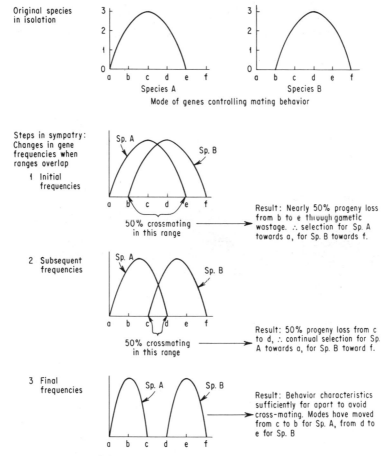

Fig. 68. Diagram of hypothetical development of sexual isolation through shifts in behavioral characteristics following range overlap between species whose hybrids are infertile. Hypothetical units of behavior are indicated by the letters a through f. Note that originally Species A had its mode at c and Species B at d.

matically the probable steps in this process. The speed would vary with the extent of cross-mating, the percentage viability of the hybrids, and the differences in behavior pattern at different stages of the process.

An illustration of the process of removing overlapping bands occurs in two nearctic frogs belonging to the genus *Microhyla* (Blair, 1955). The ranges of these two frogs, *Microhyla carolinensis* and *M. olivacea,* overlap along a narrow band in Oklahoma and Texas. In this area of overlap the species hybridize in at least some localities (Fig. 69). The chief factor which tends to reduce hybridizing seems

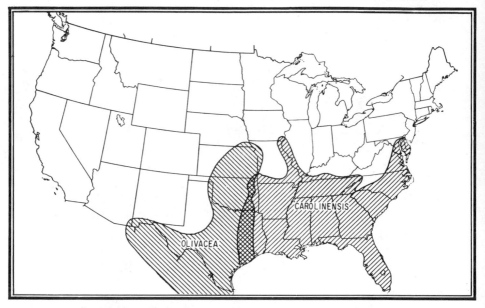

Fig. 69. Ranges of the two frogs *Microhyla olivacea* and *M. carolinensis.* (Adapted from Hecht and Matalas 1946, and Blair 1955.)

to be differences in mating call. Through a study of mating calls Blair found a most interesting phenomenon. In the area of overlap and adjoining areas east and west of it, the calls of the two species differ greatly in the average of both frequency and duration and differ completely when these two factors are considered as a unit (Fig. 70). In distant non-overlapping parts of the two ranges, however, the calls of the two species are almost identical.

A reconstruction of the past history of these two species indicates that a parent *Microhyla* species became divided during the Wisconsin glacial advance into a southeastern population which evolved into *M. carolinensis* and a southwestern population which evolved into *M. olivacea.* Following glacial retreat these two species spread northwestward and northeastward, respectively, eventually meeting in or near the present zone of overlap. Until the time of meeting the

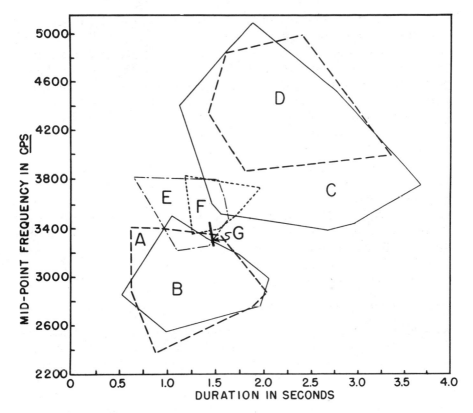

Fig. 70. Comparison of *Microhyla* mating calls by polygons constructed from scatter diagrams. A, *carolinensis* from the overlap zone; B, Texas-Oklahoma *carolinensis* from east of the overlap zone; C, Texas-Oklahoma *olivacea* from west of the overlap zone; D, *olivacea* from the overlap zone; E, *carolinensis* from Florida; F, presumed hybrids from the overlap zone; G, *olivacea* from Arizona. (After Blair.)

mating calls of the two species were presumably only slightly different, *M. carolinensis* as in E (Fig. 70), and *M. olivacea* as in G. Because of selection against hybrid individuals, the differences between the calls of the two species became intensified and now, in the overlap area, the call of *M. carolinensis* (A) is lower and shorter than that of *M. olivacea* (D).

In a complex of seven Australian species of the frog genus *Crinia*, Littlejohn (1959) found evidence of a similar history of call differentiation. Of the seven species, four have become sympatric and in these the calls are sharply different. Only average differences occur between the calls of allopatric species.

The distinctive color patterns occurring in certain fish during the breeding season (for example, the red-bellied and the black-nosed daces), the "booming" pouches of the males in the American prairie chicken group, the sound producing organs, sexual sensory developments, and perhaps the curious development of genitalic structures in many arthropods, and the structural differences in the flowers of closely related orchids in which each species is adapted for pollination by a distinctive insect, all may be correlated with the development of barriers to cross-mating.

In summary, the processes leading to species fission by geographic isolation begin with ecological changes bringing about range division and the formation of allopatric species (species whose ranges do not overlap). These may subsequently expand their ranges or reverse ecological changes may occur in the environment causing the once-fragmented ranges to move together. After this congregation of species, sexual isolation evolves which is the final step in the evolution of mature daughter species.

COLONIZATION

The idea basic to colonization is that individuals of a species disperse across one of the peripheral areas unsuited to the species, reach a suitable ecological area as yet unpopulated by the species, and colonize this latter area. This colony, cut off from all but infrequent gene exchange with its parent population, then develops in virtual isolation and evolves into a different species. Except for the mode of establishing the disjunct population, colonization presumably effects an increase in number of species in the same manner as does a division of the range.

The occurrence of this process is proven by the distinctive species inhabiting oceanic islands far from and never connected with the mainland, which nevertheless support a varied biota that must have originated on the mainland. The biota of the Galapagos Islands, the Hawaiian Islands, and many others must have originated in this manner (Mayr, 1942).

In addition to these striking cases of long-distance colonizations, short-distance examples are numerous. The list includes many West Indies insect species closely related to mainland species (Ross, 1959c), the unusual insular subspecies of *Peromyscus maniculatus* on the islands of British Columbia (McCabe and Cowan, 1945; Cowan and Guiguet, 1956), and several birds and frogs on Tasmania (Mayr, 1942; J. A. Moore, 1954). One might consider that colonial populations having an irregular but moderately frequent arrival of additional members from the parent population would not evolve into distinctive species. The continuous arrival of new immigrants might be considered a sort of link which would preserve enough genetic continuity between colony and parent range to nullify the differential effects of partial isolation. Yet the fact remains that new species have evolved or subspecies differentiated on islands a comparatively short distance from continents.

The natural attainment of genetic isolation by insular species under these conditions is demonstrated by the phenomenon called double colonization. One example concerns the hornbill bird species *Acanthiza pusilla* and *A. ewingi*. The latter is an endemic Tasmanian species which evidently arose from an early colonization by the Australian *A. pusilla*. Tasmania can be reached from Australia by two successive island-to-island jumps each of only 50 miles. *A. pusilla* occurs both on the Australian mainland and Tasmania, but on Tasmania it does not interbreed with *A. ewingi* (Mayr, 1942). Mayr concluded that colonists of *A. pusilla* dispersed to and colonized Tasmania and there evolved into a distinct species *A. ewingi* which is now genetically isolated from its original Australian parent. J. A. Moore (1954) reported a similar case of insular speciation involving two frogs *Crinia signifera* and *C. tasmanica*. The former occurs both on the Australian mainland and Tasmania, and individuals from one area cross successfully with mates from the other area. *C. tasmanica* occurs only on Tasmania. Although a close relative and an obvious derivative of *C. signifera, C. tasmanica* will not cross with it and apparently evolved from an old colonization of Tasmania by *C. signifera*. Mayr (1942) gives additional examples of double invasion in many parts of the world.

The use of the word "double" might in itself imply that in a "double colonization" only two dispersals from continent to island did indeed occur. The short distance from Australia to Tasmania makes this circumstance highly unlikely, nor is it a necessary postulate to explain the case. It might be argued that if other invasions had occurred, either more than two species would be present on the island, or the island species would never have developed. Other information, however, offers a more plausible explanation of insular species evolution based on a premise of probable multiple colonization.

Let us assume a hypothetical example involving a bird such as the hornbill of Australia which might occasionally reach an island such as Tasmania either by being swept there by storm or by fortuitous wandering. Successive colonizations could follow these theoretical steps:

(1) Initial colonization will be possible only when a male and female reach the island during the same breeding season and at the same locality. When this combination occurs and the pair mate and raise a family, the first colonization begins.

(2) The genetic composition of the island colony will change independently of the parent colony because the ecological setting will be slightly different, thus exerting slightly different selection pressures. The original genetic make-up of the colony will be different from the parent population because it will contain only the genetic make-up of two parent individuals rather than the entire gene pool of the parent population. Thus a genetic divergence will arise between the parent population and the colony. Vagrants reaching the island during the initial stages of this divergence would presumably interbreed freely with members of the colony. The total number of the latter would be so large in proportion, however, that genetic differences of an occasional vagrant would be absorbed and diluted with rapidity.

(3) The genetic divergence between the colony and the parent population would reach a point at which only limited genetic compatibility existed between them. Vagrants reaching the colony would mate with members of the colony, but the offspring from these unions would be chiefly sterile, hence few of them would be able to reproduce normally. Thus if the number of vagrants remained constant, their effect on the gene pool of the colony would diminish with the passage of time.

(4) When the genetic divergence reached such proportions that the colony was completely incompatible genetically with the parent species, vagrants would undoubtedly continue to mate with members of the colony, even though all progeny of such matings were completely sterile. As previously cited observations in *Drosophila* and *Microhyla* indicate, it is a commonplace for allopatric species to cross-mate when members of closely related species accidentaly meet, and further it appears that *sexual* or behavorial isolation (at least between closely related species) is a result of contact between the main populations of the species involved. Because our island colony, now a new species, would be in contact with its parent species only through an occasional vagrant, there would be only negligible selection pressure towards the evolution of sexual isolating mechanisms. Also, because vagrants would presumably arrive

only one at a time in any one locality, they would mate with a local member of the island species rather than have an opportunity to mate with each other. Even if an odd family of vagrants became established, their progeny would be rendered ineffective by cross-mating with members of the island species. At this stage the parent species would become re-established as a second invasion on the island only if a small band reached it and if the band kept together as a breeding unit.

(5) When the divergence between the island and parent species became sufficiently great that a state of sexual isolation prevailed between them, the situation would revert to stage 1, when a pair of the parent species could start a continuing second colonization of the island.

There would be a period embracing all of stages 1 through 4 when sporadic vagrants could have reached the island without leaving any tangible trace. If a "double invasion" were ultimately accomplished, the record would give evidence only of the first and last arrivals.

The series of steps listed above are patterned after the requirements of animals such as birds or termites in which both the male and female must be present during the breeding season. The situation would differ in certain respects in the case of animals such as other insects, snakes, or mammals in which a vagrant gravid female could establish a family. With these the more important factor would be population size. A large island population would tend to swamp the relatively minute proportion of vagrant progeny either by amalgamation into the population or, if hybrid progeny were sterile, by exterminating them because of chance cross-mating.

Theoretically this series of colonizing events could be repeated again and again, giving rise ultimately to many colonial species. E. O. Wilson (1959) postulated that such multiple invasions have been an important factor in the evolution of the ant fauna of Melanesia.

Continental reinvasion. It is tacitly assumed by Mayr (1942) and others in the cited examples of the double invasion of islands, that the species common to both continent and island was the parent and that the species on the island was the offspring. This view is emphasized even more strongly by those who believe that such insular species become "less well adapted" than their continental parents (Brown, 1957) and are therefore unable to invade the continent successfully. In all cited examples of double invasion, there is no evidence to contradict the different interpretation that both species evolved on the island from a parent which colonized the island before them and that one of the insular species so produced subsequently colonized the mainland. This latter course is a possibility for a number of insular West Indian species of both plants and animals which have become established successfully in Florida (Neill, 1957).

Possibilities of species fission by colonization. The possibilities for increase in number of species by colonization are manifold, essentially a product of the multiplication of dispersal possibilities by the number of barriers to species range extension. The manner by which plants and animals become dispersed across inimical ecological areas is extremely varied and has been discussed at length by Hesse, Allee, and Schmidt (1951), Allee, Emerson, Park, Park, and Schmidt (1950), Savile (1956), and Darlington (1957). By far the greatest amount of dispersal which might lead to colonization is passive: by rafting following floods, by wind, or by other agents. Some animals may cross barriers actively. Flying birds may wander or be blown over mountains or water barriers, or wander far from their normal range (Fig. 71), fish occasionally may swim

Fig. 71. Unusual wandering of a neotropical bird, the groove-billed ani *Crotophaga sulcirostris sulcirostris.* The "x's" indicate unusual northern or eastern records; those indicated also with an arrow represent the unusually numerous dispersals noted in 1952. (Adapted from Tordoff 1952, and other sources.)

through waters which normally are not occupied by that species, and mammals may similarly wander long distances into new territory. The present disjunct distribution of certain conger eels probably came about by such wanderings (Fig. 72).

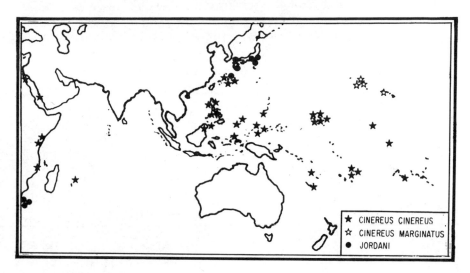

Fig. 72. Known distribution of two species of conger eels of the genus *Conger*. Note the disjunct African populations of both species. (After Kanazawa.)

The number of barriers is extremely difficult to assess. In general every distinctive ecological area of a continent or an ocean is a barrier to those species which cannot exist in it. However, attempts to correlate patterns of species fission and present ranges with existing barriers encounter difficulties imposed by a dynamic past. As Stebbins (1950) pointed out, colonizations which today seem improbable because of the great distances involved may have occurred at some time in the past when the barriers between areas were narrower than at present. Also, areas now disconnected may have been connected in the past. On the basis of present geography the Santa Cruz jay *Aphelocoma insularis* appears to be a colonist. It is possible, however, that formerly Santa Cruz Island was connected to the Californian mainland and that the Santa Cruz jay is the product of a past range disjunction of the mainland species *A. californica* race *obscura* (Pitelka, 1951).

Instances of geographic disjunction therefore fall into three categories: range disjunction, colonization, and a great number of doubtful cases which might be the product of either process.

TIME AND SPECIES FISSION

The length of time required for isolated sister populations to develop
evolutionary independence in a genetic sense appears to vary greatly
between different taxonomic groups and even between closely
related species. The moss *Grimmia patens* (Steere, 1938) and the
amphibian *Rana sylvatica* (Smith, 1957) suggest disjunctions of at
least 10,000 years without discernible change. The peculiar range
of the sword moss *Bryoxiphium norvegicum* (Fig. 73) suggests an

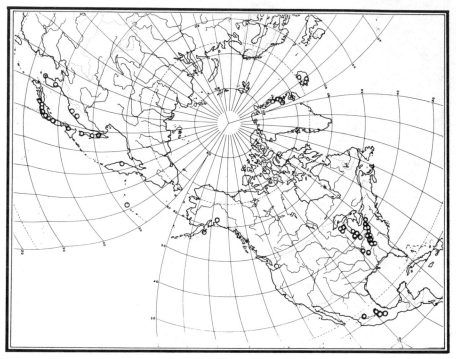

Fig. 73.   The distribution of the sword moss *Bryoxiphium norvegicum*. The
wide separation of its populations suggests a disjunction of perhaps several
million years if not a great deal more. (After Löve and Löve.)

even longer disjunction, perhaps of several million years, with little
discernible change (Steere, 1937; Löve and Löve, 1953). Judged
on the basis of morphological similarity, a similar span of separation
has not produced distinctive species in many boreal North American
stoneflies and caddisflies each of which has a northeastern population and a widely disjunct Ozarkian population. An example of the

stoneflies is *Allocapnia pygmaea* (Fig. 74).

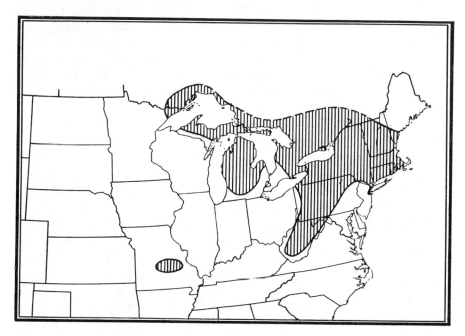

Fig. 74. Distribution of the winter stonefly *Allocapnia pygmaea* showing the disjunct population in the Ozark mountains of Missouri.

Certain disjunct Ozarkian populations, however, have evolved into species which are distinctive on a morphological basis. Three examples are the winter stonefly *Allocapnia sandersoni* and the caddisflies *Hydropsyche piatrix* and *Glyphopsyche missouri*. Each of these species is most closely related to a sister species occurring considerably to the north and east (Ricker, 1952; Leonard and Leonard, 1949). In all three examples the Ozark species differs from its northeastern relative in slight but constant morphological differences comparable in both type and magnitude with differences between closely related pairs of allied sympatric species.

The time when the Ozark Mountain populations originally became separated from the more northeastern populations of the same species is unknown, but the small amount of discontinuity in structure between those which have evolved into sister species, coupled with their geographic location, suggests that these disjunctions were associated with events of the Wisconsin glaciation. The analysis of the substages of the Lake Michigan lobe of this glacial stage by Frye and Willman (1960) is highly suggestive that (1) the disjunct Ozark populations which are apparently conspecific with their northeastern relatives became separated during the latter part of the Woodfordian substage, about 15,000 years ago, and (2) the disjunct Ozark populations which appear to be distinct species became separated during the latter part of the Altonian substage, about 28,000 years ago (Fig. 75).

In several animal groups in North America, conditions brought about by the Wisconsin glaciation seem to have caused a division of certain parent species into southeastern and southwestern daughter populations, the actual separation occurring probably from 35,000 to 50,000 years ago. In certain instances these daughter populations have again come into contact, perhaps only a few thousand years ago, and the results indicate that some of these formerly separated populations have developed into species independent in a genetic sense. One of the best known examples is the two species of narrow-mouthed frogs *Microhyla olivacea* and *M. carolinensis* discussed on p. 164 (Fig. 69).

In beetles of the genus *Trox*, Olson, Hubbell, and Howden (1954) found evidence of the evolution of five allopatric species correlated with Pleistocene events in southeastern North America, especially in the general area of Florida. If their suggested correlations are correct, the youngest species are about 30,000 years old and the older and more distinctive species range up to 500,000 years old.

In American cave beetles of the genus *Pseudanophthalmus* occurring in southern Indiana and adjacent Kentucky, Krekeler (1958) found that with few exceptions closely related species occurred along the same stream system. In two of these exceptions the distribution of related species coincided with the course of former streams disrupted during the Pleistocene. He concluded that two species, *P. bloomi* and *P. barberi,* evolved from daughter populations dating probably from the Teays river system during Nebraskan or Kansan time and that *P. jeanneli* may have arisen from a colonization in late Pliocene time.

The Olympic salamander *Rhyacotriton olympicus* of coastal western North America may present a different example. This species (Stebbins and Lowe, 1951) has a northern subspecies occurring chiefly in Washington and a distinctive spotted southern subspecies in northern California and southern Oregon with the large intervening area populated solely by intergrading forms

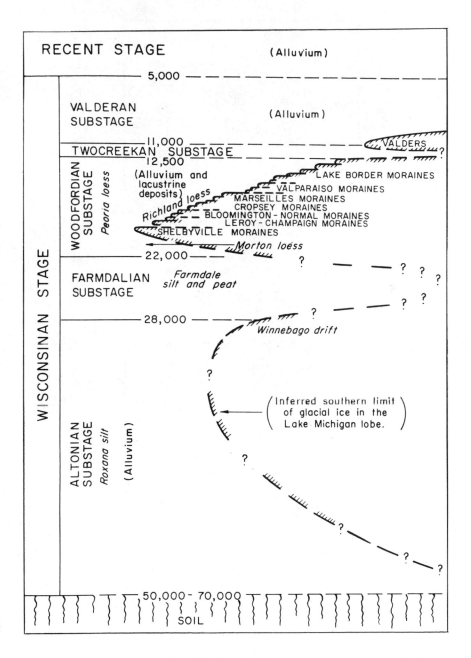

Fig. 75. A graphic representation of the advances and retreats of the ice margin of the Lake Michigan glacial lobe during the Wisconsin stage. Suggested dates are derived from radiocarbon determinations. South is to the left; the farthest ice advance shown is in the vicinity of Shelbyville, Illinois. Presumably the various ice advances coincide with periods of cooler weather considerably to the south of the glacial margin itself. (After Frye and Willman.)

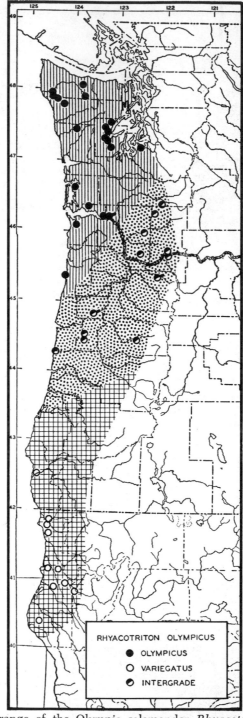

Fig. 76. The range of the Olympic salamander *Rhyacotriton olympicus* of coastal western North America. (From Stebbins and Lowe.)

(Fig. 76). Probably the original parental species had a somewhat similar range which was broken into a northern and a southern segregate by ecological changes associated with glacial fields in the Cascade and Siskyou Mountain ranges. The two isolated populations presumably evolved distinctive characteristics, but when the two populations rejoined following dissipation of the glaciers, they were still compatible genetically and are now in the process of fusing into a relatively homogeneous intermediate whole. If such a series of events took place, the separation was sufficient to produce differences but was not long enough to produce two species in this complex of salamanders.

Obviously the time required for the evolution of distinctive sister species varies with and within the taxonomic group. In most species 15,000 years would seem to be insufficient. In some species 35,000 to 50,000 years would seem to be long enough; but in still others even this length of time is not enough. The rate of differentiation of sister species is apparently influenced by two factors: degree of isolation and rate of becoming genetically incompatible.

Degree of isolation. Theoretically, complete and sustained isolation between sister populations would bring about the most rapid genetic divergence. Such absolute isolation undoubtedly occurs in organisms having low vagility and in colonies established on extremely remote areas such as highly isolated oceanic islands. Between other isolated sister populations some dispersal undoubtedly occurs. How much such occasional mixing slows down the process of genetic divergence can only be guessed.

This probability of dispersal between separated populations leads into a related question: Will certain degrees of partial isolation be sufficient to cause species fission? Certain populations of the Canada goose *Branta canadensis* suggest a negative answer (Hanson and Smith, 1950). Four of the breeding populations of this species are restricted to discrete areas around Hudson Bay (Fig. 77). Almost all the birds in any one area follow the same flyway, winter in the same southern region, and the following spring return with their young to breed in the same restricted area around Hudson Bay. There is some mixing of birds between flocks, but this, calculated from banding returns, is no more than 5 per cent (Hanson, personal communication). Presumably this behavior pattern of the Canada goose is of long standing and may antedate Wisconsin time, but to date there appears to be no tendency for the various flyway groups to become distinctive races.

Although degree of isolation is an important aspect of species

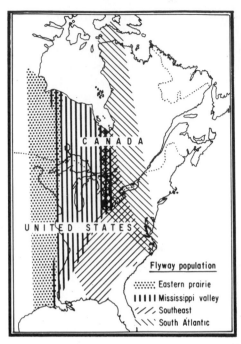

Fig. 77. Map showing roughly the main ranges of the four populations of Canada geese nesting in the Hudson-James bay region. The range of the Mississippi Valley geese overlaps the range of the Southeast population chiefly in fall; the range of the South Atlantic population overlaps the range of the Southeast population chiefly in spring. The western limits of the range of the Eastern Prairie population extend farther west than indicated here. The eastern limits of the range of the South Atlantic population probably extend farther east in some areas than indicated. (After Hanson and Smith.)

fission, it seems that comparative information about it must await future investigation.

Becoming genetically incompatible. The great differences between groups in becoming genetically incompatible are shown in striking fashion by many associated plants and their insect predators. The eastern sycamore *Platanus occidentalis* and its *Erythroneura* leafhopper predators have undoubtedly had a common history of past isolations, yet the sycamore has persisted as only one species while its original *Erythroneura* companion has evolved into six. The plant and the insects apparently have different rates for becoming genetically incompatible, and these rates are influenced by selective factors and intrinsic genetic mechanisms.

Two isolated sister populations would normally be under slightly different selection pressures. Presumably the amount of genetic differentiation would be proportional to such selective differences. Relative size of populations would exert some effect on genetic divergence, especially if one population were large and the other small, as in the case of small remnant populations existing in local pockets (Fig. 74).

Intrinsic genetic mechanisms affecting the rate of becoming genetically incompatible have been observed in several groups. Phylogenetic lines in which genetic change tends to be accompanied by chromosomal change appear to acquire genetic incompatibility between isolated populations faster than those in which chromosome number and morphology remain constant. Thus, those *Drosophila* species having large numbers of distinctive inversions appear to have a lower interbreeding potential than species of about the same relationship without such differences in chromosome structure (Patterson and Stone, 1952). Keck (1935) and Clausen (1951) have observed examples of this effect in various plant genera. In

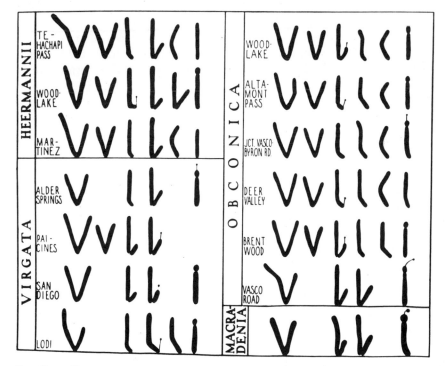

Fig. 78. Chromosome morphology of four species of the plant genus *Holocarpha* illustrating one chromosome of each pair. Note the differences between local populations of the same species. (After Clausen, *Stages in the Evolution of Plant Species*, courtesy of Cornell University Press.)

the American composite genus *Layia,* the six species having 7 gametic chromosomes can interbreed freely and successfully. In the related genus *Holocarpha,* in contrast, although the species are all closely related, each has a distinctive chromosome morphology (Fig. 78), and potential interbreeding is greatly reduced or eliminated. Clausen pointed out that these populations tend to be isolated in valleys. The occurrence of mutations in chromosome structure (see Fig. 78) apparently produces certain biotypes which are better fitted for the local environment than is the parent type with the result that a relatively homozygous local population soon evolves which can no longer form harmonious zygotes with gametes from other areas. Each such population is, as Clausen clearly recognizes, a new phylogenetic line thoroughly independent in an evolutionary sense. The decision of the systematist not to name these phylogenetic lines as species does not detract from their intrinsic evolutionary importance.

In Californian populations of certain species of *Clarkia,* Lewis (1953*a*) demonstrated conditions comparable in many respects to the *Holocarpha* populations. In *Clarkia* the species also occur in dense local colonies, have a low vagility, and also have a tendency to produce chromosomal mutations better adapted to more xeric conditions than are the parental types (Lewis, 1953*b*). Test populations of *Clarkia deflexa* (Fig. 79) indicate that many populations are genetically isolated from certain others and that one (G) may already be an independent phylogenetic line. Because several colonies are genetically compatible only with distant colonies with which they seldom if ever cross, a large number of colonies may be evolutionarily independent from a practical standpoint. In comparatively recent time the distinctive species *Clarkia lingulata* apparently evolved from such a local colony of *C. biloba* by a rapid process involving the addition of a chromosome to the genome plus chromosomal mutations involving a translocation and an inversion (Lewis and Roberts, 1956).

THE ISOLATION MACHINE

The foregoing pages attest the prevalence and importance of geographic isolation as a factor in species fission. On this basis, geographic regions having either a ring or string of islands or a series of island-like habitats in any ecological setting would constitute a veritable species machine. The combination of alternating range disruptions and conjunctions coupled with the possibilities of colo-

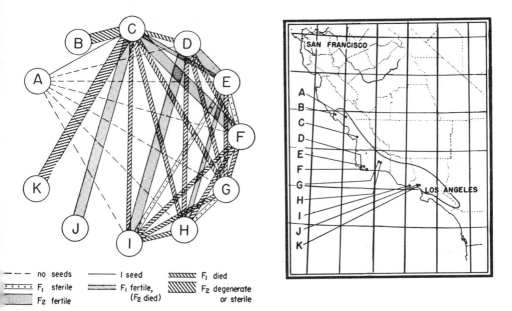

Fig. 79. Fertility relationships of populations of *Clarkia deflexa* having the geographical distribution indicated. Progenies indicated as having died without issue were in some cases victims of disease; in others they were not pollinated. (After Lewis.)

nization should set the stage for the formation of the greatest possible number of new species.

Each of these range disjunctions and colonizations, given sufficient time to change in isolation, would lead inexorably to an increase in the number of species.

Ecological Isolation

In a large number of groups of organisms there occur pairs of species which do not interbreed because some ecological difference or response separates the breeding members of one species from those of the other. For example, the closely related mosquitoes *Anopheles melas* and *Anopheles gambiae* occur together on the coast of Africa, but *A. melas* lives only in brackish or semi-saline waters, whereas *A. gambiae* lives in adjacent fresh water habitats (Ribbands, 1944). Among the North American flycatchers of the genus *Empidonax*, three very similar northeastern species occur in the same general range but occupy different habitats within it, *E. traillii* being found chiefly in swamps and thickets, *E. minimus* chiefly in open woods and clearings, and *E. flaviventris* chiefly in coniferous growth (Peterson, 1947). Other examples involve differences in seasonal timing or host. Epling (Dobzhansky, 1941) pointed out that certain related species of *Salvia* flower at different periods, and Frison (1935) found that certain related species of stoneflies had different seasonal times of emergence. In both plant and animal parasites which are restricted in host requirements, it is commonplace for two closely related species to have different obligate hosts. The different requirements of the individual species must be based on associated physiological differences of some kind.

These and innumerable other examples of closely related species occupying the same geographic range but exhibiting ecological segregation have suggested to many students of evolution that a species can divide into two distinct genetic populations by *ecological isolation* without the aid of geographic isolation. The basic reasoning behind this suggestion presupposes that if a species occurred in two quite different ecological situations, the individuals in one situation would tend to interbreed as a unit, as would those in the other situation. In each situation different selection pressures would operate on the pattern of genetic change so that the two populations would move apart genetically. The tendency of each ecological population to remain separate would prevent genetic mixing between them. If this situation persisted, theoretically the two populations would become sufficiently different genetically that members of one could not interbreed successfully with the other. At this point two species would have evolved, each restricted and adapted to distinctive ecological requirements.

Except under peculiar circumstances involving either host specificity, seasonal timing, or unusual ecological gradients, there seems to be no good reason to suppose that the set of suppositions above would work. The chief drawback is the lack of any apparent reason why, within the large network comprising the range of a species, individuals from one situation would not mingle with and mate with those from another, unless the opposite ecological conditions were situated some distance apart. In this case genetic divergence of the populations would be a function of partial or complete geographical isolation, not ecological isolation (Mayr, 1942; Lack, 1944). Thus Blair (1947) reports finding no differences in gene frequencies between mice on differently colored soils only four miles apart but marked differences between populations on the same colored soils 18 miles apart.

Ecological isolation has been invoked especially to explain

peculiar situations in aquatic animals. Lake Baikal has a number of monophyletic groups of species, or species flocks, especially members of the Amphipoda, which evidently have evolved within the lake. The African rift lakes Nyasa and Tanganyika each have several species flocks; in particular the cichlid fishes of Lake Nyasa contain flocks of 23, 24, and 101 species each, a remarkable number. At present the sympatric species show considerable ecological segregation, and thus ecological isolation has been cited as the cause of species fission. Brooks (1950), however, has pointed out that there is evidence for assuming that the levels and bottom contours of the lakes changed sufficiently to bring about geographic isolation on a small scale within the present lake boundaries.

Almost all cited instances of species fission due to presumed ecological isolation prove on analysis to be explained better on the basis of fission caused by geographic isolation, followed by range movements resulting in overlapping ranges. A few circumstances do seem to support the concept of ecological factors as isolating mechanisms, as Emerson (1949) pointed out. To be effective, these circumstances need to provide a sharp, sudden break either in behavior or location within the habitat which, in turn, results in the genetic isolation of two populations. Two circumstances affording such conditions are changes in temporal cycles and host relationships.

TEMPORAL ISOLATION

The type of change suggested here would divide a population so that, in the same locality, part of the population would breed at one time and part of it at another. Furthermore, the time differences would be perpetuated so that the two breeding populations would be continuously isolated genetically.

Banta and Wood (1928) found a mutant Cladocera which had its temperature tolerance raised 10° C. Such a mutant could conceivably give rise to a strain which matured at a different season than the original population and thus set the stage for dividing the population into two time units. Muller (1942), however, believed that characters producing this result would be polygenic in nature and would become balanced in the population. They would not produce two sharply separate modes. Even if this did not occur, presumably the heterozygotes would be intermediate in nature and would destroy any sharp timing differential.

Insects having rigid developmental patterns covering a year or more do have the possibilities of a time change which would produce genetically isolated populations. The most dramatic examples are the periodic cicadas of eastern North America comprising a species flock of the genus *Magicicada.* These insects are about an inch long and frequently occur in such numbers that their combined calls make a deafening roar. A few of the species have seventeen-year life cycles, the others thirteen-year cycles, all but a few months spent as nymphs feeding on tree roots in the soil and only about two months as adults. In spite of the fact that the seventeen-year group always matures in exactly seventeen years, there is an adult brood of these insects every year, not every seventeen years as one would suppose. The ranges of some broods overlap in area (Fig. 80), so that while the adults of one brood are active and

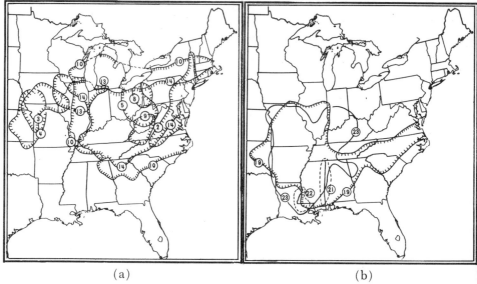

(a)   (b)

Fig. 80. The periodical cicada (a) ranges of the nine abundant broods having seventeen-year life cycles. The broods are numbered from 1-17, one for each year, hence five years elapse between the emergence of adult swarms of Broods 14 and 2; (b) ranges of four broods having thirteen-year old cycles. The broods are numbered from 18 to 30. Only broods 19 and 23 are abundant and widespread. (Adapted from Marlatt.)

mating above ground, nymphs of other broods may be growing in the soil directly beneath.

Eleven of the 17 seventeen-year broods are extensive, the others are either scattered or small in extent. Brood 11 occurs only in a small area of the New England states. Up to 1921 Brood 12 had only six locality records scattered from Maryland to Illinois. The years of emergence of the more important broods form an irregular seventeen-year clock composed, in succession, of two eastern, two western, one central, one widespread, three central, one western, and a widespread brood (Fig. 80a). Here are the elements of at least 11 interbreeding populations isolated from each other by time and perhaps each possessing the potential of developing into a separate species.

In the thirteen-year species of *M. tredecim* there are only two large broods, 19 and 23, separated in time of emergence by nine and four years (Fig. 80b). Only one other abundant brood is known, 22, confined to a small southern area. Although the number of broods is smaller in this species, there seems an excellent probability that at least broods 19 and 23 are sufficiently isolated in time to evolve eventually into distinctive species.

The results of these implications are as yet unknown. The different broods may have come into existence because of local freakish weather, but how old they are and how much they differ genetically remains to be discovered. The taxonomic complexities of individual broods are only now being analyzed extensively (Alexander and Moore, 1958), and this analysis will undoubtedly shed much light on their evolution.

Species fission by cyclic isolation of another sort is suggested from the study of sawflies and crickets (Ghent and Wallace, 1958; Bigelow, 1958). A monophyletic cluster of four species of nearctic sawflies belonging to the genus *Neodiprion* illustrates this type of temporal isolation. All four species feed on pine, have a short adult life span, and a rigid life history of one generation a year. Three of the species (*N. virginianus, N. taedae,* and *N. pratti*) overwinter as fully mature larvae, and the adults emerge and mate in spring, whereas the only other species of the cluster (*N. maurus*) overwinters in the egg stage, the larvae pupate in late summer, and the adults emerge and mate in the autumn (Ross, 1955). Most other species in the genus overwinter as larvae, indicating that this is the ancestral condition for the *N. virginianus* cluster. At present *N. maurus* occurs in the same area and on the same host species as a subspecies of *N. pratti*. The circumstances suggest very strongly that the species *N. maurus* arose as a colony of *N. pratti* (its sister species) in which for some reason the larvae pupated in autumn instead of going into hibernation and that the new seasonal timing became established in succeeding generations. The species *Neodiprion hetricki,* belonging to another group of four species, exhibits exactly the same situation as *N. maurus* (Ghent and Wallace, 1958).

It is possible that both *N. maurus* and *N. hetricki* evolved through geographic isolation and that their changed seasonal adjustments occurred during that evolution. The circumstances of both cases, however, suggest the greater probability of evolution through sympatric temporal isolation.

Bigelow (1958) based his similar concept of temporal isolation on two closely related species of field crickets of the genus *Acheta*. In *A. pennsylvanicus* winter is passed in the egg stage, and in *A. veletis* it is passed in the late nymphal stage. As a result there is extremely little overlapping in the period of adult emergence of the two species. On the basis of laboratory rearings the two species appear to be completely isolated sexually. Bigelow (1958) and Alexander and Bigelow (1960) explained the evolution of these two cricket species in the same manner as that employed to explain the sawfly examples in *Neodiprion*. They give the name *allochronic speciation* to the process.

HOST ISOLATION

In practically all groups of host-specific parasites or predators, a phylogenetic line established on one host has either changed to a new host or given rise to a daughter line on another host. Well-known examples abound in the insects. A rodent-infesting group of fleas has become established on burrowing owls (Rothschild and Clay, 1952), the moth *Platysamia columbia* evolved on larch from a parent line feeding only on angiosperm hosts (Sweadner, 1937), and two species of the sawfly genus *Nematus* transferred independently to the legume host *Robinia* from an ancestor utilizing a willow host. Dethier (1954) gives other examples, and Mayr (1947) and Emerson (1949) cite examples from other groups of animals and from parasitic plants. The physiological and genetic bases of this host transfer are poorly understood (Dethier, 1954), and the genetic situation is especially obscured because the best explanation for the meagre observed data is some type of phenotypic habituation.

In certain host transfers of this type, the possibility is very real that one species gives rise to a daughter species on a new host within the geographic and general ecological range of the parent species. As Mayr (1942, 1947) pointed out in opinions opposed to giving credence to this type of sympatric species fission, the host transfer would have to associate interbreeding males and females as an isolated breeding population on the new host. Otherwise genetic mixing would continue between populations on the two hosts, no genetic divergence would develop, and no independent phylogenetic line would evolve. In two insect groups suspected of being parents of sympatric fission species, these objections are circumvented.

In the transfer of the rodent flea to the owl, adult fleas could have been accidentally introduced on prey into the burrows by the foraging owls, the fleas could have laid eggs there, and a population of rodent fleas emerged in the owl nest. This sort of happening undoubtedly occurs frequently without a change of host, the adult fleas leaving the owl burrows in search of their normal rodent host. However, on at least one occasion the fleas adopted the owls as a host, became established on them, and evolved into a distinctive species. Presumably the owl-liking fleas maintained a series of populations in owl burrows effectively isolated genetically from the parent populations of fleas on rodents. The isolation here would be linked with the fact that the flea larvae develop and pupate in the host nest; hence each nest is almost an isolated micro-population as long as the nest is continuously occupied.

Prey brought into the nest would introduce occasional individuals of the old rodent flea species into the new owl-nest populations. Presumably here the same forces and processes would prevail as postulated for the colonization of geographically separated areas (see p. 168).

Complex multiple-host transfer is found in three North American species flocks of the leafhopper genus *Erythroneura*, almost entirely confined to the eastern deciduous forest region. In three lines of the *E. comes* flock (Fig. 81), a species feeding on grape (*Vitis*) gave rise to a sister species on redbud (*Cercis*). In the *E. maculata* flock (Fig. 82), species arising from oak-feeding ancestors became established on sycamore, maple, elm, and at least ten other host genera. In the *E. obliqua* flock, an even more complex series of host transfers have occurred. Each detectable host transfer led to the establishment of a new phylogenetic line, and some of these have evolved subsequently into two, six, or as many as 40 species (Ross, 1958*b*). In these three species flocks, totalling about 500 species, about 150 host transfers are known.

The great bulk of the species are widely distributed, frequently extending as far as their hosts. This circumstance does not fit a pattern of unusual past fragmentation of ranges. Furthermore, the earliest probable age of this cluster of flocks is the same as that of

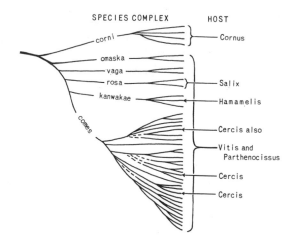

Fig. 81. Phylogenetic tree of the *comes* group of the leafhopper genus *Erythroneura*. Species names of the leafhoppers have been omitted but each apical line represents one species.

several other eastern American insect groups having a lower vagility (conducive to species fission) but nevertheless having only eight to 16 species each. Both circumstances are suggestive of host isolation as the factor producing the unusually large number of species in these three species flocks of *Erythroneura*.

The mating behavior in this genus is such that it appears to confer almost perfect genetic isolation by host. All observations to date indicate that in both sexes the stimulus for mating usually occurs after the species is on its breeding host. After the local populations become thus stratified, mating and egg-laying ensue. Thus if a group of individuals became established on and habituated to a new host, they would be fairly well isolated genetically as a breeding population from the parent species in the same locality. How the transfer is effected and the habituation becomes established is not known.

With both the fleas and the *Erythroneura* leafhoppers, circumstances of host, phylogeny, and life history indicate sympatric species fission by a host transfer mechanism.

Reviewing the evidence in bisexually reproducing organisms, it appears that, in species fission, ecological isolation does not have the same widespread importance as geographic isolation. In contrast, in organisms having either rigid host specificity or peculiarities of biological timetable, ecological isolation may be an important factor in the increase in number of species.

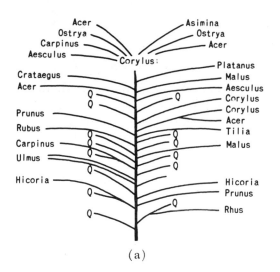

(a)

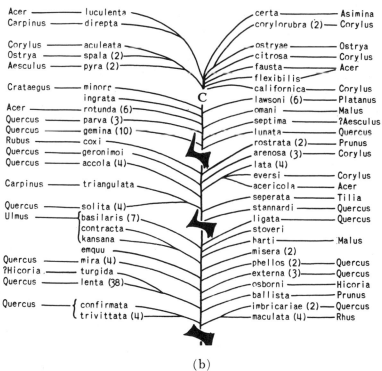

(b)

Fig. 82. (a) Phylogenetic tree of the species complexes comprising the *maculata* group of the leafhopper genus *Erythroneura* together with their known host plants. The letter C indicates a putative ancestral form occurring on *Corylus*. The black silhouettes indicate progressive changes in the style of the male genitalia. Numbers indicate the number of species in each complex. (b) The phylogenetic tree with the names of the species complexes omitted and the apparent ancestral host *Quercus* indicated by the letter Q.

Simple Hybridization

Although hybridization has been observed between a large number of plant and animal species, its role in bringing about an increase in number of species is poorly known. A few examples are reported in vertebrates and insects. Among the plants Stebbins (1950) listed only three examples (one doubtful), ending with the thought that others "will doubtless become available when more groups have been studied critically with this possibility in mind."

. One of the most plausible cases of the production of new entities by hybridization occurs in the American silkworm moths of the genus *Platysamia* (Sweadner, 1937). Two species of the genus extend through the mountainous areas from Mexico into Canada, one on each side of the arid Great Basin area: *P. euryalis* to the west and *P. gloveri* to the east. A third highly variable population, *P. kasloensis*, occupies the area to the north of the ranges of *P. euryalis* and *P. gloveri* (Fig. 83). All three species intergrade along areas of contact, but typical members are isolated genetically to a considerable degree. No sexual isolation exists, the species mating in nature just as readily between as within the species. Few of the F_1 generation reach maturity, and those that do are low in vigor. Hybrid females are sterile; hybrid males, however, are fertile and will backcross with either parent. Hence genetic interchange is possible between the species. The species *P. kasloensis* has one distinctive color character of its own, but in other color characters it is highly variable, appearing to represent what might be considered a hybrid swarm between *P. euryalis* and *P. gloveri*. Were it not for its one distinctive character and reduced interspecific fertility, *P. kasloensis* would be such a hybrid swarm, but these two features indicate that *P. kasloensis* is now potentially a third species.

The geographic distribution of the complex indicates that, at the maximum of the Wisconsin glaciation, *P. euryalis* and *P. gloveri* occurred much farther south than their present ranges, separated by the lowland Great Basin area (Fig. 83). As the ice front melted away, the two species spread northward and eventually individuals of both species colonized areas between the northern ends of their ranges and hybridized. It is highly likely that the resultant hybrid swarm was better adapted to this new area than either parent and that natural selection favored hybrid genotypes, thus perpetuating and consolidating the hybrid nature of the population.

Three Balkan firs exhibit an almost identical situation. The common fir of central Europe *Abies alba* extends through the western

Fig. 83. Distribution of the species comprising the genus *Platysamia*. The species *kasloensis* is considered to be of hybrid origin, having arisen from *euryalis* and *gloveri*. (After Sweadner.)

Balkans to northern Greece, and *A. cephalonica* extends through the mountains of central and southern Greece. Between these two species and extending considerably eastward occurs a highly variable entity *Abies borisii-regis* which is in general intermediate between *A. alba* and *A. cephalonica* and which is considered to be a hybrid species with *A. alba* and *A. cephalonica* as its parents (Mattfeld, 1930; Stebbins, 1950).

In the *Drosophila virilis* complex the cytogenetics of the subspecies *D. americana americana* can be explained only as the result of hybridization between *D. americana texana* and *D. nova-mexicana* (Fig. 84) (Patterson and Stone, 1952). The hybrid sub-

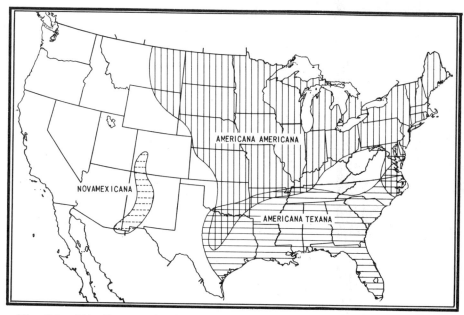

Fig. 84. Distribution of *Drosophila novamexicana* and the two subspecies of *D. americana*. The subspecies *americana americana* is a hybrid between *nova-mexicana* and *americana texana*. (Adapted from Patterson and Stone.)

species *americana* occupies such a large range with so little over-lap with the subspecies *texana* that it can justifiably be considered an incipient species resembling the *Platysamia* and *Abies* examples.

Many other plants and animals are called "hybrid species," but in most instances they are probably the result of interspecific hybridization which changed one or both parent species (introgression) but which did not produce an additional third species. In the thrips Stannard (1954) suggested that the genus *Hybridothrips* may be the result of hybridization between the allied genera *Zactinothrips* and *Zeuglothrips*. The combination of characters in certain species of the leafhopper genus *Erythroneura* can be explained most logically as a result of hybridization between two fairly different parents (Ross, 1958a). Of the 12 species of crab-hole mosquitoes comprising the Neotropical genus *Deinocerites*, Belkin and Hogue (1959) consider that at least *D. howardi* and possibly *D. epitedius* and species A. also are of hybrid origin. In woodpeckers of the genus *Dendrocopus*, Miller (1955) suggested that the southeastern *D. borealis* is a hybrid species between the widespread *D. villosus* and the southwestern *D. scalaris*. In all four of these examples it is practically impossible to know whether the probable hybrid species arose by an unusual occurrence of parallel mutations, by hybridization which simply changed one of the parent species, or by the establishment of a hybrid population which eventually became stabilized as an additional species.

Platysamia, Abies, and *Drosophila,* however, demonstrate the possibility of new phylogenetic lines arising from hybridization. The earliest theoretical stage in such a process would be a single local hybrid swarm. Examples of these are abundant, especially in the plants. In certain Illinois sand areas the two oaks *Quercus marilandica* and *Q. palustris* form extensive hybrid populations. Stebbins (1950) and Clausen (1951) cited many more. In the animals smaller numbers of examples have been recorded. Rudd (1955) reported a hybrid population of shrews and other authors have reported local hybrid populations of smaller mammals (McCabe and Cowan, 1945). Hubbs (1955) reported hybrid swarms in several species of fish. Miller (1939) recorded small hybrid populations of juncos from the mountains of southwestern United States.

An unusual aggregation of local hybrid swarms showing different proportions of parental characters occurs between two red-eyed towhees of Mexico (Sibley, 1950, 1954; Sibley and West, 1958). The northern parent, *Pipilo erythrophthalmus,* extends as a fairly uniform population into central Mexico and occurs as smaller, isolated populations east and southeast of Mexico City. The other parent is the Mexican species *P. ocai* which is known in pure form only in areas south of Mexico City. In two of these southern areas both species occur sympatrically with little or no hybridization. Hybrid swarms exist in many other areas between those occupied by typical members of either species (Fig. 85). In this figure the number zero refers to pure *P. ocai,* 24 to pure *P. erythrophthalmus,* and numbers in between to hybrid indexes indicating the average resemblance of each population to the two parental types. Sibley (1950) suggested that Pleistocene events may have caused the ranges of the two parent species to make contact and separate, thus bringing about opportunities for hybridization.

The mode of origin of these hybrid swarms presents theoretical problems. Normally species in nature either do not hybridize or, if they do, the hybrids backcross with the parents, and no discrete

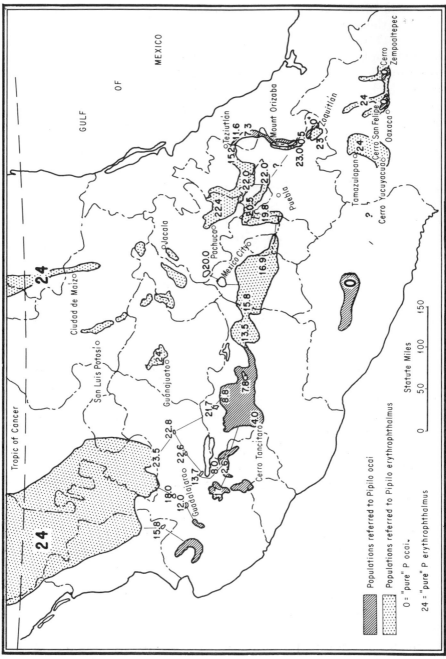

Fig. 85. Distribution of the red-eyed towhees in central Mexico. The hybrid index between the two pure species *Pipilo ocai* and *P. erythrophthalmus* ranges between 0 and 24 respectively. (After Sibley.)

hybrid unit is formed. Before hybrid species can be formed, barriers to interspecific crossing must be overcome, and factors favoring the segregation of the hybrid progeny as a unit must be present.

In plants, barriers to crossing are chiefly physiological or ecological, and presumably passive chance leads to the production of hybrid progeny. In animals, however, usually extensive behavior patterns prevent interspecific mating. Miller (1955) suggested that in birds these were circumvented if the population was so low that individuals could not find mates of the same species. Spieth (1952) and others noted that in sympatric species of *Drosophila* no mismatings occurred in mixed cultures having goodly numbers of specimens of each species. Hybridization was accomplished only by confining males of one species with females of another. Sailer (1954) found the same situation in attempting to cross two sympatric species of stink bugs, *Euschistus variolarius* and *E. servus*. Even when males and females of these opposing bug species were confined together, matings were infrequent, oviposition was reduced, and the per cent of egg fertilization was extremely low. A few hybrids were finally produced, however, and they proved to be vigorous and fertile. These hybrids possessed certain notable characters: (1) they mated more readily with each other than with either parent, and (2) hybrid to hybrid matings produced the larger number of offspring. This latter point agrees with a few observed interspecific hybrids in *Drosophila* (Patterson and Stone, 1952).

In the genus *Amaranthus*, Sauer (1957) found that various hybrid combinations were selected by the environment and that a certain hybrid type tended to predominate in each environment. The same phenomenon has been observed in other plants (Stebbins, 1950; Clausen, 1951). Darlington (1958) pointed out that certain genetic combinations resulting from hybrid crosses would be selected on a developmental basis because of ontogenetic physiological fitness.

Considering these observations, the following circumstances would favor the production of new species by hybridization: (1) local breakdown of interspecific barriers to crossing, (2) the production of hybrid combinations better fitted than the parents to thrive in the area of hybridization, and (3) any factors tending to bring about mating or more certain fertilization between hybrids than between hybrids and parents. All of these would be more likely to occur at the fringes of the range of two parental species, and they suggest that peripheral hybrid populations may develop into new phylogenetic lines distinct from the parental ones.

Spontaneous Genetic Isolation

From time to time the possibility has been discussed that individuals might acquire a non-polyploid mutation which was fertile when crossed with itself but sterile when crossed with the parent stock and that such mutations would result in the production of a new species. The theoretical probabilities militating against such a happening are great. In a completely bisexual cycle, if only one mutant individual occurred, it would be unable to produce offspring because it would have no mate except from the parent stock. The occurrence of two such identical mutations in the same place at the same time, and the mating of these two particular individuals, seems highly improbable.

Theoretically species fission of this type can occur only when the mutant gametes can be increased in number between their formation and the next mating, hence might be possible in many unicellular organisms having asexual reproduction interspersed with sexual unions or in self-compatible, self-pollinated plants.

Laven (1957, 1959) suggested spontaneous genetic isolation to explain the occurrence of cryptic or obscure species of European mosquitoes. In the house mosquito *Culex pipiens* he found (1957) that populations from northern Germany produce no offspring when crossed with populations from extreme western Europe, that the latter were intersterile with Italian and Tunisian populations, and that many other combinations of populations from different areas exhibited varying degrees of intersterility (Fig. 86). No morphological or other distinguishing attributes have yet been found between these intersterile forms, nor does any mating preference exist between them. The net result is the delineation of at least five rigidly defined but contiguous areas each having a population intersterile with its neighbor. In a genetic sense the population of each area is a true species with a sharp boundary between them.

These boundaries are maintained by sterility factors carried in the cytoplasm (Laven, 1957). Laven (1959) suggested that these arose within the parent population and, by increasing without natural selection, formed the present system of cryptic species.

Several points militate against this view. In northern Germany especially, local populations exhibit various degrees of interfertility, indicating that the intersterility factors arose as a succession of small mutants or as the accumulation of dosages of an original mutant having only slight effect. Normally such mutations would be swamped out or would gradually spread through the whole

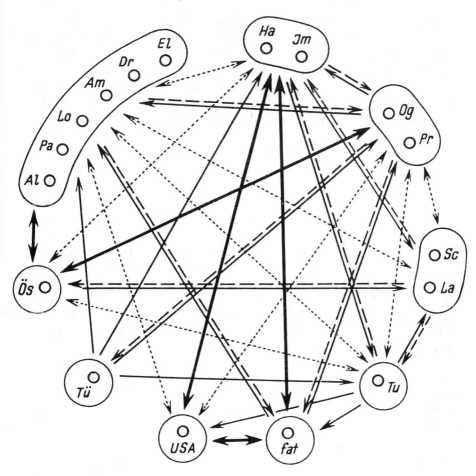

Fig. 86. Cross-breeding chart between various populations of *Culex pipiens.* *El-Al,* western Europe; *Os,* Osterberg; *Tu,* Tubingen; *USA,* Illinois; *fat,* California; *Tu,* Tunis; *Sc,La,* Italy; *Og, Pr,* Oggelshausen, Prague; *Ha, Im,* Hamburg, Immenrode. The heavy line indicates cross fertile in both directions; the thin line indicates cross fertile in direction shown by arrow; the broken line indicates cross sterile in direction shown by arrow; the dotted line indicates cross sterile in both directions. Populations within same circle are completely compatible genetically. (After Lavan.)

species range. The present system of species boundaries can be explained more logically on the basis of range movements associated with the last ice age. During that time the range of the parent species could have become divided into several or many isolated units, and in each segregate mutations leading to these intersterility factors could have become established. These factors might also have been associated with physiologically beneficial characters on which natural selection would operate positively, increasing the rate at which the intersterility factors would have become intensified and established throughout the entire isolated population. If after this evolution the segregates of the old range rejoined, the result would logically be exactly what Laven described. If this sequence is correct, then this mosquito complex is another example of species fission by typical geographical isolation.

Polyploidy

Polyploidy is the one known mutational method by which a new species can evolve in one step. Certain peculiar conditions must occur, however, before a polyploid mutation can become a polyploid population. Polyploidy results when whole new sets of chromosomes become incorporated into the genome. This happens when the chromosomes divide but the cell itself does not. Thus, in an organism having a haploid or gametic number of five chromosomes, mutation during gametogenesis might give rise to gametes having 10 chromosomes. When one of these gametes united with a normal gamete, it would result in a $3n$ or triploid instead of a normal $2n$ or diploid individual. These triploids might be viable but, with only one or two known exceptions, are always highly sterile. As a result most gametic polyploid mutations lead to no permanent lineage.

Although few in number, the triploid species of animals are of great interest in that all of them are parthenogenetic. The list includes a dozen or more species of weevils, four species of black flies, a few species of earthworms, and possibly a few others (White, 1954; Basrur and Rothfels, 1959). How the combination of parthenogenetic condition and triploidy may have arisen is a complex and unsolved problem. It has been discussed by White, Basrur and Rothfels, and by Stalker (1956). Triploids and other odd n ($5n$, $7n$) plants occur as isolated perennial individuals in many groups, as in the ferns (Manton, 1950) but, as with the animals, never form bisexual populations.

If it should happen that the polyploid gamete united with a sister polyploid gamete, a viable *and* fertile individual frequently would result which would have 20 somatic chromosomes ($4n$, or tetraploid) instead of the parental 10 somatic chromosomes ($2n$, or diploid). The chance of this type of union happening is almost zero if it relies on several polyploid gametes being produced as spontaneous mutations by different parents of opposite sexes of the same species at the same time and place.

In contrast, a somatic polyploid mutation could produce a whole polyploid organism or fruiting structure. If this were hermaphroditic, it would produce polyploid gametes of both sexes in close proximity, and if this individual were also capable of self-fertilization, the stage would be set for the production of a potentially viable and fertile polyploid population. Such a population would immediately comprise a new species because it would form an independent phylogenetic line, genetically compatible within itself but rigidly isolated genetically from its original parent.

The occurrence of polyploidy in species reproducing bisexually bears out the role of chance as has just been outlined. The infrequent cases of polyploid species in bisexually reproducing metazoan animals are confined to a few groups which are hermaphroditic, chiefly the turbellarian flatworms and the leech and earthworm groups of the Annelida. Even in some of these examples (White, 1954) there is considerable doubt as to the polyploid nature of the species. In many of the turbellarians, for example, the gametic chromosome numbers for related species are two, four, five, and eight, or two, three, and six, or three and six. This suggests strongly that the species with four and eight chromosomes are tetraploid and octoploid, respectively, and those with six are tetraploid, but it does not prove it. The added chromosomes could be the result of other processes. There seems to be no doubt concerning the tetraploid or at least polyploid nature of some earthworms belonging to the family Lumbricidae. White (1954) suggested that they may have arisen originally as parthenogenetic polyploids which later became bisexual, but this again is only a surmise. Gates (1952) suggested that several mammals are polyploid, but White attacked the reliability of his circumstantial reasoning.

In the plants, examples of polyploidy are legion and emphasize the importance of this type of evolution in this branch of the biotic world. Two factors appear to be the basis of this difference between plants and animals. In the plants, hermaphroditic structures (monoecious organisms) are the rule rather than the exception, and in many groups infertile hybrid individuals may reproduce vegetatively for many years. The combination of both conditions occurring together should give the greatest proportion of polyploid types. Stebbins (1950) pointed out that such is partially the case because the highest incidence occurs in the perennial monoecious herbs although not in the woody plants. The annual herbs and woody plants, however, do have many polyploid series at an incidence that is extremely high compared with the animals.

A high proportion of natural polyploids in plants are hybrid in composition. Winge (1917) first theorized that new species of plants could arise as the result of hybridization followed by polyploidy. His theory was verified experimentally by Clausen and Goodspeed (1925) by the artificial synthesis of the polyploid species *Nicotiana digluta* from the hybrid between *N. tabacum* and *N. glutinosa*. Unknown to these investigators, a similar case was already on record in the genus *Primula*. In Kew Gardens a perennial hybrid plant of a cross between *Primula verticillata* and *P. floribunda* was viable but sterile. After some time a polyploid shoot arose which produced fertile polyploid flowers (Digby, 1912). Since that time botanists have discovered many more cases of this sort (Stebbins, 1950), and it now appears that the great proportion of naturally occurring polyploids arose from hybrids, in other words are *allopolyploids*.

The occurrence of simple polyploids (*autopolyploids*), which arise by doubling of the parental chromosomes without hybridization, is much less frequent. In her fascinating account of the cytology and evolution of ferns, Manton (1950) found several cases of autopolyploidy but many more in which the evidence pointed to the hybrid origin of the polyploid species. Stebbins cautioned in this regard that even species suspected of being autopolyploids because of chromosomal behavior may actually be allopolyploids in which many chromosomes of the parental species of the hybrids are similar in basic structure.

All possible polyploids are not successful species. Stebbins (1950) listed many experimentally produced ones which are either sterile or virtually inviable, or both. In the laboratory, Manton (1950) produced the autotetraploid of the fern *Osmunda regalis* (a form which has not been collected in nature) and found that it was much less vigorous than the naturally occurring diploid form. She concluded that autopolyploidy in the genus *Osmunda* would give rise to no persistent types and therefore would be of no evolutionary significance.

Allopolyploidy in plants has unusual evolutionary significance in two respects. Because of it, whole sets of polyploid species have evolved to form a series of polyploid levels. A simple example in which the species differ only slightly is the European triad of fern species in the genus *Polypodium* (Manton, 1950). In these forms three fertile levels of ploidy occur, diploid, tetraploid, and hexaploid with gametic numbers of 37, 74, and 111. Sterile perennial triploids and pentaploids (3n and 5n) also occur in nature where the parent species overlap. More complex examples are found in the section *Chamaemelanium* of the genus *Viola* (Fig. 87) in which occur

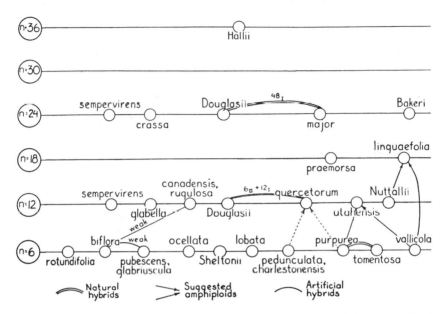

Fig. 87. Polyploid levels in the section *Chamaemelanium* of the genus *Viola*. (After Clausen, *Stages in the Evolution of Plant Species*, courtesy of Cornell University Press.)

four levels of polyploids above the diploid level (Clausen, 1951). Several levels occur also in the genus *Clarkia* (Fig. 34) but with irregular chromosome numbers because of the different numbers in the original parent species.

There is an apparent limit to the extent of polyploidy compatible with viability and fertility, probably associated with increasing problems of physiological ontogenetic adjustment with an increase in genes affecting the same processes. The great bulk of plant polyploids are tetraploids or hexaploids, but occasionally higher levels occur. In the higher plants natural species seldom exceed 12-ploids (Stebbins, 1950; Clausen, 1951). In mosses possible decaploids are the highest natural level so far found (Steere, 1954); in ferns the highest reported gametic chromosome numbers of 250 to 260 may represent as high as a 20-ploid (Manton, 1950).

Polyploidy offers unusual possibilities for the combination in one line of characteristics possessed by two or more lines so different that they would not produce fertile hybrids. Chiefly involved in this role would be inter-group hybrids and inter-generic hybrids. An example of the former is the grass *Bromus carinatus* complex representing an allopolyploid between the sections *Bromopsis* and *Ceratochloa* of *Bromus;* an example of the inter-generic type is domestic wheat, an allopolyploid of the hybrid between *Triticum dicoccoides* and *Aegilops speltoides.* Although naturally occurring polyploids of proven inter-generic parentage are few, many divergent types probably arose by this method.

Polyploidy has been of tremendous significance in increasing the number of plant species. The lowest possible estimate of polyploid species is 25 per cent with the possibility of this figure reaching 35 or 40 per cent. The percentage differs widely in various plant groups. In the mosses (Steere, 1954, 1958) and angiosperms (Stebbins, 1950) some families have little or no polyploidy, whereas others have many examples; only in the ferns (Manton, 1950) are the bulk of the families almost entirely polyploid.

The many thousands of polyploid species do not *each* represent a new phylogenetic line that arose by the process of polyploidy. Thus in *Clarkia* (Fig. 34) eight of the ten polyploid species each represent a separate polyploid origin, but the two species *C. davyi* and *C. tenella* both arose from a single polyploid line which divided into the two sister species by isolation and non-polyploid genetic divergence. In the horsetail genus *Equisetum,* the 11 fertile species listed by Manton (1950) all have a gametic chromosome number of 108, surely polyploid, but all 11 species have undoubtedly evolved by ordinary non-polyploid processes from a common polyploid ancestor having a gametic chromosome number of 108.

Species and Lower Categories

The natural processes leading to species fission are in operation constantly but not synchronously. What we observe at the present time is a cross-section through all the evolving phylogenetic lines of the world. All stages in the species fission process are represented in existing biotas. As a consequence difficulties arise in giving names to these products.

Among the phylogenetic lines diverging by the accumulation of small genetic changes, some will be represented by mature species which are demonstrably independent in an evolutionary sense, whereas others will be represented by lower levels or stages of division. Frequently, in the case of semi-distinct lines, it may be difficult to ascertain whether two lines are becoming increasingly distinct or are fusing. A puzzling and complex example of this is found in the five subspecies described in *Culicoides variipennis*, a North American biting midge of the family Ceratopogonidae (Wirth and Jones, 1957). Each subspecies occurs in a somewhat homogeneous state in a relatively limited area; some may be separated from each other on modal rather than absolute characters; and populations of an intermediate nature occur between all of the five subspecies. The relatively pure ranges of the five subspecies (Fig. 88) are chiefly allopatric, but two, *occidentalis* and *sonorensis*, overlap to a considerable extent.

Of the five subspecies, typical *C. variipennis* is the most stable, the best characterized, and probably the oldest; subspecies *occidentalis* is the next most distinctive; and the remaining three subspecies *sonorensis*, *albertensis*, and *australis* form a closely knit triad (Fig. 88). By combining these relationships with geographic distribution, a simple sequence of events can be postulated. Probably the progenitor of the present species split first into central and eastern populations. The latter eventually became typical *variipennis*. The central population subsequently divided into a far-western population which evolved into subspecies *occidentalis* and a mid-western population which was the parent of the triad *sonorensis-albertensis-australis*. The subspecies *australis* has an unusual amount of kaleidoscopic variation, reminiscent of the hybrid silkworm *Platysamia kasloensis*, and suggesting that subspecies *australis* is a hybrid entity. This can be explained by assuming that the inland ancestral population of the triad divided into two entities, a southwestern and a Great Basin population (*sonorensis*) and a Great Plains population (*albertensis*), and that finally, possibly late in the Wisconsin glacial period, the ranges of subspecies *variipennis*, *albertensis*, and *sonorensis* spread into a common south-central area. Presumably sexual isolation between these three types is as yet somewhat undeveloped, resulting locally in free hybridization and the formation of a highly variable hybrid swarm, the subspecies *australis*. The resultant phylogeny is shown in Fig. 88.

Marked ecological differences exist between the subspecies. *C. v. albertensis, australis,* and usually *occidentalis* inhabit saline situations, whereas *variipennis* and *sonorensis* breed in heavily polluted but not unusually saline breeding areas. As suggested by Wirth and Jones, the whole species may represent a somewhat freely

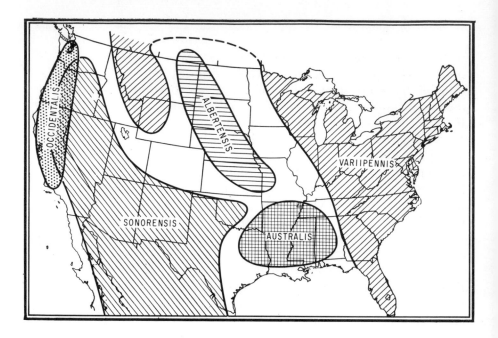

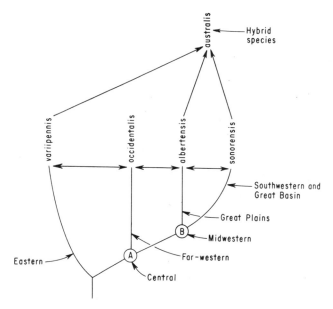

Fig. 88. Details of the *Culicoides variipennis* complex. Above are shown the ranges of the relatively typical populations of the five subspecies. Intergrading populations have been found connecting many of the adjoining peripheries. Below is shown a family tree of the five subspecies based on morphological criteria, with an indication of the postulated general range of the ancestral forms. (Based on data in Wirth and Jones.)

mixing gene pool which is segregated locally into discrete types (some of the five subspecies and possibly other as yet undetected entities) by the selective action of local environments. This concept can hardly apply to *occidentalis* and *sonorensis*, a high proportion of which maintain distinctive differences in male genitalia in the more xeric areas of California, Oregon, and Washington where their ranges overlap. Rather, these two forms suggest the situation found by Blair (1955) in his *Microhyla* studies.

Paucity of existing data makes it difficult to decide on the status of these *Culicoides* subspecies. If they represent only ecotypes selected from a common gene pool, the stability of certain types over large and diverse areas is a real puzzle. If they represent incipient species of different age levels, then younger incipient species have evolved before older ones reached a stage of sexual and genetic isolation—a situation not uncommon in plants but at present considered unusual in animals. Then the question arises: Are these entities merging or moving in the direction of evolutionary independence?

An unusually interesting situation concerns the North American garter snakes comprising the species *Thamnophis elegans* and its 13 races, which were studied by Fox (1951). This species apparently consists of two "ring species," one aquatic and one terrestrial, the two "rings" overlapping geographically to a large extent, yet separate genetically except for a single, small area straddling the Oregon-California boundary which is occupied by the race *biscutatus* common to both rings. Each ring presents the problem of interpreting its own complex parts, and in addition there is the problem of explaining the race *biscutatus* which connects the two rings. Is each ring a distinct species which in this one area hybridized to form a hybrid race, or is *biscutatus* a little-changing population of the ancestral form which gave rise to the two "rings"?

In plants of the *Potentilla glandulosa* complex, the subspecies *hanseni* is intermediate in a series of characters between the two subspecies *reflexa* and *nevadensis*. This suggests that the very distinct but geographically restricted subspecies *hanseni* may have arisen since the last glacial maximum as a hybrid between the other two subspecies. The subspecies *hanseni* occurs at intermediate elevations in the California mountains; subspecies *reflexa* occurs at lower elevations and overlaps upward into the range of subspecies *hanseni* for 2,000 feet, but the two do not interbreed because of differences in habitat and flowering dates. The alpine subspecies *nevadensis* occurs at higher elevations than the other two. The three subspecies, although interfertile experimentally, in nature appear to be quite independent, non-mixing phylogenetic lines (Stebbins, 1950; Clausen, 1951). An equally plausible alternative explanation is that the three are distinct species, that the entity *hanseni* is the most primitive of the complex, and that the entities *reflexa* and *nevadensis* evolved in opposite adaptive directions from a *hanseni*-like ancestor. The intermediate nature of *hanseni* is explained just as satisfactorily by the postulate that *hanseni* is a "living fossil" or a near-prototype as by the postulate that it is of hybrid origin.

In apomictic species and in species arising suddenly from spontaneous mutation, arbitrary taxonomic difficulties of another sort are encountered. Especially in polyploid plants, completely isolated polyploid phylogenetic lines may be so like the parents that without living material for fertility tests and cytological preparations, relationships are obscured, and identification is hazardous (Wagner, 1955).

Mayr (1942), Stebbins (1950), Clausen, Keck, and Heisey (see Clausen, 1951), and others have explained a multitude of other species and their component parts which are difficult to interpret. Because of the large number of puzzling examples there has been much argument in the literature concerning the definition and application of the terms *species, subspecies, races,* and similar categories. The preceding examples illustrate fully the nomenclatorial problem in designing a uniform system or code for listing and cataloging taxonomic entities as they are found in nature, particularly for the sliding scale in values shown by "species in the making." The only biological problem involved is to ascertain the place of these entities in relation to evolutionary and/or ecological processes. This can be done, not by deciding what name to give them, but by comparing morphological and biological data acquired by a study of specimens.

Because the primary concern of a naming system is the recording of data, it follows that the most satisfactory choice of names or categories is the one which will serve as the best vehicle to record desired data fully and clearly. This leaves much to the judgment of the taxonomist when confronted by situations representing different levels of complexity and evolutionary development. Nothing would seem to be gained by attempting to restrain or control the use of categorical names in systematics beyond the rather broad concept expressed above (Osborn, 1902).

SUMMARY

In bisexual organisms the dynamic nature of phylogenetic lines and the environment causes an inexorable increase in the number of species. Geographic isolation is the most important process in both plants and animals. Ecological isolation, simple genic mutation, and hybridization produce a limited amount of species fission and in special cases may lead to the evolution of many new species. Polyploidy in animals produces few new species but in plants is a great force in the genesis of new independent phylogenetic lines.

These processes involve two other factors of great importance: time and geomorphology.

From the viewpoint of time, the species arising through single mutations (polyploid or otherwise) come into existence in one generation. Species fission by other processes involves change through numbers of generations, few for such rapidly evolving species as those in *Holocarpha* or *Clarkia,* up to many thousands for slower changing organisms.

The relationship of geomorphology to species fission is of the greatest importance. The processes involving solely genic mutation, polyploidy, colonization, and perhaps certain types of hybridization can occur without any change in the environment. The processes involved in ecological isolation may be initiated by short-term or local weather changes, but need nothing more than the annual fluctuations normal to the area. Processes involving range fission or range congregation, however, require geomorphic changes which bring about long-term and stable changes in climatic and other environmental conditions. This is the only mechanism which will produce marked and sustained shifts in range boundaries and thereby lead to range fragmentation or to the congregation of ranges previously separated.

These processes and mechanisms have been increasing the number of phylogenetic lines since sexual life originated, although only a portion of the products survived. Extinctions have continuously reduced the total number which came into existence. Judged from information in groups having a seemingly good fossil record (Fig. 89), at various times and in various groups this extinction produced a startling decrease. How many phylogenetic lines came into existence during biologic time is difficult to estimate because the fossil record in most groups is meagre. About 1,500,000 species are known today, 365,000 plants and the rest animals (Jones, 1951;

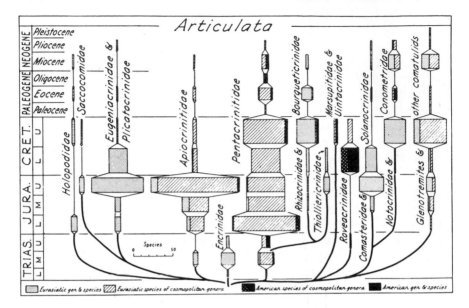

Fig. 89. The numbers of the echinoderm class Crinoidea known from various times, illustrating the drastic reduction of species which has occurred. Only a few species exist today. (After R. C. Moore.)

Sabrosky, 1952). Adding estimates of species yet unknown, the actual total may be as high as 2 to 5 million. It seems reasonable to suppose that the total number formed through all biologic evolution has been many times greater (Simpson, 1952; Teichert, 1956).

The Evolution

of Communities

8

The millions of species of plants and animals that evolved formed the species mixtures constituting the biological communities of the world. These communities, however, are not random mixtures of species. The species living together today exhibit various degrees of adjustment to each other as well as to their physical habitat. Some of these interspecific adjustments are so intimate that they can be no happenstance but must have come about by a process of evolution. The conclusion seems obvious that, first of all, species mixtures occurred, then some sort of order evolved within these mixtures. Questions relevant to this situation are: How did the first species mixtures occur, how many species had to occur in a mixture before some sort of order evolved, what kind of order evolved first, and what influences were involved? The first prerequisite to investigating these questions is an understanding of the kinds of order that occur in natural situations. In pursuing this inquiry, examples have been drawn chiefly from continental life because, in many respects, life in these habitats is known better than life in the oceans.

Under natural conditions, living continental species form different kinds of interlocking landscapes in such areas as prairie, forest, desert, lakes, and streams. The type of vegetation, that is, whether it is desert, prairie, or forest, is determined by climatic factors of temperature, rainfall, and evaporation. In the main, forests occur in regions with high rainfall, prairies in regions having lower total or seasonal rainfall, and deserts where rain is scant and evaporation high. The type of vegetation in the landscape is therefore a reflection of the climate, and, in general, widely separated areas having similar climates have similar aspects of landscape. These major types are called *biomes,* and are the largest ecological units. Each of these biomes contains smaller units. A forest, for example, may be well drained and high with a preponderance of oaks and hickories; in another place it may be low and swampy, with elms, gums, and other trees different from those in the better-drained areas. Each of these fairly uniform areas is considered by the ecologists as a biological unit of natural areas and is called a *community.* Each community consists of a set of species that persists year after year. The species living in similar communities are practically the same. Thus oak-hickory communities in Wisconsin, Indiana, Missouri, and Oklahoma each contain very nearly the same species of organisms.

Although an elm or gum forest community contains a fair proportion of the species found in an oak-hickory community, it lacks many species found there but possesses instead species distinctive to itself. Going further afield, a prairie community has a species make-up differing greatly from that of a forest community, and both have almost no species in common with marine communities.

Within each community there exists a vital relationship between many species. In a forest many species of both plants and animals feed on the forest trees, shrubs, and herbs, and are dependent on them for existence. Certain insects feed on the parasitic fungi, other insects feed on the plant-eating insects, and still other species may parasitize these predators. The squirrels and birds have their bird and mammal predators and their insect and tick parasites. Many species of shrubs and herbs are able to live only in the shade of the trees and in this way are as dependent on the trees as are the species which feed on the trees. This relationship is obligatory only in one direction. The trees would live just as well without the organisms which feed on them or the understory species which depend on them. Some relationships, however, are obligatory in both directions, as for example that between plants and the animals which pollinate them.

This brief survey of biotic communities shows that they differ from random mixtures of species because they are ordered in two different ways. First, a community contains only those species which are adapted to live in the ecological conditions prevailing in the locale of the community. Second, an intricate web of various relationships exists between the different species comprising the community. These relationships may be obligatory with regard to one or both species involved or they may appear to be relationships between what are actually casual neighbors. The community is therefore a mixture of species held together by a combination of common ecological tolerances and by interspecies relationships which are either partially or entirely obligatory.

The origin and evolutionary history of these relationships would therefore seem to be the crux of community evolution. Each instance of a relationship existing between two species may be considered as one unit of community structure, and each unit may have an evolutionary history independent of that of other units. A community embraces thousands of such units, and the evolution of these units will collectively represent the evolution of the community. The sequence of events in this evolution is (1) the evolution of many species, (2) the congregation or mixing of some of these species, and (3) the subsequent evolution of the relationships characteristic of modern biotic communities.

THE CONGREGATION OF SPECIES

The dynamics of the earth's crust, so important in the increase in number of species, have been the chief causal agents in bringing about a congregation of species. Topographic and climatic changes not only divide the ranges of some species but also unite similar ecological areas which were previously separated. Thus the successive submergence and emergence of parts of the Central American isthmus would first unite, then divide the oceanic areas of the region and conversely divide then re-unite the land areas on either side of the break. Each union of a similar area would result in a congregation of the species in the joined areas. Oscillatory changes of lesser degree have produced the same effect many times. It seems reasonable that this process of alternating change has been going on since the first cluster of species evolved on the earth. On this premise, mixtures of a few primeval species came into existence early in the evolution of life, and mixtures involving more and more species have since occurred many times in many places.

THE EVOLUTION OF COMMUNITY RELATIONSHIPS

The relationships between species in a community may be grouped into three categories: (1) *exploitation*, in which one species lives at the expense of another, including chiefly the predator-prey relationship, (2) *mutualism*, in which one or both species benefit from the relationship but neither suffers, and (3) *coexistence*, in which species live together in some measure of actual or potential competition for the same necessities such as light, moisture, space, and nutrients.

Considering that the first mixtures of species contained only a few kinds which were probably quite similar ecologically, the interesting question arises: How many species would have to inhabit an area before modern community relationships would evolve? Investigations in this realm are necessarily speculative because neither the primeval organisms nor the primeval communities of the past are still in existence. In their stead it is necessary to seek present-day species and circumstances illustrating seemingly similar simple phenomena and to assume that the general selection and survival factors now in operation would have been those in operation when life began. The evidence derived from these available sources indicates strongly that coexistence and exploitation could and probably did materialize as features of community structure in mixtures of only a few species.

Coexistence

Broadly speaking, all the species living in the same community are coexisting, although they exhibit many degrees of interrelationship. The kind of coexistence discussed in this section is the relationship existing between the members of the community which utilize the same space and food. This would include, for example, all the trees in a community, all the herbivores, or all the carnivores.

Within each of these general types, the food-procuring or other activities or habits of each species may be slightly different. This results in a staggered utilization of the commodity in potentially short supply. Common examples include seasonal succession of insect species having the same host, diurnal rhythms of hunting animals, or insect species each feeding simultaneously only on roots, leaves, stems, or flowers of the same plant host. This situation is commonly said to avoid competition, but it does not. The competition is simply less direct, hence called indirect, in comparison with a situation in which competitors utilize the commodity in short supply simultaneously, side by side, and in the same fashion. Instances of indirect competition would seem in general to be specialized conditions which evolved from conditions of direct competition.

A surprisingly large number of species are in direct competition. Especially among the insects, many species may feed on the same host at the same time without any discernible differences in food utilization among the competitors. It seems reasonable to suppose that this kind of mixture of competing species is the simple one from which specialized forms of coexistence arose and also that it is the kind most like the first primeval mixtures of species.

Several investigators, following the generalization called Gause's Law by Lack (1947) that no two species can occupy the same niche at the same time, have theorized that such mixtures could not exist. This generalization is highly unrealistic because it is doubtful if natural conditions are ever as idealized or static as the generalization requires (which was explained in Chapter 6).

Competitive mixtures of this sort are found today, and several sets of pertinent experiments based on laboratory "communities" of two or three species indicate that such mixtures could have occurred in primeval communities. The multi-species composition of competitive mixtures could have been maintained by either unusual competitive balance or oscillations of ecological factors.

UNUSUAL COMPETITIVE BALANCE

In tests for competition between two species of *Tribolium* flour beetles, Park (1954, 1955) found that under some combinations of temperature and humidity all the replicate tests did not have the same results (Fig. 90). In some of these experiments the "loser" in 90 per cent of the tests won in the other 10 per cent, and in another set of experiments the "loser" in about 66 per cent of the tests won in the other 33 per cent.

Comparing two species of *Drosophila*, Sokoloff (1955) found an even more delicately balanced competitive equilibrium between *Drosophila pseudoobscura* and *D. persimilis*. Although *D. persimilis*

Treatment	Type of Effect	Species Favored	Per Cent of Replicates in Which Favored Species Wins	Per Cent of Replicates in Which Unfavored Species Wins	No. of Replicates
HW..........	One-way	*T. castaneum*	100	0	29
HD..........	Alternative	*T. confusum*	90	10	29
TW..........	Alternative	*T. castaneum*	86	14	28
TD..........	Alternative	*T. confusum*	87	13	30
CW..........	Alternative	*T. confusum*	71	29	28
CD..........	One-way	*T. confusum*	100	0	20

Fig. 90. Consequences of interspecific competition between two species of *Tribolium* flour beetles at six combinations of temperature and humidity. H, T, C, indicate hot, temperate and cold, respectively; W, D, indicate wet and dry respectively. (From Park.)

interfered with the production of *D. pseudoobscura* more than the reverse, *nevertheless* even at extremely high population densities both species survived.

In both of these instances, if the food supply was periodically replenished (as it is normally in nature), both species of each pair would coexist indefinitely. In the *Tribolium* species the usual "loser" would exist as small local populations; in the *Drosophila* species both would exist side by side.

ECOLOGICAL OSCILLATIONS

In his *Tribolium castaneum* versus *T. confusum* experiments, T. Park (1954) found that at certain combinations of temperature and humidity one species was invariably the sole survivor, whereas at other combinations the second species was the sole survivor (Fig. 90). The extreme "weather" conditions in these experiments were 30° C. and 70 per cent R.H. versus 24° C. and 30 per cent R.H. In the hot moist cultures, *T. castaneum* eliminated *T. confusum* only after coexistence for more than a year, and in the cool dry cultures *T. confusum* eliminated *T. castaneum* only after coexistence for more than half a year. If the two species coexisted in a climate having annual fluctuations ranging between these extremes, first one species then the other would tend to predominate, resulting in an oscillating relative abundance of the two and continued survival of both.

In experiments with two parasites of the azuki bean weevil *Callosobruchus chinensis*, Utida (1957) found that the system of two parasites generated ecological variables which allowed both parasites to coexist. When the host density is high the parasite *Neocatolaccus mamezophagus* predominates and presumably outcompetes the other parasite *Heterospilus prosopidis*. However, when high *Neocatolaccus* incidence reduces the host population to a low density, *Heterospilus* outcompetes *Neocatolaccus* (Fig. 91). The

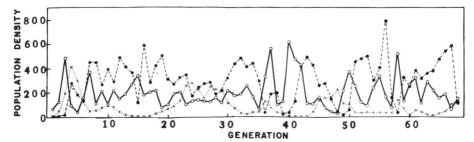

Fig. 91. Population fluctuation in a host and its two insect parasites. The hollow circles and thick line indicate the host *Callosobruchus chinensis*. The solid circles and broken line indicate the parasite *Neocatolaccus mamezophagus*. The crosses and dotted line indicate the parasite *Heterospilus prosopidis*. (From Utida.)

reason for this reversal is that the *Heterospilus* adult parasites have a greater ability to find host larvae, which live inside the beans. Thus the relation between host and parasites causes an oscillation in host density; one parasite excels when it is high, the other when it is low. This automatic but simple system accounts for the indefinite coexistence of the two competitive parasites without variation in "climate."

PRIMEVAL COEXISTENCE OF DIRECT COMPETITORS

On the basis of the experimental results and observations above, it seems logical to suppose that mixtures of primeval species would have coexisted, even if they were only slightly different ecologically. No likely environment of these creatures would have been without variables, and almost certainly no two species would have been exactly alike physiologically and therefore ecologically. The good chance of competitive balance or "losers" winning locally, plus the certain chances of dual survival when two species are adapted to opposite ends of their environmental range together indicate that coexistence undoubtedly occurred between primeval forms of life in direct competition for space and food.

It is to be expected, however, that in primeval communities

competition was an important element which set in motion selection pressures leading either to specializations toward indirect competition or to the origin of food chains.

INDIRECT COMPETITION

A simple type of competitive interference leading to indirect competition is illustrated by two mites (Acarina) studied by Lienck and Chapman (1951). In New York the closely related two-spotted mite *Tetranychus bimaculatus* and the European red mite *Paratetranychus pilosus* feed together on unsprayed apple trees. *Paratetranychus pilosus* normally reaches its maximum abundance about August 1 and *Tetranychus bimaculatus* about September 5. In 1950 an acaricide applied very early in the season to a series of orchards almost eliminated the *Paratetranychus* but had no discernible effect on the *Tetranychus*. Under these conditions the *Tetranychus* reached a greater abundance, and its time of peak abundance was appreciably earlier (Fig. 92). In unsprayed orchards the lower population and later peak of abundance of *Tetranychus bimaculatus* would therefore appear to be due to the competitive interference of *Paratetranychus pilosus*. Under prolonged competition the greater survival of the late season *Tetranychus* populations would presumably initiate selection pressures tending to stabilize genetically the later appearance of the species.

Exploitation

As Elton has stressed (1927), the organizational backbone of a community is its food chains, showing which species feed on which (referred to as *trophic levels*). It might seem that very different species must have had to evolve before one species could feed on another, but this is not a necessary postulate. Many unicellular organisms feed on other species of unicellular organisms, so that it is not necessary for the aggressor species to be a monster in order to prey on another. It is probable that the first such predator was a unicellular species which started feeding to a limited extent on the partially grown stages of another somewhat similar fellow species in the community. The predatory individuals presumably matured faster or reproduced better than others, and from this situation natural selection led to a wholly predatory species. Inferential support for the evolution of predatism between closely related species comes from many observations.

In the *Tribolium* populations studied for competitive effects, the

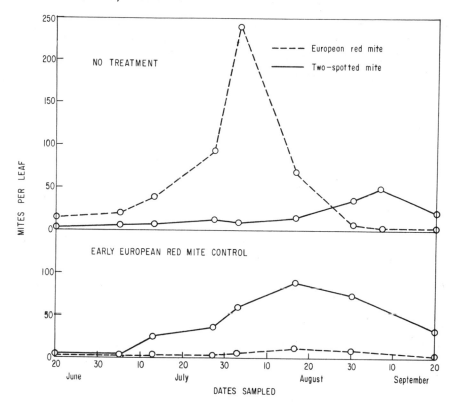

Fig. 92. Seasonal population trends of the European red mite and the two-spotted spider mite. Above, on untreated apple trees when both species were present; below, on trees treated by pre-blossom sprays in which the European red mite was virtually eliminated. (After Lienk and Chapman.)

numerical density is related to the fact that the active forms (larva and adult) eat the passive forms (egg and pupa) whenever they encounter them. This goes on indiscriminately when two species of *Tribolium* coexist in the same sample, so that each species is partly a predator on the other. With only a slight change in relationship, one species could become a habitual predator, the other species its habitual prey.

The predatory habit has evolved between closely related species many times. In certain bees (Apoidea) the adult of one species lays its eggs on the food gathered by a provisioning species, a type of predatism known as *social parasitism*. Social parasitism has evolved independently in many different subfamilies and tribes of bees. Frequently the parasite bee lives only at the expense of one of its close relatives (Fig. 93) (Michener, 1944; Linsley, 1958). The parasitic bees of the genera *Psithyrus* and *Sphecodes,* for example, are morphologically so similar to the bees they parasitize that the ancestral parasitic species in each genus undoubtedly started out simply as a "lazy" or cuckoo bee laying its eggs on the provisions of a sister species. This might readily be traced to a situation in which two previously allopatric species having identical nesting habits came to occupy the same range so that the nest-finding instincts of one would frequently lead it to the nests of the other.

The discovery of a host for the parasitic conifer *Podocarpus ustus* of New Caledonia illustrates another case of one species becoming a predator on a closely related form. This unique gymnosperm, a woody shrub with some chlorophyl in its leaves, was found growing out of a specimen of *Dacrydium taxoides,* a closely related tree member of the same family Podocarpaceae (de Laubenfels, 1959).

The First Communities

From the foregoing observations one may conclude that as soon as geomorphic changes resulted in a mixing of species, these mixtures evolved into the first biological communities which had the same fundamental characteristics as those occurring today. Competition, chance inherent differences in the species, and innate ecological differences within the range of the mixtures would interact and constitute the mechanisms of this evolution. Without much doubt, the first relationships which evolved were coexistence and exploitation or the predator-prey relationship. It seems probable that even in mixtures of only a few species both of these patterns of inter-species relationships were evolving simultaneously.

From these community relationships emerged an ecological aggregation progressing through time. Each aggregation is a mixture of species held together by ecological forces, in part obligatory as in exploitation and in part simply coincidental because of the similar ecological tolerances of the species. However, each individual phylogenetic line in this ecological aggregation has either a potential or a constant influence on the success of other companion phylogenetic lines.

EVOLUTION OF COMPLEX COMMUNITIES

After communities became established they gradually became more complex until now they are vastly richer in species and far more

Bees that are Social Parasites		Their Bee Hosts	
Genus	Family	Genus	Family
Sphecodes	Halictidae	*Halictus*	Halictidae
Stelis	Megachilidae	*Heriades*	Megachilidae
		Hoplitis	Megachilidae
Chelynia	Megachilidae	*Anthidium*	Megachilidae
		Heriades	Megachilidae
		Hoplitis	Megachilidae
		Osmia	Megachilidae
Dioxys	Megachilidae	*Anthidium*	Megachilidae
		Osmia	Megachilidae
		Megachile	Megachilidae
Coelioxys	Megachilidae	*Megachile*	Megachilidae
Nomada	Anthoporinae*	*Andrena*	Andrenidae
		Halictus	Halictidae
		Nomia	Halictidae
Holcopasites	Anthophorinae	*Pseudopanurgus*	Andrenidae
		Calliopsis	Andrenidae
Neopasites	Anthophorinae	*Dufourea*	Halictidae
Townsendiella	Anthophorinae	*Conanthalictus*	Halictidae
		Hesperapis	Halictidae
Oreopasites	Anthophorinae	*Nomadopsis*	Andrenidae
Epeolus	Anthophorinae	*Colletes*	Colletidae
Triepeolus	Anthophorinae	*Mellisodes*	Anthophorinae
		Svastra	Anthophorinae
		Anthophora	Anthophorinae
Epeoloides	Anthophorinae	*Macropis*	Melittidae
Melecta	Anthophorinae	*Anthophora*	Anthophorinae
Xeromelecta	Anthophorinae	*Anthophora*	Anthophorinae
Zacosmia	Anthophorinae	*Anthophora*	Anthophorinae
Ericrocis	Anthophorinae	*Anthophora*	Anthophorinae
		Centris	Anthophorinae
Psithyrus	Apinae*	*Bombus*	Apinae

* Anthophorinae and Apinae are subfamilies of Apidae.

Fig. 93. Genera and families of bees which are social parasites and the genera and families of their known host bees. (Adapted from Linsley.)

intricate in ecological relationships than their primeval prototypes. Basically the change in communities is simply an expression of the dynamic nature of their constituents. Species are dynamic systems of populations, changing with time. Because the community is an aggregation of variables, the relations between these variables will also change with time in proportion to the variables themselves. If one competitor becomes more successful than another, or a host becomes more resistant to a parasite, then their relationship within the community will change.

This dynamic quality of the community plus its diversity of relations makes its evolution difficult to analyse. Many of the problems are in a sense similar to those encountered when explaining the evolution of the species (Chapters 3 through 6), in which change in genetic composition is integrated with natural selection and all the while is coupled with species fission leading to an increase in the number of species. Thus, within the community many sets of changes may be occurring simultaneously, some types of change involving the whole community, others only parts of it.

The increase in taxonomic diversity and ecological intricacy found in modern communities is accompanied by changes in the processes of community evolution. The community reactions leading to coexistence and exploitation have been modified and, in at least some circumstances, form a self-perpetuating host-prey system. Selection pressures having their first roots in the community structure itself have led to new community relationships, exemplified by the differentiation of dominants and subdominants, the origin of mutualism, and the origin of protective devices and mimicry. These facets of community evolution are illustrated by the simplest type of community change, that is, the changes occurring in a community progressing through time in a geographic area that is relatively stable ecologically.

Indirect Competition

One of the basic considerations in a community is that the amount of nutrient material available limits the amount of living matter which can exist in a unit volume or area. The greater the number of species inhabiting that unit, the less average nutrient material is available per species. In the aggregation of species in communities many stratifications have evolved, each tending to divide in some manner this finite total amount of food among the species dependent on it. In time stratification, some species are active at one time and others later. Each uses the production of, or material available in a different period of the day or year. In other stratifications some species feed on different parts of the food supply. With a grass, fungi will feed inside its cells, some insects will feed on its pollen, others only on its leaves, others inside the stem, and mammals will eat the whole exposed plant. Similarly a host of predators may utilize different parts of one of the mammals, as do a great variety of intracellular, intra-organ, and external parasites, and larger vertebrate predators will eat the whole animal. Indirect competition has evolved in a remarkable number of peculiar instances, discussed at length by many authors as examples of adaptive radiation.

There is considerable weight of opinion for the belief that all indirect competition is the result of direct competition, as is illustrated in the case of two mites which feed on apple (Fig. 92). Data from other sources imply the same conclusion. Lack (1947) studied the Darwin finches of the Galapagos Islands and marshalled much evidence supporting the hypothesis that in these birds food specialization was correlated with an increase in number of species living together. Thus (Fig. 94) a species existing alone on one island may eat a fairly general diet, whereas on another island in company with a competing species, it may eat only a specialized part of the wider diet while competing species feed primarily on the other part. In the species of finch with the new, restricted feeding habits certain correlated structures have apparently changed also, notably the depth and strength of the beak.

Divergence of opinion exists concerning the mechanics of this specialization. Some believe that it takes place at the edges of the meeting ranges of the two species and progresses as the area of overlap enlarges (Brown and Wilson, 1956). These authors cite as evidence the characters and the ranges of the rock nuthatches *Sitta neumayer* and *S. tephronota,* illustrated by Vaurie (1950, 1951). In the region of overlap the beak proportions and head stripes of the two species are much more different than is the case in the non-overlapping parts of the range (Fig. 95). Brown and Wilson infer that this morphological change is correlated with food specialization brought about by a competitive relationship between the two species. An almost identical phenomenon was demonstrated by Blair (1955) concerning a displacement of characters associated with sexual behavior in the *Microhyla* frog species of Texas, as was explained in Chapter 7. It seems only reasonable that selection pressures could exert an analogous effect on feeding habits also.

In contrast, many potentially competing species already have sympatric ranges without any sign of food specialization. If competition later became acute, then theoretically it would lead to food specializations after the competing species had formed a more or less homogeneous competitive mixture. The specializations of the Galapagos finches surely began in this fashion because vagrants

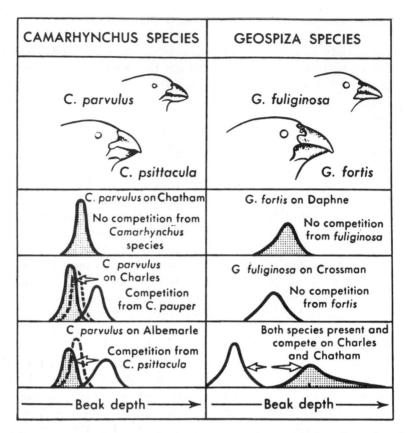

Fig. 94. Adaptive shifting of beak structure in the tree finches *Camarhynchus* and ground finches *Geospiza* of the Galapagos Islands. Competition between species has apparently led to changes in beak depth as indicated by the changes in modes on the different islands. (From Simpson, Pittendrigh, Tiffany, *Life: An Introduction to Biology,* Harcourt, Brace & World, 1957. Based, with permission, on data and figures in Lack, *Darwin's Finches,* Cambridge University Press, Cambridge, 1947.)

from one island to another had to build up coexisting populations of different species before competition would be generated and provide a basis for the operation of natural selection.

The prevalence of coexistence between potential competitors suggests that some food specializations may owe their evolution to non-competitive selection pressures. If non-competitive factors such as weather and predators were the chief pressures affecting natural selection, then any mutant specializations conferring advantages in relation to these ecological factors would be selected rigorously, much more so than specializations conferring competitive advantages. If, for example, a prey species appeared earlier or later in

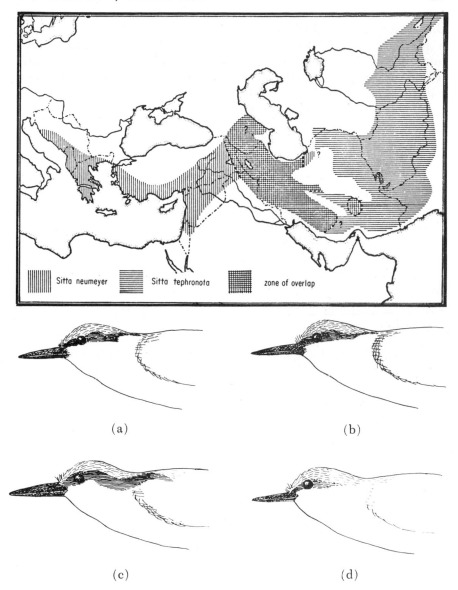

(a)

(b)

(c)

(d)

Fig. 95. Adaptive shifting of beak structure and head pattern in rock nuthatches of the genus *Sitta*. Above, ranges of the species *S. neumayer* and *S. tephronota* showing area of overlap. Below, heads and beaks of the same two species. (a) *S. tephronota* from Ferghana; (b) *S. neumayer* from Dalmatia; (c) and (d) *S. tephronota* and *S. neumayer,* respectively, from western Iran where they occur together. Note the beak similarity between the two species where they occur separately, and the much stouter beak in *S. tephronota* where they occur together. The same displacement of the dark stripe through the eye may be linked with sexual selection. (Above, after Vaurie; below, modified from Vaurie.)

the season, or bored deeper into a host, and in this way avoided a parasite, or predator, or an inimical climatic condition, then mutants bearing these changes would persist in the species and would bring about a specialization relating to food. From their nature alone it might be difficult to determine whether some of these changes had occurred because of non-competitive or competitive selection pressures.

The indeterminate nature of these observations is illustrated by studies of Broadhead and Thornton (1955) on a group of closely related psocid insects (Corrodentia) in an English forest. Three closely related species of *Elipsocus* inhabit the branches of several tree species; *E. westwoodi* and *E. hyalinus* feed only on algae, thus being in direct potential competition, whereas *E. mclachlani* may feed on algae but usually feeds on lichens, thus having only slight competitive relations with the other two. Although Broadhead and Thornton (see also Broadhead, 1958) found evidence that the populations were below a level which would bring about active competition, there is definite evidence of two points of specialization:

(1) *mclachlani,* the lichen feeder, has evolved a behavior pattern which actively chooses feeding sites where lichen is present, and

(2) *hyalinus* and *westwoodi,* the alga feeders, occur in markedly different densities on several tree species although presumably eating the same food (Fig. 96).

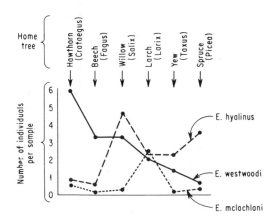

Fig. 96. Relative frequency of three species of *Elipsocus* on trees in Yorkshire. (Based on data from Broadhead and Thornton, 1955.)

There is a suggestion here that some selective action may be involved, producing the beginnings of a differential specialization in feeding sites between *hyalinus* and *westwoodi*. Also larch is the one tree species harboring these three potential competitors, and this suggests some sort of competitive interaction which might have been the basis for past selection pressures resulting in the evolution of *E. mclachlani* into a specialized lichen feeder. However, it is equally plausible that the lichen-feeding arose from spontaneous mutations that endowed ancestral *E. mclachlani* with the ability to digest lichens, that the lichen-feeding individuals reproduced in greater quantities than the others, and that they thus established selection pressures leading to an associated behavior pattern.

Direct Competition

In modern communities examples of direct competition are legion. In some cases the competition is passive, as in most plants, but in others competition is accompanied by combative actions. In Hawaii, for example, the Mediterranean fruit fly *Ceratitis capitata* is parasitized by four small hymenopterous wasps belonging to the genera *Opius* and *Tetrastichus*. All lay their eggs in the fly larvae. The newly hatched larvae of *Opius* have long, sharp mandibles. If more than one parasite egg (including an *Opius*) is laid in a fly larva, the *Opius* larvae thrash about and kill one another until only one is left. They usually kill most of the much smaller *Tetrastichus* larvae as well (Willard and Mason, 1937).

The elemental mechanisms of competitive balance and ecological oscillations probably account for many observed existing examples of direct competition. In many examples, circumstantial evidence certainly points to ecological oscillations. Of the six Illinois species of *Erythroneura* leafhoppers living in direct competition on the eastern sycamore *Platanus occidentalis*, *E. lawsoni* is the most abundant in most of the localities in Illinois, but in certain localities any one of four other species may predominate (Fig. 47). Further, the proportionate rankings of the six species may change on the same tree from year to year. In Illinois, temperatures fluctuate annually in a moderately uniform fashion over the whole state, but rainfall and humidity fluctuate greatly and in bizarre kaleidoscopic fashion from locality to locality in the same year (Fig. 97). This varying structure of the weather, correlated with slight physiological differences in the leafhopper species, could well explain the competitive coexistence of five of these six species.

Unrealized competition is another mechanism that comes into play with increased number of species and more complex food chains in modern communities. Andrewartha and Birch (1954)

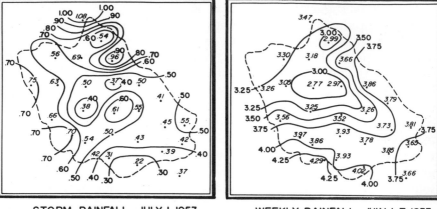

STORM RAINFALL, JULY 1, 1953   WEEKLY RAINFALL, JULY 1-7, 1953

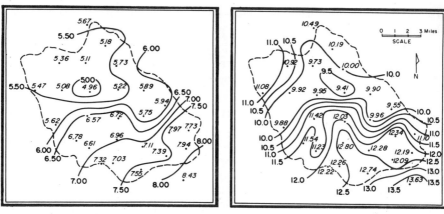

JULY 1953 RAINFALL   JUNE-AUG. 1953 RAINFALL

Fig. 97. Variation in rainfall on 100 square miles in Illinois during a day, week, month, and summer. Numbers in *italics* are rain measures at individual stations; numbers in arabic style are calculated isohyetal contours. (After Huff and Neill.)

explained at length their conviction that inimical weather plus the action of predators and parasites usually reduce populations of animals below the levels of competition for space and food. This thesis has an immediate application to communities.

Based on outbreak data concerning economic insects, Glen (1954) suggested as a general maxim that in a simple biotic system such as the few insect species found on a pure stand of an agricultural crop the crop-feeding insect species could increase to outbreak proportions readily and rapidly but that in a complex community this was not so likely to happen. The simple system would have few predator species which would depress the prey populations, but a complex community would have a large assemblage of pred-

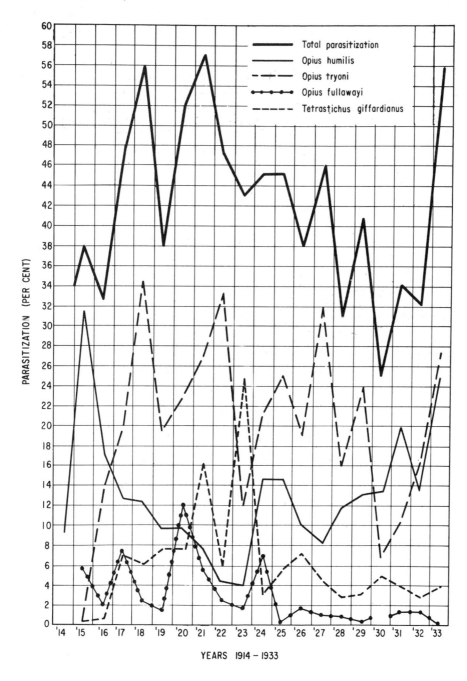

Fig. 98. Percentage of parasitization of the Mediterranean fruit fly in Hawaii from 1914 to 1933 by four parasites indicated on the chart. The total parasitization did not go below 24.9 per cent, or above 56.4 per cent. (Adapted from Willard and Mason.)

ators which collectively would maintain a steady depression of the prey species. In the parasites of the Mediterranean fruit fly in Hawaii, just discussed, the populations of each parasite varied greatly from 1915 to 1933, but the total parasitism (upper line) fluctuated much less (Fig. 98). It is highly likely that the population of the fruit fly would have periodically reached higher levels if it had been parasitized by only one species of wasp rather than by four. In contrast the observations of Burnett (1960) concerning population fluctuations of the white fly *Trialeurodes vaporariorum*, parasitized by a single species of wasp *Encarsia formosa*, indicate that even one parasite may, under special conditions, keep the prey species at low population levels for long periods of time.

A different dimension of the same principle is illustrated by other studies made in Hawaii on the parasitism of a tephritid gall fly *Procecidochares utilis* by three parasitic wasps. Bess and Haramoto (1959) found that the proportionate abundance of each parasitic species varied greatly in different vegetational and rainfall zones but that in each zone the total parasitism was remarkably similar (Fig. 99). This example indicates that multiple parasitism tends to equalize host densities along ecological gradients as well as in time.

Observed low population densities in natural habitats frequently bear out the absence, or at least apparent absence, of competition between coexisting species. At no time during the ten years of collecting for *Erythroneura* on sycamore in Illinois were trees found to be heavily infested with the leafhoppers. Of the six sycamore leafhopper species collected, five were predominant in at least some collections, but the sixth, *E. bella*, was never predominant (Ross, 1957). It seems probable that vicissitudes of weather, parasites, and predators normally deplete the populations of these leafhoppers to a point far below the competitive level, at least in some parts of the range, and that this has resulted in the long-term survival of a species of possibly lower competitive value, such as *E. bella*, in coexistence with the others.

Two maxims appear from these data concerning the coexistence of species in direct competition:

(1) If populations over the entire community range are habitually at levels producing inter-specific competition, coexistence will be possible only for species best adapted to some recurring variant of the ecological pattern of the community.

(2) If populations are habitually or locally below levels producing interspecific competition, any number of potentially but not actually competing species may coexist.

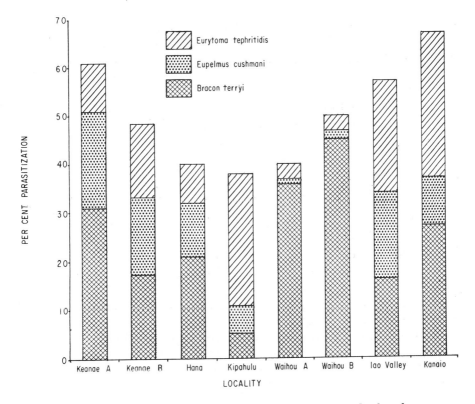

Fig. 99. Parasitization of the gall fly *Procecidochares utilis* by three parasites at different localities representing different ecological communities in Hawaii. (After Bess and Haramoto.)

Considering the dynamic aspects of population densities, especially the irregularity and ephemeral nature of unusually high densities (Fig. 50), it is highly likely that non-competitive conditions prevail in far more cases than now suspected. This mechanism may be the reason for the survival of many closely related phylogenetic lines for long periods of time as is the case in the insects, molluscs, and some other invertebrates.

THE COMPLEX PREDATOR-PREY SYSTEM

Increase in the number of prey species in the community makes it possible for more species of competing predators to coexist. Because each species has different ecological responses to a dynamic weather pattern, population oscillations of different prey species do not rise and fall synchronously. As a result, if one prey species is at a low ebb, another probably will be abundant, and the gross food supply for the predators may change only slightly. Thus in years when prey rodent populations are low, red foxes eat a larger proportion of insects (Scott and Klimstra, 1955).

Conversely, the larger the number of predator species of all categories, the more the prey populations are kept below the level of competition and the larger the number of prey species which can coexist.

These two reactions lead theoretically to the conclusion that an increase in number of species and in complexity of food chains automatically tends to perpetuate the host-prey complexity.

AGE OF HOST-PREDATOR RELATIONSHIPS

Many host-predator relationships are between extremely distantly related groups. In the marine Mollusca which feed on microorganisms, the predatory relationship may be extremely old and may perhaps trace back to a pre-Cambrian time when the ancestors of the Mollusca were closely related to the ancestors of the microorganisms. In other cases of distant relationship between host and prey the predatory relationship is not this old. In the case of insects feeding on plants, for example, the insects and the plants represent two specialized phylogenetic lines whose common ancestor was back in the far pre-Cambrian time, probably a billion years ago. The host-predator relationship between them represents a much more recent change in food habits on the part of the insects long after insects as such came into being. The cynipid gall wasps of the genus *Cynips* and allied genera make galls in plant tissues, but the ancestors of these wasps were parasites of other insects. After cynipids had evolved from other parasitic Hymenoptera, therefore, one line made the transfer of food habits from insect larvae to plant tissue, probably from a form parasitizing a leaf-mining or twig-boring insect. The plant-inhabiting Cynipidae comprise so many species, however, that the host transfer to plants must have occurred at least as long ago as earliest Cenozoic time or more probably in Mesozoic time.

The complex food chains in a modern biotic community therefore represent food relationships of various ages, ranging from very ancient to relatively recent changes in community relationships. Being a dynamic situation, similar changes are undoubtedly taking place now.

It is generally conceded that the predator species in any one feeding level (called a *trophic level*) can consume on the average only 15 to 20 per cent of the mass of the food species. This percentage, however, refers to total weight of predators in relation to total weight of prey. The number of species involved bears no relation to these weight proportions. A single species of mammal may be preyed upon by dozens of species of internal and external parasites, and 20 or 30 species of trees comprising a forest may be preyed upon by many hundred species of insects. The number of species involved is a function of the evolutionary rate of increase in number of species and of species survival in the individual taxonomic groups.

Dominants and Subdominants

After communities reached some critical stage of complexity, the members of the community became segregated into two classes: dominants and subdominants. In biotic communities some species or group of species produce special ecological conditions which, superimposed over the general climatic and edaphic conditions of the area, have a profound limiting effect on the occurrence of other species in the community. These influential species are known as dominants, and they often are the species at the base of many food chains of the community. The non-dominant species are called subdominants.

Examples of such dominants are common. In the temperate deciduous forests of eastern North America and other parts of the world, various aggregations of tall deciduous trees constitute the dominants of their respective communities. The dense summer shade of these trees superimposes a curious set of conditions on denizens of the community, increasing the humidity, decreasing temperature extremes, and reducing the sunlight materially for all organisms occurring within the canopy. In winter and spring, when the trees are without leaves, the sunlight within the tree cover is much greater. Many subdominant shrub and herb species of plants grow only under these conditions, for example members of the genera *Aesculus, Smilax, Trillium, Collinsia, Laportea,* and the woodland species of *Viola, Dentaria,* and *Cornus*. In their evolutionary history these plants have evidently become adapted to the understory conditions of the deciduous forests where they form a stratum of distinctive and competitive organisms and a base for extensive food chains. The situation holds for birds and other animals which may utilize trees for nesting sites or shelter.

In the humid coniferous forests such as those of northwestern North America, various species of evergreen conifers are the dominants. These forests modify the humidity, temperature, and sunlight conditions during the summer and continue to modify humidity and sunlight conditions during the winter. As a result of the year-round dense and continuous shade cast within the tree canopy, only a sparse understory subdominant biota exists except in small glades where a large tree has fallen and a shaft of sunlight reaches the ground. In other types of communities this highly modifying action of the dominant species is either less evident or less understood. This is especially so in grassland and aquatic communities. In grassland communities the dominant species are grasses and other herbs which bring about ecological influences concerned chiefly with the soil, involving extreme competition for water and the kind of soil cover available for other organisms. Here can grow only those plants which are hardy to sunlight throughout the year and which are able to compete in some way for space and water with the dominant species. Here also tree-nesting birds and mammals would be excluded.

In marine communities the system of dominant and subdominant species may be of an entirely different nature. All the communities have a common dependence on the currents and their load of plankton and other nutrient material. At least along the shore and on the bottom of relatively shallow seas, distinctive communities are indicated by assemblages of larger organisms. The dominant species in these assemblages or communities are those which first colonize the area and make it possible for other organisms to live there. For example, tube-making worms bind or overlay sandy or muddy substrates and form a firm anchoring area and in this way make possible the existence of other organisms which could not exist on the bare substrate. Above these bottom communities are free-swimming or floating aggregations of species which presumably have a community structure based chiefly on food chains. In these nektonic communities, the plankton could well be considered dominants. The situation in fresh water communities seems comparable.

The role of the dominant organisms in the community may be threefold: (1) they may be important in the food chains; (2) they may prevent the establishment of other types of dominants; and (3) they usually superimpose on the community special ecological conditions in addition to or modifying those of the general climate or substrate. It is possible that this third role has some expression in all communities, but more information is needed before reaching conclusions.

The dominant species themselves are dominant simply because they are the species best adapted to living in the area under the ecological conditions prevailing in the area, including not only conditions of the climate and substrate, but also of competition, predatism, and other biotic features of the community. However, because of the predominance and importance of dominants, many units of the community have a starkly real dependence on them. From an evolutionary standpoint the conditions superimposed by the dominants have been just as important in creating selection pressures as have been conditions due to other causes.

Mutualism

The many recorded cases of commensalism and symbiosis certainly arose in response to community relationships and hence followed the evolution of communities. The manner in which each instance of mutualism evolved is usually simple to deduce. Emerson (1949) has explained many examples.

An excellent example of mutualism is the combination of the flowering plants and the animals which pollinate them. Because of complementary and synchronous selection pressures, complex flowering structures evolved in plants simultaneously with specialized pollen- or nectar-feeding and flower-visiting habits in insects and certain vertebrates. The result is a mutualistic co-adaptation in which the plant benefits by being pollinated and the animal by having a source of food. Undoubtedly the pollination relationship started with a situation such as that found today in the sawflies. Adult sawflies may feed on leaf pubescence or on other insects, but all of them feed also on pollen. In the northern temperate regions, early season forms feed especially on pollen and nectar of *Alnus* and *Salix*, although the larvae of these sawfly species may feed on other plants. Although these plants are considered primarily as wind pollinated, there is no doubt that much pollination is accomplished by the feeding of the sawfly adults. It is a small step from this situation to one in which most of the pollination would be done by the insects, resulting in selection pressures which would favor any changes in the flower that would increase or insure visits of insects.

Many botanists (for example, Bessey, 1915; Hutchinson, 1926; Cronquist, 1951) point out that the evolution of different flower types has followed parallel lines in many entirely separate evolutionary lines of plants, including such developments as radial symmetry of petals, fusion of petals into a flower tube, insertion of stamens on the tube, and bilateral symmetry of flower such as orchids, snapdragons, and peas (Fig. 100, numbers 3, 8, and 14). Leppik (1956, 1957*a, b*) presents the interesting idea that these flower changes were correlated with the evolution of pattern and

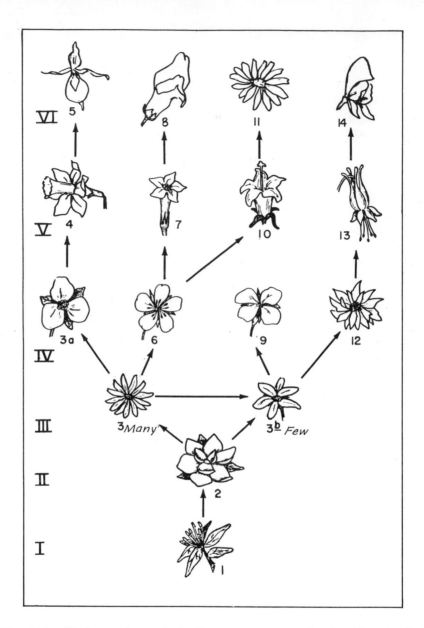

Fig. 100. Phylogenetic trends in flower patterns correlated with mutualistic evolution after insect pollination became established. Roman numerals indicate levels of general type of flower adaptation: I, amorphous; II, blobs of color; III, radial design; IV, differentiation of shapes within the radial design; V, evolution of specialized shapes; VI, evolution of specialized types including non-radial types (bilateral symmetry as in 5, 8, and 14) and return to an over-all radial design in heads containing many individual flowers (as in 11). Phylogenetic trends which can be assumed are indicated by arrows. (After Leppick.)

color discrimination in their insect pollinators, hence also the idea that in many parallel lines of plants changes at the same evolutionary level were occurring at the same time.

Among the insects, adults in each of several families of flies, moths, butterflies, and bees had concurrently become highly specialized for feeding on nectar and/or pollen of flowers. Following Leppik's theory, it is highly likely that many phylogenetic lines of plants and many phylogenetic lines of insects evolved mutualistic specializations at more or less the same rate because of their interdependent nature. This complex plexus of correlated evolutionary lines is a remarkable example of the action of selection pressures engendered because different kinds of organisms were living together. These are truly community selection pressures.

The intricacies of these community pressures can be realized more fully when one understands that most present-day communities contain many hundreds of species of flowering plants, representing all of Leppik's types plus many uniquely specialized species, and many hundreds of insect pollinators, representing all the major pollinating types. In whatever manner these different types of flowers and pollinators evolved, both primitive and specialized forms live together as a group of coexisting species in the same biotic community.

The two outstanding instances in which large wind-pollinated groups (the sedge-grass complex and the amentiferous dicotyledons) have arisen from insect pollinated ancestors surely are the product of the cessation of previous community selection pressures through a change in habit or habitat on the part of the plants. The amentiferous dicotyledons, exemplified by the oaks and beeches (Fagaceae) and birches (Betulaceae), bloom early. As blooming began to take place earlier and earlier, presumably fewer and fewer insects would be active, and, as a result, wind pollination became more effective than insect pollination. It is likely that progenitor species of grasses and sedges invaded areas having a small or insignificant biota so that insect pollination would have been less reliable than wind pollination. These events would explain the selection pressures leading to the loss of conspicuous floral parts which is presumed to have occurred in both groups (Lawrence, 1951; Tippo, 1938).

An interesting sequel is the reverse evolution which has taken place in the sedge *Dichromena ciliata*. A denizen of Central American forests, this sedge is now pollinated by insects, and in response to the selection pressures attendant to this situation the upper leaves below the fruiting body have become white and form a typical flowerlike structure (Fig. 101) (Leppik, 1955).

Fig. 101. The sedge *Dichromata ciliata* in which the leaves at the base of the flowering structure resemble a flower. (From Leppick.)

The "guests" of ants and termites include beetles, flies, mites, and other predators, but some of them undoubtedly classify as commensals or some type of symbiont (Emerson, 1949). The scavengers which feed on refuse in the nest (some of the flies and beetles) would classify as commensals. Some of the predators and parasites secrete exudates which the hosts lick from special body areas and, by contributing this much to the diet of the ants, may be considered some kind of a symbiont. It is easy to rationalize the evolution of these exudatory areas by the colony guest as a means of protection in the ant colony.

The echeneid fishes (*Remora* and its allies) which attach to sharks and other fish by means of a sucker-like disc on the echeneid's head are another excellent example of mutualism. Some echeneids feed on zooplankton and smaller fishes; they may attach themselves to sharks and other fish merely to rest or to be transported to new feeding grounds. A second group of echeneids feed chiefly on scraps from their host's meals and the host's feces. A third group, especially *Remoropsis pallidus*, feeds almost entirely on ectoparasites or sea lice which the echeneids scrape from the skin of the host. These three stages represent an evolution in habits from commensalism in which only the echeneids benefit, to symbiosis in which both the echeneid and its host benefit (Strasburg, 1959).

The mutualistic cleaning activities of *Remoropsis* are examples of a highly developed symbiosis which may be an established working relationship in every coastal marine community. Limbaugh (1961) and others have shown that at least the young of many species of smaller fishes and a number of small, slender shrimps habitually clean a large assortment of larger fishes. The cleaners remove and eat external parasites, wound tissue, and bacterial and fungus growths from the fishes which are groomed. That this relationship is not a casual one is demonstrated by the specializations in behavior and structure which have evolved in connection with cleaning symbiosis. The cleaners usually have bright colors and patterns which contrast with their background, man set stations, and often go through conspicuous acrobatic displays. They have pointed snouts and tweezer-like teeth, ideal for the cleaning habit. The fish which are cleaned habitually visit the same spot, often daily, and assume ungainly but docile attitudes when being cleaned. In tropical waters the cleaners enjoy almost complete immunity from predation by the species they clean; in temperate waters the cleaners may be eaten by their clientele. Limbaugh pointed out that this cleaning symbiosis may represent a relationship having a profound influence on the species composition and population structure of at least the fish component of all coastal marine communities.

All of these mutualistic relationships arose only because of the mixture of species in the same community and are therefore definitely part of community evolution.

Protective Devices

A conspicuous characteristic of a community is the phenomenon of protective devices. These include disagreeable secretions, distasteful substances, malodors, nettling hairs, thorns, and other devices in both plants and animals, and protective form or coloration, warning coloration, and mimicry in animals. These characteristics confer on their possessors some protection from predation, hence selection pressures leading to their evolution would follow immediately in the footsteps of the evolution of food chains. It is therefore likely that this aspect of community evolution began in simple aggregations of species, in fact as soon as one group of organisms began feeding on another.

Certain types of protective devices must have followed others. The secretion of disagreeable substances must have preceded and established selection pressures for the differential survival of conspicuously marked mutants, which would be the forerunner of warning coloration. Only when warning colors had evolved in some species would selection pressures have been set up for other species to evolve patterns mimicking these protective schemes (Fig. 102). Likewise no selection pressures would have existed leading to the evolution of stick-like or leaf-like animals until sticks and leaves themselves had evolved.

It seems certain, therefore, that not only did selection pressures

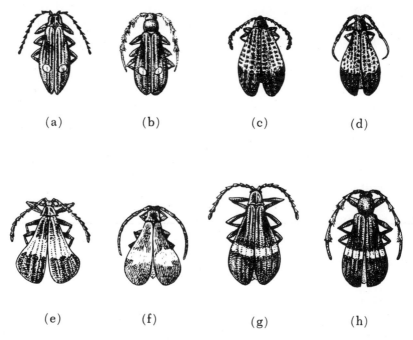

(a)   (b)   (c)   (d)

(e)   (f)   (g)   (h)

Fig. 102. Warning coloration and mimicry in Neotropical insects. In each of these four pairs of insects the species to the left is a distasteful lycid beetle exhibiting warning coloration, and the species to the right is a cerambycid beetle mimicking a lycid species living in the same community. Lycidae: (a), (c), (e), (g), *Calopteron* species. Cerambycidae: (b), (h), *Pteroplatus* species. (d) *Lycidola.* (f) *Lycomimus.* (After Linsley.)

favoring protective devices arise early in community evolution but also that these pressures led to a wider and more varied expression of protective devices as communities became more complex.

CHANGE IN SPECIES COMPOSITION

As the community progresses through time, even in a static geographic situation, its species composition changes, either by subtraction or addition. These changes in turn affect the ecological complexity of the community and the evolutionary selection pressures acting within the community.

Extinction

From both the historical and fossil record we know that certain species once living are now extinct, but in many cases we know little about the reasons or mechanism of the extinction. Great numbers of plants and animals known only from fossils have perished through the eons (Fig. 89). The Labrador duck *Campto rhynchus labradorius* is one species which seems to have become extinct recently without the influence of man. However, the great majority of known species which have become extinct recently owe their demise to man's activities, usually either by his reducing the area of the habitat below that required by the species, as in the possible extinction of the ivory-billed woodpecker *Campephilus principalis* of southeastern North America, or by his introducing competitors or predators, as with the dodo *Didus ineptus* of Mauritius. It seems safe to speculate that under natural conditions the number of established species in a community suffers only small or infrequent reductions due to extinction.

Increase in Number of Species

Although range fission may be the most important single factor leading to an increase in the number of species, an increase can and probably does occur in a community which is relatively static geographically. The following mechanisms, most of them explained in the preceding chapter, contribute to this increase.

COLONIZATION THROUGH DISPERSAL FROM
A SIMILAR BUT DISTANT COMMUNITY

Thus the present West Indian fauna of over 50 species of the leafhopper genus *Empoasca* undoubtedly reached the Antilles chiefly by overwater dispersal from South and Central America, and some of the same species may have spread from the West Indies to become established in southern Florida (Caldwell and Martorell, 1952; Ross, 1959c). In many instances of this kind, including both plants and animals, vagrant species new to the community may be close relatives to and competitors with established species. Emerson (1949) points out that myriads of dispersals never become established in the community because, for one reason or another, the latter is unsuited ecologically to the vagrant. However, if the vagrant does have ecological tolerances which suit it to the community it reaches, then the species stands a good chance of becoming established. One of the best examples of this is the establishment of northern European beetles accidentally introduced into Canada (Lindroth, 1957).

EXTENSION OF ECOLOGICAL TOLERANCE
IN NEIGHBORING SPECIES

It seems inevitable that chance mutations or other genetic changes would occasionally fit a species living in one community to extend its range into a neighboring one. In the caddisfly genus *Triaenodes* the more primitive members of certain lines are members of small stream communities, but one species, *T. tarda*, has become adapted to lakes also and is now a common member of northern lake communities (Ross, 1959b). Another species in the same genus, *Triaenodes injusta*, has also become almost completely restricted to lakes (Ross, 1959a). In each instance a species. of *Triaenodes* successfully extended its range from one distinctive aquatic community to another. A striking example involving a climatic shift is found in the mosquito genus *Aedes*. Its subgenus *Aedimorphus* contains 94 species which occur only in tropical and subtropical communities, and a single species, *A. vexans*, which has become adapted to temperate and boreal situations and is an abundant Holarctic component of many northern communities (Stone, Knight, and Starcke, 1959). The hybrid population of *Amaranthus* in the San Joaquin delta in California studied by Tucker and Sauer (1958) is one of many examples in plants in which a hybrid population has arisen and successfully colonized an adjacent community different from those communities inhabited by the parental forms.

The Old World grasses of the *Dicanthium annulatum* complex afford another interesting example of species wandering due to genetic change (Fig. 103) (Celarier, Mehra, and Wulf, 1958). Present forms of this complex apparently began as a diploid species in India. This species presumably hybridized with a closely related

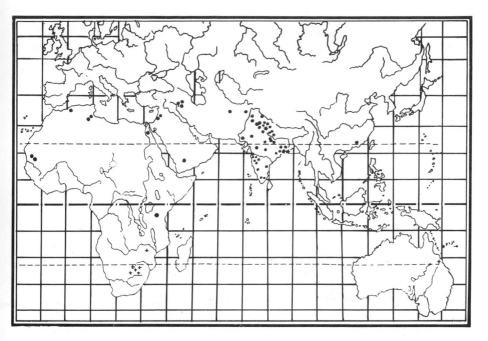

Fig. 103. Geographic distribution of the polyploid races of the *Dicanthium annulatum* grass complex. Stars indicate diploids (thought to represent the ancestral home in and near India); circles indicate tetraploids; and "plus" signs indicate hexaploids. (From Celarier, Mehra, and Wulf.)

one, and the hybrid in turn gave rise to a tetraploid species strongly resembling the diploid. The tetraploid, however, spread far beyond the range of the diploid and eventually colonized practically the entire Old World tropics from China to central Africa. On the southern edge of its range in Africa the tetraploid apparently hybridized with another species (possibly the related South African *D. aristatum*). From this union a hexaploid species arose which now has a range in South Africa to the south of the tetraploid species. Thus through hybridization and polyploidy a species with a small range has given rise to a series of polyploids that have dispersed into and colonized a large area and undoubtedly a goodly number of different ecological communities.

SYMPATRIC ORIGIN OF NEW SPECIES

As was mentioned in the preceding chapter, new species may arise by various mechanisms other than geographic isolation: polyploidy in certain plants and a few animals, host transfer mechanisms in the case of host-specific species, displacement of seasonal timing in species having rigidly cyclic life histories, and perhaps certain results following hybridization. That these new species may be a potent factor in the community ecology is well illustrated in eastern North America by the *Erythroneura* leafhoppers. Four species of this genus are the only serious etiolating insects on the honey locust *Gleditsia triacanthos,* an important tree of the forest edge community. They constitute a monophyletic cluster whose ancestor must have become established on *Gleditsia* by a host transfer from some other host. *Ilex decidua,* an important shrub of the floodplain community, likewise is etiolated chiefly by three or four species of *Erythroneura,* but each of these undoubtedly resulted from separate transfers from some other host (Ross, 1953).

In the plants polyploidy may also give rise to small species flocks living and competing in the same community, but more frequently the new polyploid species occur in different communities or at most overlap only slightly with the parental types (Manton, 1950).

This brief summary directs attention to the fact that, even while members of a community are evolving ecological specialization because the community is already a complex mixture of species, the number of species in the community is continually increasing, thus creating greater taxonomic complexity with its attendant changes in many types of selection pressures.

SUMMARY

The material outlined in this chapter depicts the probable events which take place when geomorphic changes bring about the congregation of species. From the first mixing of these different organisms, selection pressures of various types resulted automatically, and these pressures led inexorably to various interspecific relationships typical of present-day communities, including food chains, food and habitat specializations, mutualism, and protective devices. These interrelationships become more intricate as the communities become more complex. The species composition of the community may increase in a limited number of ways while the community remains geographically intact, thus generating additional complexity.

The increase in the complexity of interspecific relationships, especially those leading to an elaboration of food chains, leads to a community structure which is largely dependent on the dominant species of the community and which tends to perpetuate its taxonomic diversity.

Origin of Biomes

and Succession

9

The relatively simple community considered in the preceding chapter to explain the evolution of basic community relationships is only a small unit in comparison with the many diverse communities of the biotic world. The transition from one to many communities appears to have occurred chiefly by the processes of alternate community division and reunion, brought about by geologic and climatic change (together comprising geomorphic change) and accompanied by simultaneous species fission.

The normal action of geomorphic change would produce such results. If a new arm of the sea, a drastic change in climate, or some similar happening divides a uniform ecological area, it will split the range of the whole community and all the species restricted to it. Each such division therefore sets the stage for the formation of new daughter communities differing in that they have many, perhaps hun-

243

dreds of different but closely related species. That such events have happened in the past can be demonstrated by comparing geologic maps for successive times (Fig. 104).

Present-day communities give abundant evidence of community fission. The biotas of central Florida and of south central Texas have

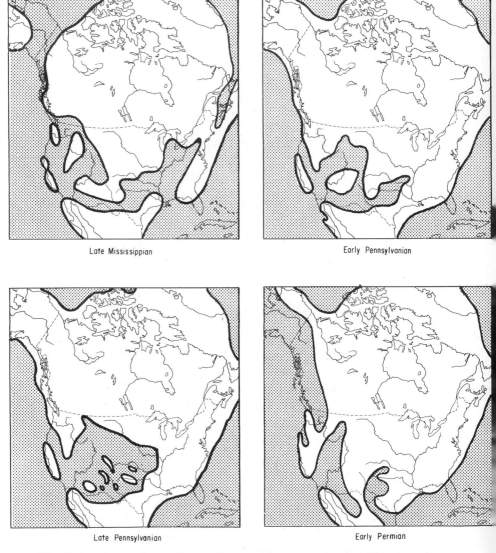

Late Mississippian

Early Pennsylvanian

Late Pennsylvanian

Early Permian

Fig. 104. Successive paleographic maps of North America showing alternate fission and reunion of both terrestrial and marine community sites. (Adapted from Dunbar, *Historical Geology*, 2nd. Ed., John Wiley & Sons, 1960.)

so many elements in common that the two areas certainly represent a community which was split by Pleistocene events (Fig. 105)

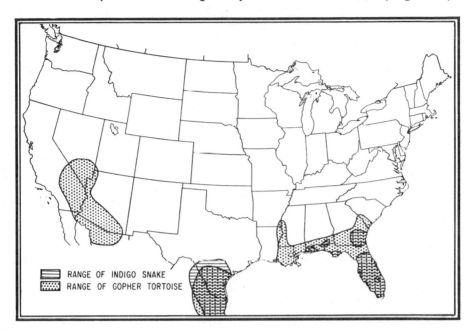

Fig. 105. Range of the indigo snake *Drymarchon corais* and of the gopher tortoises *Gopherus polyphemus* in the East, *G. berlandieri* in Texas and eastern Mexico, and *G. agassizi* in the West. (After Conant and Blair.)

(Neill, 1957). A division producing such community fragments would have followed the southern movement of a community formerly continuous to the north of the present fragmented ranges. A community movement of this type has been demonstrated for five lizards which now occur together some distance south of the locality in which all five lived together during the warmer Sangamon interglacial period of the Pleistocene (Fig. 106) (Etheridge, 1958).

The occurrence of closely related species in physically similar communities on either side of Central America attests to the former continuity of these marine areas before the elevation during Pliocene time of the Central American land barrier which now separates them. To cite only a few examples, Walton (1950) recorded the marine crayfish *Parapylocheles glasselli* from the Pacific waters of Mexico and its close relative *P. scorpio* from the Caribbean Sea; and another marine crayfish *Xylopagurus cancellarius* from the Pacific waters of Colombia and its close relative *X. rectus* only from

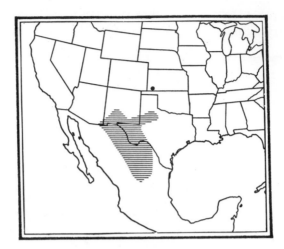

Fig. 106. The region (shaded area) where the five reptiles *Crotaphytus collaris, Hollbrookia texana, Phrynosoma cornatum, Phrynosoma modestum,* and *Eumeces obsoletus* now occur together. The black dot indicates where the five occurred together during the Sangamon interglacial period of the Pleistocene, the location of the Cragin Quarry beds. (After Etheridge.)

the Caribbean. Chace (1958) described a squillid crustacean *Lysiosquilla grayi* from the western Atlantic, which he thought most closely related to *L. decemspinosa,* a species occurring in similar habitats only in the Pacific waters of Peru and Costa Rica. According to Morrison (1959) at least five genera of tropical or subtropical salt marsh snails include pairs of very closely related species, one on the west Atlantic and one on the east Pacific shores of the Americas, indicating that the rise of Central America divided not only the aqueous marine communities existing between North and South America, but the beach and salt marsh communities also. Hopkins (1959) pointed out evidence in Mollusca indicating past divisions of marine communities in the Bering Sea region.

Geomorphic action leads to reunion as well as division of communities, as is shown in Fig. 104. Also biotas can move in more than one direction. In contrast to the lizard example in Fig. 106, collections of fossil fish found in an Oklahoma deposit of probably Illinoian (mid-Pleistocene) age contain an aggregation of species which now occur together only considerably north and east of the fossil locality (Fig. 107) (Smith, 1954). Alternating community movements are reflected in the mixtures of closely related species now living within the same area. The forest-floor inhabiting milliped genus *Brachoria* (Fig. 108) is especially suggestive of such a history,

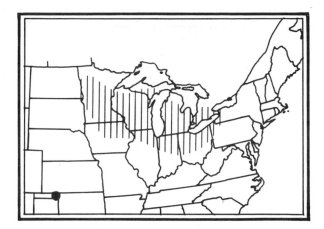

Fig. 107. The region (shaded area) where twelve fishes of the Berends Pleistocene fauna now occur together. The black dot indicates where these species occurred together during an earlier and presumably cooler period of the Pleistocene. (From C. L. Smith.)

having 25 species all confined to a small part of the climax deciduous forests of eastern North America (Keeton, 1959; Hoffman, 1959). In this forest occur many genera of trees, each having a number of closely related sympatric species, suggestive of past community divisions and fusions. Corroborating evidence is found in many groups of aquatic organisms which are restricted to streams within the eastern deciduous forest or its northern ecotone areas. The stone-fly genus *Allocapnia* contains about 15 sympatric species (Frison, 1935, 1942; Ricker, 1952), and the caddisfly genera *Pycnopsyche, Neophylax, Hydropsyche,* and many others contain comparable numbers (Ross, 1944; Betten, 1950). The sympatric eucalyptus tree species of eastern Australia suggest successive community splitting and fusing, as do the many closely related sympatric species of caddisflies occurring in the same region (Mosely and Kimmins, 1953).

Every community fission would not result in the fission of all its contained species. As was pointed out in Chapter 7, a complex of factors influences the rate of change between isolated populations. We would therefore expect that if the divided parts of the community reunited, some of the original phylogenetic lines would have evolved into separate daughter species; others would not. This circumstance seems to explain the fact that, in the temperate deciduous forest of eastern North America, the sycamore genus *Platanus* contains only a single species, but the monophyletic cluster of *Ery-*

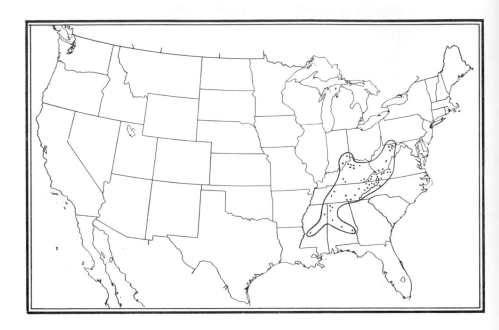

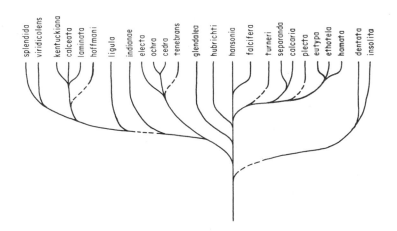

Fig. 108. Total known localities and range of the milliped genus *Brachoria*. Within this small area occur twenty-five species, many of them sympatric, which evidently evolved within this small area. Above is shown the range of *Brachoria* and below is shown the phylogenetic history of this geographically restricted evolutionary development. (Modified from Keeton.)

throneura leafhoppers feeding on *Platanus* has six species (Ross, 1957). Similarly in the same forest the tree genus *Gleditsia* contains only a single species which is host to another monophyletic cluster of four species of *Erythroneura* leafhoppers.

In contrast, the eastern Nearctic species of the sawfly genus *Neodiprion* are more nearly equal in number to the species of their host genus *Pinus*, perhaps indicating a more nearly comparable increase in number of species of insect and host.

At various times changes involving only slight ecological magnitude undoubtedly fragmented the range of only a portion of the species in the community. Different species have inherent differences in ecological tolerence. For this reason, it is quite within reason to suppose that climatic changes of only a small magnitude which might occur across the range of a community would effectively split the range of only those species with certain narrow limits to their ecological tolerance. However, the same change would have no such dividing effect on species having wide ecological tolerances. Figure 109 depicts hypothetically the effect of a small change

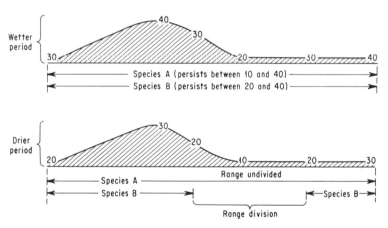

Fig. 109. Differential effect of assumed changes in rainfall on the contiguity of two hypothetical species differing in rainfall requirements. Note that in the assumed drier period (below) the range of Species A remains intact; that of Species B is divided.

in rainfall on two species, one having a narrow and the other a wide tolerance for this factor. The indicated change in rainfall divides the range of the species having the narrower tolerance but not that of the other.

These examples are the results of two mechanisms acting independently and bringing about an unequal increase in the number of species in different phylogenetic lines within a community. The mechanism based on rate of genetic change would bring about a disproportionate increase in the number of species in lines which changed rapidly. The mechanism based on breadth of ecological tolerance would bring about a disproportionate increase in the number of species having narrower ecological tolerances.

EVOLUTION FROM COMMUNITY TO BIOME

As the process of community splitting and fusing continues, more and more species are mixed or at least brought into contact. This action increases the possibilities for additional sympatric species fission through host-transfer mechanisms, hybridization, and subsequent allopolyploidy. It also adds more complexities to the predator-prey and competitive relationships. It seems highly unlikely that this mixing of species would result in a simple addition of the two sets of species because in certain of the highly competitive groups some species would surely become extinct. Simpson (1947, 1950) expressed the opinion that in the mammals the extinction following faunal interchange is considerable. It seems likely that if this high rate of extinction does occur in the mammals, it may be associated with relatively large absolute size, combative habits, and the behavior pattern called territoriality because evidence from many insect groups agrees better with the concept of a remarkably small degree of extinction following a mixing of species (Ross, 1957).

Such extinction as does occur following faunal mixing is usually attributed to competition for food or living space or to changes in the available physical environment which exceed changes in ecological tolerances made by the species. Breeding habits are another factor which may lead to extinction. If two species come together which are genetically incompatible but not sexually isolated from each other, one of them might be obliterated from progressive areas of range overlap. This is happening in the case of two European hares, *Lepus timidus* and *L. europeus,* whose ranges abut. *L. timidus* is a montane and northern species and *L. europeus* is a more widespread lowland form. When the latter was introduced into the northern range of *L. timidus* in Sweden, *L. europeus* became established there and eliminated the local population of *L. timidus*. The mechanism for this elimination was discovered experimentally by Notini (1941, 1948), who found that the two species cross-mate freely but the hybrids are sterile. Because the mating season of *L.*

europeus starts earlier than that of *L. timidus,* it seems probable that, as *L. europeus* spreads into the range of *L. timidus,* more females of the latter would be cross-mated and hence leave no productive progeny. In this way the gradual range extension of *L. europeus* is causing a progressive extinction of *L. timidus* (Udvardy, 1951).

From the standpoint of community evolution, the most far-reaching effects of community mixing are the resulting patterns of distribution and abundance of community dominants. Dominant species producing communities of different types (such as forest versus grasslands) may outcompete each other in different areas, or dominant species producing communities of the same type may predominate in different local or regional areas. Examples of these patterns have been illustrated in detail for many plant communities.

Local predominance of dominant species is illustrated in studies of 56 hill prairies in Illinois containing over 40 species of grasses. Evers (1955) found that the dominant plants were tall grasses of the genera *Andropogon, Bouteloua,* and *Sorgastrum. Andropogon scoparius* was predominant in all but a few prairies; *Bouteloua curtipendula* was predominant only in part of one prairie although it grew in 47 others; *Andropogon gerardii* was predominant in scattered patches of several prairies and grew in a total of 37; and *Sorgastrum nutans* was predominant in two prairies and grew in 21 others. The interesting point in these figures is that although in almost every instance one species of grass predominated in a particular prairie, this species never excluded all other grasses, and in many instances the two most abundant species approached numerical equality.

An example of the regional predominance of different dominant species occurs in the forests of Ohio. Sears (*in* Shelford, 1926) (Fig. 110) indicated that five major combinations of dominants, all deciduous hardwood trees, form an intermingled, crazy-quilt pattern over the state. Similar patterns of local differences in dominants have been given by many authors.

The total ranges of the important dominants mentioned by Sears and of a few hardwood dominants in adjacent areas (Fig. 111) show that species which predominate in certain areas normally occur as less numerous members of the dominant class far beyond where they comprise the bulk of the vegetation.

Whittaker (1956), analysing the forests of the Great Smoky Mountains of Tennessee and North Carolina, emphasized the fact

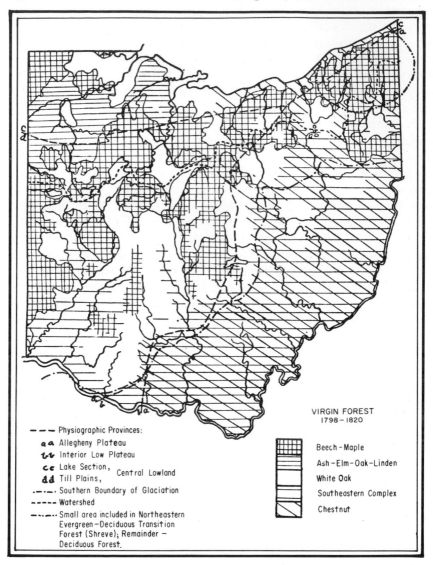

Fig. 110.   Five combinations of dominant deciduous trees in Ohio. (After Sears *in* Shelford.)

that different species of trees form a continuum over the surface, one combination gradually merging into the next (Fig. 112) (see also McIntosh, 1958). In Whittaker's examples the distances between diverse combinations are short because the area is mountainous and contains extreme ecological types in close proximity. If this same type of intergradation were stretched out over flatter

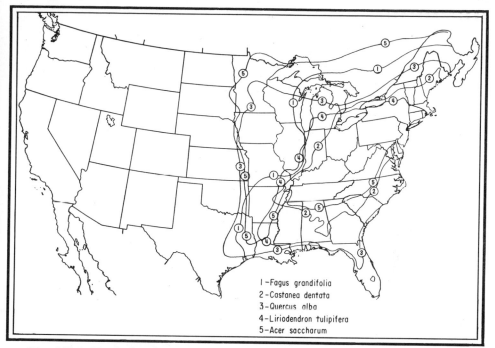

Fig. 111. Total distribution of five of the species of hardwood deciduous trees which are dominant species in smaller areas within their total range. (Modified from Munns.)

terrain, it would undoubtedly produce the conditions found in the transect across the Ohio forests mapped by Sears.

These interlocking and overlapping aggregations of species described by Whittaker undoubtedly arose from a process of splitting and amalgamation which originated from a fairly simple community. The result, however, no longer comes within the definition of a community as "a relatively uniform area biologically." In Fig. 112, the combination at station 1 is a mixed *Tsuga-Tilia* forest; stations 2 and 5 are mixed *Tsuga-Tilia-Acer* forest; stations 3 and 4 are chiefly evergreen coniferous forest with *Tsuga* the chief dominant; stations 6 to 10 are deciduous hardwood forest with *Quercus borealis, Acer* or *Acer-Quercus alba* as the principal dominants; and stations 11 and 12 are again evergreen coniferous forest with *Pinus* species as dominants.

Of the deciduous stations 6 to 10, each has a distinctive feature. Station 6 is predominantly the black oak *Quercus borealis* with only a scattering of many other kinds of trees; station 7 is just as predominantly the red maple *Acer rubrum;* and station 9 is a mixture

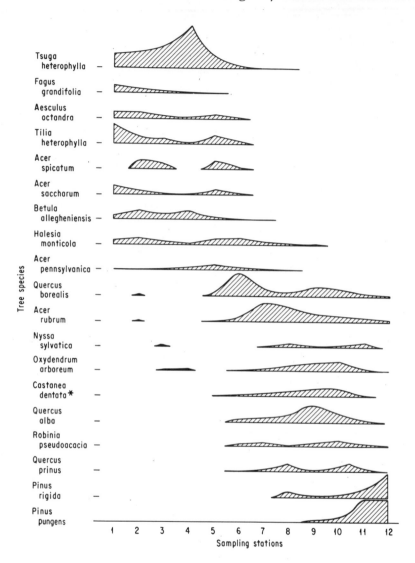

Fig. 112. Histograms showing the relative abundance of the more important trees in the forest communities of the Great Smokey Mountains. * This species now absent from area. (Adapted from Whittaker.)

of these two dominants plus an even more abundant third dominant, the white oak *Quercus alba.* Stations 8 and 10 are more nearly equal mixtures of five or six species. If the condition in any one station covered a considerable area, it would be identifiable as a forest type comparable to one of those plotted in Fig. 110. Each of these conditions is one of the "relatively uniform areas" which are usually called communities. In Fig. 112 each station represents a different community.

The whole spectrum of Fig. 112 exemplifies the concept of biomes as landscape aspect areas and as ecological units. This series of stations contains radically different vegetational types: (1) the extremely dense evergreen coniferous forest dominated by hemlock (*Tsuga*), (2) the relatively open evergreen forest dominated by the two species of *Pinus,* and (3) the deciduous forest with its dense summer shade when the trees are in leaf and sparse winter shade when the trees are without leaves. In each of these three types the dominants superimpose different ecological conditions over the general climatic and edaphic characteristics of the area and between each type a corresponding difference exists in the ground biota and other subdominant elements of the community. Each of these major types is a *biome.* As Fig. 112 shows also, the distinctive biomes merge gradually from one into another, the intermediate areas being called *ecotones.* Although in mountainous regions a small area frequently contains several biomes in close proximity, in more level country each biome tends to be an extensive area. Thus, as a rule, the more level the country, the fewer and more extensive are the biomes, and, by the same token, the wider are the ecotone areas.

Adjoining biomes may be much more sharply separated than is the case of the biomes just described from the Great Smoky Mountains. Sharp separation is illustrated by the biomes of the Kaibab Plateau in Arizona. Rasmussen (1941) described the piñon pine-juniper biome as occurring between about 5,500 to 6,500 feet elevation, the Rocky Mountain yellow pine biome between about 6,500 to 8,200 feet, and the fir-spruce biome between 8,200 to the summit, 9,200 feet. A chart of the dominant species (Fig. 113) emphasizes the relatively small overlap between the three biomes.

The biomes described by Whittaker and Rasmussen are each adapted to different climatic conditions involving temperature, humidity, and rainfall. The correlation of these with altitude is due to the rapid changes of the climatic factors with changes in elevation. In some cases edaphic factors may be the agents separating biomes. An excellent example from the Sonoran desert of Arizona is described by Yang and Lowe (1956). The two distinctive biomes in the area occur under an identical macroclimate, but the palo verde-sahuaro (*Cercidium-Cereus*) biome grows in the lighter and more rocky soils on the upper parts of the slopes, and the creosote

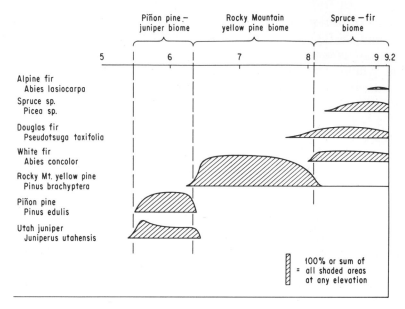

Fig. 113. Histograms showing the relative abundance of the dominant tree species in the Kaibab National Forest, Arizona. Numbers refer to elevation in thousands of feet. (Adapted from Rasmussen.)

bush-bur sage (*Larrea-Franseria*) biome grows on the finer soil which has washed to the foot of the lower slopes and valleys. Yang and Lowe point out that water content and availability are remarkably different in the two types of soil and that these differences are probably the basic reasons for the differences in vegetation.

In the subdivisions within the biome (the *associations* of Shelford) the abundant dominants are different species, but in each subdivision the set of dominants superimposes essentially the same modifications on the general environment. The biome may therefore contain several communities differing in specific rather than general properties.

Distinctive terrestrial biomes and their constituent communities are therefore chance units based on the competitive superiority of certain types of plants and the effect which the resulting dominant plant species have in modifying the general ecological conditions within the area of their dominance.

As is evident from the analyses of Moore (1958) and Hedgpeth (1957), the bottom marine communities may be and have been classified along much the same lines as terrestrial communities.

Comparable community aggregations undoubtedly exist in the water layers, but perhaps because of a lack of data no consensus of opinion has been reached as to how these communities should be delineated or what basis should be used in their delineation.

This situation is not surprising. Any system of communities is the result of historic evolutionary processes superimposed on environmental gradients. Because the ecological gradients are different on land, on the ocean bottom, and in the sea, it is entirely conceivable that in each of these realms quite different criteria will eventually be used for community segregation and delineation.

EVOLUTION WITHIN THE BIOME

Considering biomes in the northern temperate regions, especially the grassland, deciduous forest, and evergreen coniferous forest biomes, one might be led to believe that the evolution of biomes was associated with the evolution of taxonomic units of plants such as the grasses and conifers. This is far from the case. The dominant vegetation growing under the same ecological conditions may produce essentially the same tempering of the basic ecology for a very long span of geologic time, but the taxonomic composition of the vegetation may change radically and frequently. Thus vegetation that can be described as a luxuriant evergreen tropical rain forest has been in existence since Devonian time, but the kinds of trees comprising it have changed many times. Comparing fossil floras far-distant in time which we believe occupied essentially the same ecological situation, we see that the community dominants and therefore the communities themselves were quite different taxonomically at these various times.

In Devonian and Mississippian times, the equivalent of the present-day evergreen tropical rain forest included as its dominants chiefly tree ferns, scale trees, and pteridosperms. In the Mesozoic there was another combination of dominants in the tropical rain forests: tree ferns, cycads, and conifers. The present-day tropical rain forests lack scale trees and pteridosperms and have only rare cycads; the tree ferns are abundant only locally; their dominant species are chiefly angiosperms.

The changes occurred gradually through time, for some cycads occurred in Paleozoic forests, and remnants of these and the tree ferns still persist as minor elements of present-day forests. If we had a continuous record of one of these "community columns" moving through time, we would undoubtedly find it impossible to draw any sharp line at points where one community ended and another began. Each major type would merge gradually into the next. These types would be definable as associations comparable to those existing side by side today.

These transects through time might not correspond to actual borings "through time" made in pollen profiles or well drillings. The latter may cut through sections of many different biomes, such as marine versus terrestrial types or tundra versus deciduous forest, because the ranges of the biomes moved in unison with their necessary ecological conditions.

Although having a short life in relation to that of the biome, individual sets of communities or associations may exist for many millions of years. In his review of the fossil flora of the West Indies, Hollick (1924) showed that the generic elements of the early and middle Cenozoic floras are identical with those of the present. Furthermore, in genus after genus the Cenozoic species appear to be identical with or remarkably similar to existing Neotropical species occurring in the West Indies and adjacent Central and South America. Hollick concluded that the present northern Neotropical evergreen rain forest has continued with only minor changes in species composition since early in the Cenozoic.

These records show that, since land floras became well established, large evergeen trees of some sort have dominated uninterruptedly tropical land areas of low elevation having abundant available moisture throughout the year. In an ecological sense conditions beneath this tree canopy have therefore changed little if at all since mid-Paleozoic. To subdominant organisms living in the understory portion of the community it would not matter whether tree ferns, cycads, conifers, or angiosperms were the agents producing the shade. In the present-day Brazilian evergreen rain forest this principle is well illustrated by the bromeliad epiphytes and by the mosquitoes living in the water which collects in bromeliad leaf axils. Veloso *et al.* (1956) showed that each species of bromeliads is dependent not on specific tree species but on physical conditions of light and humidity, which in turn are determined by distance from the ground. Production and distribution of bromeliad-inhabiting mosquito species are not related to the species of bromeliads but to the water-holding capacity of the bromeliads, the level of bromeliad occurrence, and density of suitable bromeliads in a unit area of forest. Thus two levels of subdominants, the bromeliads and the mosquitoes, are dependent, not on the taxonomic composition of the forest, but on the physical conditions superimposed on the area by the dominant trees. The large number of both bromeliad and mosquito genera and species occurring in and restricted to this biome is testimony of the long evolutionary persistence of the physical environmental conditions necessary for their existence.

It is possible that the understory club mosses in the present-day tropical rain forests have had an even longer unbroken history in their ecological situation. Species of *Lycopodium* may trace back both phylogenetically and ecologically to their possible progenitor *Lycopodites*, a fossil genus associated with tropical rain forests of Pennsylvanian age. If so, the club moss component of the understory has evolved little, even though in a taxonomic sense the dominant tree species have changed radically many times.

Certain understory herbs of the northern boreal coniferous forest illustrate the independence of dominant and subdominant species in a geographic transect as opposed to a time transect. In the Sierra Nevada mountains of western North America this forest comprises the red fir association overwhelmingly dominated by red fir *Abies magnifica* and having small percentages of four other large dominant trees, *Pinus monticola* and *contorta*, *Abies concolor*, and *Tsuga mertensiana*, in almost every stand (Oosting and Billings, 1943). The dominant species have only a comparatively limited distribution outside the association. Seven small subdominant herbs are especially characteristic of the floor of this forest. Of these only *Sarcodes sanguinea* is restricted to the vicinity of the Sierra Nevada (Fig. 114). *Pirola dentata* var. *integra* and *P. picta* extend northward and eastward to British Columbia and Wyoming; *Corallorrhiza maculata* and *Pterospora andromedea* are transcontinental through the boreal coniferous forest; and *Pirola secunda* and *Chimaphila umbellata* extend throughout practically the entire boreal coniferous forest biome in both North America and Eurasia. Thus four of the seven characteristic subdominants of the red fir association studied by Oosting and Billings (1943) have ranges greatly exceeding those of any of the dominant species of the association.

From these examples it would seem that, as long as the community dominants were of the same physical type, taxonomic changes in dominants have no effect on the general selection pressure exerted on understory species. This means that, as long as ecological constancy prevailed, the evolution of the dominants and the evolution of the subdominants would be independent. If a rare dominant tree species became endowed with some biological advantage resulting in that species supplanting another tree in the community hierarchy of dominants, this change would have

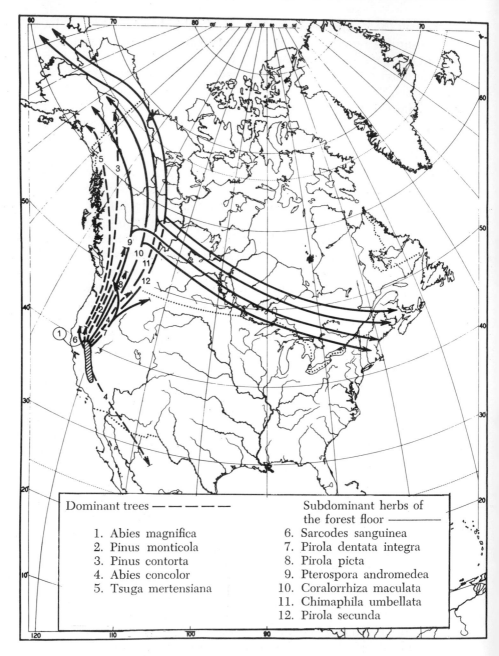

Fig. 114. Diagram of the distribution of the five dominant trees and seven subdominant herbs of the Sierra Nevadan fir forest, indicated by the small hatched area. (Compiled from Munns and Oosting and Billings.)

no effect on a shrub species, a salamander, or a cockroach living beneath these trees. Conversely, the shrubs, salamanders, and cockroaches could change either into new types or into a larger number of species, and this would have no direct effect on the evolution of the dominants.

If the various components of a community did evolve in unison, theoretically it would be the result of either pure coincidence or some intimate biological connection between particular species in the community.

For example, the demise of a tree fern species which was the sole and obligatory host of an insect species would automatically remove that insect; reduction of dominant species having branches below the crown would reduce understory epiphytic ferns and other plants; the evolution of some special kind of seeds would set up selection pressures in understory organisms leading to utilization of these seeds as food.

The long geological history of certain biomes may be associated with the evolution of dominant species which became extremely well adapted to their environment, were seldom outcompeted, and persisted virtually unchanged for long periods of time. These almost changeless dominants are encountered in many biomes. Chaney (1954) and Pierce (1957) believed that *Pinus resinosa* (Fig. 115*b*), one of the dominant pines of northeastern North America, is almost exactly like its Cretaceous counterpart, *Pinus resinosipites* (Fig. 115*a*). Chaney (1940) believed that the sycamore *Platanus*

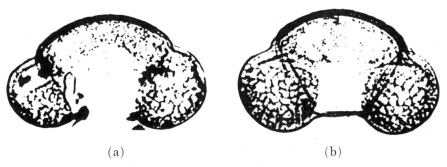

(a)   (b)

Fig. 115. Lateral views of grains of pine pollen. (a) the Cretaceous species *Pinus resinosipites;* (b) the recent species *P. resinosa.* (From Pierce.)

occidentalis of eastern North America is virtually identical with the species which occupied the same general area in Oligocene. Pierce (1958) showed that pollen characteristics of many Cretaceous trees are remarkably similar to those of existing species (Fig.

116). Many of the abundant dominant genera of freshwater stream communities trace back in the fossil record to the Cretaceous (Ross, 1956), and those of marine communities to the Paleozoic (Shrock and Twenhoffel, 1953).

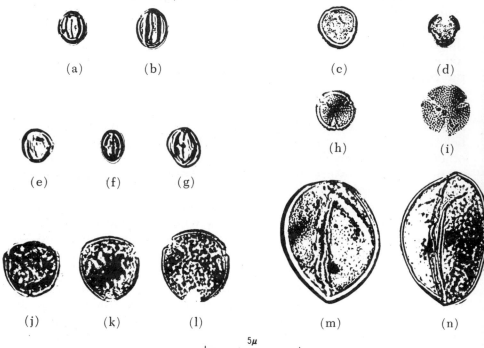

Fig. 116. Pollen grains of Upper Cretaceous plants in Minnesota and of Recent species to which they bear a striking resemblance. (a), Cretaceous species resembling (b), *Menispermum canadense.* (d), Cretaceous species resembling (c), *Platanus occidentalis.* (e), (g), Cretaceous species resembling (f), *Lithocarpus densiflora.* (i), Cretaceous species resembling (h), *Hamamelis vernalis.* (j), (l), Cretaceous species resembling (k), *Quercus laurifolia.* (m), Cretaceous species resembling (n), *Magnolia virginiana.* (Photographs courtesy of R. L. Pierce.)

Marine organic reefs, because of the wonderfully rich fossil record of their constituent species, afford an excellent example of community change through time. As in the past, circulation of warm marine waters across shallow, wave-agitated areas commonly produces ecological conditions ideally suited to flourishing benthonic communities of shelled organisms. Existing reefs have an abundant fauna and flora which continuously contributes to the reef deposits in the form of calcareous shells and skeletons. Wave action usually moves these fragments back and forth until they reach a protected area or are swept over the edge of the reef platform to be deposited on its flanks. In this way, a vertical and commonly also a lateral growth of the reef gradually comes about. The association of algae in a reef deposit indicates deposition within the photic zone. Reefs are most abundant in shallow waters of the temperate and tropical regions, but they are also found in water as deep as 100 fathoms (Teichert, 1958) and within a few hundred yards of the Antarctic ice shelf in peculiar areas of elevated temperature (Bullivant, 1959). The reefs provide an ecological setting of food and protection in which lives a remarkable assemblage of worms, fish, and many other diverse organisms (Fig. 117) (Moore, 1958).

Reef communities have persisted since the beginning of the Cambrian to the present, although their faunal and floral components and their geographic locations have changed continuously. Presumed "algal heads" (*Eozoon*), formed of encrusting layers of calcareous material in late Pre-cambrian strata in Glacier National Park, Montana, are believed to represent the oldest "reefs" (Fenton and Fenton, 1933). In early and middle Cambrian times, the Archaeocyathinae, of unknown biologic affinities but similar in many respects to calcareous sponges, grew in large dense colonies forming extensive reefs in many areas.

At the end of the early Ordovician time many new kinds of reef-forming organisms evolved. The middle and later Paleozoic reefs (bioherms) have faunas and floras with increasingly complex colonial corals (tabulates and tetracorals), calcareous algae, bryozoans, brachiopods, trilobites, echinodermal fragments, and gastropods. In the Silurian and Devonian, stromatoporoids (encrusting hydrozoans) became another important reef-building organism. Crinoids flourished in Mississippian and Pennsylvanian shelf areas and together with colonial tetracorals and algae formed many of the reefs of that time. In Permian times, aberrant productid brachiopods (*Prorichthofenia, Leptodus,* and *Scachinella*), cemented their shells to the substratum and to one another. They occurred in many of the large reefs along with corals, sponges, crinoids, and bryozoans (Newell *et al.,* 1953).

Many major Paleozoic reef builders became extinct during the late Permian, and new faunal and floral components built reefs during the Mesozoic and Cenozoic. In the Tethyan seas of southern Asia, Europe, and North Africa, stromatoporoids, algae, sponges, and hexacorals came to be the dominant faunas of many of the

Fig. 117.   Side view of the vertical face of a coral head on the Great Barrier Reef, Australia. (From Manton and Stephenson.)

reef assemblages. By Cretaceous time, specialized massive pelecypods or Rudistids formed reefs of wide extent in the low latitudes. In the Cenozoic, development of the present "coral reef"
environment took place. This included the specialization of the
symbiotic algae-hexacoral association and the encrusting Lithotha-
mian calcareous algae which together provide the physical framework for existence of many other invertebrate groups such as the
regular echinoids, branching bryozoans, and certain gastropods
and pelecypods.

These reef communities have thus formed a true biome in which,
as in the tropical rain forest, newly evolved dominants presumably
produced the same physical and ecological environment as the
species they replaced. Thus taxonomic change in the dominants
probably led to no change in the selection pressure acting on the
subdominants, with the result that evolution of the subdominants
would have been generally independent of evolution in the dominants.

Other communities existing over a shorter span undoubtedly
exemplify the same principles. The temperate deciduous hardwood
forests (Chaney, 1940) have been in existence probably since earliest Cenozoic time and the more xeric-adapted subtropical sclero-
phyllous tree and shrub communities probably since Eocene time
(Axelrod, 1958). Many of the present-day dominants in these
communities are remarkably similar to the fossil forms first associated with the community. It seems highly likely that in these
communities, as postulated for the tropical rain forest and coral
reef communities, the subdominant species evolved independently
of the dominants.

The biome may therefore be considered as a series of overlapping
communities moving through time, occasionally dividing and reuniting with a consequent increase both in constituent species and
ecological complexity. In this moving column species additions
and deletions occur irregularly and in large measure independently, and the evolution of the subdominant species is independent
of that of the dominants. As long as the dominant species, regardless of taxonomic composition, produce the same environmental
effects, the whole preserves its identity as a relatively stable ecological unit.

COMMUNITY SUCCESSION

If life should be removed in some way from a particular ecological setting, certain types of communities would colonize the denuded area, then be succeeded by others, until finally one community would appear to persist indefinitely. The early communities in this succession are termed subclimax communities; the last stage is the climax community.

A simple example of succession occurs on abandoned dirt roads in the east-central United States. The bare soil is colonized first by annual grasses such as *Aristida;* within a year or two perennial herbs and grasses such as *Andropogon* invade the area, crowd out further growth of *Aristida,* and form a solid sod; after a few more years shrubs and small trees such as *Rubus* and *Sassafras* become established, gradually crowd out the *Andropogon* and convert the area into a low-canopy community; and still later larger tree species such as *Fraxinus* gradually replace the shrubs and begin a series of tree communities ending in a beech-maple (*Fagus-Acer*) or oak-hickory (*Quercus-Hicoria*) climax community. This entire development may occur in fifty to a hundred years.

Many examples of succession have been described for plant communities (Shelford, 1913; Park, 1949), but in many instances investigators disagree on the exact course of succession in a particular area. Certain disagreements involving forest communities have been pointed out by Baker (1934) who observed that two simple reasons explain much of the difficulty: (1) the exact course of succession may be different locally or regionally depending on numerous ecological variables, and (2) our observations either lack the necessary detail or have been made over too short a time span to afford an adequate knowledge of many succession series. The general theory of succession, however, is well substantiated and raises some interesting points concerning the evolution of communities. That time alone is not the controlling factor in succession has been demonstrated by the observations of Yount (1956). He measured the growth of diatoms in Silver Springs, Florida, contrasting the results from areas giving poor diatom growth with those giving excellent growth. He found that early stages of succession were characterized by having a diverse diatom flora of 20 to 25 species whereas the climax condition had less than 12 species. In areas of high productivity the climax condition appeared in forty-six days but in areas of low productivity the climax did not develop for over two hundred days. When these times are compared with productivity charts (Fig. 118), it seems evident that the climax condition did not develop until a moderate amount of growth had accumulated, in short, until the subclimax species had changed the ecological nature of the area to some minimum degree.

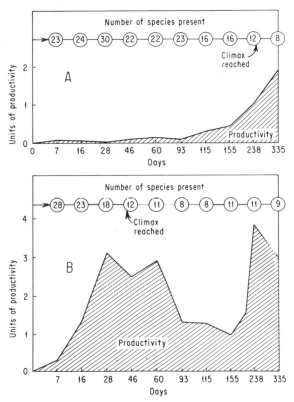

Fig. 118. Growth of diatoms in Silver Springs, Florida, A, under poor growth conditions, and B, under excellent growth conditions. The histograms represent the total productivity of all species combined in units of mass; the lines of numbers represent the highest number of species occurring at each time interval. (Data from Yount, 1956.)

In terrestrial communities the substrate may be modified to an unusual degree during the various stages of succession, as in the colonization and later community development on sand dunes in the eastern deciduous forest (Fig. 119), and the covering of small northern lakes through the famous sphagnum bog series (Fig. 120). In this bog series the sphagnum moss grows out from the shore over the water; on this floating moss mat herbs and shrubs grow, making a second community; after this growth has attained

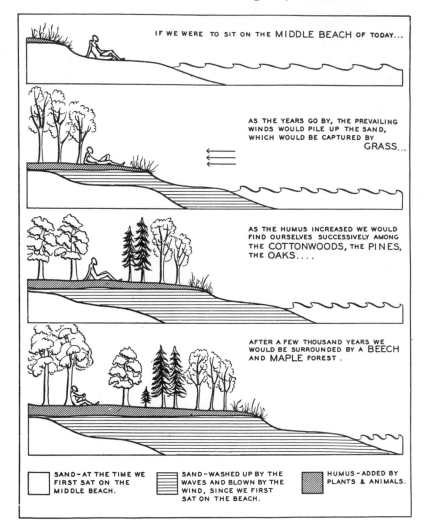

Fig. 119.   Diagram of community succession from open sand to beech-maple climax in the dune region of northern Indiana. (From Allee, Emerson, Park, Park, and Schmidt, *Principles of Animal Ecology,* W. B. Saunders Co., 1949. Adapted from Buchsbaum.)

a certain height and density, larch seedlings become established, new herbs and shrubs grow in their shade, and a new community is formed, this time with trees as its dominants. All this time the pond is filling up with decayed organic matter derived from pollen and other material falling into the open water and dead moss being pressed down from the top. When the pond is thus filled

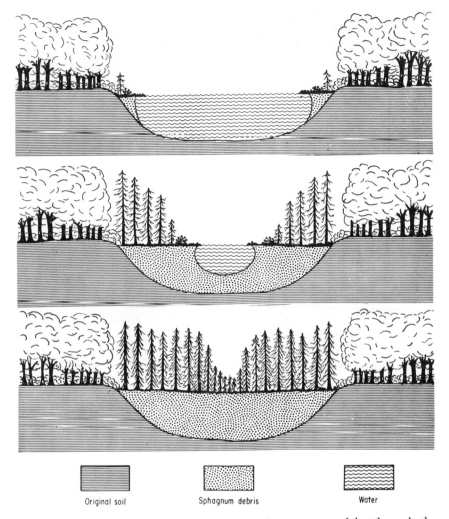

Original soil   Sphagnum debris   Water

Fig. 120. Diagram of community succession from an open lake through the sphagnum bog series to tamarack forest.

and converted to soil, oak, pine, or spruce seedlings spring up, gradually displace the larch, and become the dominants of the final stage in the succession, the climax forest of the general area. The estimated time involved in this succession is at least several thousand years, varying with the initial depth of the pond.

The same mechanisms of succession occur in all of these examples. Throughout any one series of community successions, the seeds of all plants from all the communities reach or fall on the area occupied by all the communities. Seeds of climax species falling on areas in the early stages of succession either will not germinate, or the seedlings die (Went, Juhren, and Juhren, 1952). Seeds of subclimax species falling in the climax area have the same fate. However, when the organisms growing in one of the subclimax communities have either added sufficient humus to the soil, or produced sufficient shade, or brought about some other critical effect, then the progeny of the organisms in the next successional stage can reproduce and grow better than those of the community occupying the area. This change then eliminates that particular subclimax community in that area. In abandoned farm roads, for example, the bare soil itself is perfectly suitable for growing the climax trees if shade is added, as is done artificially with canopies in raising seedling stock of forest trees.

Billings and Mark (1957) pointed out that in subclimax grassy "balds" the climax may be slow to colonize the subclimax but ordinarily will do so eventually. Baker (1934) cited a similar example involving great areas of aspen woods in Colorado which persist because seeds of the usual coniferous dominants disperse short distances. Hence, the true climax must "inch in" around the periphery of the aspen woods. This is truly a slow process. The ultimate in delayed succession occurs on certain Great Basin balds in which subclimax grass communities have become virtual climaxes because no seed source is available for *Pinus ponderosa,* the normal climax dominant in that area (Billings and Mark, 1957). In this instance local conditions cause a normally subclimax community to become a temporary climax because that community is the final one which succeeds others in that particular area.

These examples of temporary climax communities emphasize that dominant species of the grass bald and aspen subclimax communities are perfectly able to maintain themselves indefinitely if not subjected to competition from dominants of the true climax for that area. In other words, the subclimax community does not have some finite time limit after which it disintegrates. Its dominant organisms persist until better-adapted organisms crowd them out.

Aquatic Succession

Fresh water and marine communities are strikingly different from terrestrial communities regarding succession. In both aquatic habitats, if an area is denuded it is replaced rapidly by the same community as the one erased. For example, in an Illinois stream reduced by drought to a few stagnant pools, almost the full original complement of fish and aquatic invertebrates recolonized the stream within a few months after normal stream flow was resumed (Larimore, Childers, and Heckrotte, 1959). If successional communities occur, they would appear to be ephemeral ones composed of unicellular organisms and those of the type studied by Yount (1956) (Fig. 118). In these areas, the single subclimax period lasted from forty-six to two hundred days, in sharp contrast to the fifty to one hundred years often required for the development of even the most short-lived series of subclimax communities leading to a terrestrial climax community.

Following denudation, a complete aquatic community may be attained by the step-by-step addition of units of food chains. In north temperate streams a full year might be required for reconstitution of bottom communities because many of the species have only one generation a year, and dispersal is accomplished only by one stage of the life history. In marine habitats, bottom communities may be reconstituted through the successive colonization of species forming necessary means of attachment for others.

Geologic Age of Subclimax Species

If succession were a one-way process, terrestrial climax communities would gradually cover all the areas of the earth, and no areas would remain for the persistence of species able to exist only in subclimax communities, but this is obviously not the case. Subclimax plants and animals contain many species groups and sometimes genera, such as the grasses *Digitaria* and *Danthonia,* which must be of considerable geologic age, dating back certainly to the Oligocene and perhaps to the Cretaceous, and which probably have occurred in the same subclimax relationship for most if not all of this time. It is reasonable to conclude therefore, that if individual, ephemeral subclimax communities disappear a certain time after becoming established in each locality, a constant succession of freshly denuded or inundated areas must have been available to these subclimax organisms for many millions of years, and these fresh areas must have been within dispersal distance of the older areas. In other words, some processes must operate constantly to reverse the normal direction of succession.

Reversal of Succession

The proposition of reversing succession is simply that of affecting a community so that the area it occupies becomes more suitable for a community of an earlier successional age. Factors producing this condition can be classified into non-biotic and biotic factors.

NON-BIOTIC FACTORS

These may be divided into short-term and long-term factors. Short-term factors include the effects of catastrophes and weather (as distinct from climate); long-term factors include geomorphic changes.

Short-term events. Catastrophes and weather include fire, tidal waves, landslides, scouring and silting by floods, high winds, formation of oxbows and ponds by local shifts in stream channels, severe droughts, unsual temperature drops, and all similar events which disrupt the biota of a community. These are chiefly terrestrial events. Others having comparable effect undoubtedly occur in marine environments. Volcanoes and earthquakes contribute catastrophic factors on land and presumably do the same on the ocean floor. Because of an extreme paucity of knowledge concerning the effects of these factors on marine biota, however, it is necessary to base the following discussion on terrestrial examples.

Fire may have been of greater importance in maintaining sequences of subclimax areas than is generally conceded. Studying the effects of fire in the Florida Everglades, Robertson (1954) found that about 70 per cent of the 100 or more endemic herbs and low shrubs of the Everglades region occur only in communities whose existence is dependent on frequent fires. Watchers in the Everglades region saw fires start from lightning strikes in sawgrass and in tree islands. In all, fires attributed to lightning in the Everglades area numbered 12 in 1951 and 11 during the first half of 1952. Some of these fires were extinguished by the rain accompanying the electrical storm, but several became widespread. Robertson concluded that a checkerboard of frequent fires has been the principal factor maintaining the present subclimax areas in the Everglades for the full geologic life of these communities. Reasoning from these observations it is possible that most if not all of the extensive pine forests of the southeastern and south central United States may owe their continued existence to the destruction of deciduous hardwood seedlings by fire.

Natural fires have been recorded for many other areas. Prebble

(1959) expressed the opinion that fire is important in establishing or perpetuating birch, poplar, jack pine, white pine, red pine, and lodgepole pine in Canada, that much of the forested area in Canada is subject to severe lightning storms, and that on numerous occasions scores or hundreds of lightning fires might be burning at the same time. During the summer of 1940, about 18 forest fires were caused by lightning during a single summer night's electrical storm in Glacier National Park, Montana. Lightning fires have been observed repeatedly in the American short grass prairie (Shantz, 1956). It seems highly probable, therefore, that fire has been a constant and possibly the most important factor in providing suitable areas for the maintenance of many subclimax communities.

The other factors in this category need little comment. Each may be especially important in a particular region. Landslides, for example, are common in mountainous terrain, and shifting stream beds with subsequent oxbow and sand bar formation are common in wide, flat river valleys. Drought is frequently most important if associated with high winds, and this combination is most effective in areas of loose soil or low rainfall. Weaver (1954) (Fig. 121) cited many cases in which this combination has destroyed large areas of the dominant *Andropogon* grasses in the tall grass prairies of central United States and describes the subclimax communities which became established in their place. Wind alone is especially effective in forested areas of predominantly shallow-rooted species, but in the violent form of tornadoes or hurricanes it will level vegetation of any type.

Volcanoes produce a variety of effects. Their extrusions on snow banks may produce mud flows which denude large acreages just as a flood will, as has happened in Mt. Lassen National Park, California. The ash and lava flows kill vegetation and produce bare areas which may not be colonized until they are considerably weathered. The meager biota of the lava hills of the Pinacate lava cap in northwestern Mexico attests to this. This lava cap originated sometime in the Pleistocene and, although it has in patches weathered to black soil, it is inhabited by only a small proportion of the flora and fauna found in the neighboring desert (Dice and Blossom, 1937; Smith and Hensley, 1958).

The sum total of these short-term events accounts for the continuity through time of a series of different areas suited for the establishment of new local communities of early, short-lived stages of succession. These mechanisms account for the occurrence of a large number of subclimax communities.

Fig. 121. Native prairie under different grazing conditions. Above, with light to moderate grazing on prairie almost entirely composed of *Androgopon* grasses and other climax plants. Below, with heavy grazing with the climax *Andropogon* species replaced by blue grass *Poa pratensis* and ironweed *Vernonia sp.* (From Weaver.)

Long-term events. The examples of succession on the sand dunes and the sphagnum bogs concern phenomena which arise only through the action of long-term events. In certain arid areas new bare sand dunes may indeed arise continuously and apparently *ad infinitum* through local wind action, but sand areas in the deciduous forest of eastern North America with its relatively high rainfall have a different history. These sand areas and the bogs bring out some interesting aspects concerning the life of communities.

The large upland sand areas in the temperate deciduous forest of central North America resulted chiefly from the deposition of sand by the tremendous rivers of melt-water issuing from the spent Wisconsin ice sheets, and strong winds during the period of glacial decay. Many of these sand areas are unstable to the point that unusual wind, rain, or drought lead to fresh exposures of sand surfaces, and this is followed by the establishment of a new series of local successions leading from bare sand to hardwood forests. Many of the plants and animals of the earliest stages apparently require sand for their existence. As this process of succession continues, organic material is constantly being incorporated into the upper layers of sand, which in some localities have reached the state of sandy loams. Many herbs which do not require sand thrive on these loams and out-compete the obligate sand dwellers. It is only a matter of time before the upland sands of this area will lose their distinctive physical character whereupon the upland sand community will no longer be represented in the region. The habitat itself will not be present again until another glacier and its rivers, or some equally drastic change, reworks the present and future loams and deposits large amounts of pure sand. Local streams will continue to create new sand bars along their courses, but these sand bars support only river edge plants, not the more xeric types found on the upland sand areas.

Comparable upland sand areas were undoubtedly left as the aftermath of glaciers preceding the Wisconsin ice sheets. What happened to the sand biota of these areas when the sandy habitats presumably turned into loam soils? We can get some clues from the known distribution of some of the species confined to the Illinois sand areas. Each sand species of the herb *Lithospermum* has a wide distribution and occurs to the west in sandy prairie communities (Fernald, 1950). The grass *Aristida tuberculosa* occurs slightly to the west and north but chiefly in the sandy areas along the Atlantic coast (Hitchcock and Chase, 1950). The majority of the distinctive insects which in Illinois are obligate to sand areas are either chiefly plains species or are known from even farther west (Riegel, 1942). Only one of the abundant leafhoppers (*Polyamia rossi*) has not been found to date in any other area (DeLong, 1948). Thus if these Illinois sand areas and their distinctive species disappeared and new sand areas later came into existence, it is probable that the present subclimax communities would be almost fully reconstituted. Forms such as *Lithospermum* and many insects would colonize the new sand areas from western prairie communities, and forms like *Aristida tuberculosa* might come in from eastern communities. The few species now absolutely obligate to the area (the leafhopper *Polyamia rossi* might be one) would have become extinct, and the new community would conceivably differ from the old only in lacking these few species.

This example of the sand areas points to the possibility that a community which is highly distinctive because of its particular combination of species, may completely disappear, then later be almost completely reconstituted upon the recurrence of specific ecological conditions.

The sphagnum bogs in central North America are likewise products of glaciation. They occur in basins gouged in the earth by ice action. When they filled with water these basins formed ponds or lakes with only a slight current or none at all. In the central part of the continent these bogs are gradually disappearing because of plant succession and drainage. Presumably no additional ones will be formed until another ice sheet again extends southward. Whereas this community is distinctive as a unique combination of organisms in central North America, the individual species all have a wide range in contiguous non-bog communities to the north (Forest Service of Canada, 1949). Thus when all the central bog communities disappear, the species will not vanish. If the pot-hole lakes and ponds again form in the area, the same species could colonize them and reconstitute the sphagnum-tamarack community.

Undoubtedly geologic events have made many other unusual but ephemeral topographic features which, during their relatively short lives, have supported communities composed of an unusual combination of species, each species occurring elsewhere in some other community. In an evolutionary sense the chief interest of these unusual types is to illustrate the fortuitous nature and plasticity of communities, to highlight the fact that many species do occur in more than one distinctive community, and to emphasize the short geologic life of some types of communities, such as the tamarack bogs, compared with the long geologic life of such types as the tropical rain forest or the marine organic reef.

Other long-term geomorphic events produce new denuded areas which support simply the successional communities normal for the area. Receding glaciers leave in their wake gravel and boulder beds which are colonized by the same plants which colonize nearby areas denuded by stream scouring or landslides. A retreating or advancing ocean shore creates either new areas for open beach communities or new areas for marine communities. In themselves such actions do not provide entirely new types of habitats that set the stage for the evolution of new types of life, as maintained by Axelrod (1958); such actions simply contribute to local reversals of the succession which is normal for the area. The chief difference is that the geomorphic event would likely create much larger areas for subclimax colonization than would local events.

BIOTIC FACTORS

In a number of communities the unusual increase of plant-feeding species leads to sufficient local or regional modification of the vegetation that earlier stages of succession become established on the area. One of the best examples is overgrazing by livestock in which the climax grasses of the prairie areas may be cropped too severely and perish; the entire community of climax plants and undoubtedly the obligate climax animals would disappear with the dominants. Subclimax communities then colonize the areas. Weaver (1954) described the mechanics of this destruction of climax plants which leads to greatly reduced shade on the soil surface and thus effects a reversal of succession (Fig. 121).

Destruction of vegetation likewise occurs naturally during grasshopper and locust outbreaks in both the Old and New Worlds. In the short grass region of North America these insect outbreaks have commonly reduced the grass cover to such an extent that wind has been able to loosen and drift the soil, uprooting some plants and burying others. These changes have resulted in large areas becoming available for colonization by organisms belonging to the earliest successional stage.

It is almost certain that periodically through geologic time grazing species of vertebrates have produced overgrazing with its consequent reversal of succession just as commercial livestock do now. Normal concentration of grazing around watering places would produce small, almost continuously overgrazed local areas, and any coincidence of abundant grazing populations with a drought-produced small grass supply would certainly produce extensive over-grazed areas. It seems reasonable to believe that these biotic factors coupled with ordinary weather cycles provided continuous areas for many subclimax communities.

Biotic or abiotic factors acting alone, however, may produce different kinds of subclimax communities. In the reversal of succession described by Weaver (1954), if the climax *Andropogon* prairie is overgrazed, it is first replaced by subclimax blue grass *Poa pratensis*, which forms a uniform prairie cover; if this is overgrazed, several species of herbs such as *Verbena* and *Vernonia* may become abundant members of the blue grass prairie community. These are not the same subclimax stages which follow complete destruction of the vegetation by fire or excessive wind or drought. The succession following these catastrophic events consists of communities of annual grasses, then perennial grasses other than *Poa pratensis*, and finally the *Andropogon* climax. Thus certain communities probably owe their existence solely to biotic factors acting with local and unusual intensity on the climax community. Such communities are a product of the complexity of the community structure.

Studies of phytophagous insects in Canadian forests indicate a similar but more limited action of biotic factors in reversing succession (Blais, 1952, 1954; Ghent, Fraser, and Thomas, 1957; Morris, 1958). The spruce budworm *Choristoneura fumiferana*, the caterpillar of a Nearctic moth which is always present throughout the balsam fir and spruce forests of eastern Canada, is usually present in low densities but occurs in outbreak numbers when two conditions coincide. These two conditions are an almost pure dense stand of balsam fir and a preponderance of mature trees in the stand. Under these conditions the spruce budworm may completely defoliate the trees for several successive years and kill all but the very young ones. Winds usually fell the dead stems. In this area a new community springs up composed of very small balsam and spruce trees (already present before defoliation) and a rank growth of shrubs or shrubby herbs including *Ribes, Rubus, Corylus,* and *Aralia,* plus many understory herbs including *Lycopodium* and *Linnaea* (Ghent, Fraser, and Thomas, 1957). This community has subclimax angiosperm shrub species as its dominants but contains well-advanced young growth of balsam and spruce up to several feet high, which are the dominants of the climax. On this basis it would seem as if the spruce budworm attack had moved the succession back from late in the climax to a stage late in the preclimax community or to a stage very early in the climax community. In contrast (1) the particular genera mentioned (*Ribes, Rubus,* and so on) and the understory herbs are also typical forest glade species, and (2) in succession following complete denudation by fire the coniferous forest often follows a preclimax community having the aspen *Populus tremuloides* as its dominant. Thus the budworm attack has apparently reversed the succession but has produced a subclimax community different from the usual one which follows complete denudation of the area.

Other insects occurring as outbreaks in coniferous forests produce much the same results. From an evolutionary standpoint this series of events is similar to wind action because areas of forest leveled by wind are often colonized in exactly the same fashion as when the trees are killed by insect outbreaks. Both insects and wind act most effectively on large, over-age trees and in a measure can be considered together as a mechanism bringing about a sort of cycle between the climax and some kind of pre-climax community.

Plant diseases which have virtually exterminated particular species of trees in North America have had only a limited ecological effect. A fungus pathogen has almost eliminated the chestnut *Castanea dentata* from the eastern deciduous forest. Certain organisms restricted to this host have also been removed. Where the chestnut grew in nearly pure stands, the succession was reversed to a certain extent as described for the balsam fir forests, but other hardwoods filled the gap in the climax community. Where chestnut trees were well mixed with other species only small glades were produced, as would happen with the fall of a specimen of any dominant tree species in the community. Losses of elms because of the diseases phloem necrosis and Dutch elm disease produced the same results. Thus except for associated host-specific species, the loss or great reduction of these species resulted in neither permanent change in the general ecological conditions of their respective communities nor the introduction of new repetitive series of subclimax stages that might serve for the perpetuation of species confined to them.

A review of the foregoing material on terrestrial community succession brings out the conclusions that (1) subclimax communities and their constituent species have existed through a long part of geologic time, undoubtedly in some form ever since complex biotic associations came into existence; (2) mechanisms of various kinds continually reverse succession and so produce new areas suitable for the persistence of subclimax species; (3) all the stages of succession in a given area, including the climax, may form a recurring cycle of communities, although the cycle may be highly irregular because of the many variables which affect it; and (4) under special ecological conditions new communities, short-lived in a geologic sense, may be formed from species living in other communities.

From these considerations of succession it is clear that any one area is occupied not by one community alone but recurrently by a system of successive communities. The same idea is expressed by calling the entire system one community, as is implicit in the *life zone* terminology of some authors, but because climax and subclimax communities of the same successional series may be radically different it is simpler to consider each distinctive subclimax stage as a separate community. Because the subclimax communities are distinctive for a given biome and merge imperceptibly with the climax types, it seems most feasible to consider these successional communities as a part of the biome in which they occur.

Evolution of Subclimax Species

A great many subclimax species occur in more than one biome and consequently have ranges quite different from those of species which are restricted to a single biome. In the species of three-awned grass *Aristida,* which are common subclimax species in the Nearctic eastern deciduous forest biome, some extend considerably beyond the biome and are also components of subclimax communities in central and western grassland areas. Five of these *Aristida* species are illustrated in Fig. 122; *A. dichotoma* and *A. ramosissima* occur only in the deciduous forest biome, but *A. biramosa, A. curtissii,* and *A. oligantha* occur considerably west of it (Hitchcock and Chase, 1950).

More extensive ranges of subclimax organisms occurring in the eastern deciduous forest include the side-oats grama grass *Bouteloua curtipendula* and the sandbur *Cenchrus pauciflorus,* both distributed from the Atlantic to the Pacific and from southern Canada to Argentina, and the wild cherries *Prunus americana* and *P. virginiana* (Fig. 123), which extend through other biomes to the north and west.

Many species of animals have ranges which likewise extend over subclimax areas of several biomes and, as Shelford and Olsen (1935) pointed out, may range over both subclimax and climax communities. The black bear *Ursus americanus,* the cottontail rab-

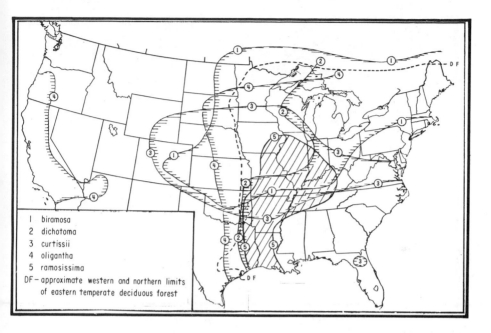

Fig. 122. Ranges of five species of the grass genus *Aristida*. (Adapted from Hitchcock and Chase.)

bit *Sylvilagus floridanus,* the coyote *Canis latrans,* and insects such as wide-ranging mosquitoes and sawflies are but a small number of many examples in North America.

Certain of the plants in this category are of unusual interest because they are subclimax species in one biome and dominants of some climax communities in another biome. Thus the two American grasses *Andropogon scoparius* and *A. gerardii* are subclimax plants in the eastern deciduous forest biome but are dominant species in the long-grass prairie biome immediately to the west and subclimax components again in the swale communities of more xeric biomes even farther west. The American *Aristida oligantha* is a grass of early stages of succession in Illinois and eastward but a co-dominant with *Andropogon gerardii* in prairie communities of Oklahoma (Ray, 1959).

These wide-ranging subclimax organisms differ markedly in evolutionary potential from species whose ranges more or less concide with a single biome. In the first place, the selection pressures influencing genetic change in species with a wider ecological range will come from a wider spectrum of ecological situations and thus

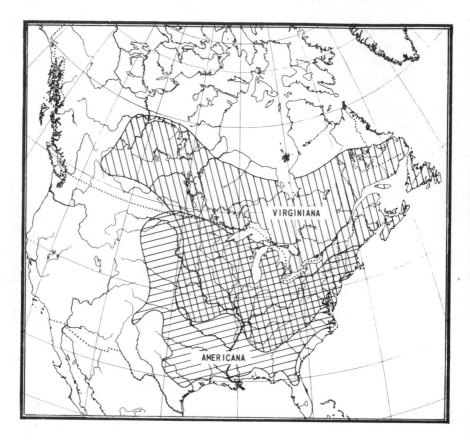

Fig. 123. Ranges of two species of the genus *Prunus* common in subclimax communities of the eastern temperate deciduous forest. (Adapted from Munns.)

may contribute to changes different from those resulting from the influences of only one biome. In the second place, the pattern of species fission and the resulting increase in number of species will also be different in the more widespread species. These would result from two opposing mechanisms. An ecological change of sufficient magnitude to divide the climax species of the biome might not be sufficient to divide the ranges of more widespread subclimax species because the latter would presumably have a wider ecological tolerance than the climax species. In contrast, the more widespread subclimax species, because of the greater area of its range, would be subject to possible geographic fragmentation that might not occur in a single biome. As a result, subclimax species may have an entirely different evolutionary history than climax species.

EVOLUTION OF SUCCESSION

The most plausible explanation for the evolution of community succession is that it arose as a competitive relationship such as gave rise to seasonal succession. Let us consider a simple case in which two species A and B evolved in isolation and then occupied the same area. Let us assume first that A germinated better on bare ground and B germinated better where A was already growing, and second that B eventually outcompeted A. B would gradually supplant A over the range of A in which B could live. Because it is highly improbable that two species would have identical ranges, A would continue to exist along one periphery of the range of B, and for a short time in any new denuded areas occurring within the range of B. This latter arrangement is the subclimax-climax relationship. The competitive restriction of A to a subclimax position and B to a climax position would change the selection pressures acting on the two species and theoretically lead to adaptations establishing each species more firmly in its respective position. A would presumably evolve toward faster maturation and greater seed or spore dispersal, B toward longer life and possibly larger stature.

If subsequent events divided the range of this two-species system so that A divided into 1A and 2A, both ecologically similar to A, and B into 1B and 2B, and these divided units again mixed, two communities would have come into existence, the subclimax composed of 1A and 2A, and the climax composed of 1B and 2B.

It is also possible that the original mixture contained many species, and that, through the same mechanism as the one described, the subclimax and climax components came into existence as mixtures of species rather than as single species.

Support for this thesis is found in the successional microcommunities occurring in certain microhabitats. Three overlapping but distinct microcommunities of this type occur in cattle droppings (Mohr, 1943). Mohr found that the first stage is dominated by a group of five or six species of extremely rapidly growing fly maggots and lasts about five days; the second is dominated by a few slower growing species of maggots and ends about fifteen days later; and the third is dominated by even more slowly growing beetle larvae and extends until the dung is reduced to little more than soil (Fig.

124). A remarkable set of behavior patterns have evolved parallel with this set of successional events. In the first stage there is a remarkably timed succession of ovipositing flies, starting at the very instant that the dung is dropped. The first fly species is on

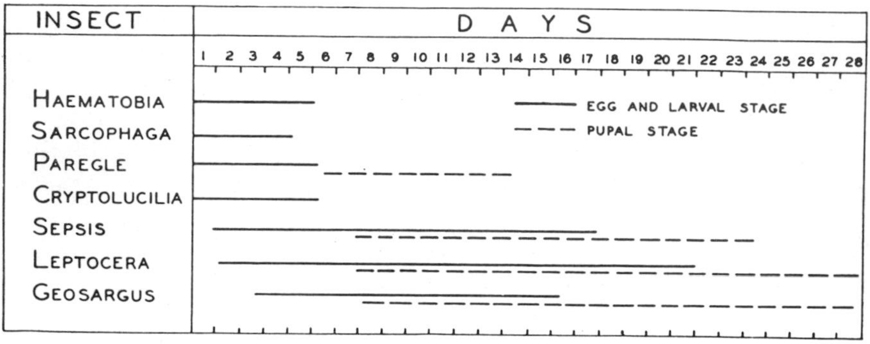

INSECT	D A Y S
	1 2 3 4 5 6 7 8 9 10 11 12 13 14 15 16 17 18 19 20 21 22 23 24 25 26 27 28
Haematobia	—————— ——— EGG AND LARVAL STAGE
Sarcophaga	———— — — — PUPAL STAGE
Paregle	————— — — — — — — —
Cryptolucilia	—————
Sepsis	——————— — — — — — — — — — — — — —
Leptocera	————— — — — — — — — — — — — — —
Geosargus	———— — — — — — — — — — — — —

Fig. 124. Predominant fly maggots of the first two microcommunities in freshly dropped cattle droppings. The upper four species belong to the first stage of succession. (From Mohr.)

the cake only one or two minutes, the next set less than an hour, and the others up to six hours (Fig. 125).

The key species of the first microcommunity and many of those in the second occur only in this microhabitat. The various species, however, are related not to each other but to species with other habits. The various species therefore colonized the microhabitat independently, then, after forming a species mixture, evolved habits which resulted in the present community structure. Although this example is not an exact replica of successional communities in plants, there is considerable indication that the members of the first dung microcommunity bring about changes in the medium making it more readily available to invaders of the second micro-community.

After a series of subclimax stages have evolved, it is always theoretically possible for new species to colonize the system or old species to evolve new properties, and to bring about a modification of successional relationships.

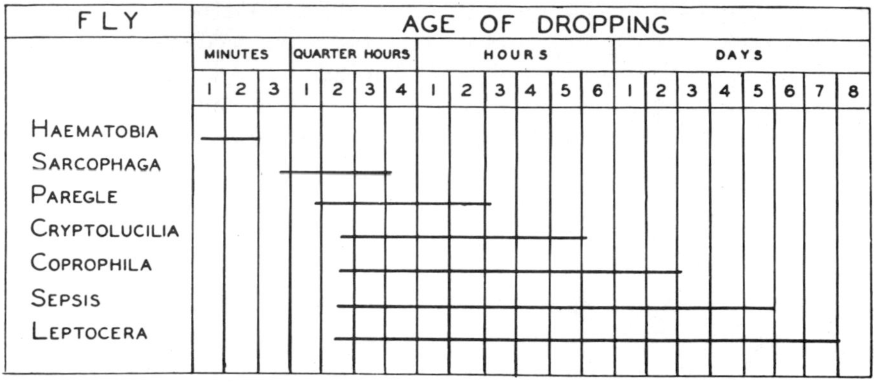

FLY	AGE OF DROPPING			
	MINUTES	QUARTER HOURS	HOURS	DAYS
	1 2 3	1 2 3 4	1 2 3 4 5 6	1 2 3 4 5 6 7 8
HAEMATOBIA				
SARCOPHAGA				
PAREGLE				
CRYPTOLUCILIA				
COPROPHILA				
SEPSIS				
LEPTOCERA				

Fig. 125. Period during which adult ovipositing flies were present on fresh cattle droppings. The upper four species were members of the first successional stage; the lower three species were members of the second. (From Mohr.)

ORIGIN OF NEW TERRESTRIAL BIOMES

Since the appearance of the first biome many additional ones have come into existence. Three principal processes have led to the origin of the new biomes:

(1) Colonization of areas in which no life previously existed.
(2) Substitution of dominants which change the physical aspect of the biome.
(3) Changes of climate resulting in new combinations of dominants, each combination having different physical characteristics.

These processes are an expression of the dynamic nature of both the species making up communities and the environment.

1. Colonization of Abiotic Areas

Few large areas in the world today lack life. Summit areas in the highest mountain systems, limited polar areas, and a few desert areas do lack life, but less extreme ecological settings have at least a scattering of living organisms. When the tropical rain forest or its earliest equivalent was the only terrestrial biome, the opposite of the present terrestrial condition must have held. Except for the areas of the earth's land surface having abundant year-around rain and warm climates, the entire surface was uninhabited. Since that time a remarkably varied and diverse biota has evolved and gradually inhabited the colder and drier habitats.

Following the tropical rain forest, the first of these new biomes may have been a coniferous forest which existed in Pennsylvanian time or even earlier and which adapted to cooler or drier climates than the rain forest proper. Evidence of this forest consists of the highly fragmentary fossils thought to be coniferous and assigned to *Taxeopsis, Taxodiella, Sboromirskia, Paleotaxus* and other genera (Andrews, 1955) and the primitive Pityales (Axelrod, 1959). Certainly fossil evidence suggests that such a coniferous forest existed by early Mesozoic when genera occurred which are more typical of conifers today (Knowlton, 1919) and which were the hosts of wood-boring beetles belonging to existing families or superfamilies (Ross, 1956*b*).

At a still later time the more xeric grassland and desert biomes arose, many elements of the desert biota in particular evolving into highly specialized and, to our eyes, wierd forms such as the Cactaceae of the New World and the cactus-like Euphorbiaceae of the Old World.

In each new colonization the first requisite was a genetic change in some pre-existing species which endowed its possessor with the ability and behavior to live "farther out" in areas too inimical ecologically for its parents to colonize. Once a species was able to live in the new environment it would come under extreme selection pressures which would favor the establishment of any mutant types better adapted to the new situation. In some instances such conditions have doubtless led to unusually rapid evolution, perhaps leading to the cactus-like desert plants or the highly specialized giraffes and mammoths. The theoretical mechanics of such evolution were considered in Chapters 4 and 5.

A well-documented analysis of the colonization of a new area was made by Axelrod (1958), in which he described the evolution of the semi-desert biomes of southwestern North America from ancestral elements of the tropical rain forest. According to his hypothesis, somewhat arid conditions occurred in the Southwest as early as Middle or Late Cretaceous time. By late Cretaceous or Paleocene time species in such genera as *Quercus, Ficus, Sabal, Platanus,* and *Xanthoxylum* had colonized at least the periphery of these areas. These species would have had a greater tolerance to less humid conditions than those required by their parent species. After the Paleocene these plants colonized progressively more xeric sites in southwestern North America (Fig. 61) and evolved many adaptations to life under xeric conditions such as water-storage, seasonal deciduousness, and extremely short life in annuals. The present product of this series of events is the live oak, piñon-juniper, and other woodland associations of southwestern North America, and their respective successional stage communities.

In reconstructing the evolution of these and other biotas (Axelrod, 1958; Chaney, 1947; MacGinitie, 1953) no attempt was made to trace the evolutionary patterns of individual successional communities. Such a segregation would indeed be impossible from fossil evidence alone because not only are successional stages, including the climax, usually mixed intimately in the same area and hence contributing jointly to local fossil deposition, but also preclimax successional stages are short-lived temporally and in the geologic record would not be found separately except in varve deposits. However, in both MacGinitie's and Axelrod's studies the fossil species match so closely the composition of some living successional communities that the mid-Cenozoic semi-desert plants could very well have been organized in the same community structure we find at present. The fossil evidence is comprised chiefly of woody species which are therefore representative of later successional communities. Preclimax shrub communities are represented by the genera *Ceanothus, Cercocarpus,* and *Arctostaphylos.* Undoubtedly the earlier and chiefly herbaceous communities also existed but Axelrod mentions that herbaceous types were "largely unrecorded."

Information concerning the behavior of existing succession combined with fossil evidence of studied floras supports three simple principles concerning the community colonization of abiotic areas:

(1) Members of the first stage subclimax community, the normal bare ground invaders, would be the first organisms to extend their range onto previously uninhabited ground. Only after these had become established would species of the next community in the normal succession have any opportunity to extend their ranges into the newly colonized areas and in essence follow the ecological extension of the first colonizing community. This process would be repeated for each community in the succession. Based on the assumption that later subclimax stages in the parent area cannot initiate growth on bare ground within that area, it is unreasonable

to suppose that they would be able to initiate growth on adjacent bare areas having even more rigorous conditions.

(2) New colonizing communities contain only a few of the species present in their respective parent communities. Examples of this thesis are found in the large genera of North American grasses associated with early stages of succession in temperate deciduous forest and adjacent grassland biomes. *Stipa* and *Aristida* have many species in both mesic and xeric communities, *Panicum* has a very large number in mesic communities but few in xeric ones, and *Festuca* and *Paspalum* are restricted almost entirely to mesic communities. If these five genera originated as mesic types (as seems likely), then originally several species of *Stipa* and *Aristida* spread into and colonized previously uninhabited areas, while only a few of *Panicum* and none of *Festuca* and *Paspalum* did so. In these same communities grass-feeding leafhoppers (Cicadellidae) parallel the grass examples. In particular, the genera *Deltocephalus* and *Hebecephalus* have many species in mesic communities but few or none in xeric ones, whereas the genera *Flexamia* and *Athysanella* have many species in mesic communities and also a large number in xeric communities.

Another example of reduced number of species in colonizing communities is found along the western edge of the North American temperate deciduous forest. Eastward roughly from the western range limit of *Quercus alba* this forest contains many species of trees, but westward the number of tree species drops sharply. In western Minnesota and the Dakotas, the climax is predominantly *Quercus macrocarpa,* often occurring in almost pure stands. Furthermore, on a transect west from Missouri the wooded areas contain chiefly *Gleditsia, Juglans,* and *Celtis.* The trees on the edge of these western areas are those able to exist under more xeric conditions than their eastern neighbors and undoubtedly represent the encroachment of the deciduous forest upon the tall-grass prairie biome. The small number of species in these truly colonizing communities contrasts strikingly with the larger numbers found in more eastern and more mesic communities.

(3) Communities of a later successional stage may not become adapted to as great ecological extremes as communities of an earlier successional stage. Axelrod points out that in California the more shrubby chaparral occupies more xeric sites than the live-oak woodland, although the chaparral community is also a subclimax stage following burning of the live-oak woodland. Axelrod offers fossil evidence that earlier in the Cenozoic the chaparral may have

been more restricted to the area occupied by the live-oak woodland. On this basis, it is possible that more recently the chaparral community has become adapted to xeric conditions beyond the limit to which the live-oak woodland has become adapted. If such is the case, then where the woodland does occur, the chaparral is a true subclimax community, but in areas slightly too xeric for the woodland, the chaparral would be the climax community. This concept gives a rational explanation for the previous observation that many species may be members of a subclimax community in one area and of a climax community in another. The concept leads further to the idea that a community may be a subclimax stage under certain conditions and the climax stage under others.

2. Substitution of Dominants

During the history of life, dominants in biomes such as the tropical rain forest and marine organic reefs have changed without changing the general physical nature of the community. In other instances, dominants supplanting the old have changed the physical nature of the community drastically. The part thus changed has in essence become a new biome.

The effect on the community of substituting even a single dominant species is shown strikingly by the introduction of the European perennial herb, St. John's wort, *Hypericum perforatum*, into the arid grazing areas of Australia and California (Holloway, 1957). In California the native dominants in range land communities are arid-tolerant annual grasses. The *Hypericum* out-competed these grasses for water and virtually supplanted them wherever the *Hypericum* spread. Thus a grass community was converted into one dominated by a luxurious shrubby herb growing to a height of up to five feet and casting a dense shade.

The possible effect of adding additional species to the same community is shown by several insect species introduced as control agents for this *Hypericum*. These insects were imported first into Australia, then into California, in an effort to reduce the weed. A leaf-feeding beetle *Chrysolina gemellata* proved to be especially effective in reducing the extent of the *Hypericum*. The beetle did not exterminate its host but reduced it to a negligible part of the vegetation or to small ephemeral patches. Thus this one species of plant predator has effected another substitution of a dominant, suppressing the *Hypericum* to the point that the area has reverted to being primarily an annual grassland.

A similar example explained by Bess and Haramato (1958) is afforded by the tropical American plant *Eupatorium adenophorum.* commonly known as pamakani. When introduced into Hawaii in 1860 it thrived and spread over the grassland areas, forming impenetrable thickets ten feet high which killed the grass. The change in the dominant converted the grassland into a dense shrubland (Fig. 126, top). A Mexican tephritid fly *Procecidochares utilis,* which makes large galls on the *Eupatorium* stems and branches, was introduced into the Hawaiian area in 1945. In a few years the fly practically eliminated the *Eupatorium* from the more open and drier areas, which reverted to grassland. In other areas, notably some of the wetter slopes, the *Eupatorium* was less affected by the fly. In this example the net result of the two successive introductions was the initial threatened extinction of one biome by the substitution of a dominant, then a checking effect by a plant predator which has resulted in a new shrub community being added along the wetter edges of the somewhat reduced original grassland (Fig. 126, bottom).

The examples cited above concern species artificially introduced into the biomes, but nonetheless they give a good indication of the effects of changes in community dominants and in host-parasite (prey-predator) relationships. There is every reason to believe that comparable changes in community and biome structure have occurred many times and in many places due to the natural dispersal of organisms from one part of the world to another.

The possible origin of the angiosperm temperate deciduous forests of the Holarctic region presents an interesting set of speculations. In Cretaceous pollens of Minnesota, Pierce (1957, 1958) found evidence suggesting that the Cretaceous forests of that area were chiefly pine and other conifers, with a smaller, presumably subdominant element of angiosperm trees. Many belonged to extant genera such as *Magnolia, Platanus, Hamamelis, Quercus,* and *Tilia.* This situation is highly suggestive of two possibilities. One is that the forest was much like that of the pine woods of southeastern United States, in which the preponderance of pine may be maintained to a large extent by natural fire (see p. 272). If so, the Minnesota observations may be one of the earliest indications so far observed of the occurrence of natural fires.

A second possibility is that the aggregation of species described by Pierce was the true climax of that community and that since then the angiosperm trees have supplanted the pines as the final dominants.

Fig. 126. Hawaiian hills (above) in which pamakani *Eupatorium adenophorum* has completely replaced grasses, and (below) after pamakani had been destroyed in open areas by the gall fly *Procecidochares utilis*. (From Bess and Haramoto.)

If this latter is so, then it adds another concept to the subject of subclimax and climax stages. It could well be true that the deciduous hardwoods did not crowd out the pines to the point of extinction but over at least part of the range became a new climax community superimposed on the previous succession which had stopped at the pine community.

We have a little evidence here, therefore, that new types of organisms may form new climax communities on top of old ones. This really is not a strange concept because it is inherent in the evolution of community succession in the first place. It simply emphasizes the idea that in a dynamic system even the units which appear the most stable can and undoubtedly do undergo a change in status.

3. By Climatic Change

The dominant species of a biome live together because their ecological tolerances are similar *under existing conditions.* Under certain other conditions these tolerances might not coincide and the species would not occur together. The opposite is equally possible. A simple type of climatic change which would produce these results is illustrated by the hypothetical example shown in Fig. 127. The

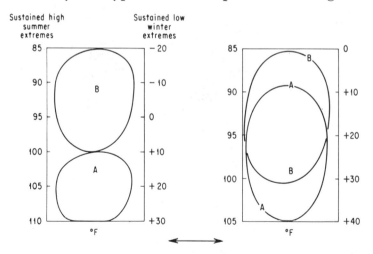

Species A — Heat tolerant species killed by winter extreme of 10
Species B — Cold tolerant species killed by summer extreme of 100

Fig. 127. A hypothetical chart illustrating how the ranges of two species, A and B, would alternately separate and overlap under climatic oscillations between a condition of greater annual extremes of temperature (left) and more moderate conditions (right).

heat resistant, cold susceptible species A would have no range overlap with heat susceptible, cold resistant species B in a climate having great seasonal extremes. If the climate moderated with resulting cooler summers and warmer winters, the two species would have extensive range overlap. These hypothetical climates could conceivably move in either direction, resulting in separation or congregation of species.

Fossil evidence indicates that both of these processes have resulted in past changes in biome composition and change.

SEPARATION

The arid southwestern flora analysed by Axelrod (1958) is an excellent example of the evolution of communities by separation. Axelrod pointed out that today this flora represents at least five moderately distinctive associations (Figs. 128 and 129): (1) a California live oak and pine woodland, chiefly in California, (2) an insular oak and pine woodland, on northwestern Baja California and islands off the coast of southern California, (3) a Lagunan oak woodland in lower Baja California, (4) a Sierra Madrean woodland of evergreen oaks, piñon, and juniper, extending from central Mexico to southern United States, and (5) a piñon pine-juniper woodland in and around the Great Basin area.

In the Cenozoic fossil records, components of these five associations were not segregated in this fashion but occurred in the same localities. Every included species was not found in every fossil find, but several distant stations such as Sonoma, California and Florissant, Colorado, contained large assemblages of species which included distinctive members of practically all the derived modern communities. Axelrod believed that orogenic movements in the mid-Cenozoic brought about greater regional differences in climate, particularly extremes in aridity and winter temperatures and that this in turn brought about a differential separation of the various plant species according to their adaptive characteristics.

The grassland biomes of central North America probably arose in somewhat the same fashion. Prior to the Miocene the Great Plains areas were either inundated or of lower elevation and warmer climate than now. The more xeric of the terrestrial areas presumably supported a semi-desert woodland merging into a temperate deciduous forest to the north and east. During the Miocene this central area was elevated to a height of 3,000 to 6,000 feet and became colder. This probably produced a climate in which most of the species in the older biomes could not survive, and, as a result, these species disappeared from the area. The grasses and other herbs now constituting these grassland biomes may very well be the only members of the old biomes which were hardy to both the new cold and the new xeric conditions. It is also likely that these species were members of the subclimax communities of the older

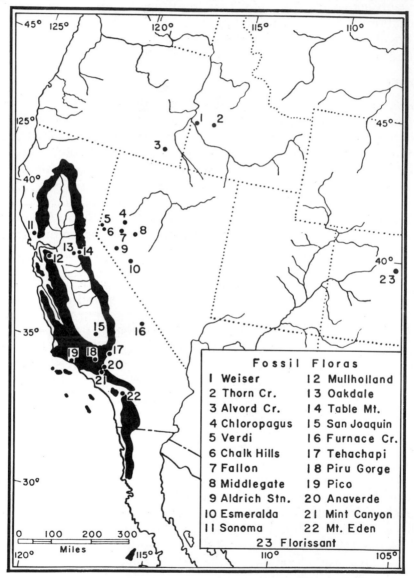

Fig. 128. Occurrence of present California woodland and chaparral (black) and records of related Cenozoic vegetation (numbered dots). (From Axelrod.)

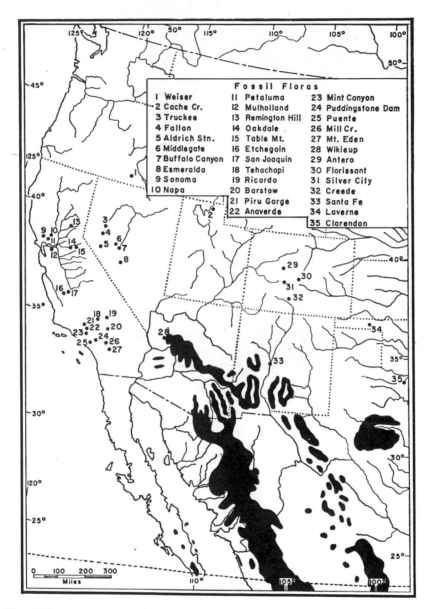

Fig. 129. Occurrence of present Sierra Madrean woodland (black) and records of related Cenozoic vegetation (numbered dots). Note that sixteen of the fossil localities in Fig. 128 contain records for this set of communities also. (From Axelrod.)

biomes, as many still are today. Thus climatic changes would result in what might be termed either a new biome by separation or a new biome from old ingredients. This latter is reminiscent of the subclimax sand communities in the neighboring temperate deciduous forest.

CONGREGATION

If biomes and associations can arise by separation, there is a theoretical possibility that the separated units might reunite. If, for example, in the future the climate of southwestern North America reverted to the more uniform one of Oligocene time, would the five existing associations intermingle to form somewhat the same single biome represented by the Madro-Tertiary flora of earlier Cenozoic time?

The question of a reunion of biomes may be of special interest in questions arising from the geographic displacement of biomes during maximum ice advances of the Pleistocene. Did the various biomes maintain their taxonomic characteristics as we now know them and simply condense in distinctive narrow bands, or did they reunite to a considerable extent to form biomes unlike any now in existence? Two circumstances favor the latter view. In the first place during the ice maxima spruce pollen was deposited in several localities near the Gulf Coast, many hundreds of miles south of existing spruce stands. In the second place, the eastern states south of the ice unquestionably had a climate *different from any present eastern climate,* and therefore more than likely they had forests with a combination of species different from any now extant. Perhaps the result was somewhat like the Cretaceous forests suggested by Peirce, probably with many more species than those earlier forests but having a mixture of conifers and hardwoods which would seem unusual to a student of existing biomes.

SUMMARY

Geomorphic changes may cause a simultaneous range fission of all the species in a community and in this manner bring into existence two daughter communities composed of different if closely related species. If later geomorphic events reunite these communities, competition between dominant species results in the establishment of different communities existing side by side.

The continued operation of this mechanism of alternating community fission and .reunion has led to the formation of the successional communities which follow denudation and of biomes, the largest existing ecological units. A much more complex series of successional stages has evolved in terrestrial biomes than seems to be the case in aquatic ones.

The evolution of these interlocking communities forming biomes and their successional stages has been accompanied by a remarkable increase in complexity within the community. In spite of this, the addition or extinction of a single critical species may cause drastic changes in the ecological structure of the entire biome. In several biomes, however, the taxonomic composition of the dominants has changed radically many times, but the general physical and ecological nature of the biome has remained unchanged. Because of this situation, the dominants and subdominants of the communities comprising these biomes have evolved independently.

Comparative

Evolution of Biomes

10

Each major biome occurs over a considerable portion of the earth, and the various biomes differ from each other in their individual characteristics. Some, such as the northern coniferous forest or taiga, have an almost continuous range, whereas others such as the tropical rain forest occur as widely separated fragments. In some of the fragmented biomes the individual parts may be taxonomically similar; in others they may be markedly different.

Geomorphic changes of the earth's surface have continued to divide certain ecological areas and to effect a congregation of others. These actions on world-wide biomes have at times been on a truly grand scale, both in geographic extent and in the tremendous amounts of time involved in separations or unions. Abundant examples from the fields of evolutionary change and biogeography illustrate the fact that, during this time, each phylogenetic line may have had an individual rate of change and an individual dispersal pattern. In a biome progressing through time, therefore, all the phylogenetic lines do not change and disperse in unison, but each line may do so differently from the others. The result of this situation is that many of the data for the study of the comparative evolution of biomes are drawn from studies of emergent evolution and biogeography.

The emphasis in these two fields is on the evolution and dispersal of taxonomic units, such as a genus, family, or class of plants or animals. Because the larger taxonomic units include species inhabiting many biomes, the analysis of these taxonomic units gives comparative information on floras or faunas as a whole but information which cuts across rather than coincides with ecological units. The communities making up the biomes contain species from many unrelated taxonomic groups. Hence the evolution of the biomes must be reconstructed from ecologically similar but frequently phylogenetically unrelated species whose evolutionary history is in some measure known.

When such reconstructions are attempted, it is apparent that the evolution and dispersal of many species in a biome have been affected either synchronously or similarly by certain ecological factors. Thus the comparative evolution of biomes is a complex mixture of similarities and differences in the response of their component species to changes in ecological and geographic events occurring through time.

As a result of the interaction of a dynamic biota with a dynamic geomorphology, each biome continues to evolve along its own distinctive pattern which is determined by (1) a mixing effect caused by alternating divisions and fusions and (2) a differential evolution of the isolated parts.

THE MIXING PROCESS

Applied to biomes as a whole, the mixing process has three important variables: intercontinental connections, climatic zonation, and dispersal availability.

Intercontinental Connections

Geologic and biogeographic evidence proves that in the past certain continents have alternately been connected by land bridges and separated by seas. From the standpoint of the past history of particular biomes it is essential to know which continents now disconnected were once connected and vice versa, as well as when the connections existed. Definite information is difficult to obtain because of current disagreements concerning the history of the continental masses, disagreements which are not only highly controversial but extreme in divergence of view. The different hypotheses are treated in more detail in Chapter 1; only information pertinent to this chapter is summarized here.

One hypothesis maintains that the continents have occupied the same relative positions since the origin of life, and that since the course of organic evolution began, connecting corridors between various continents such as the Bering bridge, the Isthmus of Panama, and the Asiatic-Australian bridge have arisen or sunk many times (Fig. 130). These connections would have acted like gates opening and closing at different times.

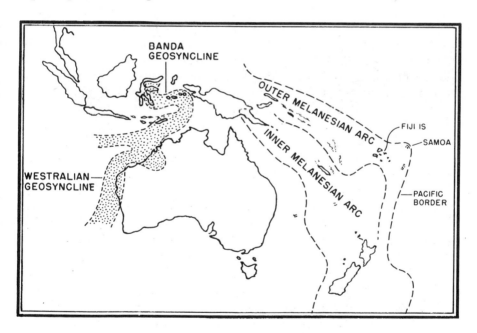

Fig. 130. Geomorphic features of the connecting link between Asia and Australia. The Banda geosyncline and the Melanesian arcs are thought to have been unstable several times. (From Ross, compiled from various sources.)

The opposing hypothesis holds that the continents have drifted over the face of the globe and have had entirely different spatial relations with each other during the evolution of current taxonomic groups. According to one interpretation of this continental drift hypothesis, all the continents formed a single land mass as recently as middle Cenozoic time, and since then this mass has fractured and drifted apart to form the present continents (Wegener, 1924). If this were true, dispersal in the past would have been essentially inter-regional. More recent views concerning continental drift, however, express the opinion that little drifting has occurred since Cretaceous time, that only a small amount of continental drifting occurred in the northern hemisphere since Permian time, but that considerable drifting occurred in the southern hemisphere during the Mesozoic (Irving, 1959; Runcorn, 1959).

It seems, therefore, that whatever the outcome of these controversies, dispersal patterns for Cenozoic and late Mesozoic times can be reckoned on the basis of the present positions of the continents. Prior to late Mesozoic time the picture of intercontinental biotic interchange is clouded by uncertainties regarding the crustal history of the earth. Because of these circumstances the discussion in the remainder of this chapter concerns the later Mesozoic-Cenozoic eras. The general ideas expressed would hold for any period of changing land bridges, but the examples would be different if the juxtaposition of the land masses were different.

With the exception of Antarctica the continents now form three definitely north-to-south systems: North and South America, western Eurasia and Africa, and eastern Eurasia and Australia. The equator being at right angles to these axes, the climates of the world are stratified like rings, the warmest being at the equator, the coldest at the poles. If a member of the tropical Pacific littoral biome dispersed at the present through natural waterways to the Atlantic tropical littoral biome, it would have to go around either the southern tip of South America or the northern part of North Amerrica, or island-hop in the Bering Sea or North Atlantic. If this species could not exist outside tropical conditions, it would not be able to disperse through the cold waters of either route. However, the Central American land bridge which separates the parts of this marine biome connects the tropical rain forest and other continental biomes of southern North America and northern South America. This situation exemplifies the complementary action of land bridges—they have an opposite result on the terrestrial and marine biomes. If a land bridge rises, it connects land biomes and divides marine biomes; if it sinks, it divides the land biomes and connects marine ones.

Biotic traffic between the Old and New Worlds apparently occurred chiefly near the poles because elsewhere the continents are far apart. The proximity of the northern portions of the northern continents favors freer biotic interchange at higher latitudes by various over-water dispersal methods in addition to the probability that land connections existed. In the southern hemisphere somewhat the same relationship exists between Australasia, Antarctica, and the tip of South America.

Traffic north and south has depended greatly on the existence of land connections between North and South America, between southeastern Asia and Australia, and between Africa and areas north or northeast of it. Biotic exchange in the regions of these connections has been augmented by over-water dispersals.

Enough geologic and biogeographic evidence has accumulated to indicate that certain of these land connections have occurred several times (Simpson, 1947, 1950), but when and for how long these connections remained on each occasion is open to speculation and greatly in need of critical investigation. The number of times different connections occurred simultaneously is not known either, a subject on which available evidence is not conclusive. The only safe assumption at present is that overland dispersals between the continents followed an irregular and opportunistic pattern depending on the land connections in existence at any one time.

Climatic Zonation

At the present time the climate of the earth forms zones roughly paralleling the equator, constantly warm and frost-free through the tropics, becoming less warm away from the tropics, and culminating in frigid conditions at the polar areas. Over geologic time, however, the earth's climate in the higher latitudes has fluctuated over a fairly wide range. We live at the moment in a cool but not the coldest part of that fluctuation. Through extrapolation from the ecological tolerances of their living relatives, fossils can be used to provide a thermometer for these oscillations over the last 500 million years (Schuchert, 1924; Durham, 1950). More recently, measurements of certain radioactive isotopes of oxygen and other elements have contributed information on these temperature changes (Lowenstam and Epstein, 1954; Emiliani, 1955). Combined information from these sources suggests ocean tempera-

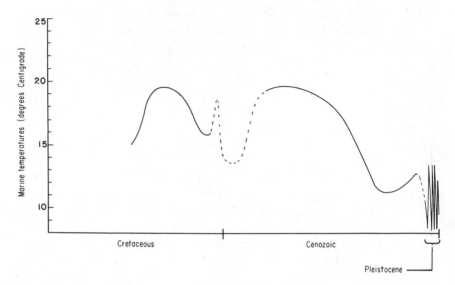

Fig. 131. Suggested temperature trends during the latter part of Cretaceous and Cenozoic time, combining data for the Cretaceous from Lowenstam and Epstein (1954), the Cenozoic from Durham (1950) and Dorman and Gill (1959), and the Pleistocene from Emiliani (1955). These authors stress that the values represent trends and should not be construed as indicating absolute climatic measurements.

ture trends from middle Cretaceous time to the present (Fig. 131) in which the warmer periods have been fairly long and the cooler periods fairly short.

As was stressed by Axelrod (1952) these climatic temperature bands are roughly at right angles to the three continental bands running from the southern through the northern hemispheres, and may have been in this relative position for a long time. On the basis of the known distribution of marine fossils, Stehli (1957) believes that Permian climatic zonation was parallel to the present.

Current investigations on rock paleo-magnetism (Irving, 1959; Runcorn, 1959) have resulted in the suggestion that the poles have wandered considerably throughout the history of the earth (Fig. 11). The projected figures indicate only slight wandering since the Miocene, a total of only about 15° of wandering since the Cretaceous, but much greater wandering before these times. All theories therefore seem in agreement that the direction of climatic zonation has apparently been the same from at least late Cretaceous time to the present.

Under conditions of these hypotheses exchanges of tropical terrestrial communities from the Americas to Asia or Australia would have occurred only when tropical climates extended north to latitudes of the Bering bridge. Estimates concerning climates at the Bering bridge indicate that the latest tropical conditions occurred during Upper Cretaceous time (Emerson, 1952) and the latest subtropical conditions during Eocene time (Durham, 1950). Since then climates in that area have become gradually cooler, and the climate during the latest probable dates of bridging in the Pleistocene probably ranged between temperate and subarctic. If all these premises were true, we would expect the similarity between existing Eurasian and North American species to be greatest to the north and to decrease towards the south. In his analysis of the insects of the order Collembola, Mills (1939) pointed out that this proportionality does actually exist.

The north and south movement of temperature bands coupled with intercontinental connections at only the polar end of the continental systems in the northern hemisphere explains the movements of many tropical groups. Three other dynamic sets of factors produce climatic zonation which may be at right angles to these temperature rings and hence cause drastic deviations from a simple annular pattern of dispersal. These three sets of factors are rainfall patterns, mountain systems, and ocean currents.

RAINFALL PATTERNS

The relatively high relief of existing mountain systems and other factors influencing world wind directions together have resulted in great inequality of rainfall on different parts of the earth. This rainfall pattern (Fig. 132), does not coincide with the temperature bands, more often than not forming arid and humid bands running generally from north to south. Because organisms are usually adapted to live under only a narrow set of rainfall conditions, these rainfall bands act as rigid barriers to the free movement of organisms. These bands may therefore be just as important a factor as temperature banding in limiting opportunities for intercontinental dispersal.

MOUNTAIN SYSTEMS

Mountain systems have a unique effect in relation to intercontinental connections in that they may negate the restricting effects of other factors. Mountain systems trending north and south have cooler climates at higher elevations, and toward the equator afford avenues of dispersal for cool-adapted forms across regions which at lower levels would be too warm for the species to exist. Cool-adapted terrestrial organisms have seldom dispersed across the

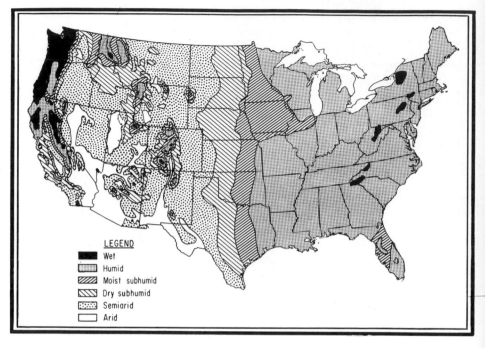

Fig. 132.   Moisture bands in the United States. (Adapted from U.S.D.A.)

equator (de Beaufort, 1951; Darlington, 1957), but when they
have done so it has undoubtedly been through the cool habitats
of mountain chains (Ross, 1956a).

Mountains have been of especial importance in the intercontinental mixing of freshwater communities. Many of these occur only
in swift, cold streams associated with mountains. The intercontinental and inter-regional dispersal of these communities is therefore dependent on chains of hill or montane country connecting
various areas. That such terrain has at times connected all the
major portions of the earth is well shown by certain insect components of these communities. The net-winged midges comprising
the family Blepharoceridae occur only in cold, rapid streams but
do not extend into truly arctic regions. The present range of all
species is restricted to widely separated mountain systems (Alexander, 1958), yet each subfamily has a wide distribution (Fig.
133). Past conditions in the more northern mountains must have
approximated those in the more southern mountains now occupied
by Blepharoceridae and thus provided intercontinental and inter-regional avenues of dispersal for these forms.

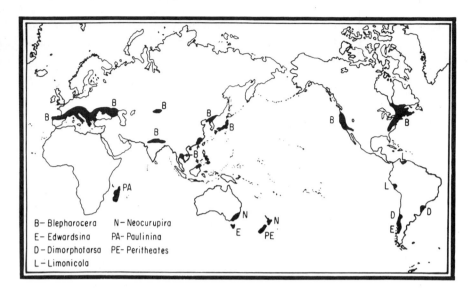

Fig. 133. Geographic distribution of seven genera of net-winged midges of the family Blepharoceridae. (After Alexander.)

OCEAN CURRENTS

These play the same modifying role in providing avenues of dispersal across temperature zones as do mountain systems but are of especial importance in the dispersal of marine forms. Cool and warm ocean currents traverse practically all parts of the ocean and connect many of the major oceanic basins. It is certain that similar ocean currents have existed since the beginning of life. As a result the widespread dispersal of marine organisms has always been more probable than comparable dispersals of terrestrial organisms.

Dispersal Opportunities

Changes in geomorphology and climatic zonation thus provide opportunities for members of different biomes to spread to various parts of the world at different times. Representatives of marine biomes have greater opportunities for dispersal than do those of terrestrial biomes. The latter are frequently rigidly restricted geographically by ecological factors. As a result the changes in land bridges and in climatic zonation produce a curious, intermittent, gatelike set of dispersal opportunities which have allowed first one terrestrial biome then another to disperse between continents (Fig. 134).

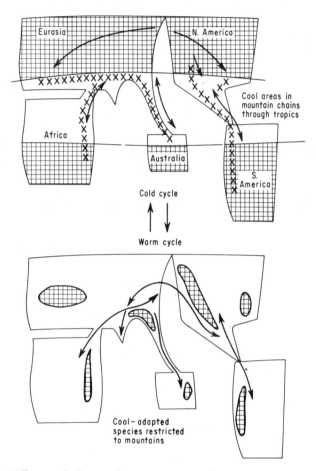

Fig. 134. Differential dispersal opportunities for temperate versus tropical biotas during cold and warm periods of the earth. Arrows in the top drawing indicate dispersal paths of cool-adapted species, and the arrows in the figure at the bottom indicate dispersal paths of warm-adapted species. Note the restriction of dispersal of tropical species between the New and Old Worlds during cold periods and the isolation of temperate species during warm periods.

Large segments of terrestrial and fresh water biomes are separated from each other by land areas which form dividing agents as effective as oceans. In the case of the mountain stream biome, the western North American segment is as effectively separated from the eastern segment by the flat central area of the continent as it is from the segment in northeastern Asia by the Bering Sea. In terrestrial and freshwater biomes, therefore, inter-regional mixing on the same continent may be governed by a set of factors comparable to those involved in intercontinental mixing.

Dispersal Availability

When a bridge connects two segments of a biome, one would expect that all the species on each side would disperse across it, resulting in a thorough mixing of the components of the two previously separated regional units. There is some evidence that this may occasionally happen. Known fossils of the holarctic, middle Cenozoic, temperate deciduous forest recorded by Chaney (1940) contained sufficient species common to both North America and Eurasia to indicate a fairly complete panmixia. However, for every case like this there are many that indicate a much lesser degree of mixing. Two factors cause a reduction from complete mixing: the ecological nature of the bridging area and the geographic distribution of species in the biome.

The connecting area may be within the limits of ecological tolerance of only a few of the many species living at either end of it. To cite an inter-regional example, in North America the Rocky Mountain and the Appalachian mountain systems were connected during the Pleistocene and are connected at present by a non-mountainous area having cold lakes and streams. During this time a few species of montane caddisflies such as *Rhyacophila acropedes* and *angelita* spread from the Rocky Mountains to the Appalachian Mountains. Only those which were able to live in the slower cold streams of the flatter country dispersed in this fashion. Many other eastern and western species which appear to be completely restricted to faster mountain streams either did not spread over the routes or failed to persist in their new homes (Ross, 1956a). An example from the monotremes explained by de Beaufort (1951) also fits this concept. In early Cenozoic times populations of the form ancestral to *Echidna* and *Zaglossus* spread over New Guinea and Australia; during isolation in later Cenozoic time, *Echidna* evolved in Australia and *Zaglossus* in New Guinea. During the Pleistocene connection between these areas *Echidna* reached southern New Guinea and Tasmania, but *Zaglossus*, which lives only in the mountains, could not reach Australia because the connection was entirely lowland in nature.

Thus only the species able to exist under climatic or biotic conditions of various kinds occurring on a connection are able to cross it. Simpson (1947) has given the apt name "filter bridge" to terrestrial connections, which probably fits all land connections sufficiently narrow and intermittent to be considered as bridges.

Only those members of a biome in actual geographic contact with bridging areas can cross them. Thus of the many northern species of the rodent genus *Citellus,* only the most northerly and holarctic species *C. undulatus* appears to have made a recent crossing of the Bering bridge between Siberia and Alaska (Fig. 135) (Burt and Grossenheider, 1952; Rausch, 1953). In each of many North American genera in divers groups only one species now extends into Alaska and is in a position to cross the Bering bridge should the climate change slightly. In the large caddisfly genera *Hydropsyche* and *Triaenodes* only *H. riola* and *T. tarda* extend into Alaska, and of the many nearctic pines only *Pinus contorta* extends into the vicinity of this region (Munns, 1938; Flook, 1959).

A remarkable parallel exists between these present-day examples and indications of what happened in the past. In a surprising number of instances only one species of a moderately large genus has dispersed over a land bridge and become established in another regional association of its parent biome. This is suggested whenever all the species in each regional unit are monophyletic. Examples in the caddisflies include the North American genus *Pycnopsyche* in the eastern deciduous forest, the entire American branch of *Agapetus,* and the Australian branch of *Agapetus.*

Virtual proof of past dispersals of only one species per group is demonstrated in the caddisfly genus *Wormaldia.* One subgenus consists of a number of Asiatic species and one species, *W. mohri,* in the Great Smoky Mountains of eastern North America. The American species is closely related to *W. kisoensis,* the only known Japanese species, although it is distinct from it in many features. When the phylogeny and geographic distribution for the subgenus are correlated, it is evident that the evolution of the subgenus centered around China and that late in this evolution a northern species evolved which dispersed into North America and to Japan, the two migrant populations giving rise to *W. mohri* and *W. kisoensis* respectively (Fig. 136) (Ross, 1956a). In another family of caddisflies, the genus *Himalopsyche* illustrates the initial evolution of a single northeastern Asiatic branch and the subsequent dispersal of this one distinctive line into North America. The single American species of *Himalopsyche* lives in Californian streams.

Fig. 135. Distribution of the ground squirrels of the genus *Citellus*. The northern hatched area is the North American range of the Holarctic species *C. undulatus,* the lower area the combined ranges of the other 19 Nearctic species. (Adapted from Burt and Grossenheider and from Rausch.)

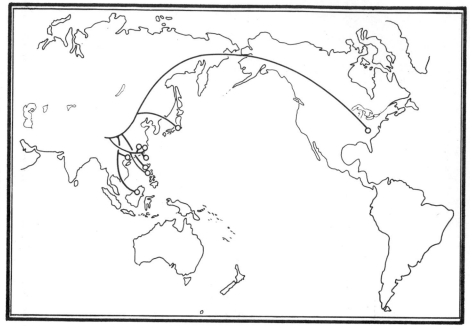

Fig. 136. The phylogenetic tree of the caddisfly genus *Wormaldia* subgenus *Doloclanes* superimposed on the known distribution of the species. The circle in Japan represents *W. kisoensis,* that in eastern North America *W. mohri.*

The sawfly genus *Taxonus* shows the same features but with dispersal in the opposite direction. The genus apparently evolved in the eastern deciduous forest of North America where several species now occur. A single species occurs in Europa, and it is a member of one of the more highly specialized North American branches of the genus. Kinsey (1930, 1936) postulated that a single species of the gall wasp genus *Cynips* dispersed from western North America to Eurasia and became the parent of the Palearctic species of the genus.

This parallel between present conditions and probable past occurrences, especially remarkable in examples concerning the Bering bridge region, suggests that only slight ecological changes accompanied the formation of many connections between the continents, and the bridges usually were of a narrowly restricted ecological type.

The correlation of several "one-per-genus" dispersals suggests the importance of peripheral communities in biome dispersal.

In his remarkable studies on termite distribution, Emerson (1952) pointed out that in each of several subfamilies related genera arose in South America and that, probably in Cretaceous time, representatives of only one genus spread into North America and ultimately into the Old World. Seevers (1957) postulated an almost identical circumstance in the beetles which live as guests in the termite colonies. In the beetle subtribe Perinthina (Fig. 137), only a single

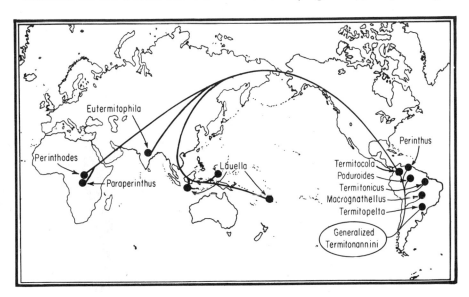

Fig. 137. Distribution of the genera of the subtribe Perinthina of the family Staphylinidae. Lines indicate the phylogeny and paths of dispersal. (After Seevers.)

line dispersed, in the tribe Termitohospini two lines dispersed, and in the subtribe Corotocina also two lines dispersed (Fig. 138).

With these termites and their beetle guests, the apparently correlated dispersal of several lines indicates that an entire community dispersed as a unit. Many other related South American genera, however, did not disperse. This difference in dispersal behavior may be correlated with biome structure. Biomes are a system of overlapping associations or communities in which the peripheral communities may be similar in physical nature to the others but different in taxonomic composition (see Chapter 9). If a land bridge of limited ecological characteristics became available for dispersal, it would probably be similar ecologically to the peripheral community which it touched. Under these circumstances only species in these peripheral communities would spread across the bridge.

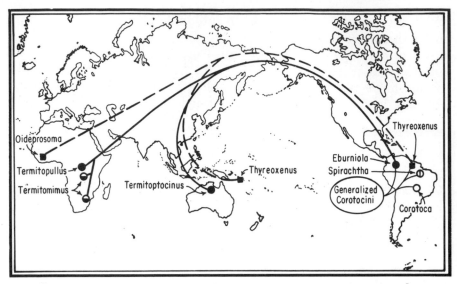

Fig. 138. Distribution of the genera of the subtribe Corotocina of the family Staphylinidae. Lines indicate the phylogeny and paths of dispersal. (After Seevers.)

Subclimax versus Climax Dispersal

Because most subclimax species occur throughout every associa-tion of the biome and many occur in the subclimax communities of several biomes, subclimax species in general have an inordinately greater chance of being adjacent to land bridges than the climax species restricted to only a few associations of a single biome. This circumstance has resulted in many apparent paradoxes of distribu-tion which have puzzled students of biogeography. For example, the scrub mallees of Australian deserts are dominated by certain species of *Eucalyptus* and other indigenous shrubs and trees which occur only in Australia, whereas their counterparts, the semi-desert scrub of southwestern North America, are dominated by New World shrubs and trees. In contrast to this taxonomic divergence, genera such as the grasses *Danthonia* and *Aristida* are abundant in both places (Coaldrake, 1951).

Sawflies of the genus *Dolerus* which feed on *Equisetum* and grasses provide another example of paradoxical distribution. Many species of *Dolerus* abound in the temperate deciduous forest of eastern North America, but unlike many leafhoppers, grasshoppers, and other insects endemic in the same areas, many of these *Dolerus* species extend across North America and Eurasia, and others have their closest relatives in Europe and Asia (Ross, 1929; Benson, 1952).

The grass genera *Danthonia* and *Aristida* and the genus *Dolerus* are subclimax organisms, and illustrate the wide geographic range commonly found in the components of subclimax communities. The distribution of these organisms is sufficiently extensive to highlight an interesting aspect of biome evolution, namely, that species of the subclimax communities have had a greater amount of intercontinental mixing than have species restricted to the climax communities. Among invertebrates inhabiting temperate climates, two insect genera afford excellent examples. In the leafhopper genus *Macrosteles,* many species feed on subclimax herbs such as *Urtica* and subclimax grasses, and much intercontinental mixing has occurred (Fig. 139) (Moore and Ross, 1957). However, in the sawfly genus *Neodiprion,* confined to climax or near-climax coniferous hosts, present evidence indicates only a single intercontinental dispersal and in addition only little inter-regional dispersal between the eastern and western parts of North America (Fig. 140) (Ross, 1955).

Information concerning the insect fauna of the grasses *Aristida* and *Danthonia* indicates that even with subclimax species we cannot draw too wide a generalization. Although the two grass genera have dispersed between North America and Australia, all their North American leafhopper fauna has not. Certain members of the North American leafhopper genera *Unoka* and *Flexamia* feed on species of these two grass genera but have not been found on any other continent. Either the grasses dispersed before the leafhopper species began living on these hosts, or at the time of dispersal the grasses had either a greater vagility or wider tolerances than the leafhoppers.

Three genera of grass-feeding leafhoppers abundant in subclimax communities of the eastern deciduous forest of North America exemplify the dispersal effects of differences in ecological tolerances. The genus *Polyamia* occurs almost wholly in communities in or near the range of the eastern deciduous forest and apparently has never dispersed to any other continent. The tribe Balcluthini (in reality only one well-marked genus or supergenus) and the genus *Exitianus* also occur in these same eastern communities but, like the grasses *Aristida* and *Danthonia,* occur also in a wide array of central and western communities in both arid country and at elevations up to 10,000 feet. Unlike *Polyamia,* the Balcluthini and

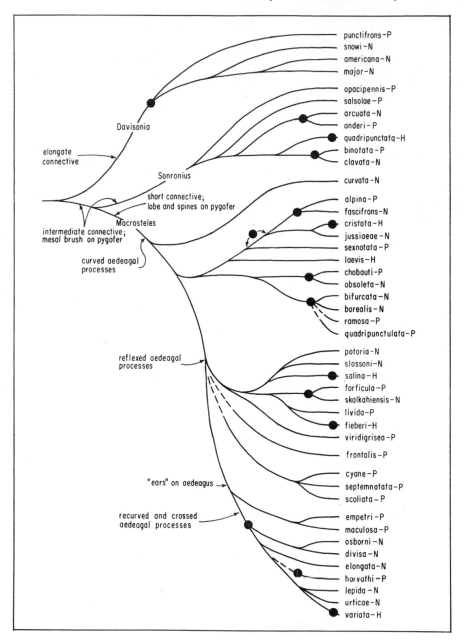

Fig. 139. Phylogenetic tree of the leafhopper genus *Macrosteles*. Black circles indicate the minimum number of intercontinental dispersals between Asia and North America necessary to explain the present distribution. H indicates holarctic; N indicates nearctic; P indicates palearctic. (After Moore and Ross.)

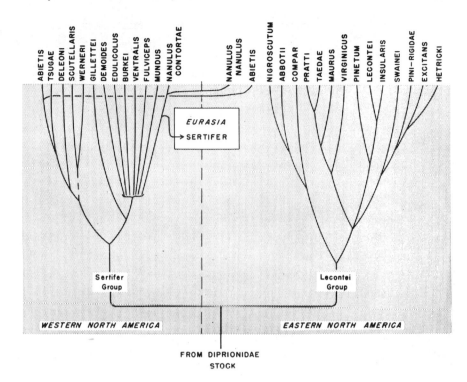

Fig. 140. Phylogeny and dispersal chart of *Neodiprion*, a genus of sawflies which feed on conifers. This indicates rigid regional restriction of the eastern and western groups, with a fairly recent dispersal to Asia and, even more recently, the dispersal of two species from west to east.

Exitianus have dispersed to all continents of the world (Oman, 1949; Evans, 1947*a,b*).

A situation embodying these differentials in dispersal possibilities is found in the North American mouse *Peromyscus maniculatus* and its ectoparasitic fleas *Monopsyllus thambus*, *M. wagneri*, and *Orchopeas leucopus*. The mouse has an extensive range including many subclimax communities. Two of its ectoparasites, *Monopsyllus wagneri* and *Orchopeas leucopus* are also widespread, but *Monopsyllus thambus* occurs only in the extreme northern portion of the mouse's range (Fig. 141) (Holland, 1958). Should this mouse disperse into South America, its two widespread fleas would probably go with it, but *Monopsyllus thambus* certainly would not.

The extensive ranges and relatively frequent dispersal of many subclimax species may explain some situations which have been considered puzzling, for example the Cenozoic dispersal of horses

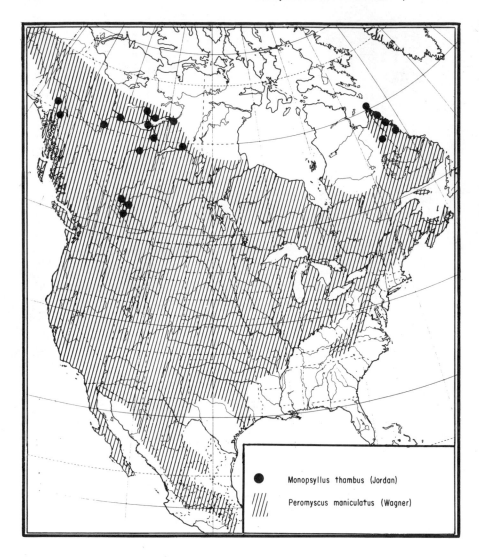

Fig. 141. Distribution of the widespread mouse *Peromyscus maniculatus* and its Arctic flea *Monopsyllus thambus*. (From Holland.)

into South America without evidence of grassland extension from North to South America. It is possible that horses were successful in subclimax communities having abundant grasses, and that the horses dispersed into South America in company with the many subclimax grass genera now common to both Americas.

REGIONAL EVOLUTION

Because the factors affecting the evolution of communities are extremely numerous and complex, it is reasonable to suppose that the total of these factors would never produce the same results in any two isolated segments of a biome. The truth of this postulate becomes evident when parts of a biome on different continents are compared with respect to relative increase and extinction of species.

Extinction

According to Chaney (1940), the holarctic and continuous temperate deciduous forest had a fairly uniform taxonomic composition during middle Cenozoic time. The existing large isolated segments of this forest are now different from each other. In the western European segment many plant genera are no longer present, whereas in both the Asiatic and the eastern North American segments most of the earlier genera have survived. This difference reflects a differential regional extinction of certain ancestral elements.

In the mammals this sort of regional extinction has been commonplace (Simpson, 1947). In many examples such as the horses, the representatives in one region of the biome became extinct, then colonization from the other region repopulated the first region with close relatives of the extinct forms, and these colonists in turn became extinct.

Increase in Number of Species

Differential evolution of this type is exemplified by certain insects of the temperate deciduous forest. In the European and Asiatic segments of this biome the leafhoppers comprising the genus *Erythroneura* have a known fauna of about 100 distinctive species, all belonging to a closely knit series of species groups. Members of two of the groups apparently dispersed into North America in middle Cenozoic time, and these have since evolved into several distinctive groups together containing over 400 species. Obviously some special set of circumstances favoring an unusual increase in the number of species (probably a host-transfer mechanism, p. 187) occurred in the North American region and not in the other continents. Why this happened in only one region is not known, but it does illustrate the point that many evolutionary developments come about only in one area even though apparently equally propitious circumstances occur in other areas also.

Some investigators have suggested that the number of species increases in direct proportion to the size and age of the area (Willis, 1922). The example of *Erythroneura* above indicates the fallacy of this "age and area" theory, because in this group of *Erythroneura* the older fauna on the larger Eurasian area has only about a fourth the number of species found in the younger fauna in the single, smaller North American segment.

Regional differentiation on a relatively small scale of evolutionary divergence occurs in two groups of grass-feeding leafhoppers. In one, the compact *Stirellus* group, four genera including *Stirellus* and *Gillettiella* occur in North America, and about a dozen genera including *Aconura* and *Paivanana* occur in Eurasia (Oman, 1949). In the other, the *Doratura* group, *Athysanella* and *Driotura* occur in North America, whereas *Doratura* and possibly others occur in Eurasia. Evidence from phylogeny and distribution suggests that early Cenozoic members of each group dispersed between Eurasia and North America and since then have evolved on each continent into a number of readily identifiable but otherwise similar genera inhabiting comparable grassland communities. All of these genera are relatively southern in distribution, which may explain the apparent lack of intercontinental dispersal since the evolution of the present-day genera.

An important mechanism contributing to the increased diversity of isolated regions of a biome concerns colonists from other biomes. A biome is continually enriched by species from adjoining biomes which become adapted to live in it. Isolated sections of a biome have different neighbors, and the act of colonization is undoubtedly highly random and unpredictable. The unequal result is demonstrated by the desert biome. The African region was colonized by a branch of the spurge family Euphorbiaceae, which has since evolved into many cactus-like species. The American regions of the desert biome were colonized by the cactus family Cactaceae which has also evolved into many prickly species.

A less striking example occurs in the widespread grass-feeding leafhopper subfamily Hecalinae. Several American lines became xeric-adapted and now, in the form of the genera *Memnonia, Hecullus,* and *Dicyphonia,* are distinctive elements of the arid prairie biomes of central and southwestern North America. From mesic grassland leafhoppers allied to *Deltocephalus*-like lines evolved distinctive xeric American genera such as *Lonatura* and *Unoka* (Delong, 1948; Ribault, 1952; Oman, 1949) which are likewise members of the same prairie biomes. The fact that these xeric forms occur only in North America suggests that the grassland biomes to which they belong have had only incomplete intercontinental mixing, if any, since these leafhoppers became established in the more xeric grassland communities. In the grasshoppers (Orthoptera) many similar examples from many continents (Roberts, 1941; Uvarov, 1943; Rehn, 1958) emphasize the importance of colonization in contributing to regional diversity.

Conservative Elements

In contrast to the examples above, many plants and invertebrate animals seem to exhibit a pronounced evolutionary conservatism throughout widely separated regions. In the cool, temperate, rapid stream biome, the caddisfly genus *Sortosa* dispersed into all the continents, apparently during Cretaceous time, and has existed subsequently as isolated geographic units. Since that time each separate branch has evolved into a distinctive subgenus. A daughter genus *Wormaldia* of nearly similar ecological traits dispersed throughout the northern hemisphere, probably in early Cenozoic time, and the isolated branches of this group have evolved into moderately distinctive species groups. In spite of a great difference in age and the widespread nature of the regional units of this biome, the geographic segregates of these genera have undergone little change either ecologically or in number of species.

Within the temperate deciduous forest biome many of the ferns have been an equally conservative element. The fern components of the different regions of the biome are strikingly similar, and this would seem to be due to small amounts of change since the regions became separated rather than to fairly recent dispersal.

PHYLOGENY AND AGE OF BIOMES

The alternation of intercontinental or inter-regional mixing and the evolution of the isolated regional segments produce biomes having a reticulate phylogeny. Typical stages in this phylogenetic pattern are available for study because biomes are of different ages and exhibit different stages of development.

The oldest existing biomes are those of the sea. Peterson (1914, 1918) and Ekman (1953) presented a great deal of information concerning marine communities and ecological and geographic associations of marine species. Too little is known about marine biomes, however, to attempt an analysis of their regional phylogeny.

The phylogeny of existing terrestrial biomes can be outlined in a moderately comprehensive fashion. The oldest terrestrial biome is the tropical evergreen rain forest, occurring in continuously warm and humid areas. Through geologic time and by various evolutionary mechanisms, plants colonized other areas, certain colonizations proceeding toward adaptation to drier conditions, other colonizations proceeding toward adaptation to colder conditions. Through such developments the major biomes evolved, possibly in the order tentatively suggested in Fig. 142. Certain branches of

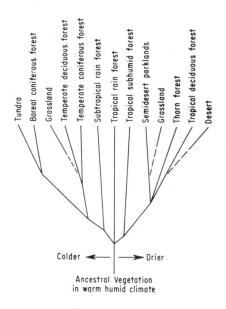

Fig. 142. Tentative suggestion of the phylogeny of the major terrestrial biomes.

the diagram seem to be well founded. The careful and detailed analysis of Axelrod (1958) indicates clearly that the semi-desert woodland-chaparral biomes of southwestern North America evolved from a tropical subhumid forest.

The youngest terrestrial biome is probably the tundra or paramos. It is characterized universally by the short growth form of its plant life, including trees, shrubs, and herbs. Few if any genera occur only in tundra. Many of the tundra plant species in both northern and southern hemispheres belong to widespread genera such as

Festuca, Arabis, Draba, Cerastium, and *Pedicularis.* It is virtually certain that, since these genera evolved, tundra conditions have not extended in a continuous belt across the equator. It is therefore equally certain that in each region these plants have moved independently from adjacent communities into tundra areas. The genera mentioned above and the great bulk of other tundra genera contain many species inhabiting stream bank or subclimax communities of temperate or boreal biomes. The present tundra would therefore appear to be populated by subclimax and stream bank species arising in lower latitudes or elevations. It is reasonable to suppose that these colonizing species were those with the wider ecological tolerances and therefore were the most widely distributed both ecologically and geographically.

The tundra biome may therefore be regarded as a former subclimax aggregation which has become a series of climax communities by the independent colonization of distant areas. The remarkable taxonomic similarity of distant regions of this biome is not due to a joining of regions of the biome with a subsequent mixing of biotas. It is due to the initial widespread nature of the species which did the colonizing.

The next theoretical stage in biome phylogeny would be the evolution of climax species especially adapted to the ecological situation of the biome and restricted to it. Certain desert biomes seem to represent this stage.

The cactus desert biome of southwestern North America and certain areas such as Jamaica in the dry parts of the American tropics (Asprey and Robbins, 1953) are physically and visually similar to certain African deserts which are dominated by cactus-like Euphorbiaceae. The vegetation of both associations produces an overlay of similar ecological conditions and thus may be classified as the same biome. Taxonomically the situation is completely the opposite. The Cactaceae evolved in the western hemisphere and, with the exception of some species of *Rhipsalis* in Africa and Ceylon which are probably introduced (Lawrence, 1951), are rigidly confined to the Americas. The Euphorbiaceae is a large cosmopolitan family in which cactus-like forms evolved in the eastern hemisphere and have apparently never dispersed from it. Each of these cactus-like associations therefore arose independently from different ancestral types, and the resulting communities owe their ecological similarity to the convergent evolution of dominants rather than to phylogenetic affinities. In other words, this biome is polyphyletic in origin.

Interwoven Biome Phylogeny

Should ecological conditions in areas between the New and Old World cactus-like deserts change in such a manner that the two deserts came into contact, the two associations would merge and form a single biome of greater taxonomic heterogeneity than that of either present association. This presupposes that species comprising the two associations have similar or widely overlapping ecological tolerances and that most of the mixing species would become adjusted to coexistence rather than undergoing wholesale extermination of species. Even in case of considerable extinction it is likely that some species from each original association would survive, increasing at least the taxonomic heterogeneity of the mixture as regards genera and families. After such a mixing had occurred it would be impossible to determine its history from a study of the biome itself. It would be necessary to trace the phylogeny and dispersal of the individual species of the biome in order to unravel the history of the mixing.

The temperate deciduous forest is an example of a biome following such a mixing. This forest consists of three major, well-separated units, one in western Europe, one in eastern Asia, and one in eastern North America. The close taxonomic affinities of plants in all three areas, with many genera such as *Quercus, Acer, Ulmus* and *Tilia* represented by related species in all three, plus abundant fossil records show that at one time these units were connected as a single system. Since the last separation of the regional units many different species have evolved in the isloated regions, but except for a few groups such as the mammals no great evolutionary changes seem to have occurred.

With present knowledge it is impossible to ascertain how many times this temperate deciduous forest biome has divided and reunited in the past, or how many of its components mixed at each contact. During this time the components of the biome undoubtedly became interwoven in intricate fashion because species would be associated or separated because of ecological rather than phylogenetic affinities.

A comparison of the Old and New World regions of the tropical rain forest draws attention to features arising from long regional isolation (probably since Cretaceous time) following many previous mixings. Many of the slowly changing genera such as the plant genera *Piper* and *Ficus* occur in both regions. More commonly the same families occur in both regions, but, as in the order Cycadales, the individual genera occur in only one or the other. In some plant groups entire families are restricted to one region, as the Pandanaceae in the Old World and the Cyclanthaceae in the New World. The large plant family Bromeliaceae is restricted to the New World except for the single species *Pitcairnia Feliciana* which occurs also on the west coast of Africa (Lawrence, 1951). This lone colonist would seem to indicate the extreme infrequency of over-water dispersal of terrestrial organisms from South America to Africa and the relatively absolute isolation of these intercontinental segregates of the present tropical rain forest.

Biome Extinction and Resurrection

When tropical or subtropical climates presumably prevailed as far north as the Bering Sea area in the Cretaceous and Eocene, mountainous areas may not have been as high as at present. If boreal forests or tundra communities had evolved previously, they might have become extinct because of the disappearance of sufficiently cold areas in which to live. In this event, the cold region biomes of today would be the result of another colonization of cold areas by species living in adjacent biomes. No direct evidence has yet been presented on this possibility, but it is nevertheless a very real one. It fits Axelrod's contention (1959) that many upland plant species adapted to rigorous conditions evolved much earlier than the record indicates, yet because of poor conditions for their fossilization may never be known.

Indirect evidence for the extinction of past biomes adapted to cool climates lies in the greater number of species which occur in tropical regions as compared with the number found in temperate and arctic regions. This latitudinal differential, well known to Wallace (1878) and more recently treated by Darlington (1957) and Fischer (1960), can be explained best on the assumption that areas for the survival of tropical biomes have always been available, whereas temperate and arctic areas have periodically become so reduced that many older temperate and arctic biomes became extinct. Although tropical areas have been relatively stable climatically, most of them have been unstable geologically. As a result, connected and disconnected island arcs, elevated then peneplaned mountains, and other geomorphic events have produced in the tropics a continuous succession of isolating and congregating conditions leading to an equally continuous evolution of more and more species and ecological communities.

The Age of the Process

The alternation of intercontinental mixing and regional isolation has undoubtedly been a major factor in biome evolution over many geologic periods. Indirect evidence can be found dating back as early as Pennsylvanian and Mississippian times of the Paleozoic. Schuchert (1924) mentioned that the tree species of the coal measures (Pennsylvanian in age) were remarkably alike in distant locations such as central North America and Europe. These Paleozoic floras probably represented the same well-mixed stage of biome phylogeny as the present-day temperate deciduous forest or the taiga. Various elements had undoubtedly evolved in isolated regions of the tropical biome and then intermingled across bridging areas. Because these processes are automatic when a dynamic biota occurs in an area of dynamic geomorphology, it is reasonable to assume that they have been important in biome evolution ever since the most primitive biomes came into existence perhaps two billion years ago.

The Geotectonic

Factor

11

The products of organic evolution are the result of the interplay between a spontaneously dynamic biota and a spontaneously dynamic environment. Without the dynamic nature of the biota, evolution would not have occurred. Without the particular kind of dynamics present in the environments on the earth, either evolution would have followed an entirely different course or life itself might not have evolved. The environmental dynamics owe their ultimate basis to geotectonic events which have been alluded to only briefly in the preceding pages.

The dynamics of the earth's crust produce dynamic environments. Facets of this changing environment affecting evolutionary processes include the rise and subsidence of land bridges, changes in climatic zonation and extremes, and the formation of new soils and new climates. These changes are the product of two great general forces which oppose each other to affect the configuration of the earth's surface: the elevating and levelling processes. Each has its distinctive action on the surface and through this its effect on the biotic environment.

THE ELEVATING PROCESS

The most conspicuous results of the elevating process are the mountains, but these are only one of many related phenomena. The process should more properly be called crustal deformation, for it includes not only great upthrusts which produce mountains, but also warping and faulting of the surface and upwellings of molten materials from the interior of the earth.

Mountains produce high elevations, hence cool temperatures on the land surfaces which precipitate large amounts of moisture from clouds moving across them. This results in decreasing precipitation on the lee side of the mountains and produces in the mountains themselves cooler and more moist habitats than exist in the surrounding country. This dual effect is especially marked in the western part of North America where much of the moisture comes from the Pacific Ocean. Successive mountain chains running roughly north and south provide cool temperate to near arctic conditions southward into areas which are subtropical at sea level, but they also produce rain shadows which result in extremely xeric areas on the eastern side of each range. Deflection of winds produces similar changes, resulting in greater or lesser rainfall depending on the moisture content of the winds or in temperature changes.

Mountain-like ridges arising from the ocean floors undoubtedly influence the direction of ocean currents and in this way affect the temperatures prevailing in different areas and at various depths in the ocean. These effects are not, however, limited to the ocean itself. Upwellings of cold water at the surface may cause precipitation from air moving above it. The Humbolt current is such a cold upwelling, and it reduces rainfall for thousands of miles along the western coast of the tropical and subtropical Americas. The warm surface Japanese current in the North Pacific produces the opposite effect, contributing to the unusually warm and humid condition of the western coast of North America northward from San Francisco.

At times great areas of the continents have been raised to considerable heights. The Great Plains region and the Colorado plateau in North America were elevated possibly 4,000 or 5,000 feet in middle Cenozoic time. Large areas of Africa were similarly elevated. It is likely that when these areas were raised, entirely new ecological conditions came into existence, differing from all previous ones in unique combinations of climatic conditions.

Frequent slight warpings of the crust have produced less spectacular changes in levels in many areas. Many of the land bridge regions such as the Bering Straits area and the Banda geosyncline area (Fig. 130) seem to have been either raised and lowered or alternately exposed and submerged many times (Fig. 143). Combined with changes in sea level, slight warpings have caused areas such as the lower Mississippi valley of North America to alternate between being a shallow continental sea and a low elevation terrestrial area. Such a series of changes coupled with some irregularities in topography could readily produce the succession of islands and connected land shown in Fig. 104.

Sea level changes contributing to these events have been most extreme during periods of glaciation. When the maximum amount of water was in the form of ice on the continents, the ocean level was lowered some 600 feet. At this low point the present British Isles were connected by a broad land mass with continental Europe (Beirne, 1952), and many present islands of the South Pacific were part of the Asiatic mainland (Umbgrove, 1947) (Fig. 144). The weight of the ice itself caused some warping of the underlying continents, adding another factor to the changes in water level.

The same orogenic activities which produce mountains on a continent produce many of the islands between continents. Igneous material spewing from volcanoes erupting out of the bottoms of the oceans have built the Hawaiian Islands and others situated far from continents. A combination of upthrust, down-warping, and volcanic activity along what seem to be permanent strips of weakness in the crust may have periodically produced series of islands where intercontinental isthmuses now stand. The present Central American corridor between North and South America has probably had this type of history (Simpson, 1950).

The speed at which these crustal movements progress is not always easy to measure. The volcano Parícutin in Mexico erupted in 1943, continued erupting until 1952, and built up a cone over 1,500 feet in height. Thrusts are expressed chiefly as earthquakes. Cloos (1954) pointed out that the unusually severe 1872 quake in the mountains of California produced an increase in elevation of six feet, evidenced today as the fault at Lundy Creek (Fig. 145). He calculated that a sudden rise like this every few thousand years would produce the 6,000 foot rise of the Sierra Nevada range in about five million years.

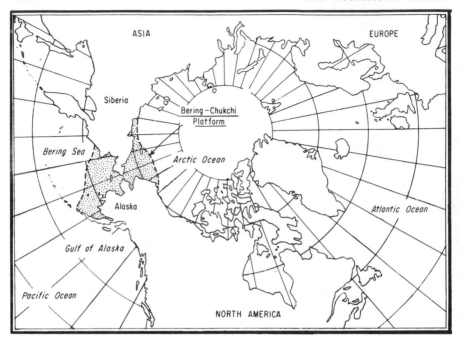

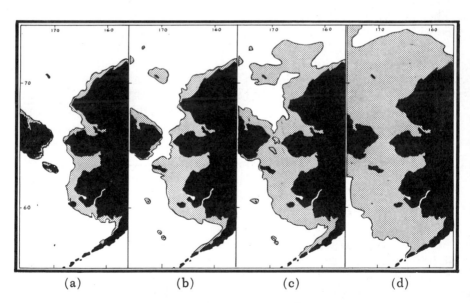

Fig. 143.   The Bering Bridge. Above, its present location, the Bering-Chukchi platform. Below, its state of emergence when the sea level was at various depths below the present level. (a), 75 feet; (b), 120 feet; (c), 150 feet; and (d), 300 feet. (From Hopkins.)

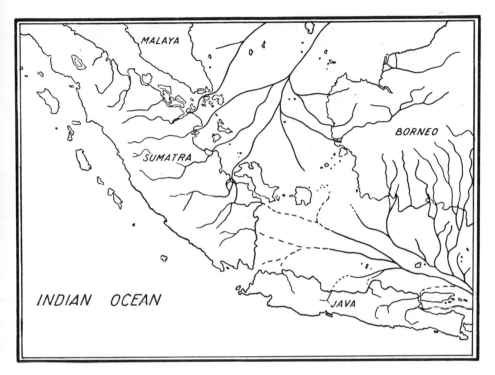

Fig. 144. The drowned rivers of Sundaland, southeastern Asia. These indicate that this entire area was above water when the Pleistocene ocean was at its lowest level. (From Umbgrove, *The Pulse of the Earth*, courtesy of Martinus Nijhoff.)

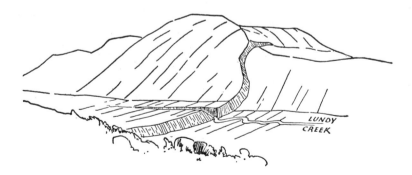

Fig. 145. The beheaded valley of Lundy Creek, near Mono Lake, California. The rift was caused by the earthquake of 1872. (From Cloos, *Conversation with the Earth*, courtesy of R. Piper & Co.)

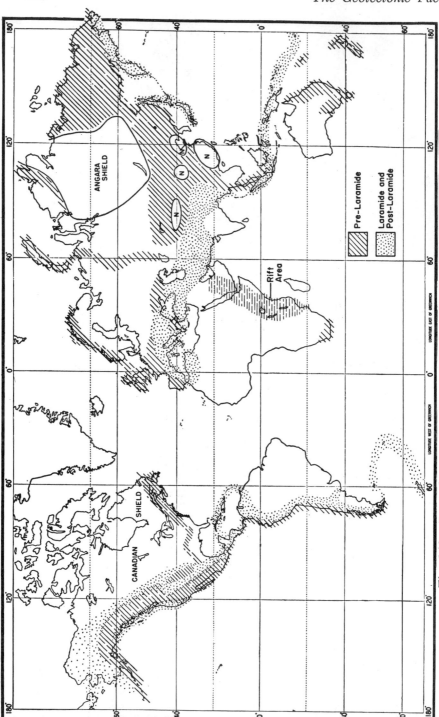

Fig. 146. Principle areas of mountain-making and associated features. *N*, stable nuclei of southern Asia. (Adapted from Umbgrove.)

Although crustal movements take place slowly in terms of our own sense of time, sufficient time has elapsed since the origin of life on the earth for myriads of these crustal movements to occur. In some areas, such as the Paleozoic Arbuckle Mountains of Oklahoma, orogenic movements have been few, and no new major upthrusts have occurred since the Paleozoic. In other areas crustal changes have been frequent, forming orogenic belts in which mountain building has been fairly continuous since pre-Paleozoic times (Fig. 146) (Umbgrove, 1947; Love, 1939).

There is good evidence in the geologic record (Schuchert, 1924) that whereas mountain building has been almost continuous, it has not always been of the same intensity. This activity has reached high peaks during some periods, with long intervening periods of lesser activity. The Laramide orogeny during the late Cretaceous and early Cenozoic, seems to be one such period of increased orogenic activity, as have been late Pliocene and Pleistocene times. Umbgrove (1947) believed that these successive active times are cyclic phenomena which he described as "the pulse of the earth." King (1958) suggested that the Mesozoic and Cenozoic orogenic phenomena of western North America form a single long cycle. Attempts to ascertain past oceanic temperatures give indications of a climatic cycle of about 75 million years (Fig. 131), considerably shorter than that proposed by King and more nearly like that proposed by Umbgrove. However, even between the orogenic "revolutions" mountains did rise locally and crustal elevations did occur.

The net effect of crustal movements is to increase topographic contrasts on the earth's crust and as a direct result of that to increase ecological contrasts. At the height of the elevating process, through a combination of high mountains, intense rain shadows, and other effects, the greatest extremes of hot and cold, humid and xeric conditions would also occur. These extremes would be expressed as (1) the greatest variety of different climates which would exist together at one time, and (2) the greatest proportionate expanse of cold climates and xeric climates and the smallest expanse of hot, humid climates. In such times, areas of tropical rain forest would be at a minimum whereas areas of warm xeric climates and of temperate or arctic climates would be at a maximum.

THE LEVELLING PROCESS

As soon as crustal elevations occur, the action of wind, water, and ice immediately start wearing them down. The erosion which progresses has an extremely complex action (Lobeck, 1939). The erosive power of water varies with the gradient, the volume, and the abrasive materials suspended in it. Ice may be an active flowing agent as in a glacier, abrading the surfaces over which it moves, or it may freeze in cracks and through expansion disintegrate the surface. The action of wind, like that of water, varies with velocity and the scouring materials which it carries. In all cases the efficiency of these agents is affected by the texture of the surface layers, harder rocks being generally more resistant to erosion than softer formations.

These levelling factors are dependent on the dynamics of the atmosphere, either as transport for water vapor and the consequent production of rain, or as a mechanical agent for moving erosive particles. Because the atmosphere is also one of the primary factors which permits the existence of life on the earth, life and the leveling process have a primary factor in common.

All of these erosive agents become more effective as the landscape becomes more rugged because the ruggedness is associated with greater elevation which automatically increases the gradients. That in turn increases the erosive power of water and ice. Thus as mountains go higher, erosion goes faster; as the mountains are worn away, erosion goes more slowly. However, erosion would never come to a complete stop while any land remained about the level of the seas.

The ridges along the ocean floor may be eroded to some extent by the major ocean currents and may change in ways comparable with surface features. Submarine ridges presumably wear away and affect the course of the very currents that eroded them. This would produce a dynamic character in the "climates" of the ocean.

Geological evidence from many sources indicates that during periods of minimum crustal unrest, these levelling forces flatten or peneplain large areas of the earth. Under these conditions ecological conditions change in the direction opposite to those produced by unusual elevation. Climatic extremes of xeric and cold become modified, and climates over the entire area are thought to approach a fairly even tropical or subtropical humid condition. Under these conditions the tropical rain forest would presumably reach its maximum geographic extent, and the xeric and cold biotas would presumably be at a minimum, restricted to local areas having mountainous terrain or exposure to unusual coastal oceanic currents. The oceanic temperature indications diagrammed in Fig. 131 seem to indicate that these periods of widespread warm climates have been much more extensive than those of cold climates.

EFFECT ON EVOLUTION

The dynamics of the crust may have been instrumental in keeping earth climates within the range of the ecological tolerances of life. The obverse is certainly true. Life has evolved within the climatic limits that have existed.

The most obvious effect of these geotectonic factors has been to produce a constant changing and shifting of climates and physical conditions with time over the entire earth including the oceans. The geographic extent of particular sets of ecological conditions have moved, contracted, and expanded, or even disappeared, depending on the prevalent direction of geotectonic influence. The geographic ranges of organisms adapted to these conditions have moved with the conditions. Some of the most important evolutionary processes occur because of these shifting geographic ranges:

(1) Before the origin of life, pre-life stages may have developed in isolation and then, when previously separated pools or seas united, combined to form the next step toward a living organism.

(2) In both plants and animals the great bulk of present-day species owe their origin to geographic isolation. This isolation has occurred because of a splitting of ranges (almost entirely by climatic shifts) or by the colonization of isolated areas whose separation is maintained by topographic irregularities.

(3) The greatest number of species not created by geographic isolation are the allopolyploid species arising from plant hybrids. The contact between the parental species is usually due to the overlapping of previously separated species ranges brought together by climatic shifts or land bridge formation.

(4) The evolution of biotic communities as integrated mixtures of species resulted from the congregation of species formed chiefly in isolation which were then brought together by climatic changes after the species had evolved.

(5) The evolution of simple biotic communities into a series of successional stages and biomes came about by various processes, the most important of which was the splitting and reunion of communities and their segregated parts by oscillations of climatic zones.

Crustal changes have also produced areas having new types of edaphic and climatic characteristics. These areas have furnished opportunities for the evolution of new types of organisms adapted to live under the novel conditions.

It is obvious that without the crustal disturbances which constantly counter the action of erosion, organic evolution would have been entirely different. If crustal movement ceased now and only levelling forces operated, the surface of the earth would gradually become peneplained even though high uplands might erode to form low mountains as a transitory product of the erosion. Climates would approach relative uniformity over the whole world. As more extreme climates disappeared, so would the species and communities restricted to them. With climatic change going only in one direction, the ranges of the remaining species would come together but not divide, and no new geographic isolates would form. As ecological diversity diminished, so would the opportunities for geographic isolation through colonization because climatic barriers between similar but distant areas would disappear. One by one, islands would erode away, removing other opportunities for colonization. As species became extinct, few new ones would evolve to take their places. Presumably comparable processes would occur in the oceans. The trend would be backwards, toward fewer and fewer species occurring in fewer and fewer communities.

What if crustal disturbances had never occurred since the initial time when conditions favored the origin of pre-life organic compounds? Without the mechanism provided by crustal movements for dividing and reuniting areas, life might not have evolved at all. If it had, only marine life would have evolved because erosion would have worn away any original continents, and there would have been no exposed land.

Even in this continuous ocean, life would have been quite different. Without barriers arising periodically to divide species ranges there would have been no increase in the number of species through the mechanism of geographic isolation. A few species might have arisen by the occurrence of polyploid series or curious genetic devices, but based on the behavior of present polyploid series this process could not have gone far.

THE "GEOTECTONIC MACHINE"

The dynamic changes of the earth's topography and climate have acted as a veritable machine which has brought about a continual increase in the number of different kinds of living things and a subsequent congregation of these into biotic communities. As was discussed in Chapter 2, many conflicting theories have been advanced to explain the cause and nature of the crustal unrest producing these changes.

Whether this geotectonic force is gravitational pressure following contraction, convection currents beneath the crust, mechanics of an expanding crust, or something else, the fact remains that it is one of the basic forces influencing the direction of organic evolution.

The Organization

of Matter and Life

Organic evolution has followed a course which can best be described as a mixture of peculiar types of randomizing and ordering processes. Mutation may be considered a randomizing process because it tends to produce an infinite number of different kinds of individuals. Natural selection may be considered an ordering process because it reduces this number of kinds to those which can succeed under specific environmental conditions. The advent of bisexual species was another such ordering process because it made interbreeding populations rather than individuals the units in natural selection.

Each ordering process appears to have arisen from the situation produced by the preceding kind of randomization. Each new set of randomizing and ordering relationships, however, is superimposed on a previous set, so that finally different sets operate contemporaneously. Within certain limits each set operates independently, but all sets influence each other to some degree. The total product is therefore extremely complex.

The origin of life in the first place was the result of a series of such processes extending back to the origin of the elements. Viewed in this light both prebiological and biological evolution merge into a single connected series of processes and events.

Whichever theory of the origin of the present universe is correct, most investigators seem agreed that the first step in the evolution of the present universe was the formation of hydrogen from lesser units of matter. The randomly distributed atoms of hydrogen which resulted apparently had some sort of mutual attraction and ultimately formed great galactic gas clouds. Various natural forces, such as momentum, the laws of turbulence, and the force of gravitation, brought about an increased orderliness within this galactic cloud, resulting in the formation of high density gas balls which evolved into the stars of the galaxy.

After the evolution of stars, a curious mixture of randomizing and ordering occurred. The gravitational properties of the star and the nuclear properties of hydrogen lead to a tremendously hot structure which gives off energy as heat and light (randomizing) but converts the hydrogen into elements of higher atomic weight (ordering). Stars have a curious evolution, leading finally to a random scattering of most or all of their products into the residual galactic gas and dust cloud. These materials again come under ordering influences resulting in the formation of new stars composed chiefly of hydrogen but containing some of the heavier elements. The added elements in the star cause it to follow a different pattern of nuclear evolution, and in this evolution new and heavier elements are formed. Thus the product of one evolutionary process automatically changes the specific course and the specific products of the next cycle in the same process. In this scale our sun is a third generation star.

The origin of the planets of the solar system is still a matter of conjecture. Their high percentage of heavier elements is highly unusual in celestial bodies and suggests that the planets arose from remnants of a twin star of the sun. When they are understood, the processes leading to the formation of the planets will undoubtedly prove to have been predicated by preceding events and the action of logical processes of randomization and ordering.

The chemical and physical properties of the earth's crust, oceans, and atmosphere set the stage for a chemical evolution leading to the formation of life. This evolution was an increase in chemical order predicated by the properties of the compounds originally present in reactive mixtures in or on the earth. Some sort of natural selection occurred, favoring the compounds which were larger and mutually attractive and which formed stable mixtures. Many of these compounds had inherent physical properties which, under certain ecological conditions, resulted in orderly aggregations of large numbers of molecules. There seems little doubt that this ordering property of certain molecules was a necessary attribute for the evolution of life.

At some point in this chemical evolution, mixtures of compounds occurred which had three properties: (1) absorbing selected compounds from the environment, (2) using these to duplicate one or more master compounds, and (3) in the final reaction of this process producing a by-product which acted as a catalyst or enzyme starting the whole process again. This series of reactions would have been a conditioned ordering—certainly an ordering, but one which would occur only in a suitable environment having a renewable supply of nutrient materials.

As with the evolution of the stars, so there may have been many cycles of organic ordering in the world before life evolved. In this event each cycle undoubtedly produced chemical "building blocks" such that the next cycle of this organic ordering process followed different specific pathways and produced different specific products.

ORDERING IN LIFE

When life did evolve, it was an orderly and highly precise system of integrated molecular machines, organized as individual units or cells which absorbed nutrients from their environment, increased in size, then inexorably divided into daughter cells exactly like their parents. These daughters followed just as inexorably the same cycle of growth and reproduction. At this stage it would seem that life might be organizing all the organic material in the world into myriads of individuals of exactly the same kind.

The replication at reproduction was not, however, always perfectly exact. Mutations unquestionably have always occurred at random intervals in any reproducing line. Mutations produce new kinds of individuals, hence the effect of mutation is to increase continuously the randomness of the population.

This kind of randomizing brought natural selection into play as an ordering influence on living organisms. Because living organisms had the property of inexorable increase and the necessities of life were limited, all organisms could not go on reproducing forever. The habitable world had a finite carrying capacity. The occurrence of mutations resulted in inequality between different individuals, based on physiological differences and hence expressed as differences in ecological fitness. The automatic expression of natural selection has continuously tended to eliminate mutations less suited to the environment, resulting in the survival or "selection" of the better adapted types and eventual elimination of the others. This sifting type of ordering is the only one operating in clonal organisms.

Simultaneously, natural selection effected a second type of ordering. Because of the selective advantages resulting from a combination of different beneficial mutant types in the same individual, natural selection favored any device in which this combining came about. The evolution of sex resulted. The sexual mechanism established a rigid order by uniting the individuals of a species into an interbreeding system, the phylogenetic line. Within this organization the criterion of genetic compatibility became a new factor, screening, and thus ordering, genetic mutation.

The dynamic nature of phylogenetic lines in conjunction with the factor of genetic incompatibility formed the foundation for the next kind of randomness. Various circumstances, especially the geotectonic factor, led to an increase in the number of species, a new randomizing effect. This process has been going on since sex became established and has resulted in the formation of many million different species. The production of more species tended to reduce the order of species themselves by increasing the hybridization between them. Hybridization between species occurs in varying degrees thus introducing a randomizing element composed of an increase in the genetic variability within each species. Again by the action of natural selection, however, a number of processes have evolved which tend to reduce hybridization and thus promote a more rigid ordering of individuals into discrete species progressing through time.

The geotectonic factor, however, congregates species in addition to splitting them, and this congregation of species set in motion evolutionary developments resulting in a new kind of order, that of multi-species systems or biotic communities. In these communities the evolution of certain of the inter-species relationships such as food chains, commensalism, and symbiosis has resulted in an obligatory coexistence, which is a rigid kind of organizational orderliness. Other inter-specific relationships such as competitive coexistence are caused and maintained by the similar ecological tolerances of different species and result in an increase of the number of different species in any one organizational or trophic level, which is another phase of randomness. It is a peculiar property of these systems that the more complex the prey-predator levels become, the larger is the number of potentially competing species that can coexist. This phenomenon arises from several mechanisms and is an expression of increased ecological stability.

Although each evolutionary process in community evolution is in itself fairly simple, the effect of these processes brings about a highly complex and dynamic situation. If, for example, one of two competing species in a community evolves into a predator of the other species, this change would lessen the competitive selection pressures acting on the second species and increase the selection pressures associated with being preyed upon. If other predators were already present, the newly evolved predator would enter into a competitive relationship with them. The increase in number of predators might lead to the evolution of food specializations among them, such as the divergence between dogs, cats, and shrews. This is the mechanism of adaptive radiation. It is an increase in randomness in producing more ecological types of organisms but is an increase in orderliness in reducing the number of species belonging to any one of these ecological types. These examples are a few of many kinds of processes showing that every change in relationships within the community or in the relative success of any species brings about changes in the details of selection pressures acting on many other species in the community. Thus change in itself produces a reorientation of the specific paths of evolution which originally caused the change.

Concurrently with splitting or congregating species, the geotectonic factor splits and congregates the communities of which the species are a part. The splitting of communities is in the direction of randomizing by means of increasing the number of different kinds of communities. However, the congregating action of the geotectonic factor results in the emergence of still another kind of order typified by the biome. Because of competitive advantages, certain organisms become the dominant ones in the community. These dominants superimpose peculiar ecological properties on the over-all climatic and edaphic characteristics of the area, such as the shade pattern in an evergreen coniferous forest. When daughter communities are formed by the splitting of parental communities, they have the same general type of dominant species. If these daughter communities later come in contact, the various new pairs of species may intermingle sufficiently that all trace of the original daughter communities is lost. Thus, although the number of communities does not increase, the species mixtures in the communities become more random. However, an ecological ordering effect is superimposed on the community because only those non-dominant species can exist that are adapted to the ecological conditions produced by the dominant species.

Natural selection among dominant species has effected another ordering influence. Only a limited number of types of dominants have persisted, each type producing a different landscape or its aquatic equivalent. Each of these landscape aspect areas is called a biome, and each is maintained solely by the competitive advantages of its dominants.

Within each biome, especially terrestrial ones, past congregations of communities have led to the evolution of community succession, representing the order in which denuded areas are rehabilitated by various communities of organisms.

Changes in soil or climate may result either in a randomizing effect because of the separation of certain species of one biome into several new biomes or in an ordering effect through the union of previously separated biomes. If habitable new climates come into existence, some of the species in a neighboring biome will colonize the new area, and if the dominants which become established in these new areas are of a different physical character than those in older areas, a new biome will result. These developments constitute a randomizing agent because of the evolution of new communities and biomes.

Each of the randomizing and ordering processes has a complex action, and all of them operate constantly and simultaneously. As a result, individuals in a modern ecological community come under a reticulate set of selection pressures, acting on the individual, respectively, as a member of a local population, as a member of a species, as a member of an ecological community, and as a member of a biome. A change produced by evolution in any one of these roles may affect the response to selection pressures in other roles or may affect the evolution of other populations or species which have any direct or indirect relationship with the changing unit. As a result the biota of the world is now extremely diverse, and the inter-relationships within and between the parts are sufficiently complex that they defy complete analysis by present methods.

In this fluctuating matrix of change there is one facet of stability. The processes themselves operate on fixed principles, such as the laws of natural selection. The specific products of the evolutionary processes are highly opportunistic and subject to the laws of chance. So many factors, for example, are involved in the persistence of species that it is impossible now to predict which species will become extinct in the future. It is likewise impossible to predict what new species will form or what new ecological relationships will evolve. In this way evolution does not lead to rigid determinism.

Observations and information which are available, however, do indicate that first chemical compounds, then life, then species, then the intricate webs of biotic communities evolved in an inevitable yet opportunistic manner. Starting from simple mixtures of matter, this entire progression of evolutionary processes advanced by a finite series of steps. In this sequence each process followed inexorably from the circumstances preceding it and in turn produced conditions which made the next process inevitable.

REFERENCES

Abelson, P. H. 1954. Paleobiochemistry. Carnegie Inst. Wash. Yearbook 53:97–101.

Aldrich, J. W., and A. J. Duvall. 1958. Distribution and migration of races of the mourning dove. Condor 60:108–128.

Aldrich, L. T. 1956. Measurement of radioactive ages of rocks. Science 123:871–875.

Alexander, C. P. 1958. Geographical distribution of the net-winged midges (Blepharoceridae, Diptera). Tenth Intern. Cong. Ent. Proc. 1:813–828.

Alexander, R. D. 1957. The taxonomy of the field crickets of the eastern United States (Orthoptera: Gryllidae: *Acheta*). Ent. Soc. Amer. Ann. 50:584–602.

Alexander, R. D., and R. S. Bigelow. 1960. Allochronic speciation in field crickets, and a new species, *Acheta veletis*. Evolution 14:334–346.

Alexander, R. D., and T. E. Moore. 1958. Studies on the acoustical behavior of seventeen-year cicadas. Ohio J. Sci. 58:107–127.

Allee, W. C., A. E. Emerson, O. Park, T. Park, and K. P. Schmidt. 1949. Principles of animal ecology. W. B. Saunders Co., Philadelphia.

Allee, W. C., and K. P. Schmidt. 1951. Ecological animal geography. John Wiley & Sons, Inc., New York.

Allison, A. C. 1955. Aspects of polymorphism in man. Cold Spring Harbor Symposia Quant. Biol. 20:239–255.

Anderson, E. 1949. Introgressive hybridization. John Wiley & Sons, Inc., New York.

Anderson, E., and D. DeWinton. 1935. The genetics of *Primula sinensis*. IV. Indications as to the ontogenetic relationship of leaf and inflorescence. Ann. Bot. 49:671–688.

Anderson, E., and T. W. Whitaker. 1934. Speciation in *Uvularia*. Arnold Arboretum J. 15:28–42.

Andrewartha, H. G., and L. C. Birch. 1954. The distribution and abundance of animals. Univ. Chicago Press, Chicago.

Andrews, Henry N., Jr. 1955. Index of generic names of fossil plants, 1820–1850. U. S. Geol. Surv. Bull. **1013**:1–262.

Asprey, G. F., and R. G. Robbins. 1953. The vegetation of Jamaica. Ecol. Monog. **23**:359–412.

Axelrod, D. I. 1952. Variables affecting the probabilities of dispersal in geologic time. Amer. Mus. Nat. Hist. Bull. **99**:177–188.

―――. 1958. Evolution of the Madro-Tertiary geoflora. Bot. Rev. **24**:433–509.

―――. 1959. Evolution of the psilophyte paleoflora. Evolution **13**:264–275.

―――. 1947. The genus *Crepis*. Part I. Univ. Calif. Publ. Bot. **21**:1–198.

―――, and J. A. Jenkins. 1943. Chromosomes and phylogeny in *Crepis*. Univ. Calif. Publ. Bot. **18**:241–292.

―――, and G. L. Stebbins, Jr. 1937. The American species of *Crepis*: their relationships and distribution as affected by polyploidy and apomixis. Carnegie Inst. Wash. Publ. **504**:1–200.

Bailey, I. W., and C. G. Nast. 1943. The comparative morphology of the Winteraceae. II. Carpels. Arnold Arboretum J. **24**:472–481.

Baker, F. S. 1934. Theory and practice of silviculture. McGraw-Hill Book Co., Inc., New York.

Baldwin, P. H. 1945. The Hawaiian goose, its distribution and reduction in numbers. Condor **47**:27–37.

Banta, A. M., and T. R. Wood. 1928. A thermal race of Cladocera originating by mutation. Fifth Intern. Cong. Genet. Proc. **1**:397–398.

Barr, A. R. 1957. The distribution of *Culex p. pipiens* and *C. p. quinquefasciatus* in North America. Amer. J. Trop. Med. and Hygiene **6**:153–165.

Barraud, P. J. 1934. The fauna of British India, including Ceylon and Burma. Diptera. Vol. V. Family Culicidae. Taylor and Francis, London.

Basrur, Parvathi K. 1959. The salivary gland chromosomes of seven segregates of *Prosimulium* (Diptera: Simuliidae) with a transformed centromere. Can. J. Zool. **37**:527–570.

Basrur, V. R., and K. H. Rothfels. 1959. Triploidy in natural populations of the black fly *Cnephia mutata* (Malloch). Can. J. Zool. **37**:571–589.

Bayer, F. M. 1955. Remarkably preserved fossil sea-pens and their Recent counterparts. Wash. Acad. Sci. J. **45**:294–300.

Beadle, G. W. 1945. Biochemical genetics. Chem. Rev. **37**:15–96.

———. 1955. Gene structure and gene function. Mo. Agric. Expt. Sta. Res. Bull. **588**:10–38.

Beirne, B. P. 1952. The origin and history of the British fauna. Methuen and Co., London.

Belkin, J. N., and C. L. Hogue. 1959. A review of the crabhole mosquitoes of the genus *Deinocerites* (Diptera, Culicidae). Univ. Calif. Publ. Ent. **14**:411–458.

Bell, A. W. 1959. *Enchytraeus fragmentosus*, a new species of naturally fragmenting oligochaete worm. Science **129**:1278.

Benson, R. B. 1952. Hymenoptera 2. Symphyta. Section (*b*). Royal Ent. Soc. London, Handbooks Ident. Brit. Insects **6**(*2b*):51–137.

Benzer, S. 1955. Fine structure of a genetic region in bacteriophage. Nat. Acad. Sc. (U.S.A.) Proc. **41**:344–354.

Bernal, J. D. 1951. The physical basis of life. Routledge and Kegan Paul, London.

Bess, H. A., and F. H. Haramoto. 1958. Biological control of pamakani, *Eupatorium adenophorum*, in Hawaii by a tephritid gall fly, *Procecidochares utilis*. I. The life history of the fly and its effectiveness in the control of the weed. Tenth Intern. Cong. Ent. Proc. **4**:543–548.

———. 1959. Biological control of pamakani, *Eupatorium adenophorum*, in Hawaii by a tephritid gall fly, *Procecidochares utilis*. 2. Population studies of the weed, the fly, and the parasites of the fly. Ecology **40**:244–249.

Bessey, C. E. 1915. The phylogenetic taxonomy of flowering plants. Mo. Bot. Gard. Ann. **2**:109–164.

Betten, Cornelius. 1950. The genus *Pycnopsyche* (Trichoptera). Ent. Soc. Amer. Ann. **43**:508–522.

Bigelow, R. S. 1958. Evolution in the field cricket, *Acheta assimilis* Fab. Can. J. Zool. **36**:139–151.

Billings, W. D., and A. F. Mark. 1957. Factors involved in the persistence of montane treeless balds. Ecology **38**:140–142.

Blair, W. F. 1947. Estimated frequencies of the buff and grey genes (G,g) in adjacent populations of deer-mice (*Peromyscus maniculatus blandus*) living on soils of different colors. Lab. Vert. Biol. Univ. Mich. Contrib. **36**:1–16.

————. 1955. Mating call and stage of speciation in the *Microhyla olivacea- M. carolinensis* complex. Evolution **9**:469–480.

————, and W. E. Howard. 1944. Experimental evidence of sexual isolation between three forms of mice of the cenospecies *Peromyscus maniculatus*. Lab. Vert. Biol. Univ. Mich. Contrib. **26**:1–19.

Blais, J. R. 1952. The relationship of the spruce budworm (*Choristoneura fumiferana*, Clem.) to the flowering condition of balsam fir (*Abies balsamea* (L.) Mill.). Can. J. Zool. **30**:1–29.

————. 1954. The recurrence of spruce budworm infestations in the past century in the LacSeul area of northwestern Ontario. Ecology **35**:62–71.

Blum, H. F. 1951. Time's arrow and evolution. Princeton Univ. Press, Princeton, New Jersey.

————. 1955. Perspectives in evolution. Amer. Scient. **43**:595–610.

Bondi, H. 1952. Cosmology. Cambridge Univ. Press, Cambridge, England.

Boudreaux, H. B. 1957. Fertility of hybrids from spider mite strain crosses. Mimeog., publ. by author.

————. 1959. A viruslike transovarian factor affecting morphology in spider mites. J. Insect Path. **1**:270–280.

Broadhead, E. 1958. The psocid fauna of larch trees in northern England —an ecological study of mixed species populations exploiting a common resource. J. Animal Ecol. **27**:217–263.

————, and I. W. B. Thornton. 1955. An ecological study of three closely related psocid species. Oikos **6**(1): 1–50.

Brock, T. D. 1959. Biochemical basis of mating in yeast. Science **129**:960–961.

Brooks, J. L. 1950. Speciation in ancient lakes. Quart. Rev. Biol. **25**:30–60, 131–176.

Brown, A. W. A. 1960. The resistance problem, vector control, and WHO. Ent. Soc. Amer. Misc. Publ. **2**(1):59–67.

Brown, W. L., Jr. 1957. Centrifugal speciation. Quart. Rev. Biol. **32**:247–277.

————, and E. O. Wilson. 1956. Character displacement. Syst. Zool. **5**:49–64.

Bullivant, J. S. 1959. An oceanographic survey of the Ross Sea. Nature **184**:422–423.

Burbidge, M., and G. Burbidge. 1958. Formation of elements in the stars. Science **128**:387–399.

Burnett, T. 1960. Effects of initial densities and periods of infestation on the growth-forms of a host and parasite population. Can. J. Zool. **38**:1063–1077.

Burns, V. W. 1959. Synchronized cell division and DNA synthesis in a *Lactobacillus acidophilus* mutant. Science **129**:566–567.

Burt, W. H. 1958. The history and affinities of the Recent land mammals of western North America, *in* Zoogeography. Amer. Assoc. Adv. Sci. Publ. **51**:131–154.

————, and R. P. Grossenheider. 1952. A field guide to the mammals. Houghton Mifflin Co., Boston.

Cain, S. A. 1944. Foundations of plant geography. Harper & Brothers, Publishers, New York.

Caldwell, J. S., and L. F. Martorell. 1952. Review of the auchenorhynchous Homoptera of Puerto Rico. Part I. Cicadellidae. J. Agric. Univ. Puerto Rico. **34**(1):1–132.

Calvin, M. 1959. Round trip from space. Evolution **13**:362–377.

Camin, J. H., and P. R. Ehrlich. 1958. Natural selection in water snakes (*Natrix sipedon* L.) on islands in Lake Erie. Evolution **12**:504–511.

————, C. A. Triplehorn, and H. J. Walter. 1954. Some indications of survival value in the Type "A" pattern of the island water snakes of Lake Erie. Nat. Hist. Miscellanea (Chicago Acad. Sc.) **131**:1–3.

Carlson, J. G. 1956. On the mitotic movements of chromosomes. Science **124**:203–206.

Carson, H. L. 1959. Genetic conditions which promote or retard the formation of species. Cold Spring Harbor Symposia Quant. Biol. **24**:87–105.

Cassidy, H. G. 1957. Fundamentals of chromatography. Interscience Publishers, New York.

Celarier, R. P., K. L. Mehra, and M. L. Wulf. 1958. Cytogeography of the *Dicanthium annulatum* complex. Brittonia **10**:59–72.

Chace, F. A., Jr. 1958. A new stomatopod crustacean of the genus *Lysiosquilla* from Cape Cod, Massachusetts. Biol. Bull. **114**:141–145.

Chaney, R. W. 1940. Tertiary forests and continental history. Geol. Soc. Amer. Bull. **51**:469–488.

————. 1947. Tertiary centers and migration routes. Ecol. Monog. 17:139–148.

————. 1954. A new pine from the Cretaceous of Minnesota and its paleoecological significance. Ecology 35:145.

Christensen, H. N. 1955. Possible role of chelation between alkali metals and pyridoxal in biological transport. Science 122:1087–1088.

Clark, A. H. 1930. The new evolution. Zoogenesis. Williams and Wilkens, Baltimore.

Clarke, J. F. G. 1952. Host relationships of moths of the genera *Depressaria* and *Agonopterix*, with descriptions of new species. Smithsonian Misc. Coll. 117(7):1–20.

Clausen, J. 1951. Stages in the evolution of plant species. Cornell Univ. Press, Ithaca, New York.

Clausen, R. E., and T. H. Goodspeed. 1925. Interspecific hybridization in *Nicotiana*. II. A tetraploid *glutinosa-Tabacum* hybrid, an experimental verification of Winge's hypothesis. Genetics 10:279–284.

Cloos, Hans. 1954. Conversation with the earth. Alfred A. Knopf, Inc., New York.

Coaldrake, J. E. 1951. The climate, geology, soils, and plant ecology of a portion of the County of Buckingham (Ninety-mile Plain), South Australia. Commonwealth Sc. Ind. Res. Org. Australia Bull. 266

Cole, LaM. C. 1951. Population cycles and random oscillations. J. Wildlife Management 15:233–252.

Colless, D. H. 1956. The *Anopheles leucosphyrus* group. Royal Ent. Soc. London Trans. 108:37–116.

Conant, R. 1958. A field guide to reptiles and amphibians. Houghton Mifflin Co., Boston.

Cowan, I. M., and C. J. Guiguet. 1956. The mammals of British Columbia. British Columbia Prov. Mus. Handbook 11:1–413.

Crick, F. H. C. 1954. The structure of the hereditary material. Scient. Amer. 191(4):54–61.

Crombie, A. C. 1947. Interspecific competition. J. Animal Ecol. 16:44–73.

Cronquist, A. 1951. Orthogenesis in evolution. State Coll. Wash. Res. Studies 19(1):3–18.

Darlington, C. D. 1958. Evolution of genetic systems. Oliver and Boyd, London.

Darlington, P. J., Jr. 1938. Experiments on mimicry in Cuba, with suggestions for future study. Royal Ent. Soc. London Trans. **87**:681–696.

―――. 1957. Zoogeography: the geographical distribution of animals. John Wiley & Sons, Inc., New York.

Darwin, Charles. 1859. On the origin of species by means of natural selection. John Murray, London.

de Beaufort, L. F. 1951. Zoogeography of the land and inland waters. Sidgwick and Jackson, London.

Deevey, E. S. 1949. Biogeography of the Pleistocene. Geol. Soc. Amer. Bull. **60**:1315–1416.

de Laubenfels, D. J. 1959. Parasitic conifer found in New Caledonia. Science **130**:97.

DeLong, D. M. 1948. The leafhoppers, or Cicadellidae, of Illinois (Eurymelinae-Balcluthinae). Ill. Nat. Hist. Surv. Bull. **24**:97–376.

Demerec, M. 1955. What is a gene?—twenty years later. Amer. Nat. **89**: 5–20.

Dethier, V. 1954. Evolution of feeding preferences in phytophagous insects. Evolution **8**:33–54.

Dice, R. L., and P. M. Blossom. 1937. Studies of mammalian ecology in southwestern North America with special reference to the colors of desert mammals. Carnegie Inst. Washington, Washington, D. C.

Digby, L. 1912. The cytology of *Primula kewensis* and of other related *Primula* hybrids. Ann. Bot. **26**:357–388.

Dingle, H. 1954. Science and modern cosmology. Science **120**:513–521.

Dobzhansky, T. 1937. Genetics and the origin of species. Columbia Univ. Press, New York. See also revised edition, 1941.

―――. 1946. Genetic structure of natural populations. Carnegie Inst. Yearbook **45**:162–171.

―――. 1948a. Genetics of natural populations. XVI. Altitudinal and seasonal changes produced by natural selection in certain populations of *Drosophila pseudoobscura* and *Drosophila persimilis*. Genetics **33**:158–176.

―――. 1948b. Genetic structure of natural populations. Carnegie Inst. Yearbook **47**:193–203.

―――. 1951. Genetics and the origin of species. 3d ed. Columbia Univ. Press, New York.

————. 1955. Evolution, genetics, and man. John Wiley & Sons, Inc., New York.

————. 1958. Evolution at work. Science **127**:1091–1098.

Dorman, F. H., and E. D. Gill. 1959. Oxygen isotope paleotemperature determinations of Australian Cainozoic fossils. Science **130**:1576.

Dougherty, E. C. 1955. Comparative evolution and the origin of sexuality. Syst. Zool. **4**:145–169, 190.

Downey, J. C., and W. H. Lange, Jr. 1956. Analysis of variation in a recently extinct polymorphic lycaenid butterfly, *Glaucopsyche xerces* (Bdv.), with notes on its biology and taxonomy. So. Calif. Acad. Sc. Bull. **55**:153–170.

Dunbar, R. W. 1959. The salivary gland chromosomes of seven forms of black flies included in *Eusimulium aureum* Fries. Can. J. Zool. **37**:495–525.

Durham, J. W. 1950. Cenozoic marine climates of the Pacific coast. Geol. Soc. Amer. Bull. **61**:1243–1264.

Du Toit, A. L. 1937. Our wandering continents. Oliver and Boyd, London.

Edwards, F. W. 1941. Mosquitoes of the Ethiopian Region. III. Culicine adults and pupae. British Museum (Natural History), London.

Edwards, V. C., R. M. Lockley, and H. M. Salmon. 1936. The distribution and numbers of breeding gannets (*Sula bassana* L.). British Birds **29**:262–276.

Ekman, S. 1953. Zoogeography of the sea. Sidgewick and Jackson, London.

Elton, C. S. 1927. Animal ecology. The Macmillan Co., New York.

————. 1958. The ecology of invasions by animals and plants. Methuen and Co., London.

Emerson, A. E. 1949. Section V. Ecology and evolution, *in* Allee *et al.* 1949: 598–729.

————. 1952. The biogeography of termites. Amer. Mus. Nat. Hist. Bull. **99**:217–225.

Emiliani, C. 1955. Pleistocene temperatures. J. Geol. **63**:538–578.

Errington, P. L. 1945. Some contributions of a fifteen-year local study of the northern bobwhite to a knowledge of population phenomena. Ecol. Monog. **15**:1–34.

―――――. 1954. On the hazards of overemphasizing numerical abundance in studies of "cyclic" phenomena in muskrat populations. J. Wildlife Management **18**:66–90.

Etheridge, Richard. 1958. Pleistocene lizards of the Cragin Quarry fauna of Meade County, Kansas. Copeia 1958:94–101.

Evans, J. W. 1947a. A natural classification of leafhoppers (Jassoidea, Homoptera). Part 3. Jassidae. Royal Ent. Soc. London Trans. **98**:105–271.

―――――. 1947b. A new leafhopper from Victoria (Homoptera, Jassidae). Nat. Mus. Victoria Mem. **15**:126–127.

Evers, R. A. 1955. Hill prairies of Illinois. Ill. Nat. Hist. Surv. Bull. **26**:367–446.

Farstadt, C. 1953-7. Maps published *in* Canadian Insect Pest Survey, 1953–57.

Felix, K. 1955. Protamines, nucleoprotamines and nuclei. Amer. Scient. **43**:431–449.

Fenton, C. L., and M. A. Fenton. 1933. Algal reefs or bioherms in the Belt Series of Montana. Geol. Soc. Amer. Bull. **44**:1135–1142.

Fernald, M. L. 1929. Some relationships of the floras of the northern hemisphere. Intern. Cong. Pl. Sciences Proc. **2**:1487–1507.

―――――. 1950. Gray's "Manual of Botany." Ed. 8. American Book Co., New York.

Fieser, L. F. 1955. Steroids. Scient. Amer. **192**(1):52–60.

Fischer, A. G. 1960. Latitudinal variations in organic diversity. Evolution **14**:64–81.

Fisher, R. A. 1930. The genetical theory of natural selection. Clarendon Press, Oxford.

Flook, D. R. 1959. An occurrence of lodgepole pine in the Mackenzie District. Canadian Field-Naturalist **73**:130–131.

Ford, E. B. 1955. Rapid evolution and the conditions which make it possible. Cold Spring Harbor Symposia Quant. Biol. **20**:230–238.

Forest Service of Canada. 1949. Native trees of Canada. 4th ed. Dept. Mines and Resources, Dom. Forest Service, Ottawa, Canada.

Fowler, W. A. 1956. The origin of the elements. Scient. Amer. **195**(3):82–91.

Fox, S. W. 1956. Evolution of protein molecules and thermal synthesis of biochemical substances. Amer. Scient. **44**:347–359.

————. 1957. The chemical problem of spontaneous generation. J. Chem. Educ. **34**:472–479.

————. 1959. Origin of life. Science **130**:1622.

————. 1960. How did life begin? Science **132**:200–208.

————, and K. Harada. 1958. Thermal copolymerization of amino acids to a product resembling protein. Science **128**:1214.

————, K. Harada, and Jean Kendrick. 1959. Production of spherules from synthetic proteinoid and hot water. Science **129**:1221–1223.

————, J. E. Johnson, and A. Vegotsky. 1956. On biochemical origins and optical activity. Science **124**:923–925.

————, and M. Middlebrook. 1954. Anhydrocopolymerization of amino acids under the influence of hypothetically primitive terrestrial conditions. Federation Proc. **13**:211.

Fox, W. 1951. Relationships among the garter snakes of the *Thamnophis elegans* rassenkreis. Univ. Calif. Publ. Zool. **50**:485–530.

Fraenkel-Conrat, H., and R. R. Porter. 1952. The terminal amino groups of conalbumin, ovomucoid, and avidin. Biochim. Biophys. Acta **9**:557–562.

Frison, T. H. 1935. The stoneflies, or Plecoptera, of Illinois. Ill. Nat. Hist. Surv. Bull. **20**:281–471.

————. 1942. Studies of North American Plecoptera. Ill. Nat. Hist. Surv. Bull. **22**:235–355.

Fruton, J. S. 1950. Proteins. Scient. Amer. **182**(6):32–41.

Frye, J. C., and A. B. Leonard. 1952. Pleistocene geology of Kansas. State Geol. Surv. Kan. Bull. **99**:1–230.

————. 1957. Studies of Cenozoic geology along eastern margin of Texas high plains, Armstrong to Howard counties. Tex. Bur. Econ. Geol. Rep. Invest. **32**:1–62.

Frye, J. C., and H. B. Willman. 1960. Classification of the Wisconsinan stage in the Lake Michigan glacial lobe. Ill. Geol. Surv. Circ. **285**:1–16.

Fuller, Mary E. 1934. The insect inhabitants of carrion: a study in animal ecology. Council Sc. Ind. Res. Australia Bull. **82**:1–63.

Fulton, B. B. 1952. Speciation in the tree cricket. Evolution **6**:283–295.

Gamow, G. 1948. Biography of the earth. New American Library, New York.

————. 1951. The origin and evolution of the universe. Amer. Scient. **39**:393–406.

————. 1952. The birth and death of the sun. New American Library, New York.

————. 1954. Modern cosmology. Scient. Amer. **190**(3):55–63, 108.

————. 1955. Information transfer in the living cell. Scient. Amer. **193**(4): 70–78.

Gates, R. R. 1942. Chromosome numbers in mammals and man. Science **96**:336–337.

Ghent, A. W., D. A. Fraser, and J. B. Thomas. 1957. Studies of regeneration in forest stands devastated by the spruce budworm. Forest Science **3**:184–208.

————, and D. R. Wallace. 1958. Oviposition behavior of the Swaine jack-pine sawfly. Forest Science **4**:264–272.

Glaessner, M. F. 1961. Pre-Cambrian animals. Scient. Amer. **204**(3):72–78, 212.

Glass, B. 1955. Pseudoalleles. Science **122**:233.

————. 1957. In pursuit of a gene. Science **126**:683–689.

Glen, R. 1954. Factors that affect insect abundance. J. Econ. Ent. **47**:398–405.

Glick, P. A. 1939. The distribution of insects, spiders, and mites in the air. U.S.D.A. Tech. Bull. 673:1–151.

Gloyd, H. K. 1940. The rattlesnakes, genera *Sistrurus* and *Crotalus*. Chicago Acad. Sci., Chicago.

Goldschmidt, R. 1940. The material basis of evolution. Yale Univ. Press, New Haven.

————. 1948. Ecotype, ecospecies, and macroevolution. Experientia **4**:1–22.

————. 1955. Theoretical genetics. Univ. Calif. Press, Berkeley.

Gordon, M. 1947. Genetics of *Platypoecilus maculatus*. IV. The sex determining mechanism in two wild populations of the Mexican platyfish. Genetics **32**:8–17.

Gregory, W. K. 1951. Evolution emerging, Vol. 1 (text) and Vol. 2 (illustrations). The Macmillan Co., New York.

Guiguet, C. J. 1955. Undescribed mammals (*Peromyscus* and *Microtus*) from the islands of British Columbia. Prov. Mus. Nat. Hist. Anthrop. Rep. for 1954: B64–B76.

Haldane, J. B. S. 1932. The causes of evolution. Harper & Brothers, Publishers, New York and London.

Hales, A. L. 1960. Oldest rocks. Scient. Amer. **202**(5):95.

Hall, E. R., and K. R. Kelson. 1959. The mammals of North America. Ronald Press, New York.

Hanson, H. C., and C. Currie. 1957. The kill of wild geese by natives of the Hudson-James Bay region. Arctic **10**:211–229.

————, P. Queneau, and P. Scott. 1956. The geography, birds, and mammals of the Perry River region. Arctic Inst. N. Amer. Spec. Publ. **3**:1–96.

————, and R. E. Griffith. 1952. Notes on the South Atlantic Canada goose population. Bird-Banding **23**:1–22.

———— and R. H. Smith. 1950 Canada geese of the Mississippi flyway, with special reference to an Illinois flock. Ill. Nat. Hist. Surv. Bull. **25**:59–210.

Harvey, G. T. 1954. Absence of diapause in rearings of the spruce budworm. Can. Dept. Agric., Forest Biol. Div., Bi-monthly Prog. Rept. **10**(4):1.

Hayes, W., and R. C. Clowes. 1960. Microbial genetics. Cambridge Univ. Press, New York.

Hecht, M., and Bessie L. Matalas. 1946. A review of middle North American toads of the genus *Microhyla*. Amer. Mus. Novitates **1315**:1–21.

Hedgpeth, J. W. (Editor). 1957. Treatise on marine ecology and paleoecology; Vol. 1, Ecology. Geol. Soc. Amer. Mem. **67**.

Hetrick, L. A. 1956. Life history studies of five species of *Neodiprion* sawflies. Forest Science **1**:181–185.

Hitchcock, A. S., and Agnes Chase. 1950. Manual of the grasses of the United States. 2nd ed. U.S.D.A. Misc. Publ. **200**:1–1051.

Hoagland, M. B. 1959. Nucleic acids and proteins. Scient. Amer. **201**(6): 55–61.

Hoare, C. A. 1952. The taxonomic status of biological races in parasitic Protozoa. Linn. Soc. London Proc., Session **163**(1):44–47.

————. 1955. Intraspecific biological groups in pathogenic Protozoa. Refuah Veterinarith **12**:263–258.

————. 1957. The classification of trypanosomes of veterinary and medical importance. Vet. Rev. Annot. **3**:1–13.

Hoffman, R. L. 1959. Personal correspondence.

Hoffmeister, D. F. 1951. A taxonomic and evolutionary study of the Piñon mouse, *Peromyscus truei*. Ill. Biol. Monog. **21**(4):1–104.

————, and C. O. Mohr. 1957. Fieldbook of Illinois mammals. Ill. Nat. Hist. Surv. Manual 4:1–233.

Holdaway, F. G. 1930. Field populations and natural control of *Lucilia sericata*. Nature, **25**:1–3.

Holland, G. P. 1958. Distribution patterns of northern fleas (Siphonaptera). Tenth Intern. Cong. Ent. Proc. **1**:645–658.

Hollick, A. 1924. A review of the fossil flora of the West Indies, with descriptions of new species. N. Y. Bot. Gard. Bull. **12**:259–324.

Holloway, J. K. 1957. Weed control by insects. Scient. Amer. **197**(1):56–62.

Hopkins, D. M. 1959. Cenozoic history of the Bering land bridge. Science **129**:1519–1528.

Hovanitz, W. 1954. Chromosome structure. III. Coiling in giant chromosomes (Advance notice). Wasm. J. Biol. **12**:129–131.

Hoyle, F. 1950. The nature of the universe. Harper & Brothers, Publishers, New York.

Hubbell, T. H. 1954. Relationships and distribution of *Mycotrupes*. (see Olson, Ada L., T. H. Hubbell, and H. F. Howden)

Hubbs, C. L. 1955. Hybridization between fish species in nature. Syst. Zool. **4**:1–20.

Huff, F. A., and J. C. Neill. 1957. Rainfall relations on small areas in Illinois. Ill. Water Surv. Bull 44:1–61.

Hutchinson, J. 1926. The families of flowering plants. I. Dicotyledons. The Macmillan Co., London.

Irving, E. 1959. Paleomagnetic pole positions: a survey and analysis. Geophys. J. **2**:51–79.

Isely, F. B. 1938. Survival value of acridian protective coloration. Ecology **19**:370–389.

Jackson, R. C. 1957. New low chromosome number for plants. Science **126**:1115–1116.

Jardetzky, W. S. 1954. The principal characteristics of the formation of the Earth's crust. Science **119**:361–365.

Jepson, G. L., G. G. Simpson, and E. Mayr. 1949. Genetics, paleontology and evolution. Princeton Univ. Press. Princeton, New Jersey.

Johnson, W. H. 1956. Nutrition of Protozoa. Annual Rev. Microbiol. **10**:193–212.

Jones, H. S. 1940. Life on other worlds. New American Library, New York.

Jones, G. N. 1951. On the number of species of plants. Scient. Monthly **72**:289–295.

Jones, G. N., and G. D. Fuller. 1955. Vascular plants of Illinois. Univ. Ill. Press, Urbana, Illinois.

Jordan, K. 1905. Der Gegensatz zwischen geographischer und nichtgeographischer variation. Zeits. wiss. Zool. **83**:151–210.

Kacser, H. 1956. Molecular organization of genetic material. Science **124**:151–154.

Kanazawa, R. H. 1958. A revision of the eels of the genus *Conger* with descriptions of four new species. U. S. Nat. Mus. Proc. **108**:219–267.

Katchalski, E. 1951. Poly-α-amino acids. Advances in Protein Chemistry **6**:123–185.

Keck, D. D. 1935. Studies on the taxonomy of the Madiinae. Madroño **3**:4–18.

Keeton, W. T. 1959. A revision of the milliped genus *Brachoria* (Polydesmida: Xystodesmidae). U. S. Nat. Mus. Proc. **109**:1–58.

Kennedy, G. C. 1959. The origin of continents, mountain ranges, and ocean basins. Amer. Scient. **47**:491–504.

Keosian, J. 1960. On the origin of life. Science **131**:479–482.

Kettlewell, H. B. D. 1955. Selection experiments on industrial melanism in the Lepidoptera. Heredity **9**:323–342.

———. 1956*a*. Further selection experiments on industrial melanism in the Lepidoptera. Heredity **10**:287–301.

———. 1956*b*. A resumé of investigations on the evolution of melanism in the Lepidoptera. Royal Soc. London, Proc. **145** (Ser. B):297–303.

Khalaf, K. 1954. The speciation of the genus *Culicoides* (Diptera, Heleidae). Ent. Soc. Amer. Ann. **47**:34–51.

King, P. B. 1958. Evolution of modern surface features of western North America. Amer. Assoc. Adv. Sci. Publ. **51**:3–60.

King, R. L., and Eleanor H. Slifer. 1955. The inheritance of red and blue hind tibiae in the lesser migratory grasshopper. J. Heredity **46**:302–304.

Kinsey, A. C. 1930. The gall wasp genus *Cynips*, a study in the origin of species. Ind. Univ., Waterman Inst. Scient. Res. Publ. 42:1–577.

———. 1936. The origin of higher categories in *Cynips*. Ind. Univ. Publ. Sci. Ser. 4:1–334.

Knowlton, F. H. 1919. A catalogue of the Mesozoic and Cenozoic plants of North America. U. S. Geol. Surv. Bull 696:1–815.

Knopf, A. 1957. Measuring geologic time. Scient. Monthly **85**:225–236.

Koopman, K. F. 1950. Natural selection for reproductive isolation between *Drosophila pseudoobscura* and *Drosophila persimilis*. Evolution 4:135–148.

Kornberg, A. 1960. Biologic synthesis of deoxyribonucleic acid. Science **131**:1503–1508.

Krekeler, C. H. 1958. Speciation in cave beetles of the genus *Pseudanophthalmus* (Coleoptera, Carabidae). Amer. Midland Nat. **59**: 167–189.

Kulp, J. L. 1961. Geologic time scale. Science **133**:1105–1114.

Lack, D. 1934. Habitat distribution in certain Icelandic birds. J. Animal Ecology 3:81–90.

———. 1944. Ecological aspects of species-formation in passerine birds. Ibis **86**:260–286.

———. 1947. Darwin's finches. Cambridge Univ. Press, Cambridge, England.

Larimore, R. W., W. F. Childers, and C. Heckrotte. 1959. Destruction and re-establishment of stream fish and invertebrates affected by drought. Amer. Fish. Soc. Trans. **88**:261–285.

Laven, H. 1957. Vererbung durch kerngene und das problem der ausserkaryotischen vererbung bei *Culex pipiens*. Zeits. für indukt. Abstammungs- und Vererbungslehre **88**:443–516.

———. 1959. Speciation by cytoplasmic isolation in the *Culex pipiens* complex. Cold Spring Harbor Symposia Quant. Biol. **20**:166–173.

Lawrence, G. H. M. 1951. Taxonomy of vascular plants. The Macmillan Co., New York.

Lea, A. O., J. B. Dimond, and D. M. DeLong. 1956. A chemically defined medium for rearing *Aedes aegypti* larvae. J. Econ. Ent. **49**:313–315.

Leonard, J. W., and Fannie A. Leonard. 1949. An annotated list of Michigan Trichoptera. Univ. Mich. Mus. Zool. Occas. Papers 522:1–35.

Leppik, E. E. 1955. *Dichromena ciliata,* a noteworthy entomophilous plant among Cyperaceae. Amer. J. Bot. **42**:455–458.

———. 1956. The form and function of numeral patterns in flowers. Amer. J. Bot. **43**:445–455.

———. 1957*a*. A new system for classification of flower types. Taxon **6**:64–67.

———. 1957*b*. Evolutionary relationship between entomophilous plants and anthophilous insects. Evolution **11**:466–481.

Lerner, I. M. 1954. Genetic homeostasis. John Wiley & Sons, Inc., New York.

———. 1958. The genetic basis of selection. John Wiley & Sons, Inc., New York.

Lewallen, L. L. 1957. Paper chromatography studies of the *Anopheles maculipennis* complex in California (Diptera: Culicidae). Ent. Soc. Amer. Ann. **50**:602–606.

Lewis, H. 1953*a*. The mechanism of evolution in the genus *Clarkia.* Evolution **7**:1–20.

———. 1953*b*. Chromosome phylogeny and habitat preference of *Clarkia.* Evolution **7**:102–109.

———. 1953*c*. Quantitative variation in wild genotypes of *Clarkia.* I.U.B.S. Symp. on Gen. Pop. Structure, Pavia: 114–125.

———, and Margaret E. Lewis. 1955. The genus *Clarkia.* Univ. Calif. Publ. Bot. **20**:241–392.

———, and Margaret R. Roberts. 1956. The origin of *Clarkia lingulata.* Evolution **10**:126–138.

Lienk, S. E., and P. J. Chapman. 1951. Influence of the presence or absence of the European red mite on two-spotted spider mite abundance. J. Econ. Ent. **44**:623.

Limbaugh, C. 1961. Cleaning symbiosis. Scient. Amer. **205**(2):42–49, 168.

Linderstrom-Lang, K. U. 1953. How is a protein made? Scient. Amer. **189**(3):100–106.

Lindroth, H. C. 1957. The faunal connections between Europe and North America. John Wiley & Sons, Inc., New York.

Linsley, E. G. 1958. The ecology of solitary bees. Hilgardia **27**:541–599.

———. 1959. Mimetic form and coloration in the Cerambycidae (Coleoptera). Ent. Soc. Amer. Ann. **52**:125–131.

Littlejohn, M. J. 1959. Call differentiation in a complex of seven species of *Crinia* (Anura, Leptodactylidae). Evolution **13**:452–468.

Lobeck, A. K. 1939. Geomorphology. McGraw-Hill Book Co., Inc., New York.

Löve, A., and Doris Löve. 1953. Studies on *Bryoxiphium*. The Bryologist **56**:73–94, 183–203.

Love, J. D. 1939. Geology along the south margin of the Absaroka range. Geol. Soc. Amer., Special Paper 20:116–117.

Lowenstam, H. A., and S. Epstein. 1954. Paleotemperatures of the Post-Aptian Cretaceous as determined by the oxygen isotope method. J. Geol. **62**:207–248.

McCabe, T. T., and I. M. Cowan. 1945. *Peromyscus maniculatus macrorhinus* and the problem of insularity. Royal Can. Instit. Trans. 1945:117–215.

MacGinitie, H. D. 1953. Fossil plants of the Florissant beds, Colorado. Carnegie Inst. Wash. Publ. 599.

McIntosh, R. P. 1958. Plant communities. Science **128**:115–120.

MacLulick, D. A. 1937. Fluctuations in the numbers of the varying hare (*Lepus americanus*). Univ. Toronto Studies, Biol Ser. 43.

Mahler, H. R., H. M. Baum, and Georg Hübscher. 1956. Enzymatic oxidation of urate. Science **124**:705–708.

Manton, Irene. 1950. Problems of cytology and evolution in the Pteridophyta. Cambridge University Press, Cambridge, England.

Marlatt, C. L. 1907. The periodical Cicada. U. S. D. A. Bur. Ent. Bull. 71.

Mattfeld, J. 1930. Über hybridogene Sippen der Tannen. Bibliotheca Botanica **25**(100):1–84.

Mattingly, P. F. 1953. Species hybridization in culicine mosquitoes. Royal Ent. Soc. London Proc., Ser. C, **18**:41–42.

Mayr, E. 1942. Systematics and the origin of species. Columbia Univ. Press, New York.

————. 1947. Ecological factors in speciation. Evolution **1**:263–288.

Mazia, D. 1956. The life history of the cell. Amer. Scient. **44**:1–32.

Menard, H. W. 1960. The East Pacific rise. Science **132**:1737–1746.

Michener, C. D. 1944. Comparative external morphology, phylogeny, and a classification of the bees (Hymenoptera). Amer. Mus. Nat. Hist. Bull. **82**:151–326.

Micks, D. W. 1954. Paper chromatography as a tool for mosquito taxonomy: the *Culex pipiens* complex. Nature **174**:217–221.

Miller, A. H. 1939. Analysis of some hybrid populations of juncos. Condor **41**:211–214.

———. 1955. A hybrid woodpecker and its significance in speciation in the genus *Dendrocopos*. Evolution **9**:317–321.

Miller, S. L. 1953. A production of amino acids under possible primitive Earth conditions. Science **117**:528–529.

———, and H. C. Urey. 1959. Organic compound synthesis on the primitive Earth. Science **130**:245–251.

Mills, H. B. 1939. Remarks on the geographical distribution of North American Collembola. Brooklyn Ent. Soc. Bull. **34**:158–161.

———. 1951. Facts and waterfowl. Sixteenth North American Wildlife Conference Trans.: 103–109.

———. 1953. The unity of animal populations. Ill. Acad. Sci. Trans. **46**: 197–202.

Mohr, C. O. 1943. Cattle droppings as ecological units. Ecol. Monogr. **13**:275–298.

———. 1947. Major fluctuations of some Illinois mammal populations. Ill. Acad. Sci. Trans. **40**:197–204.

Moore, Charlotte E. 1954. Atoms and ions in the Sun. Science **119**:449–456.

Moore, H. B. 1958. Marine ecology. John Wiley & Sons, Inc., New York.

Moore, J. A. 1949. Patterns of evolution in the genus *Rana, in* Jepsen, Simpson and Mayr 1949:315–338.

———. 1954. Geographic and genetic isolation in Australian Amphibia. Amer. Nat. **88**:65–74.

Moore, T. E., and H. H. Ross. 1957. The Illinois species of *Macrosteles*, with an evolutionary outline of the genus (Hemiptera, Cicadellidae). Ent. Soc. Amer. Ann. **50**:109–118.

Morgan, W. W. 1955. The spiral structure of the galaxy. Scient. Amer. **192**(5):42–48.

Morgulis, S. 1953. Introduction in "The Origin of Life," by A. I. Oparin, republication of 1938 translation: v–xxii. Dover Publications, New York.

Morris, R. F. 1958. A review of the important insects affecting the spruce-fir forest in the Maritime Provinces. Forestry Chronicle **34**:159–189.

Morrison, J. P. E. 1959. Personal letter of Jan. 9, 1959.

Mosely, M. E., and D. E. Kimmins. 1953. The Trichoptera of Australia and New Zealand. British Mus. (Nat. Hist.). London.

Muldrew, J. A. 1953. The natural immunity of the larch sawfly [*Pristiphora erichsonii* (Htg.)] to the introduced parasite *Mesoleius tenthredinis* Morley, in Manitoba and Saskatchewan. Can. J. Zool. 31:313–332.

Muller, H. J. 1925. Why polyploidy is rarer in animals than in plants. Amer. Nat. 59:346–353.

————. 1942. Isolating mechanisms, evolution and temperature. Biological Symposia 6:71–125.

Munns, E. N. 1938. The distribution of important forest trees of the United States. U. S. D. A. Misc. Publ. 287:1–9.

Neill, W. T. 1957. Historical biogeography of present-day Florida. Fla. State Mus. Bull. 2:175–220.

Newell, N. D., J. K. Rigby, A. G. Fischer, A. J. Whiteman, J. K. Hickox, and J. S. Bradley. 1953. Permian reef complex of the Guadalupe Mountains region, Texas and New Mexico: A study in paleoecology. Freeman and Co., San Francisco.

Nilsson, H. 1953. Synthetische artbildung. II. Gleerup, Lund.

Notini, G. 1941. Om harens biologi. Svensk. Jagarforb. Meddelande 4. Uppsala.

————. 1948. Hararna. Svensk. djur. Daggdjuren, Stockholm: 481–511.

Odishaw, H. 1958–1959. International geophysical year. Science 128: 1599–1609; 129:14–25.

O'Keefe, J. A., Ann Eckels, and R. K. Squires. 1959. Vanguard measurements give pear-shaped component of Earth's figure. Science 129: 565–566.

Olson, Ada L., T. H. Hubbell, and H. F. Howden. 1954. The burrowing beetles of the genus *Mycotrupes* (Coleoptera: Scarabaeidae: Geotrupinae). Univ. Mich. Mus. Zool. Misc. Publ. No. 84.

Oman, P. W. 1949. The nearctic leafhoppers (Homoptera: Cicadellidae). Ent. Soc. Wash. Mem. 3:1–253.

Oort, J. H. 1956. The evolution of galaxies. Scient. Amer. 195(3):101–108.

Oosting, H. J., and W. D. Billings. 1943. The red fir forest of the Sierra Nevada. Ecol. Monog. 13:259–274.

Oparin, A. I. 1938. The origin of life. The Macmillan Co., New York.

Ortmann, A. E., 1902. The geographical distribution of freshwater decapods and its bearing upon ancient geography. Amer. Philos. Soc. Proc. 41:267–400.

Osborn, H. 1902. A statistical study of variations in the periodical cicada. Ohio Naturalist 3:323–326.

Park, O. 1949. Section IV. The community, *in* Allee *et al.*, 1949.

Park, T. 1954. Experimental studies of interspecies competition. II. Temperature, humidity, and competition in two species of *Tribolium*. Physiol. Zool. 27:177–238.

———— 1955. Ecological experimentation with animal populations. Scient. Monthly 81:271–275.

Pathak, M. D., and R. H. Painter. 1959. Geographical distribution of the four biotypes of corn leaf aphid, *Rhopalosiphum maidis* (Fitch), in Kansas. Kan. Acad. Sci. Trans. 62:1–8.

Patterson, C., G. Tilton, and M. Inghram. 1955. Age of the earth. Science 121:69–75.

Patterson, J. T., and W. S. Stone. 1952. Evolution in the genus *Drosophila*. The Macmillan Co., New York.

Pauling, L., R. B. Corey, and R. Hayward. 1954. The structure of protein molecules. Scient. Amer. 191(1):51–59.

Petersen, C. G. J. 1914. Valuation of the sea. II. The animal communities of the sea-bottom and their importance for marine zoogeography. Danish Biol. Sta. Rept. 21:1–68.

————. 1918. The sea bottom and its production of fish food. Danish Biol. Sta. Rept. 25:1–62.

Peterson, R. T. 1941. A field guide to western birds. Houghton Mifflin Co., Boston.

————. 1947. A field guide to the birds. Houghton Mifflin Co., Boston.

Pierce, R. L. 1957. Minnesota Cretaceous pine pollen. Science 125:26.

————. 1958. Early Upper Cretaceous plant microfossils of Minnesota. Dissertation Abstracts 18(1):2 p.

Pitelka, F. A. 1951. Speciation and ecologic distribution in American jays of the genus *Aphelocoma*. Univ. Calif. Publ. Zool. 50:195–464.

Poldervaart, A., editor. 1955. Crust of the Earth (A symposium). Geol. Soc. Amer. Special Paper 62.

Prat, H. 1936. La systématique des Graminées. Ann. Sci. Nat., Ser. 10, Bot. 18:165–258.

Prebble, M. L. 1959. Personal correspondence.

Price, J. L. 1958. Cryptic speciation in the *vernalis* group of Cyclopidae. Can. J. Zool. **36**:285–303.

Rasmussen, D. I. 1941. Biotic communities of Kaibab Plateau, Arizona. Ecol. Monog. **3**:229–275.

Rausch, R. 1953. On the status of some Arctic mammals. Arctic **6**:91–148.

Ray, R. J. 1959. A phytosociological analysis of the tall-grass prairie in northeastern Oklahoma. Ecology **40**:255–261.

Reeve, E. C. R., and P. D. F. Murray. 1942. Evolution in the horse's skull. Nature **150**:402–403.

Rehn, J. A. G. 1958. The origin and affinities of the Dermaptera and Orthoptera of western North America, *in* Zoogeography, Amer. Assoc. Adv. Sci. Publ. **51**:253–298.

Rensch, B. 1929. Das Prinzip geographischer Rassenkreise und das Problem der Artbildung. Borntraeger, Berlin.

Revelle, R. 1955. On the history of the oceans. J. Marine Res. **14**:446–461.

Reynolds, J. H. 1960. Age of the elements. Scient. Amer. **202**(2):72–73.

Ribaut, H. 1952. Faune de France. 57. Homoptères Auchénorhynques. II. (Jassidae). Lechevalier, Paris.

Ribbands, C. R. 1944. Differences between *Anopheles melas* and *Anopheles gambiae*. II. Salinity relations of larvae and maxillary palp banding of adult females. Ann. Trop. Med. Parasit. **38**:87–99.

Ricker, W. E. 1952. Systematic studies in Plecoptera. Ind. Univ. Publ. Sci. Ser. **18**:1–200.

Riegel, G. T. 1942. *Cyclocephala abrupta* in Illinois. Ill. Acad. Sci. Trans. **35**:215.

Robb, R. C. 1936. A study of mutations in evolution. Part 3: The evolution of the equine foot. J. Genetics **33**:267–273.

———. 1937. A study of mutations in evolution. Part 4: The ontogeny of the equine foot. J. Genetics **34**:477–486.

Roberts, H. R. 1941. A comparative study of the subfamilies of the Acrididae (Orthoptera) primarily on the basis of their phallic structures. Acad. Nat. Sci. Philadelphia Proc. **93**:201–246.

Robertson, C. 1928. Flowers and insects. Published by the author, Carlinville, Illinois.

Robertson, H. P. 1956. The Universe. Scient. Amer. **195**(3):73–81.

Robertson, W. B. 1954. Everglades fires—past, present and future. Everglades Nat. Hist. 2:9–16.

Rogers, J. S. 1933. The ecological distribution of the crane-flies of northern Florida. Ecol. Monog. 3:1–74.

Ross, H. H. 1929. Sawflies of the subfamily Dolerinae of America north of Mexico. Ill. Biol. Monog. 12(3):1–116.

―――. 1944. The caddis flies, or Trichoptera, of Illinois. Ill. Nat. Hist. Surv. Bull. 23:1–326.

―――. 1947. The mosquitoes of Illinois (Diptera, Culicidae). Ill. Nat. Hist. Surv. Bull. 24:1–96.

―――. 1951. Conflict with *Culex*. Mosquito News 11:128–132.

―――. 1953. Polyphyletic origin of the leafhopper fauna of *Ilex decidua*. Ill. Acad. Sci. Trans. 46:186–192.

―――. 1955. The taxonomy and evolution of the sawfly genus *Neodiprion*. Forest Science 1:196–209.

―――. 1956a. Evolution and classification of the mountain caddisflies. Univ. Ill. Press, Urbana.

―――. 1956b. A textbook of entomology. 2nd ed. John Wiley & Sons, Inc., New York.

―――. 1957. Principles of natural coexistence indicated by leafhopper populations. Evolution 11:113–129.

―――. 1958a. Evidence suggesting a hybrid origin for certain leafhopper species. Evolution 12:337–346.

―――. 1958b. The relationships of systematics and the principles of evolution. Tenth Intern. Cong. Ent. Proc. 1:423–429.

―――. 1959a. The relationships of three new species of *Triaenodes* from Illinois and Florida. (Trichoptera). Ent. News 70:39–45.

―――. 1959b. Affinities and origins of the northern and montane insects of western North America, *in* Zoogeography Part I, Amer. Assoc. Adv. Sci. Publ. 51:231–252.

―――. 1959c. A survey of the *Empoasca fabae* complex (Hemiptera: Cicadellidae). Ent. Soc. Amer. Ann. 52:304–316.

Rothfels, K. H. 1956. Black flies: siblings, sex, and species grouping. J. Heredity 47:113–122.

Rothschild, M., and T. Clay. 1952. Fleas, flukes and cuckoos. Philosophical Library, New York.

Rubey, W. W. 1955. Development of the hydrosphere and atmosphere, with special reference to probable composition of the early atmosphere. Geol. Soc. Amer., Spec. Paper 62:631–650.

Rudd, R. L. 1955. Population variation and hybridization in some California shrews. Syst. Zool. 4:21–34.

Runcorn, S. K. 1959. Rock magnetism. Science 129:1002–1012.

Ruzicka, V. 1919. Restitution und Vererbung. Vortr. u. Aufs. über Entw.-mech. d. Org., H. 23.

Sabrosky, C. W. 1952. How many insects are there? U. S. D. A. Yearbook Agric., 1952:1–7.

Sager, R. 1960. Genetic systems in *Chlamydomonas*. Science 132:1459–1465.

Sailer, R. I. 1954. Interspecific hybridization among insects with a report on crossbreeding experiments with stink bugs. J. Econ. Ent. 47:377–383.

Sandage, A. R. 1956. The red shift. Scient. Amer. 195(3):170–182.

Sanger, F. 1959. Chemistry of insulin. Science 129:1340–1344.

Sanjean, J., and B. V. Travis. 1955. An eight-legged flea, *Orchopeas howardi howardi* (Baker). J. Parasitol. 41:636–637.

Sauer, J. 1957. Recent migration and evolution of the dioecious amaranths. Evolution 11:11–31.

Savile, D. B. O. 1956. Known dispersal rates and migratory potentials as clues to the origin of the North American biota. Amer. Midl. Nat. 56:434–453.

Schmalhausen, I. I. 1949. Factors of evolution. The theory of stabilizing selection. Blakiston Co., Philadelphia.

Schoof, H. F. 1952. House fly dispersion studies in metropolitan areas. J. Econ. Ent. 45:675–683.

Schrödinger, E. 1953. What is matter? Scient. Amer. 189(3):52–57, 168.

Schuchert, C. 1924. A textbook of geology. Part II. Historical geology. 2nd rev. ed. John Wiley & Sons, Inc., New York.

―――. 1955. Atlas of paleogeographic maps of North America. John Wiley & Sons, Inc., New York.

Scott, T. G., and W. D. Klimstra. 1955. Red foxes and a declining prey population. Southern Ill. Univ. Monog. Series 1:1–123.

Sears, P. B., and Kathryn H. Clisby. 1952. Two long climatic records. Science 116:176–178.

Seevers, C. H. 1957. A monograph on the termitophilous Staphylinidae. Fieldiana, Zoology, 40:1–334.

Serra, J. A. 1958. Chromosomic units of genetic determination. Revista Portug. de Zoologia e Biologia Geral 1:131–195, 219–271, 273–291.

Shantz, H. L. 1956. History and problems of arid lands development, *in* The future of arid land. Amer. Assoc. Adv. Sci., Washington, D.C.

Shelford, V. E. 1913. Animal communities in temperate North America. Geog. Soc. Chicago Bull. 5:1–368.

————. 1926. Naturalist's guide to the Americas. Williams and Wilkins Co., Baltimore.

————. 1951. Fluctuation of non-forest animal populations in the upper Mississippi basin. Ecol. Monog. 21:149–181.

————, and W. P. Flint. 1943. Populations of the chinch bug in the upper Mississippi valley from 1823 to 1940. Ecology 24:435–455.

————, and S. Olson. 1935. Sere, climax and influent animals with special reference to the transcontinental coniferous forests of North America. Ecology 16:375–402.

Shrock, R. R., and W. H. Twenhoffel. 1953. Principles of invertebrate paleontology. 2nd ed. McGraw-Hill Book Co., Inc., New York.

Sibley, C. G. 1950. Species formation in the red-eyed towhees of Mexico. Univ. Calif. Publ. Zool. 50:109–194.

————. 1954. Hybridization in the red-eyed towhees of Mexico. Evolution 8:252–290.

————. 1960. The electrophoretic patterns of avian egg-white proteins as taxonomic characters. Ibis 102:215–284.

————, and D. A. West. 1958. Hybridization in the red-eyed towhees of Mexico: the eastern plateau populations. Condor 60:85–104.

Simpson, G. G. 1940. Antarctica as a faunal migration route. Sixth Pacific Sci. Cong. Proc. 2:755–768.

————. 1944. Tempo and mode in evolution. Columbia Univ. Press, New York.

————. 1947. Holarctic mammalian faunas and continental relationships during the Cenozoic. Geol. Soc. Amer. Bull. 58:613–688.

————. 1949. The meaning of evolution. Yale Univ. Press, New Haven.

————. 1950. History of the fauna of Latin America. Amer. Scient. **38**: 361–389.

————. 1951. The species concept. Evolution **5**:285–298.

————. 1952. How many species? Evolution **6**:342.

————. 1953. The major features of evolution. Columbia Univ. Press, New York.

————, C. S. Pittendrigh, and L. H. Tiffany. 1957. Life: An introduction to biology. Harcourt, Brace & Co., New York.

Sinsheimer, R. L. 1957. First steps toward a genetic chemistry. Science **125**:1123–1128.

Smith, C. L. 1954. Pleistocene fishes of the Berends fauna of Beaver County, Oklahoma. Copeia **1954**:282–289.

Smith, P. W. 1956. The status, correct name, and geographic range of the boreal chorus frog. Biol. Soc. Wash. Proc. **69**:169–176.

————. 1957. An analysis of post-Wisconsin biogeography of the prairie peninsula region based on distributional phenomena among terrestrial vertebrate populations. Ecology **38**:205–218.

————, and M. M. Hensley. 1958. Notes on a small collection of amphibians and reptiles from the vicinity of the Pinacate lava cap in northwestern Sonora, Mexico. Kansas Acad. Sci. Trans. **61**:64–76.

————, and S. A. Minton, Jr. 1957. A distributional summary of the herpetofauna of Indiana and Illinois. Amer. Midl. Nat. **58**:341–351.

————, and Dorothy M. Smith. 1952. The relationships of the chorus frogs, *Pseudacris nigrita feriarum* and *Pseudacris n. triseriata*. Amer. Midl. Nat. **48**:165–180.

Sokoloff, A. 1955. Competition between sibling species of the *pseudo-obscura* subgroup of *Drosophila*. Ecol. Monog. **25**:387–409.

Spassky, B. 1957. Morphological differences between sibling species of *Drosophila*. Univ. Texas Publ. 5721:48–61.

Spencer, W. P. 1947. Mutations in wild populations of *Drosophila*. Advances in Genetics **1**:359–402.

————. 1949. Gene homologies and the mutants of *Drosophila hydei, in* Jepsen, Mayr, and Simpson 1949:23–44.

Spieth, H. T. 1952. Mating behavior within the genus *Drosophila* (Diptera). Amer. Mus. Nat. Hist. Bull. **99**:395–474.

Stadler, L. J. 1954. The gene. Science **120**:811–819.

Stalker, H. D. 1953. Taxonomy and hybridization in the Cardini group of *Drosophila*. Ent. Soc. Amer. Ann. **46**:343–358.

————, 1956. A case of polyploidy in Diptera. Nat. Acad. Sci. (U.S.A.) Proc. **42**:194–199.

Stannard, L. J., Jr. 1954. *Actinothrips* (*Hybridothrips*) *oneillae*, new subgenus and species. Ent. Soc. Wash. Proc. **56**:71–74.

————, 1957. The phylogeny and classification of the North American genera of the suborder Tubulifera (Thysanoptera). Ill. Biol. Monog. **25**:1–200.

Stebbins, G. L., Jr. 1942. The genetic approach to problems of rare and endemic species. Madroño **6**:240–258.

————. 1950. Variation and evolution in plants. Columbia Univ. Press, New York.

————. 1959. The role of hybridization in evolution. Amer. Phil. Soc. Proc. **103**:231–251.

Stebbins, R. C., and C. H. Lowe, Jr. 1951. Subspecific differentiation in the Olympic salamander *Rhyacotriton olympicus*. Univ. Calif. Publ. Zool. **50**:465–484.

Steere, W. C. 1937. *Bryoxiphium norvegicum*, the sword moss, as a preglacial and interglacial relic. Ecology **18**:346–358.

————. 1938. Critical bryophytes from the Keweenaw Peninsula, Michigan, II. Annales Bryologici **11**:145–152.

————. 1954. Chromosome number and behavior in arctic mosses. Bot. Gaz. **116**:93–133.

————. 1958. Evolution and speciation in the mosses. Amer. Nat. **92**: 5–20.

Stehli, F. G. 1957. Possible Permian climatic zonation and its implications. Amer. J. Sci. **255**:607–618.

Steinberg, D., M. Vaughan, and C. B. Anfinsen. 1956. Kinetic aspects of assembly and degradation of proteins. Science **124**:389–395.

Stern, C. 1929. Über die additive Wirkung multipler Allele. Biol. Zentralbl. **49**:261–290.

Stone, A., K. L. Knight, and H. Starcke. 1959. A synoptic catalog of the mosquitoes of the world (Diptera, Culicidae). Ent. Soc. Amer., Thos. Say Foundation **6**:1–358.

Strasburg, D. W. 1959. Notes on the diet and correlating structures of some central Pacific echeneid fishes. Copeia **1959**:244–248.

Strong, C. L. 1959. The amateur scientist. Scient. Amer. **200**(2):143–152.

Sweadner, W. R. 1937. Hybridization and the phylogeny of the genus *Platysamia*. Carnegie Mus. Ann. **25**:163–242.

Szent-Györgyi, A. 1956. Bioenergetics. Science **124**:873–875.

Taylor, J. H., P. S. Woods, and W. L. Hughes. 1957. The organization and duplication of chromosomes as revealed by autoradiographic studies using tritium-labeled thymidine. Nat. Acad. Sci. (U.S.A.) Proc. **43**:122–128.

Teichert, C. 1956. How many fossil species? J. Paleo. **30**:967–969.

————. 1958. Cold- and deep-water coral banks. Amer. Assoc. Petrol. Geol. Bull. **42**:1064–1082.

Theorell, H. 1956. Nature and mode of action of oxidation enzymes. Science **124**:467–472.

Thiel, R. 1957. And there was light. Alfred A. Knopf, Inc., New York.

Thomas, C. A., Jr. 1956. New scheme for performance of osmotic work by membranes. Science **123**:60–61.

Thornton, W. A. 1955. Interspecific hybridization in *Bufo woodhousei* and *Bufo valliceps*. Evolution **9**:455–468.

Tippo, O. 1938. Comparative anatomy of the Moraceae and their presumed allies. Bot. Gaz. **100**:1–99.

Tordoff, H. B. 1953. Groove-billed ani in Great Plains in 1952. Wilson Bull. **65**:202–203.

Trager, W. 1953. Nutrition, *in* Insect Physiology, by K. Roeder. John Wiley & Sons, Inc., New York.

Tucker, J. M., and J. D. Sauer. 1958. Aberrant *Amaranthus* populations of the Sacramento-San Joaquin delta, California. Madroño **14**:252–261.

Tuttle, O. F. 1955. The origin of granite. Scient. Amer. **192**(4):77–82.

Udine, E. J. 1941. The black grain sawfly and the European wheat stem sawfly in the United States. U. S. D. A. Circ. **607**:1–9.

Udvardy, M. D. F. 1951. The role of interspecific competition in bird ecology. Oikos **3**:98–123.

Umbgrove, J. H. F. 1947. The pulse of the earth. 2nd ed. Martinius Nijhoff, The Hague.

Upjohn Company, The. 1958. The cell. Published by the Upjohn Co., Kalamazoo, Mich.

Urey, H. C. 1952. The planets. Their origin and development. Yale Univ. Press, New Haven.

Utida, S. 1957. Population fluctuation, an experimental and theoretical approach. Cold Spring Harbor Symposia Quant. Biol. **22**:139–151.

Uvarov, B. P. 1943. The tribe Thrinchini of the subfamily Pamphaginae, and the interrelations of the Acridid subfamilies (Orthoptera). Ent. Soc. London, Trans. **93**:1–72.

————. 1951. Locust research and control 1929–1950. Colonial Res. Publ. **10**:1–67.

Valentine, J. M. 1932. *Horologion*, a new genus of cave beetles (Fam. Carabidae). Ent. Soc. Amer. Ann. **25**:1–11.

————. 1952. New genera of anophthalmid beetles from Cumberland caves (Carabidae, Trechini). Geol. Surv. Alabama, Mus. Paper **34**: 1–41.

Van de Kamp, P. 1954. The nearest stars. Amer. Scient. **42**:573–588.

Vaurie, C. 1950. Notes on Asiatic nuthatches and creepers. Amer. Mus. Novitates **1472**:1–39.

————. 1951. Adaptive differences between two sympatric species of nuthatches. Tenth Intern. Ornith. Cong. Proc.:163–166.

Veloso, H. P., P. Fontana, Jr., R. M. Klein, and R. J. de Siqueira-Jaccoud. 1956. Os anofelinos do sub-gênero *Kertezia* em relação à distribuição das bromeliáceas em communidades florestais do município de Brusque, Estado de Santa Catarina. Mem. do Inst. Oswaldo Cruz **54**(1):1–86.

Wagner, M. 1868. Uber die Darwinsche Theorie in Bezug auf die geographische Verbreitung der Organismen. Sitzber. bayer. Acad. Wiss. (Math-natur.) **1868**(1):359–395.

Wagner, W. H., Jr. 1955. Cytotaxonomic observations on North American ferns. Rhodora **57**:219–240.

Wakeland, C. 1958. The high plains grasshopper. U. S. D. A. Tech. Bull. **1167**:1–168.

Wald, G. 1954. The origin of life. Scient. Amer. **191**(2):45–53.

Wallace, A. R. 1878. Tropical nature and other essays. The Macmillan Co., New York.

Walton, B. C. 1950. Some new and rare Pacific pagurids. Wash. Acad. Sci. J. **40**:188–193.

Warburg, O. 1956. On the origin of cancer cells. Science **123**:309–314.

Watson, J. D., and F. H. C. Crick. 1953. The structure of DNA. Cold Spring Harbor Symposia Quant. Biol. 18:123–131.

Wave, H. E. 1958. Personal correspondence of Jan. 7.

Weaver, J. E. 1954. North American prairie. Johnsen Publ. Co., Lincoln, Nebraska.

Wegener, A. 1924. Origin of continents and oceans. Methuen and Co., London.

Weinstein, L. H., W. R. Robbins, and H. F. Perkins. 1954. Chelating agents and plant nutrition. Science 120:41–43.

Wenrich, D. H., I. F. Lewis, and J. R. Raper. 1954. Sex in microorganisms. Amer. Assoc. Adv. Sci., Washington, D.C.

Went, F. W., G. Juhren, and M. C. Juhren. 1952. Fire and biotic factors affecting germination. Ecology 33:351–364.

Westerhout, G. 1959. The radio galaxy. Scient. Amer. 201(2):44–51.

Westoll, T. S. 1949. On the evolution of the Dipnoi, *in* Jepsen *et al.*, 1949: 121–184.

White, M. J. D. 1954. Animal cytology and evolution. 2nd ed. Cambridge Univ. Press, Cambridge, England.

Whiting, P. W. 1955. Some interactions of mutant eye-color factors in the wasp *Mormoniella*. Penn. Acad. Sci. Proc. 29:242–245.

Whittaker, R. H. 1956. Vegetation of the Great Smoky Mountains. Ecol. Monog. 26:1–80.

Willard, H. F., and A. C. Mason. 1937. Parasitization of the Mediterranean fruitfly in Hawaii, 1914–33. U. S. D. A. Circ. 439:1–17.

Willis, J. C. 1922. Age and area; a study in geographical distribution and origin of species. Cambridge Univ. Press, Cambridge, England.

Wilson, E. O. 1959. Studies of the ant fauna of Melanesia. VI. The tribe Cerapachyini. Pacific Insects 1:39–57.

Wilson, J. T. 1959. Geophysics and continental growth. Amer. Scient. 47: 1–24.

Winge, O. 1917. The chromosomes. Their number and general importance. Compt. Rendu Trav. Lab. Carlsberg 13:131–275.

Wirth, W. W., and R. H. Jones. 1957. The North American subspecies of *Culicoides variipennis*. U. S. D. A. Tech. Bull. 1170:1–35.

Wright, B. S. 1960. Predation on big game in East Africa. J. Wildlife Manag. 24:1–15.

Wright, S. 1949. Adaptation and selection, *in* Jepsen, *et al.*, 1949:365–389.

Yang, T. W., and C. H. Lowe, Jr. 1956. Correlation of major vegetation climaxes with soil characteristics in the Sonoran desert. Science **123**: 542.

Yount, J. L. 1956. Factors that control species numbers in Silver Springs, Florida. Limnol. and Oceanogr. **1**:286–295.

Zinder, N. D. 1953. Infective heredity in bacteria. Cold Spring Harbor Symposia Quant. Biol. **18**:261–269.

Index

B

C